Interculturalism and Performance

for Bharati, in memoriam

© 1991 Copyright by PAJ Publications

Library of Congress Cataloging in Publication Data
Interculturalism and Performance
ISBN: 1-55554-057-0 (cloth)
ISBN: 1-55554-058-9 (paper)

Printed in the United States of America

The publishers gratefully acknowledge a generous grant from The Rockefeller Foundation for the publication of this book. Additional funds were made available by the New York State Council on the Arts.

Interculturalism and Performance

Writings from PAJ

Edited by Bonnie Marranca and Gautam Dasgupta

PAJ Publications
New York

Editors' Note

Many of the selections in this anthology have appeared in other PAJ books and in *Performing Arts Journal*. Essays or interviews by these authors first appeared in "The Interculturalism Issue" (PAJ 33/34, 1989): Carl Weber, Daryl Chin, Johannes Birringer, Bonnie Marranca, Frantisek Deak, Per Brask, Gabrielle Cody, J. Ndukaku Amankulor, Andrzej Wirth, Mead Hunter, Richard Schechner. Past issues of *Performing Arts Journal* featured the work of the following contributors: Edward Said (PAJ 37, 1991), Diana Taylor (PAJ 38, 1991), Gautam Dasgupta (PAJ 30, 1987), Edith Turner (PAJ 30, 1987), Peter J. Chelkowski (PAJ 4, 1977), Tadashi Suzuki (PAJ 23, 1984), Frederick Turner (PAJ 35/36, 1990). The selections by these authors were especially prepared for this book: John J. Flynn, Una Chaudhuri, Chidananda Dasgupta, editors' preface and epilogue. Victor Turner's essay was first published in his *From Ritual to Theatre: The Human Seriousness of Play* (PAJ Publications, 1982).

PAJ Publications gratefully acknowledges the support of The Rockefeller Foundation, particularly its former assistant director, Steven D. Lavine, in making possible our Interculturalism research project. This three year project began in 1988, with the preparation of PAJ 33/34, culminating now in the publication of *Interculturalism and Performance: Writings from PAJ*. The publishers/editors wish to thank Scott Walters of PAJ Publications for his valuable assistance in the production work on this book.

Contents

III   KINDS OF HISTORY

EPILOGUE

PREFACE

Thinking About Interculturalism

Bonnie Marranca

WHEN SADDAM HUSSEIN DECLARED at the start of this new year that there would be no end to what might become "the theatre of our operations," no one could have imagined the extent to which war as spectacle would dominate the lives of cultures and continents, on a scale of global spectatorship unprecedented in human history. Before the Gulf War started, we had barely settled down from the euphoria of watching on television the revolutions that brought enormous political and cultural transformation to Eastern and Central Europe.

That part of Europe had been so fixed for decades in its icy grimace that many had forgotten "Europe" was not an undifferentiated entity, but a world of diverse cultures, encompassing Anglo-Saxon, Latin, Arabic, Teutonic, Slavic, Nordic, Celtic, Gypsy, and Semitic peoples, to choose only a sampling of those who, historically, have created the idea of Europe. Looking toward the Soviet Union, part Europe, part Asia, we have stopped counting by now the number of ethnic populations who want to break away from Kremlin centralization. Increasingly, there are items in the press on ancestral homes long-forgotten in contemporary history books: Moldavia, Transylvania, Swabia, Herzegovina, Slovenia, Nagorno-Karabakh. When last did we speak of Bohemia? Long-suppressed ethnic rivalries, and dangerous nationalist tendencies are producing rising tensions in countries experiencing the first taste of freedom in the post-war era. The world is opening up to us, and closing in on itself at the same time, as people and

9

places alternately exalt local, regional, and global affiliations. If strong ethnic identification is aligned to progressive politics in the U.S., in many other parts of the world it is feared as reactionary. All around us the old divisions of political life are being challenged.

In Latin America, several countries are slowly moving toward democracy after years of military rule, and in South Africa the promise of an end to apartheid can at last be envisioned. In Korea, in Japan, in Singapore, and in India the expansion of new economies is modernizing the lives of many Asians. Some brave Chinese people tried to make a democratic revolution, but they did not succeed in toppling the old men in their palaces. While everyone was looking in another direction, toward the Middle East, they put Wang Dan on trial. And the Soviets quickly moved their tanks into Latvia, cutting down the young filmmaker who was documenting their brutality. But there is no place to hide in the world any longer. Everyone is watching.

As we look toward 1992 the European countries are preparing to unite in a new European Community, which will surely change the nature of North American-European relations. Europe, the old world, the longest link in the political, cultural, and economic chain that has bound the United States to the continent, and it to us for over five centuries, is about to reorganize itself as a new world.

Nearly 500 years ago America was called the ''New World.'' Its ways and wonders were studied, classified, traded, and marveled at for centuries, influencing people all the world over, in the natural and human sciences, economics, art, politics, philosophy, and history. St. Jean de Crèvecoeur, equally at home whether on his colonial farm in the lower Hudson Valley, or in the high-heeled Parisian circles of the *philosophes*, thought he had discovered here the ''New Man.'' His independent American wife was, of course, a new woman.

On the eve of the Revolution, in Crèvecoeur's world there were foreign peoples, chiefly from Great Britain, Holland, Sweden, France, Belgium, Germany, Switzerland, Africa, and the Caribbean living in the English colony. Less than a century earlier, downriver near the Dutch-ruled Manhattan, of the European-descended population that numbered less than 2000, nearly 18 languages were spoken. Farther west, in territories that would remain for some time un-united with the new states, the language of Spain ruled.

America, now a nation with an immigrant population of 40%, more than any other country in modern times, is again reconstituting the idea of the ''New Man'': *homo multiculturans*. America has always been a culture of more ethnic diversity than any in the West, and, singularly, it has been for

10

centuries the land where people have come to escape their own histories and cultures, even as they cling fiercely to those values and symbols left behind. There is more than a little truth in William Gass' contention that the only history America can have is a geographical one.

In the last two decades especially, the flow of refugees moving over the surface of the globe, now thought to number about 15 million, has focused attention on cultures everywhere, forcing each country to address its own questions of identity and definition. At no time in memory have more people throughout the world publicly argued changing beliefs in nationalism, internationalism, ethnicity, and culture, in the face of global interdependence in economic, military, cultural, and environmental spheres. Against this background, the conflict in the Gulf signals a new definition of "world war."

We began 1991 sitting around the television, which circles the globe like Rumor, watching a war in Iraq, the alleged home of the garden of Eden. This Mesopotamian region was the cradle of civilization where the arts and sciences, mathematics, and religion grew and spread around the earth, intermingling Near Eastern, Mediterranean, and African cultures at the beginning of the exchange of ideas and skills between peoples. The epic of *Gilgamesh*, one of the earliest stories written down, told of the people of this land. It was a story of war between men, and the destruction of the landscape. *Gilgamesh* was the text behind Homer's text. One world inside another world, the future in the ancient past.

In almost every intersection of cultures, everywhere there are worlds within worlds. In the world of contemporary performance, what I shall call the "discourse of interculturalism," and by that I mean its evolving affiliations and themes, has positioned itself to reflect these crosscurrents as a strategic mode of inquiry. This is my subject.

II

What is "interculturalism"? The writings that cluster around the world of this word alternately address theory, technique, politics, aesthetics, theatrical production, critical writing. Interculturalism is linked to world view, practice, and theory/criticism—that is, the mental attitude that precedes performance, the performance process, and the theoretical writing that accompanies performance. A fairly recent addition to theatrical vocabulary, interculturalism, then, is a state of mind, as much as a way of working.

Our plan for this anthology proceeded from a genuine desire to explore the issue of interculturalism within the history of performance ideas, and to

11

articulate themes that may have been overlooked in previous writing on the subject. As editors, Gautam Dasgupta and I hoped to situate this subject in a broader frame than the social sciences approach which has characterized intercultural writings of the last decade or so. We wanted to include discussion of the idea of interculturalism within the scope of the literary essay, and in the context of different traditions of theatre. Our intention was to expand the theme beyond the East/West polemic, to treat Europe and America as intercultural spaces; to reflect on the historical avant-garde, and neglected topics such as the dramatic text, music, video, the new urban cultures. Our editorial design was to encourage a historical perspective, by giving a diverse, often contradictory, group of people the opportunity to address interculturalism as both theory and practice, in a personal, speculative manner. Overall, we set out to construct a *critique of interculturalism* in the polyvocal views of contributors from around the world.

We proceeded to commission several essays for the special double issue of *Performing Arts Journal* 33/34 (1989) from which to begin an investigation of what people in the theatre thought, wrote, and practiced around the idea of interculturalism, as they understood it. We also solicited new contributions to address specific themes, and to these essays we added selections culled from 15 years of issues of *PAJ*, and from the books we have published to date. Together, the selections comprise *Interculturalism and Performance*.

For my own part, editing became a way of analyzing the major concepts of interculturalism, as it has evolved thematically in theatre discussions over the last decade or two. Increasingly, I began to question what was written about interculturalism, and, especially, what was not written about. The discourse of interculturalism, in its specific rhetorical inflections, raises a number of profound concerns about the nature of representation, which I would like to pursue in this preface. By rhetorical inflections, I mean the variety of attachments and oppositions, spoken and unspoken, to which interculturalism as a philosophic position, has become aligned over the years. These include: theatre anthropology, social sciences, postmodernism, multiculturalism, culture studies, grass roots politics, people's theatre, new historicism, the East/West axis.

It is chiefly the discourse—the voices—circling about intercultural themes, the kind of thinking the subject has engendered, that engages me, rather than specific works. In fact, a proliferation of theoretical apparatus rather than exemplary works characterizes this school of thought, which is rooted more in academic writing than in the voices or manifestos of artists, as was the case, say, with Surrealism. Interculturalism, though, may be more method or critical perspective than style.

Ironically, no recent theatre work, the form which by nature takes as its subject *representation,* has generated as much controversy around the notion of interculturalism, as the 1988 publication of Salman Rushdie's novel, *The Satanic Verses.* The Ayatollah Khomeini condemned the novel and called for the execution of Rushdie as an enemy of Islam. Did he not *misrepresent* Islam? Rushdie's book succeeded so brilliantly, not only as it leaped into the history of the satiric comic novel, but in the author's deeply committed mastery of conveying his own imaginative life between two cultures (an Indian-born Muslim living in England) in its pages. Here he blended the texts and textures of Asian and Western culture, dreams, history, geography. Rushdie created a new way of writing the English language, setting post-colonial India and Thatcherite Britain in Bakhtin's explosive dialogical tension.

There is no such worldly creation that one can point to in theatre (except, and in a different artistic direction, the unrealized *CIVIL warS* project of Robert Wilson), but the work which has focused the most debate around what theatre people define as intercultural issues is *The Mahabharata* of Peter Brook, also an Englishman. Less known here are the stunning orientalized productions of France's Ariane Mnouchkine. That some of the most suggestive work comes out of the intersection of British (or French) culture and a former colony is in no small measure a decisive factor in the discussion. For one cannot put on interculturalism like an imported shirt, or a new gestural vocabulary. American interculturalism has not grown out of the experience of colonialism, but from this country's own geography and changing demographics.

Though American links with India are very recent, and not extensive, India figures prominently in the writings on interculturalism, beginning with the early influence of Grotowski, and continuing today in the work of Eugenio Barba and Richard Schechner. Notwithstanding, contemporary Indian sensibility has filtered into intellectual life here in recent years through the novel rather than the theatre, in the writings of such authors, among several others, as Rushdie, Bharati Mukherjee, Amitav Ghosh, Vikram Seth, Ruth Prawer Jhabvala, and, earlier, V. S. Naipaul. A few decades ago Indian music influenced (at the same time that it did the Beatles) American avant-garde composers, of whom Philip Glass is the most prominent. In the world of performance, ''India'' exists largely in theoretical writings, or as a model for performance discipline. Its classical dance and musical forms are known and performed here, though not contemporary Indian drama.

My own view is that the far greater impact of Japan on the history of American performance has not been fully acknowledged in the discourse of interculturalism. Since before World War II and continuing into the present (from Michio Ito to the contemporary fascination with Kabuki, Noh, and Bunraku), Japanese aesthetics, design, and philosophy have had an enormous effect on avant-garde performance, centered historically in New York. Japanese influence, whether aesthetic or Buddhist, extends from Martha Graham to the Cunningham-Cage collaborative model, to Fluxus, to the Judson school, to individuals such as Nam June Paik, Yoko Ono, and Allan Kaprow who inspired the beginnings of video and performance art, and continuing up to the work of many of the experimental directors working today: Lee Breuer, Peter Sellars, Elizabeth LeCompte, Meredith Monk, Ping Chong, Robert Wilson, and puppeteers Julie Taymor and Theodora Skipitares. These artists declare their attachment to the highly stylized, refined sensibility of traditional Japanese aesthetics in many ways: the approach to narrative; the construction of theatrical space and time; conceptual use of puppets; separation of body and voice; and, in the general development of formalistic vocabularies attuned to rhythm, composition, silence, and abstraction. Weaving its way through the visual arts, multimedia, dance, and theatre, Japanese aesthetics joined with European modernism to create the New York school of avant-garde performance in the post-war era.

Interculturalism as theatrical practice divides itself into two distinct lines and it will, I believe, continue to do so more often in the years to come. Those artists inclined toward formal experimentation and abstraction as a performance mode will draw closer to Japanese aesthetics. Others who declare themselves for a politically-engaged, popular theatre will emphasize Latin American, Indian, Southeast Asian, and African affiliations. Artists of both persuasions will take it for granted that their work reflects social commitment.

The politics of this alignment is reasonably clear. The discourse of interculturalism, as it has evolved in this country, orients itself around the notion of ''people's theatre,'' in reaction to Western theatre convention and the more formalist, literary impulses of modernism. Generally, this theatre demonstrates a less formal separation of performer and audience, independence from the dramatic text of a single author, and disinterest in the work as an aesthetic object to be viewed. The more stylized, abstract theatre experimentation proposes a clear demarcation between performer, audience, and spectator decorum, and links itself stylistically to modernist movements. In this latter sense, there is no attempt to represent the Orient, just as decades earlier Brecht did not aim, in his own stylized work which drew upon Chinese acting technique, to create ''Orientalness.''

In New York, it was mainly the groups prominent in the '60s, such as The Living Theatre, The Open Theatre, (in earlier years influenced, too, by

Japanese philosophy), and The Performance Group, which concerned themselves with the autobiography of performance, social criticism, and at times, audience participation.

As we move into the decade of the '90s, avant-garde performance (coming from both theatre and visual arts directions), intercultural or otherwise, is beginning to seem more similar to the '60s counterculture events or street (people's) theatre than to the formalist, at times high-tech, modernist stance of artists who dominated thinking about theatre two decades ago. They include, for example, Mabou Mines, The Ontological-Hysteric Theatre of Richard Foreman, and Robert Wilson, whose work exemplified what I had called the Theatre of Images.

(In attempting to articulate themes that address American intercultural practice, I am aware that the perspective outlined above is shaped by my own local setting—New York—turned toward the East Coast-Europe-Orient axis which has had the most impact on performance theory and production here. On the other hand, the geographic setting of the West Coast reflects an intercultural practice shaped more decisively by Chicano culture, which has not yet been sufficiently integrated into the discourse of interculturalism. This would be a necessary step in the development of a truly intercultural national consciousness.)

It is interesting to note that if interculturalism is any proper gauge, there is a certain anti-modernist attitude in the re-evaluation of the European legacy, and a search for the "authentic," real experience elsewhere than in Western culture. That was certainly the case in the promotion of the recent Los Angeles festival which made a point of distancing itself from both New York and European performance. I note this in the sense that cultural historian Jackson Lears used to characterize a strong tendency in American culture to react against modernity. As he contends, at the end of the nineteenth century American artists and intellectuals, in shrugging off the "overcivilized" rationalist values, and aesthetics of European culture, and the effects of new technologies, looked instead toward Oriental culture, the primitive, religion, and myth, in search of the *therapeutic*. Lears' view of this turn-of-the-century turbulence offers a tempting analogy for contemporary life and artistic practice.

III

If we were to pursue the idea of interculturalism as a kind of people's theatre to its logical end point, we would confront a situation in which boundaries between actor, spectator, and spectacle blur and disentangle. It would feature only participants. Here is the precise intersection of theatre/anthropology, the staging ground of Grotowski who, as Polish critic

Konstanty Puzyna has pointed out, was the first contemporary theatre artist to link the fields of study. Grotowski, of course, was extending the project of Artaud, who looked East in search of the sacred and the mythic. The mythopoeic impulse plays a dominant role in the history of twentieth-century performance, challenged only by the Brechtian model. The essential antinomy of the twentieth-century theatre evolves from Brecht and Artaud: the world as text/the world as spectacle.

The performance trajectory Grotowski's example describes represents a profound shift from the conventional acceptance of the dramatic text in performance as revelation, to the emphasis on the creative transformation of the participant in a sacred act, from redemption (or catharsis) to the ritualistic celebration of human potential and spirit. As an anti-modernist performance vision, in the context that I have outlined above, it posits a new utopia for our time, founded on the *fin-de-siècle* turn toward physical and spiritual discipline that has framed the twentieth century.

Grotowski is the most extreme example of the contemporary urge to turn away from spectacle, spectatorship, and, by extension, aesthetics. Two decades ago Grotowski spoke of the end of such words as "theatre," "performance," "spectator," "actor." His emphasis on the holistic life (with consciousness as its supreme state), and his search for a universal human language in sacred, ritual experience intersect with the problematics of New Age philosophy. Grotowski's view of "human nature," his universalist ideal—"man precedes difference," he contends—bypasses the contemporary cultural politics of difference, and its disenchantment with humanism's claims to universality. His world is no longer that of art or theatre, but a theatreless society. It is like Rousseau's, in one respect: social science is set in conflict with theatre (representation). However, while Rousseau was interested in the *public* individual, Grotowski is concerned now with *private*, exclusive circles of initiates, suggestive of earlier spiritual and artistic movements, beginning with Symbolism.

In a 1985 essay, "PAJ, A Personal History," I suggested that a critique of theatre anthropology should begin with Rousseau, the first to link theatre and anthropology, in the modern sense, a point to which I'd like to return. Rousseau, of course, is notorious for his attack on theatre in *Letter to d'Alembert*, in which he extols a new vision of society that forbids theatre (plays). Instead, from the perspective of social scientist he imagines the *polis* as public festival, comprised only of participants making a spectacle of themselves, in democratic harmony. "Let the spectators become an entertainment to themselves; make them actors themselves; do it so that each sees and loves himself in the others so that all will be better united." But Rousseau's ecstatic vision was directed toward generating "patriotic

16

charm'' as a form of citizenship to preserve the paternalistic authority of the state, in tandem with the moral authority of the family. His body politic was intended to dramatize the values of the republican constitution—a profoundly conservative pageantry.

Generally speaking, theatre anthropology shares an obvious infatuation with social contracts (or social structures). I am troubled by the anthropological view of performance as ''social drama'' because of the implications in the notion of social order on which such drama is founded. The communal or ritual performer is not, by definition, a critical, dissenting participant in the social drama.

What I find problematic in this aspect of intercultural discourse—the valorization of the social pact, or public festival—is the disappearance of boundaries between actor, spectator, and text. In effect, the denial of spectatorship. One result of this denial is a Nietzschean, ritualistic play of mass spectacle and quasi-religious experience which carried into Artaud, then to Grotowski, and finally into the writings on interculturalism (by way of structural anthropology and ethnographic studies), coinciding with contemporary popular currents in psychology. Another outgrowth of this development is the assumption that one can ''do'' culture.

The notion of social drama has a long, complicated history in the modern world. On a personal level, I continue to return to the visionary work of Pirandello in whom the dynamics of individuality and group ethos illuminate how frighteningly ambiguous and intertwined are the strategies of performance acts, in both democratic and totalitarian systems of government. In the modern era, the urge towards self-transformation linked itself to the theatrical gesture, then moved on to the realm of ontological act. In this larger philosophic sense, performance as an existential, self-defining act, outside of theatrical activity, projects itself as phenomenological gesture. Pirandello clearly distinguished between performance as an ontological act of individuation, and the construction of a role encouraged by the prevailing social structure. Theatre anthropology and sociologies of theatre need to confront the fundamental political and philosophical issues that complicate the interactions of the individual and the group.

Early, important studies of crowd psychology coincide with the rise of mass movements in the modern era. In our own time, it is fascinating to watch the spectacle of societies in different parts of the world—particularly, in the kinds of transformations that have taken place in the Soviet Union and Eastern Europe, and from another political perspective, in the Middle East. Borders between the democratic and totalitarian political impulse frequently blur, as do theatre and spectacle, or politics and religion.

The Eastern European example is provocative, in relation to the subject

17

of theatre. From all reports, during the stages of social revolution in the Eastern European region, as life in the street became more and more compelling, and public speech encouraged, the audience for theatre, up until then the site of (albeit veiled) political discourse, dwindled. Audiences, reveling in their new role of citizenship, lost interest in theatrical representation. Acting themselves out, staging their own dramas, became more important. Gradually, however, people began to distinguish between self-dramatization and the representationalism of theatre. They realized they were two different realms of experience.

In the allusion to the Greek ideal that underlies the modern revolutionary fervor in imagining the new *polis*, the "New Man," and this has been the dream of all avant-garde movements of the twentieth century, there is an important issue which seems to be obscured in current performance theory: that *thinking is a kind of spectatorship*. Acts of thought, of contemplation, are related to judging: thinking discerns the differences between things. As Hannah Arendt, from whom we can learn a great deal on the subject of social life, has argued, only the spectator, not the actor, can know and understand the spectacle. Extending her philosophic insight, then, it becomes obvious that a performance world in which epistemology is centered in the body—in doing—only serves to reinforce the mind/body dualism. In the context of performance, this position generates another version of the nature/culture argument.

If consciousness, and the subjunctive expression of becoming as part of the order of a social community, is one of the valued aspirations of the anthropological approach to performance theory, it is important to remember that consciousness is not the same as thinking. Only thinking, which involves thinking *about* something, is a dialectical process.

The represented drama is the conventional object of thought in theatre. Yet, the play of single authorship (especially when it is contemporary) is disdained in the discourse of interculturalism which sets itself in opposition to a theatre of dramatic literature, to propose in its place a theatre of the actor's body as emblematic of community, and repository of knowledge. This strategy has not been seriously questioned in recent critical writing, nor has the obvious power play of directors who undermine the significance of the dramatic text. After all, an *auteur* is an author, too. Given our contemporary knowledge of the complexity of textuality, it no longer seems useful to encourage the view that the text only fully comes into meaning in performance, or that literary knowledge is dependent on performance knowledge in theatrical production. That intercultural writings have not made a more substantial attempt to bring into the discourse the difficult questions of dramaturgy, or to explore their own literary ambiguity, is regrettable, especially since interculturalism can be understood more broadly as a form of intertextualism. But, what is the crucial issue here: authorship or the place of literature in performance?

Not only the dramatic text of theatre, but the theatre building itself has been called into question in contemporary performance theory. Rather falsely, I believe, there has been an attempt to suggest that the mere act of working in a conventional (institutional) theatre puts one in the hands of an "elite" audience forced to be "passive" voyeurs of "consumerist" *objets d'art*. Conversely, as the argument plays itself out, the folksy informality of a theatre for a highly particularized, micro-community actively promotes social change. In reality, both kinds of performance share the same financial support in this country: the NEA, Rockefeller Foundation, foreign governments, state arts councils, universities, etc. Frequently, they share the same audiences.

Theoretically, then, the undifferentiated (counter-revolutionary?) audience in the theatre judges and consumes the aesthetic object, while the community-conscious theatre precludes judgment, and, instead spectators-as-participants are drawn into a shared experience. The outmoded "high" and "low," ruling class vs. folk, decadent or sacred opposition which underlies this view, often combining with the rhetoric of postmodernism by way of '60s-style provocation, obfuscates the very important differences between commodity entertainments and art works, between consumers and audiences, between culture and mass society. It also tends to obliterate differences between popular forms of art and those which do not appeal to popular taste. More importantly, the argument does not take into account the historical circumstances of the spectrum of art forms created at different times and places for many different social groups. (This is not only true of Western performance spaces and traditions, but those in Asia as well. In non-Western art, in addition to distinctions between classical and folk forms, and so-called "high" and "low" art, there is also a distinction between religious and secular forms.)

When it obscures these kinds of theatrical differences, when it confuses culture and art, and dismisses the contemplative, critical life of the spectator in favor of the audience-as-performer, interculturalism and theatre anthropology, as critical strategies, risk a new kind of philistinism. Much of the already published writing inscribed in the interculturalist perspective, rooted as it is in the various sciences, has developed a scientific profile, a laboratory approach to performance, and documentary attitude toward criticism. What is emphasized is technique and training, social process. The act of judgment or evaluation of the performer or performance in the context of art seems to be discouraged. For my part, I prefer Kantian disinterest to this dubious objectivity. Philosophically speaking, the struggle I have outlined is between materialism and idealism.

Ironically, as certain schools of thought in the arts here look toward other parts of the world for creative inspiration, many in Asia, and most recently, the former Soviet-bloc countries, have looked for renewal toward individualistic aspects of Western art and democratic pluralism developed within the humanist tradition. We should not underestimate the value of abstraction—from the art object, from the state, from the church, from the crowd—that has evolved in this cultural tradition. It is the private, individual "I" that many people have made revolutions to recover. This abstracted, even alienated subject is worth holding onto, more fiercely than ever, in the face of contemporary ideological pressures.

IV

The social sciences, psychology, and anthropology have had a significant impact in the scholarly discourse on interculturalism, indeed instigated its exploration and expansion in performance theory. But the scientific approach has its limits in dealing with art forms. The sciences are more attentive to process, structure, system, and research methodology, than to the moral, ethical, and aesthetic questions raised by human performance and cultural artifact. The scientific approach tends to be concerned with the "how" of activity, rather than meaning, the "why" of it. Perhaps it is time now to open up interculturalism alongside discoveries in literature, philosophy, visual art, history, geography, architecture. Anthropology, for example, is most interesting when it embraces literary values, as in the recent work of Clifford Geertz and James Clifford, and earlier, Victor Turner. Do we really need to restage the art/science—two cultures—debate in the theatre at this late date? Instead, why not bring into the world of performance all textures of creative intelligence.

Since the goals of interculturalism are so deeply linked to the concept of multiculturalism, which is rooted in the new urban cultures, we need to understand the nature of the city in history, following the ground work of someone like Lewis Mumford, or in our time Richard Sennett who, like him, confronts the new life of cities and their cultures. We might also build upon the writings of Walter Benjamin to enlarge the understanding of today's *flaneur*, our *homo performans* who inhabits cities all over the world.

In essence, writing on interculturalism would make a marvelous leap if it adopted a more cosmopolitan outlook on the galaxies of knowledge in our world. Oddly enough, while touching base quite naturally with new historicism's attention to what Stephen Greenblatt has called "the circulation of social energy," interculturalism is surprisingly ahistorical in its critical approach. It needs to develop a *historical consciousness*, having now made its large contribution to performance theory.

Unfortunately, even as it places culture at the center of its ethos, interculturalism reflects no strongly-defined theory of culture. This situation lends a certain paradoxical twist to the writing: the emphasis is more often than not on performance technique, more specifically the aesthetics of form (especially Indian or Balinese), rather than any sense of the historical-cultural-social-religious settings of these forms, past or present. Furthermore, in the turn toward other performance traditions, namely those of Hindu, Buddhist, and Muslim cultures, there is a certain dissociation from analysis of their social and religious strictures and hierarchies. The intellectual rigor applied to the critique of humanism should in fairness extend to other philosophic traditions as well. Not to do so, then, leads to the aestheticization of cultures and the de-historicization of their forms. Not to "represent" another culture is perfectly acceptable, after all it is the Brechtian option, but that conflicts with the natural linkage of interculturalism and culture studies. What, in the larger sense, can we learn from interculturalism: how is it different from other ways of representation, in both theory and practice? Is it truly a new world view or simply a new name for an evolutionary process? More to the point, what is the difference between the representation of interculturalism and the very thing itself, between "intercultural-ness" and true interculturalism?

The framework of interculturalism would be revitalized if, for example, there were input and debate from several different schools of thought in the field, as in like-minded literary and art criticism, which is more developed polyphonically. As I indicated earlier, one of the main objectives of this anthology is to open up new perspectives on our understanding of the nature and practice of interculturalism, and to articulate issues other than those which now define the parameters of its discourse.

If interculturalism as a critical enterprise is to embrace more eclectic themes, European modernism should certainly be a point of departure. For over a century, intercultural practice has been linked to avant-garde movements, in particular, literary modernism (often overlooked in intercultural writings), beginning with Symbolism and its infatuation with Orientalism. Symbolism outlines the beginning of abstraction in Western art, the point at which artists became interested in the concept of the sign, also coinciding with interest in the dance-dramas—based on the sign—of Asia. In the history of modernism, the influence of Orientalism, and the search for spiritual renewal, extends from the symbolists to Artaud, the first modern European theatre artist to turn away from the West, to Grotowski and Wilson, who represent two different paths of this symbolist legacy at

21

our turn-of-the-century..

In my view, the importance of the spiritual element in the historical development of virtually every movement in modernism throughout Europe and in the Soviet Union, has been erased in much of postmodernism's desire, which carried into interculturalism, to distance itself from modernism. This oversight misconstrues the inseparability of revolutionary politics and avant-garde aesthetics in the evolution of modernist performance. We need to investigate the deep linkages of avant-garde performance, literary modernism, and interculturalism, especially in influential individual theatre artists such as Yeats, Strindberg, Meyerhold, Brecht, Artaud; in the attraction of Russian artists to the Islamic art of Central Asia; in *fin-de-siècle* Japonisme; in the major role in experimentation played by cities of the Austro-Hungarian empire, viewed as an intercultural construct; in the movements from Symbolism to Futurism to Constructivism to Surrealism in the pre-World War II era.

French culture, due to its colonial past, and its unparalleled role in the spread of avant-garde ideals on the continent, in the Soviet Union, and in the U.S., can be an obvious point of departure for intercultural studies of a historical nature. That would bring together performance ideas and the literary text in an analytical frame. It might also take us closer to Edgar Allan Poe who was so influential for the French symbolists, and the first important American artist for whom Orientalism was an aesthetic strategy. (Perhaps it is not so coincidental that his writing is appearing increasingly in contemporary theatre works.)

On the subject of Orientalism, the world of opera, too, from Rossini's *Semiramide* to Philip Glass' *Akhnaten* is poised for inclusion in the discourse of interculturalism. Edward Said's erudite genealogy of ''imperial spectacle'' attending the Cairo premiere of Verdi's *Aida* provides a fresh opening to theatre history and criticism. Opera is an astonishingly resonant field of inquiry: plenty of primary artifacts are available; a history of theatrical theory and an entire performance tradition are in place; the contemporary repertoire offers for reconsideration a dialectical landscape of Asian, Middle Eastern, and African settings of works of numerous European composers. Not the least significant encouragement is the fact that today many of the most innovative directors in the world are working in opera.

If America does not have its own operatic history, there is a more than three-centuries-long intercultural music tradition. Black music, rooted in the mixing of African rhythms, Protestant hymns, and the European classical forms that fed into the creation of jazz is at the heart of our popular song. One cannot even begin to catalogue all of the musical exchanges revitalizing pop music, as it creates the World Beat. In the intercultural spaces of the South and Southwest especially, old ethnic traditions are coming into the mainstream. Music performance, both popular and avant-garde, should be highlighted more in the interculturalism context because it is so indigenous to American culture, and so dominant a performance mode in our time. But also, and especially significant, its roots are more in artistic expression than in theory. Theatre researchers needn't abandon this subject to ethnomusicology specialists.

Specialization may not be the best guide to the twenty-first century. In our world, knowledge has turned too compartmentalized as subjects have become foreign to their former, natural settings. To cultivate the mind once had the same meaning as to cultivate the earth. Through the process of erosion the transmission of ideas has become progressively more restricted by a kind of forced zoning regulation, while the universe of knowledge itself continually expands. As recently as last year we have seen old categories of thinking collapse in the punctured illusion of the Berlin Wall. Nothing is written in stone. In the time it has taken me to complete this essay a war has been fought that will transform another great region of the earth, in ways that we cannot yet begin to grasp. More and more of the world is revealing itself, forcing us to find untried, creative ways to apprehend the insistent dreams of cultures and continents. What is performance, and we to it, in this new world being made?

Interculturalism must of necessity become more worldly in its pursuit of global affiliations, dare to cross intellectual frontiers as casually as geographic ones. In the most profound analysis, a society is judged by the connections its people make between the urgent themes of the world. The cultivation of worldliness can only deepen and make more radical the interculturalism project, openly welcoming the wandering eye of the traveler, a philosopher without a system, to the glorious book of knowledge that is our world, our home.

New York City
March 1991

23

I   THE INTERCULTURALISM ISSUE

AC/TC

Currents of Theatrical Exchange

Carl Weber

DURING THE PAST decade a cultural phenomenon which made its first appearance in Western Europe in the fifties, finally became firmly established this side of the Atlantic, namely, the International Arts Festival. Such festivals took place during the 1984 Olympics at Los Angeles as well as in cities all over the country, from Charleston to Chicago and New York. The label indicates that they are intended to present art works and to host meetings of artists from a multitude of national or ethnic cultures. Yet there is another, probably even more constitutive aspect: essentially, these festivals are fairs, fairs in all the meanings of the term as Webster's Dictionary lists them: ''1) a gathering of people . . . for barter and sale of goods; 2) a festival or carnival where there is entertainment and things are sold; 3) an exhibition, often competitive, of . . . manufactured products; a kind of exposition.'' In other words, the arts, entertainment, and commerce become inseparably intertwined in the event.

This should be kept in mind when we discuss a phenomenon which often has been connected or traced to the proliferation of international arts festivals, especially of those presenting the performing arts, a phenomenon frequently described as ''transculturation.'' The term is as new as the phenomenon seems to appear to many observers. It is meant to signify a transfer of culture, or intercultural exchange, from one country or society to another. ''Trans-fer'' implies ''trans-port'' which, consequently, implies ''import'' as well as ''export''—all these being terms of trade and commerce. The term ''transculturation,'' however, isn't merely applied to the exchanges of art works, or between artists, that take place during festivals

27

and similar occasions all over the globe. It is more generally used to signify a cross-cultural collaboration and appropriation which brings forth art works that combine elements from separate cultures and their indigenous artistic traditions. A growing trend of such intercultural activities has become especially visible in the performing arts. The term ''intercultural'' is used in this context to signify transactions between separate indigenous cultural systems when, either unilaterally or mutually, elements of one culture are accepted or adopted in the other culture. Similarly, ''international'' trade goods and services pass back and forth between the economic systems of independent nations.

* * *

Performance is seen today by most people, most of the time, in the media of film and television, of audio and video recording. And the trend labeled ''transculturation'' has, indeed, pervaded on a global scale through the media. ''Western,'' which in this context means European or North American ideology, its values, structure, and contents are inscribed in the predominant models for performance accepted by most contemporary societies, models that partly ingest, partly destroy indigenous cultural values and forms. Indeed, non-Western cultures have already been greatly changed by the process, as can be observed in many Asian and African nations. This victorious march of ''transculturation'' across the globe—to the tunes of rock and other popular music, with the imagery of ''Dallas'' or game shows on its video screens—threatens to achieve an ultimate triumph of the Western cultural export business. Or, to put it in historical perspective, a second colonization of the so-called third world, inscribing the ideology of Western capitalism in the individual and communal minds of non-Western, non-white societies, is on its way.

The connection of ''transculturation'' with the ''transport'' and ''export'' of merchandise has always been quite obvious as far as the contemporary entertainment technology and its industries are concerned. The much older media of live performance, the theatre, dance, etc.—as old as the oldest human spiritual aspirations and activities—appear to many observers less commercialized when they undergo a process of transculturation. These media seem rather to gain from it. Aren't the international theatre festivals actively promoting and glorifying the intercultural collaboration of artists? Who would deny that the increasing exchange of performances between various cultures has beneficial effects on the artistic climate of the host nations as well as on the visitor's own culture? Who would question that the proliferating contacts between actors, authors dancers, directors, and designers from all over the globe can but broaden their perspective, stimulate their imagination, and enrich their practice?

28

There were, after all, acclaimed performance projects which combined forms of a foreign culture with features of the indigenous American theatre and dance tradition, or experiments which fused Asian myth and performance structures with Western theatrical practice, to create an intercultural theatre. Such projects include the Sondheim/Prince musical *Pacific Overtures*, the Acting Company's *Kabuki Macbeth*, or Martha Clarke's *Vienna Lusthaus* and, from the international festival circuit, Peter Brook's *Mahabharata*, to name but a few. Projects like these could certainly be cited as examples of "transculturation." They attempted a transfer of one cultural tradition to another or ventured a welding of both, while also keeping the separate identities of those cultures visible, to a degree at least, if not always intentional.

Some of the artists who embark upon such transcultural projects appear to harbor a growing belief in the emergence of a global culture that will eventually encompass all of mankind. In support of such trust, they point frequently at today's global network of communications which, of course, also promoted the all-consuming advance of Western media culture disseminated by the contemporary video and audio industry. Peter Brook, in a recent address on the occasion of the fortieth anniversary of the International Theatre Institute of UNESCO, argued for a theatre that is based on a merging of traditions (including the mix of actors from different cultures and languages in performance), where audiences are confronted with the specific as well as the universal truth by virtue of performances that blend various cultures. Such an act supposedly reflects the increasing convergence of political and social global trends.

What seems to be ignored in all this blissfully utopian thinking are the realities of the contemporary "transculturation business." As pointed out earlier, the international theatre or performance festivals are just as much trade fairs as cultural events. Most producers of projects which deserve the label of transcultural performance regard these festivals as their market of choice, if they haven't tried also to succeed in their native entertainment industry, e.g., in the American context: Broadway, Off-Broadway, and the national touring circuit. There certainly is nothing wrong with such acceptance of the market; most American theatre workers have to make their living in it, like their fellow citizens in other professions. The marketplace, however, depends on the laws of supply and demand. It will judge each product, first of all, by its sales sheets.

Quite inevitably, any "transcultural" experiment will be traded as a device that employs exotic ingredients to make the product more palatable, i.e., marketable. (The same attitude may afflict performances presented at international festivals—though festivals usually can rely on subsidized support from public or private money). What these very real, though certainly not very "cultural" conditions lead to is that a great number of transcultural projects, trying to combine, fuse, blend—or whatever you'd like to call it—features of the indigenous with those of an alien culture, arrive at performances which use the alien component as a spicy sauce to make some old familiar gruel palatable again. Quite like the Chop Suey once concocted in the Chinese railway worker camps of the West—a dish which superficially looked and smelled like Chinese cuisine while it merely tried to make edible whatever was available to the hapless cooks. More than a few among the transcultural performances mounted in recent years remind me of Chop Suey.

What is happening? The artists who created those works certainly didn't intend to compromise their efforts. What they appear to have tried for is a mistake, in my opinion, from the start. They picked a foreign motif or form and looked for its real or imagined "closeness" to our contemporary post-industrial Western society, if they weren't simply seduced by an attractive formal/sensual surface. Delighted when they found aspects they could "connect" with, they then seem to have proceeded with little if any regard for the historicity of the chosen material. Yet, awareness of a given foreign culture's historic and social conditions, and their inscription in all works of art, is paramount in our context. The neglect of such conditions, and of the ideology inscribed through them, inevitably leads to an incongruous mix of foreign and native elements which in the final analysis "refuse to fuse," adding up to a sum which is much less than its components.

One could and should of course ask: So what? Why is an amalgam of impurities necessarily bad theatre? Admittedly, it may even turn out to be impressive theatre—if it's superbly executed. It still won't be a new and different kind of performance where cultural boundaries are transcended.

The question remains if, and why, the transcending of cultural otherness should be desirable and—if it is—can it be achieved? What might be the definition of such an effort?

Webster's 1979 dictionary doesn't show an entry for "transculturation," only for "trans-," as a prefix, meaning: 1) across; to the other side of; 2) as to changing thoroughly; 3) transcending, above and beyond. Only the first meaning applies to the term "transculturation" as it is generally used, though numbers two and three offer intriguing definitions. The accepted contemporary reading appears to be more precisely expressed—at least according to Webster's—by the term "acculturation," which the dictionary defines as "the transfer of culture from one ethnic group to another." This definition describes much more fittingly the phenomenon I have been describing.

If the reader will accept the term "acculturation" along with the present-ly more popular "transculturation," he or she gains the option of using each term in a specific way. The latter would signify a genuine effort to "transculture" (as in "transcend" and "transform") both the foreign and indigenous tradition, or specific elements of them, the former an effort to "acculture" (as in "acquire" and "acclimate") a foreign culture or aspects of it. The complementing of "transculturation" with the term "ac-culturation" will help in analyzing the phenomenon to be signified by the two terms and the problems they represent.

* * *

Western performance history could be read as a narrative of transcultura-tion. For instance, when in the Roman theatre Plautus, Terence, and others adopted the New Comedy from the Greek tradition and viewed their own society through its paradigm, they created an early example of transcultura-tion. In turn, their works eventually provided the stuff of transculturation for the Renaissance authors of the *Commedia Erudita* who developed their plots and characters from the Roman model. In both instances, the works resulting from the process presented a new and different identity—the model was fused with the indigenous culture and became part of its tradi-tion. Molière adopted the structures of *Commedia dell' Arte* which Italian players had brought to France. He explored the model in his early farces un-til he had thoroughly transfigured it, and thus created a distinct form of French comedy which had absorbed the Italian tradition. Earlier, across the channel, the Jacobean theatre had embraced the new Italian stage technology. Its proscenium, its perspective design, and its machinery weren't merely copied; mediated with the indigenously developed masque, in the work of artists like Inigo Jones and Ben Jonson, an original perfor-mance mode was developed, until a Puritan Parliament put an end to all theatrical activity. When English theatres were opened again after the Restoration, the new playwrights—some of them returning from exile in France, like Wycherley—were familiar with French farce and Molière's model which they fused with whatever had survived of the Jacobean and Carolean tradition, creating the new form of Restoration comedy.

In step with a rapidly expanding inter-European commerce, transcultura-tion became a driving force in the further growth of Western theatre. The influx and the influence of numerous English acting troupes that wandered all over Central Europe during the seventeenth and early eighteenth cen-turies, eventually induced in the later eighteenth century a movement among German playwrights—in defiance of French classicism—to adopt Shakespeare and the Jacobeans as a model. Lessing was their prophet and then the young Goethe, Lenz, Schiller, and many others, created with their "Sturm und Drang" drama a striking example of transculturation. In the nineteenth century, Romanticism spread from Germany and France all over Europe; Zola's and Antoine's Naturalism was quickly adopted in every theatrical culture from the Atlantic to Moscow. The Norwegian Ibsen's dramaturgy of realism, which he evolved from the model of the French *pièce bien faite*, became the structure of choice for most playwrights in the rest of Europe and the U.S., and the system of the Russian actor and director Stanislavsky is still the preferred model of actor's training and technique in American theatre, film, and television.

* * *

Several examples of transculturation from the twentieth century may serve to identify aspects that are essential to the process. The performance of Diaghilev's Ballets Russes and their sets and costumes, designed by Bakst, Goncharova, and Larionov led to a revolution in Western European design and staging between 1910 and 1920. Their bold use of colors and shapes—derived from the folklore of Russia and its Asian provinces—was soon adopted in the French, English, German, and Scandinavian theatres and swept Naturalism's drabness from most of their stages. The European theatre had been laboring towards such a rout of Naturalism since the turn of the century. The results weren't mere copies of the Russian/French model but a "transcultured" fresh view of color and shape in stage design, and the recognition of a theatre for theatre's sake.

A decade later, a playwright appeared on the German stage who brazenly exploited the otherness of foreign cultural traditions, using them "like a quarry"—as he once explained his approach to Shakespeare—where he found contents and forms from which to construct his own works. When accused of plagiarism, he proudly agreed. Yet in plays culled in such fashion he welded whatever he had adopted with his own experimentation, providing examples of genuine transculturation. I'm talking of Brecht, of course, who appropriated dramaturgic models from England's Elizabethans, from classic Indian, and Japan's Noh Theatre, who employed motifs and structures from Villon, Kipling, Synge, lifted content from American stories as well as from Russian novels, and who absorbed performance modes from early Hollywood films and techniques of classic Chinese opera in his own theory of "Epic theatre." In the last instance, he may have misunderstood his model, though Brecht often deliberately disfigured his sources in the process and thus was blamed for blatant distortion. But there's the rub. The Chicago or London, China or Russia, on Brecht's stage were never intended to be depictions of a foreign society. The "Lehrstücke," which emulated the model of Noh theatre, weren't conceiv-

32

ed as demonstrations of a Japanese cultural tradition. All these sources were deconstructed and then again encoded within a different frame of reference and ideology. They became "sublated" in the new work, quite in the Hegelian sense.

Brecht was so impressed when, in 1935, he watched Mei Lan Fang demonstrate the skills of Peking Opera acting, that his idiosyncratic interpretation of Chinese techniques became a cornerstone of his theory of Epic theatre. Four years earlier, Antonin Artaud had seen the Balinese dancers in Paris and proclaimed their performance—as he understood it—a model for his project of a theatre purified from all contamination by literature. In both instances, the foreign tradition was embraced for virtues of its Otherness and then used to create something new, as distant from the adopted as from the indigenous tradition.

Thirty years later, Artaud's ideas received a similar transculturation when Jerzy Grotowski in Poland, Peter Brook in England, and Richard Schechner in the U.S. fused Artaud's concept of a ritualistic "pure theatre" with their own cultural tradition, in pursuit of a new kind of performance. Their theatres set themselves apart from the dominant culture's mainstream, as Artaud had tried to do, though they showed few similarities with Artaud's own experiments. The peculiar "mix" achieved in their performances transcultured not only Artaud's example, but also practices of Stanislavsky and Brecht and the findings of anthropological research.

An even more momentous transculturation had been achieved in America at the time Artaud discovered Balinese theatre. After the Moscow Art Theatre's visit to New York in the twenties, Norris Houghton had traveled to the USSR and brought home new information on Stanislavsky's theatre in the thirties, when Harold Clurman and Stella Adler had also observed the great Russian reformer's practice and discussed with him his teachings, while Russian actors, as Boleslavsky, Soloviova, and especially Michael Chekhov had brought—and taught—Stanislavsky's "system" to the American theatre community.   From these contacts grew the remarkable work of the Group Theatre which pioneered new ways to act, to direct, and to write plays, reflecting the Group's understanding of the Moscow Art Theatre model. Even more influential were the later teaching methods of former Group Theatre members Lee Strasberg, Sanford Meisner, and others who adapted/transcultured Stanislavsky's theory and practice to the exigencies of the American entertainment industry. Eventually the Stanislavsky "system," in one form or another, came to dominate all theatre training in the U.S.

The plays of Brecht in his own productions made an indelible impact on the English theatre community when his Berliner Ensemble appeared at

London's Palace Theatre in 1956. Brecht's example changed directing and playwriting in England at least as decisively as Ibsen's did after the Norwegian's work had been introduced and promoted by Archer, Shaw, Granville Barker, and others before the turn of the century. A comparison of plays and productions on British stages before and after 1956 offers abundant evidence for the successful transculturation of Brecht's East German performance model.

Since the fifties, the model has been transcultured throughout the so-called Third World. In the contemporary Brazilian theatre, for instance, the director/author Augusto Boal based much of his concept of a ''Theatre of the Oppressed'' on Brecht's theory and practice. Colombia's production of ''Nuevo'' or ''Gran Teatro,'' with director/playwrights as Enrique Buenaventura and Santiago Garcia, has been exemplary in an imaginative adaptation of Brecht's authorial and directorial approach. In Nigeria, his dramaturgy of an Epic theatre was mediated with native performance traditions by Wole Soyinka, Femi Osofisan, and other playwrights, resulting in works which accomplished successful transculturations of the Central European model. Philippine theatre groups, belonging to the trade union-supported cultural organization PETA, created remarkable performances by adopting models of Brecht and also the European Agitprop movement of the thirties.

What distinguishes all the examples mentioned is that they didn't merely flesh out the structure lifted from a foreign culture with indigenous subject matter, but they truly transformed their model. Even where early efforts still bordered on copies, soon the models became infused and mediated with native literary and/or performance traditions. Often the foreign text is deconstructed, the resultant findings then rearranged according to codes inscribed in the native culture, and an original performance text constructed. Eventually, the model ''dis-appears'' in a new text or technique, which gains its own identity of form and of content.

Such ''dis-appearance'' of an adopted model in the newly encoded text of performance, dramatic script, or theory is the mark of ''transculturation,'' as this article attempts to define it. The appropriation of a foreign performance code without change, or with merely superficial adjustments, is more accurately signified by the term ''acculturation.'' Stagings of a *Kabuki Macbeth* or *Lear*, for instance, would be examples of acculturation, whereas Akira Kurosawa's films based on Shakespeare's *Macbeth* and *Lear* represent transculturation. Jan Kott defined the distinction succinctly in a recent interview for the German theatre magazine *Theater Heute* (9/1988). He compared Kurosawa's work with Ariane Mnouchkine's experiment of presenting Shakespeare plays to French audiences in a Kabuki-derived performance style, an experiment which Kott rejected and which could be regarded as acculturation. Kott described Kurosawa's film *Ran* as a displacement of Shakespeare's fable of *Lear* "to a completely new, Japanese environment. It is an effort to rediscover the . . . structure of *Lear* within a situation that is historically and socially totally different, it is not merely a chic idea for a costume change."

Transculturation could indeed be defined as the deconstruction of a text/code and its wrenching displacement to a "historically and socially different situation." Acculturation, then, would be the inscription of a preserved foreign code in a native structure, which implies that an ideology is inscribed with it. Acculturation of a Western model in the Third World, for instance, often inscribes the concomitant gaze of the white patriarchal culture. The same goes for the uncritical adoption of non-European models to Western performance; if however, the process moves towards an analytical, critical reassessment, it may turn into an act of deconstruction and eventually lead to transculturation.

* * *

The question is, of course, whether processes as complex as the many variants of intercultural exchange in the theatre can be encapsulated by those two terms. Maybe they can't. Yet, it seems important to differentiate the modes of intercultural exchange that increasingly appear on the contemporary stage. It is especially useful in analyzing such exchanges against the context of an ever-expanding communication technology which transcends and threatens to eliminate all cultural borderlines.

One surprising phenomenon, which may have been effected by the growing communication network and the "global village" it fosters, is a proliferation of plays and performance projects which are grounded in native traditions, deliberately ethnic, often even stubbornly parochial in content and form. Like an immune system which responds to invading pathogens, theatre cultures increasingly appear to develop "anti-works" that battle the influx of foreign models which are invading the video screens. Quite in step with this phenomenon, there has been no increase—more frequently a reduction—in the number of foreign plays produced by commercial as well as subsidized theatres of many national cultures, though the rapid expansion of the international communication network would make us expect the opposite.

There is much evidence to suggest that Brecht, Beckett, Williams, Miller, and Pinter probably were the last playwrights to achieve lasting global impact and become a staple of the repertoire in most countries with a thriving theatre culture. A majority of contemporary playwrights have directed their focus narrowly on very specific issues of their native society, topics which usually fail to encounter a frame of reference with audiences who were conditioned by a different society and the inscriptions of its ideology.

Works which achieve genuine transculturation might be better suited for the crossing of cultural borders between nations/societies. The history of the modern avant-garde provides many examples of accomplished crossings. Transculturation was always closely linked with and eagerly embraced by the theatre's avant-garde. Whenever a society's stage was ripe for a change because its traditional performance codes had become obsolete, i.e., no longer responded to a perceived social reality, experimentation with ideas and forms lifted from other cultures was conducted. Emerging new modes of performance were frequently evolved from a transculturation of foreign structures and ideas.

At such times of social/cultural change, numerous efforts in acculturation were also undertaken. Successful or not, they broke the ground from which transculturation would eventually grow. Instances of acculturation often happened to supply the first exposure of a foreign model, if even in a flawed copy; artists of the avant-garde then would take up the model and reshape it. An example is *The Chalk Circle*, a play written in the twenties by the German poet Klabund, which was a commercially very successful acculturation of the old Chinese text. Brecht's *The Caucasian Chalk Circle*, written twenty years later, achieved a genuine transculturation, deconstructing the original's form and revisioning the motif to arrive at a distinctly new work in which the original Chinese fable had been dialectically sublated.

* * *

The growing number of international performance festivals is breaking down the barriers between the world's theatre cultures. An international community is emerging where those who make and those who consume theatre become increasingly familiar with the multitude of forms and issues presented on the stages of all nations. Foreign performance modes are welcomed not in spite of but because of their Otherness. The models they are offering have been investigated and, as to be expected, first used in acculturation efforts which range from simplistic application to sophisticated adaptation. Creative transculturation has happened on many occasions in the thirty-five years that have passed since the first International Festival of Theatre in Paris, in 1954, marked the beginnings of a period of extensive experimentation and fundamental change in Western performance.

The contemporary Western theatre, in spite of proliferating intercultural

36

exchanges, has been stagnant for more than a decade now. It appears to be ready and waiting for a new leap. Transculturation belongs among the projects which could propel it into such forward movement. Performances that presented acculturations introduced in recent years many models which so far haven't been thoroughly explored. New paradigms—as they were proposed, for instance, by postmodernist, poststructuralist, or feminist criticism—offer fascinating options for the project "transculturation." The theatre waits for new performance works that achieve a true sublation of the "Other" and the "Own."

Criticism, Culture, and Performance
An Interview with Edward Said

by

Bonnie Marranca, Marc Robinson, Una Chaudhuri

The publication of Edward Said's Orientalism, *followed by the more recent* The World, the Text, and the Critic, *influenced an entire generation of scholars and students in literary and culture studies. A Palestinian, born in Jerusalem, he has been an active spokesman for the Palestinians, writing and lecturing frequently on the Mid-East and international politics. A professor of English and Comparative Literature at Columbia University, Said also writes music criticism for* The Nation. *His writings on music will appear in the forthcoming* Musical Elaborations, *coinciding with his new political study* Culture and Imperialism. *In March 1990, Bonnie Marranca, Marc Robinson, and Una Chaudhuri met with Edward Said for a conversation.*

I

BONNIE MARRANCA: Since you write on music performance, tell us how you feel about this activity in your life, and how it is perceived by others in the literary world.

EDWARD SAID: I think the isolation of musical culture from what is called literary culture is almost total. What used to be assumed to be a kind of passing knowledge or literacy on the part of literary people with regard to music is now non-existent. I think there are a few desultory efforts to be interested in the rock culture and pop music, that whole mass culture phenomenon, on the part of literary intellectuals. But the world that I'm interested in, the music of classical performance and opera and the so-called high-culture dramas that have persisted largely from the nineteenth century, is almost totally mysterious to literary people. I think they regard what I do as a kind of lark. I've demonstrated my seriousness by giving a series of lectures last spring, the Wellek Lectures at the University of California at Irvine, which are normally very heavy-duty literary theory lectures. I gave them on what I call musical elaborations, of which the first lecture of three was on performance.

It was called "Performance as an extreme occasion." I was also interested in the role of music in the creation of social space. In the third lecture I talked about music and solitude and melody, which are subjects that interest me a great deal. But I don't think one can really worry about music seriously without some active participation in musical life. My own background is that of a pianist. I studied piano quite seriously when I was an undergraduate at Princeton and with teachers at Juilliard. So I think what interests me in the whole phenomenon is not so much the reviewing aspect. I prefer trying to deal with the problem of the composer and the problem of performance as separate but interrelated issues.

MARRANCA: Your music criticism seems to be different from your literary criticism. Not only is the subject matter different, but it doesn't seem to be as—let me see if I can choose the right word, because I don't want to mean it in any kind of pejorative sense—it's lighter, it's not as dense and politically engaged. Of course, it doesn't always lend itself to that, depending on the subject matter. On the other hand, the piece that you did on Verdi's *Aida* is a model for a new kind of theatre history. But it seems to me that there is something you allow yourself to do in music criticism that is not there in your literary criticism.

SAID: What I'm moved by in music criticism are things that I'm interested in and like. I am really first motivated by pleasure. And it has to be sustained over a long period of time. I don't write reviews; I think that's a debased form, to write a kind of scorecard, morning-after kind of thing about performance. So what I like to do is to go to many more performances than I would ever write about and then over a period of time, certain things crystallize out of my mind as I reflect on them and think about them and the music I'll play over. In the end, what I really find abides are the things that I care about. I don't know what those are until after a period of time has elapsed. It's a different type of occasional writing from the kind that I do in literary criticism, where I'm involved in much longer terms of debates. Whereas in this I don't really engage with too much in music criticism, because most of it is to me totally uninteresting. There are a couple of interesting music critics around. Not the journalistic ones. Andrew Porter in the *New Yorker* I think is challenging and quite brilliant at times. And then there are people who write from the extreme right wing, like Samuel Lipman, who writes for *The New Criterion*, and Edward Rothstein, who writes for the *New Republic*, who are very intelligent music critics. And that's about it. The rest is really a desert; people who write about music in a non-musicological way are quite rare.

On the other hand, I have had lots of response from young musicologists, who write me about some of the issues that come up. For example, I wrote a piece about feminism in music and the problem of that. And I've written about the problems of political power and representation over the years in some of the things I've done for *The Nation*. But my main overriding concern is a record of a certain kind of enjoyment, which I think can be given literary form, without drawing attention to itself as a kind of tour de force. "Lighter" is the word you used, I would call it glib and superficial.

UNA CHAUDHURI: Do you think that performance, as a category, has something to do with the difference?

SAID: Tremendously. That's what I'm really interested in. I think the thing that got me started was Glenn Gould. It was really the first extended piece that I wrote which appeared the year he died, or the year after he died—'82 or '83—in *Vanity Fair*. I'd long been fascinated with him. And I also was very interested in the phenomenon of Toscanini. Just because it seemed to me that both of them seemed to be musicians whose work, in a certain sense, was *about* performance. There was no attempt to pretend they were doing something else, but they had sort of fixated on the notion of performance and carried it to such an extreme degree that it compelled attention on its own, and it attracted attention to the artificiality of performance. And to the conventions of it, and to the strange—in the case of Toscanini—well, Bonnie, you write about it, too, in your essay on performance versus singing—the difference between performers who heighten the occasion and those who turn it into a kind of extension of the drawing room or social occasion. So performance is very interesting because then there's the other problem, that you don't have either in theatre, the visual and/or literary arts, in that the performance of music is so momentary—it's over!—I mean, you can't go back to it, anyway, really. And so there's a kind of sporting element that I'm trying to capture. I talked about it once with Arthur Danto who said, for example, if you read his pieces, they're all about going back over to an exhibition, leaving aside what he says and what his attitudes and his ideas are about art. I can't do that. So I have to go back, really, to my recollection. And my attempts, in my own mind, to restate it or

40

experience it in another context.

MARC ROBINSON: On the whole idea of performance, let me draw you out a bit on opera performance, especially the staging of it. For so many people in the theatre, the whole world of opera is a foggy, dead zone that most of us don't go to because the theatricality of it is so conservative. But now many of the experimental directors are going back to opera—Robert Wilson, Peter Sellars, Andrei Serban—and trying to revive it from a theatre background. Where do you see opera performance going?

SAID: Well, it's a tremendously interesting subject that excites me in many different ways. I think for the most part there is a deadness at the heart of opera performance, largely because of institutions like the Met, which for one reason or another—some of the reasons are perfectly obvious—has been dominated by what I call Italian *verismo* opera—and strengthened in this ridiculous kind of thing by the revival, that began in the '60s, of the *bel canto* tradition. The result of this is that a kind of hegemony has formed between the blue chip opera companies like the Met, and this repertory, and has frozen out a large amount of really extraordinary music. It has hardened performance style into a ridiculous conventionalism which has now become the norm. It infects everybody, even the greatest singers. It is certainly true of Pavarotti, sort of on the right; and on the left, Jessye Norman. You see what I'm trying to say? It's narcotized audiences. The thing I cannot understand is how people can sit through operas at the Met.

ROBINSON: I remember when you reviewed the Schoenberg opera *Erwartung* and were so disappointed. Didn't you say something about how it would be much more rewarding just to stay at home and stage it in your mind?

SAID: Exactly. Or watch it as a concert performance with Jessye Norman. It's the story of a woman who's going mad. And she's looking for her betrothed. The text is written—texts in operas are very interesting—by a Viennese medical student. The text is not of great literary value, but it's about hysteria and it bears an interesting relation, Adorno says, to Freud's case studies. So it is a minute, seismographic dissolution of a consciousness. Now here is this wonderful singer who hasn't got a clue what it's about, much too large in size to represent neurasthenia and hysteria and all this kind of stuff. As the opera progresses she goes deeper and deeper into the forest losing her mind and looking for her fiancé. And then it's discovered she really might be a patient in a mental institution who's run away. And right in the middle of the set—right in the middle of the stage—is this enormous grand piano. What is a grand piano doing in the middle of a forest? So

41

I opined that the reason she was going mad was that she couldn't figure out what to do with the grand piano. Which produces a kind of—I mean, you could say—it's a kind of perverse version of the opera. It's a glorious misinterpretation of the opera. That's not what's intended; it was supposed to be a deeply serious kind of thing, and it just didn't work. That's what the Met does, and I don't understand how it continues to do that.

ROBINSON: Maybe the consequence of that is there are certain works of music-theatre that simply shouldn't be staged. You always hear that with dramatic literature, there are certain "unstageable" texts—an awful lot of Shakespeare . . .

SAID: Yes, that's certainly true, but a lot of those derive from performances where the unstageability of the piece can be made evident, you know, like a late Ibsen play, *When We Dead Awaken*. It has a lot to do with musical performance as well as opera . . . That is to say, how do these—this is a sort of Gramscian phrase—how do these hegemonic canons get formed? I mean, for example, the exclusion of French opera is really quite extraordinary. There is a wonderful tradition of French music and French drama—music-drama—that just doesn't find its way onto the American stages. Think of Rameau; think of Berlioz; think of most of Rossini, aside from *The Barber of Seville*. I mean, Rossini was a French opera writer. Berlioz: you never see him. Bizet is the author of ten operas, of which *Carmen* gets fitful performances—*Carmen* is one of the great masterpieces—but precisely because it's kind of an anti-French and anti-German opera, in a way. Then there's Massenet and Fauré. Why this *verismo* and then a little smattering of Wagner—Wagner sort of turned into Italian. . . .

MARRANCA: I think the last time we spoke we talked a little bit about the Philip Glass operas, about whether you had seen *Einstein on the Beach*, *Akhnaten*, or *Satyagraha*. Are you interested in the contemporary repertoire?

SAID: I am. I've heard those and I've seen videos of them—one or two of Glass's things. It's not a musical aesthetic that moves me tremendously. It doesn't seem to me to exploit to the maximum what is available there.

MARRANCA: What about as critical material, in the sense of writing about or looking at the *Akhnaten* opera. . . . Even in terms of political themes I would have thought they'd attract your attention.

SAID: That's true. It's just . . . I don't know. I can't explain it. As I say, I work with fairly strong likes and dislikes, pleasures and so on . . . I don't derive the kind of interest from Glass that I would have found, say, in other contemporary composers, like Henze. I think Henze is a more interesting writer of opera.

MARRANCA: I was interested to read in a recent interview—one of the things you mentioned in talking about your writing—how the concepts of polyphonic voice and chorus interest you. Could you elaborate on that in terms of your own critical writing?

SAID: These are things it takes a while to fetch out of one's own interests and predilections. I seem to have always been interested in the phenomenon of polyphony of one sort or another. Musically, I'm very interested in contrapuntal writing, contrapuntal forms. The kind of complexity that is available, aesthetically, to the whole range from consonant to dissonant, the tying together of multiple voices in a kind of disciplined whole, is something that I find tremendously appealing.

MARRANCA: How do you extend it to your own essay?

SAID: I extend it, for example, in an essay I did on exile, basing it on personal experience. If you're an exile—which I feel myself, in many ways, to have been—you always bear within yourself a recollection of what you've left behind and what you can remember, and you play it against the current experience. So there's necessarily that sense of counterpoint. And by counterpoint I mean things that can't be reduced to homophony. That can't be reduced to a kind of simple reconciliation. My interest in comparative literature is based on the same notion. I think the one thing that I find, I guess, the most—I wouldn't say repellent, but I would say antagonistic—for me is identity. The notion of a *single* identity. And so multiple identity, the polyphony of many voices playing off against each other, without, as I say, the need to reconcile them, just to hold them together, is what my work is all about. More than one culture, more than one awareness, both in its negative and its positive modes. It's basic instinct.

CHAUDHURI: Do you think there are certain cultures and cultural practices that are more encouraging of polyphony?

SAID: Absolutely. For example, in music, one of the things I've been very interested in—and it occupies the last part of the three sections of my book on music, which will appear next year, is a kind of opposition between forms that are based upon development and domination. Like sonata. Sonata form is based on statement, rigorous development, recapitulation. And a lot of things go with that: the symphony, for example, I'm staying within the Western, classical world; certain kinds of opera are based upon this, versus forms that are based upon what I would call developing variations, in which

43

conflict and domination and the overcoming of tension through forced reconciliation is not the issue. There the issue it to prolong, like in a theme and variation, in fugal forms. In polyphony, like in my own tradition, the work of Um Kulthum. She was the most famous classical Arab singer of the twentieth century. Her forms are based upon an inhabiting of time, not trying to dominate it. It's a special relationship with temporality. Or the music of Messiaen, for example, the great French avant-garde composer who I think is divine. You see the dichotomy of that. On the one hand, domination/development; on the other, a kind of proliferation through variation and polyphonic relationship. Those are the culture practices that I think one could use as a typology of *other* culture practices: they're based on the whole idea of community, overlapping vs. coercive domination and enlightenment—the narratives of enlightenment and achievement that are to be found in novels.

CHAUDHURI: I'm very interested in what you say about this idea of inhabiting the time of performance, instead of dominating it.

SAID: Trying to ride it. It's a phrase that comes out of Gerard Manley Hopkins who has a very strange relationship with time in his poetry, especially the last part of his first great poem, *The Wreck of the Deutschland*. There's this whole thing where the question of whether you try to resist the time and erect the structure, or you try to ride time and live inside the time.

CHAUDHURI: I think of theatre performance as such, as somehow demanding that the time be inhabited. That is, it makes its own demands, even in the masterful performer, who may try to dominate it, but may not succeed.

SAID: Yes. There really is a difference in musical performance between people who are involved in remaking the music and inhabiting it in that way, as opposed to just dispatching it with efficiency and tremendous technical skill.

ROBINSON: It is also very much in the nature of the exile. I mean, there's a sense that you're either living in the past or living in an ideal future, and the present is such a dangerous equivocal realm where you can't place yourself, and yet you're forced to.

SAID: What's interesting about it is, of course, that you get a sense of its provisionality. That's what I like about it. There's no attempt made to pretend that it's the natural way to do it. It's giving up in a temporal sort of way to that moment.

ROBINSON: Such a balancing act too. Both in terms of time, but also in terms of the exile's relationship to the world. On the one hand, you have the wonderful worldliness or the ability to partake of so many regions. And on the other hand, the enforced isolation. How does one balance between those two?

SAID: I don't know. I don't think there's a formula for it. I think one can call it a kind of ceaseless, but unresolved, trafficking between those situations.

II

ROBINSON: The whole idea of private space connects to that and might be a topic to pursue. I'm very moved by your idea if the secular intellectual, the secular artist, partaking of the public world in a real, strong way. And yet all the changes that are going on now in Eastern Europe started me thinking about alternatives to that point of view. There was an anecdote about East German playwright Heiner Müller—he had always been in opposition to the government—who was asked by somebody from Western Europe, "Aren't you excited now that the chains are off, you're able to write your plays that really do take on the political situation, take on the government, what have you . . ." And he said, "No, actually, freedom now means freedom to read Proust, to stay at home in my library." That seems to signal a rediscovery of private space, a retreat from what used to be an enforced secularity.

SAID: Privacy for me is very jealously guarded, because so out of my control is the public dimension of the world I live in, which has to do with a peculiar sensitivity and intransigence of the Palestinian situation. And thinking about it for the last fifteen or twenty years has been very difficult for me to guard. Partly the music has been very much that way, because it's a non-verbal idiom. I've been involved in the thick of these battles over what one says, what one can say, and all that kind of stuff. The public has been so much with me it's been impossible for me to retreat into the private. Although, obviously, we all do have a kind of intimate private life. But it's not recoverable for me in any easy way. In the last couple of years—partly because I'm getting older—I've been deeply resentful of how much, quite against my will and intention and any plan that I might have had, public life has usurped so much of my time and effort. By that, I don't mean only politics. I mean teaching, writing, the whole sense of having an audience—sometimes completely unpredictable and against my will. So that inwardness is a very, very rare commodity. I'm not sure that my case is a special case. I think it may be true of more people than we suspect.

45

CHAUDHURI: Do you think that somehow a certain kind of engaged intellectual is being made to carry more cultural burden than ever before?

SAID: Well, I feel it. I can't speak for others. I find it very hard to speak for others, because I'm in a strange position. I mean, I don't have as much time for reflection. And that's why, for me, the musical experience has been so important. Because it's something that isn't changed and inflected in quite the ways that some of the other things I've been doing have been. I just feel that for the public intellectual it can be extremely debilitating. It's almost paranoid: something you say can be twisted into a thousand different forms or only one different form that can have untold consequences. And in my case, also, I have many quite different and totally impermeable audiences. I write a monthly column in Arabic for one of the largest weeklies in the Arab world. And then the constituencies you have, necessarily, in the world of European languages is also very different. So it's extremely draining, just to try to keep up with it, much less to contribute.

ROBINSON: I wonder if we're going to see some of the models of the intellectual artist change, as is the case already in Eastern Europe, with many who are now retreating from that public role—seeing it as a burden, and now evolving into a secluded hermeticism. A lot of the artists there want to rediscover beauty.

SAID: I understand that perfectly. What we live in, in a way, is what Eliot called a wilderness of mirrors: endless multiplication, without tremendous significance, but just a spinning on. And you just want to say: enough. I don't want too much to do with that. And therefore, one of the things that I find myself thinking about, not only privacy that as we talked about earlier is virtually impossible, but also looking at performance exactly like Gould, who understood this problem, and because of that, therefore, was able to focus and specialize and control what he did to the extent that it wasn't a limitless spinning out. There was this kind of—now this hasn't been written enough about or noted about Gould enough—massive effort on his part from the moment he thought about a work to practicing, preparing, and then performing it, and then recording it. He is one of the unique examples of somebody who was a public performer, whose attempt was to enrich the art of performance by, at the same time, controlling it. There is something, of course, quite cold and deadening about it, at the same time. But on the other hand, it's an interesting model to think about. Not many people do that. Most people tend to be profligate and they want more multiplication. There is a sense in which he wanted that, but he wanted to control it as much as possible. Perhaps because he feared that being on the stage had

46

already showed him what was likely to happen: that he would just become a creature of this public space.

ROBINSON: Genet might be another example, a man who was always preserving the private realm.

SAID: Exactly.

ROBINSON: In *Prisoner of Love*, he was able to understand what went on in the Middle East because of his own experience of outsiderhood.

CHAUDHURI: And also in the plays as well.

MARRANCA: Beckett, too.

SAID: But what you feel in Genet and Gould you don't feel in Beckett, that is, that there's a flirting with danger. I've never felt that about Beckett. Who can't admire him—but on the other hand, there is a kind of safety in Beckett's work that you don't find in Genet. In Genet you feel the incredible risk involved in all of his drama.

CHAUDHURI: It's also a provocation, isn't it?

MARRANCA: One of the things that strikes me about Beckett is that he's so great a writer and so overpowers theatricality that it's not necessary ever to see him performed. But Genet gains by being in the theatre . . . We've been talking about the private moment and the Eastern European situation, the sense of aloneness and solitude that somehow seems to be demanded after so strong a public life.

The death of Beckett set many people wondering about just what will come after Beckett, of course. And in some ways it seems it's the end of the universal playwright and the international dramatic repertoire. Also, because culture has become so public and so much a part of spectacle, and where there's so little emphasis on the private moment, it seems to me that drama, which is such a private, reflective, intimate form anyway, is falling further and further down in the hierarchy of forms experienced by serious people who would ordinarily have gone to theatre, those who read serious novels and go to the opera. People like Havel and Fugard became known not necessarily because they are great playwrights. They got into the international repertoire because of their politics and their symbolic value. It seems more and more that drama will be a kind of local knowledge. And in the theatre we see the ascendancy of spectacle, of performance, rather than drama. International performers like, say, Laurie Anderson or Wilson, make things that can travel in culture.

SAID: Or Peter Brook. . . . But even Laurie Anderson, and Brook in particular—what underlies them, also, paradoxically is a kind of modesty of means. It's not like a traveling opera. It has, in fact, a kind of easily-packed baggage, which you can transport from country to country and do with a small repertory, the same pieces. But I think one thing that you didn't mention about drama—that in the Palestinian situation, for example, which is the only one I can speak about with any assurance—is that the drama has a testimonial value, which is different from symbolic, when you talk about symbolic. That is to say—take Joseph Papp canceling that Palestinian play, *The Story of Kufur Shamma,* last summer. It wasn't because of the content of the play, it was Palestinians talking about their experience. That was what was threatening. And that's why he had to cancel it. So on that level it is local knowledge, but a local knowledge that is frequently engaged in translocal issues. Things that are of interest to other places. I suppose the burden placed upon the playwright and the performer is somehow to translate this local situation into an idiom that is contiguous to and touches other situations.

MARRANCA: In that way, I suppose, drama can travel. But so much of it now, when you compare the theatre of the last four, five, or six decades—what used to be considered international and of interest to an international audience—no longer appears on Broadway. For example, when was the last, say, German or Hungarian or French play on Broadway? In this sense the international repertoire is shrinking.

SAID: Although, I'll tell you, Bonnie, I was in Delphi last summer giving a talk at an international conference on Greek tragedy. I talked about Wagner, I believe. Every night there was a performance of a play in the theatre at Delphi. And I was there for two performances, the second of which was extraordinary, the performance by Wajda's troupe of a Polish-language *Antigone* . . .

ROBINSON: I saw it in Poland.

SAID: You saw it in Poland. Well, I saw it in Delphi. And the audience was entirely Greek . . . modern Greeks, obviously. It was overwhelming. It seemed to me to have there a peculiar mix of things. It was the ''OK cultural festival,'' it was the antique representation of self that was acceptable to the powers-that-be, because it's sponsored by the Greek government which is in a great crisis at the moment. It was an occasion for the local folk. OK, all that. But in addition, it was for me a very powerful theatrical experience. I don't know which performance you saw, because there were several versions. When did you see it?

ROBINSON: In Krakow in '85. It was a very bad time, politically, for Poland.

SAID: Were there transformations of the chorus?

ROBINSON: Yes. The chorus changed throughout the play—moving from bureaucrats—maybe Parliament members—to protesting students to, finally, shipyard workers, like those from Gdansk who started Solidarity. In a Polish theatre, it becomes extremely powerful. Actually, it's an event that makes me question or at least want to take issue with your idea, Bonnie, about the universality of a play.

SAID: No, I think what she's talking about—which I'm interested in—the great master theatrical talent that produces, I have to keep using the word over and over again, a masterwork of the sort that created the nineteenth-century repertory theatre, that continues into the late symbolic tragedies of Ibsen and Strindberg, and then moves into Brecht and then Beckett. There's a pedigree here that you're alluding to: people who dominate the stage. The model is one of domination. I don't regret its end, to be perfectly honest with you, because of a lot of what goes with it. In the same way that you could say, well what about the great—think of this—what about the great Austro-Germanic symphonic tradition that begins with Haydn, goes through Mozart, Beethoven, Schumann, Brahms, I suppose Wagner's in there a little bit, Mahler, Bruckner, Schoenberg . . . and then what? Nothing. It ends. And you get these local nationalists, you know, Bartok. I mean, it took place, but we can live without it. It can be respected and memorialized in various ways, but I'm not so sure of that, given the damage to other surrounding clumps it overshadows and dominates. It produces a certain canon or canonicity.

ROBINSON: Yeah, and aren't we all trashing the canon!

SAID: Not trashing. It isn't the be-all-and-end-all, is what I'm saying.

MARRANCA: I understand your point of view about attacking universality, of course, but the issue is that in drama there's almost nothing else. There are plenty of musical traditions to follow. There are plenty of great novels that are breaking out of the mode and being enjoyed by wide groups and nationalities.

SAID: Yes, that's true.

MARRANCA: But with drama, the whole thing collapses, because if there's no international repertoire, then it's a gradual decreasing of the form itself. And what's left are just the bestsellers, the topical plays that somehow travel, and then the classics. But maybe two of Ibsen, or a few of Brecht.

What I'm saying is the other traditions are so much richer, and the repertoires are so wide, but if you begin to have a form which worldwide audiences lose interest in—in terms of the new—then I think it's a problem for the form, and that that's different than, say, the situation in music.

ROBINSON: But isn't that a Romantic idea, that of an international work of art?

MARRANCA: But they still exist in art, if you look at paintings from many, many countries, a lot of it even looks largely the same, and there are good and bad works. I see nothing wrong with large groups of people in different cultures around the world appreciating the same work. That always happens in terms of fiction, for example.

SAID: The way you describe it, it certainly sounds special and peculiar to the drama. But why is it?

MARRANCA: One of the things I hinted at before is that what we are seeing now are international spectacles found in several cultural festivals, works by Brook or Laurie Anderson, whose recent piece can be just as accessible in Japan or Western Europe or Brazil, or someplace else. Often we're seeing a kind of internationalization of performance. When I use the word ''performance,'' I mean something different from the theatre. It's not textbound, it doesn't deal with a play. Performance work is highly technological, it reflects a certain transfer of pop imagery and music.

SAID: Recognizable and commodified styles.

MARRANCA: Exactly. And they are understood by people all over the world now, because of the international youth culture. And that has unseated drama somewhat . . .

SAID: And also because of film and television and all the apparatus of the culture industry.

MARRANCA: So that the great theatres now tend to remain in their own countries and build their repertoires on the classics, redo them, and are rejuvenated by new people. But we don't see this travel in theatre that we're seeing in video or visual arts, or fiction, or ''performance'' as a genre in itself.

SAID: And, of course, in music you find it in the cult of the traveling maestro or the celebrated pianist or the important diva and tenor, and so on and so forth.

ROBINSON: Maybe theatre is less suited to this kind of travel because of the holdover of the idea that a play should somehow address the issues of the people in front of it, the audiences. It's the most socially-connected of the arts, of course. And I would think people would be reluctant to give up that possibility of engagement that the theatre provides, in a much more immediate way than art, music, or TV.

CHAUDHURI: There's another way of looking at this. There has always been this dimension of locality in the theatre, this connection to a specific time and place. And it's always been special to the drama. Now, for all its power technology is not going to promote a better means of a direct collaboration with people than the theatre event. So that this ''local knowledge'' characteristic may be what will save the theatre, and give it its future.

SAID: But she mourns it. I think you really do have a nostalgia for the great figures. Or the great forms. It's a kind of Lukacsian, early Lukacs—you know, *The Soul and Form* . . . a kind of Lukacsian forlornness and melancholy, which is there. I think you're right. I'm not saying you're wrong.

MARRANCA: To tell you the truth, I'm more interested in the idea of performance than I am in drama, with a very few exceptions. Of course, as a publisher, knowing what it's like to sell books, worldwide, on a very practical basis I find a loss of interest in drama.

SAID: What does that mean? You've lost interest in the drama and you watch the performance. In other words, it would matter more to you that Vanessa Redgrave was acting in a play, rather than that the play was, say, *Macbeth*, or something like that. Is that what you mean by performance?

MARRANCA: No. I mean something else. I've lost interest in conventionalized stagings of drama. In that case, I would rather sit home with a play and not see it. Though I take a larger interest in performances such as Wilson's work, and some avant-garde performance.

CHAUDHURI: That's really a question of quality, isn't it?

MARRANCA: Yes.

SAID: See, the other part of it is, and I think it's very important for people like us, who are interested in these issues and questions, not simply to celebrate the avant-garde—that is to say, the novel, or the exciting and unusual that come along in the cases of Peter Sellars or Wilson—but also, to stimulate greater dissatisfaction and anger on the part of audiences who now sit sheepishly through unacceptably boring reproductions of masterpieces. That's the part that I find the most puzzling of all. Why is it that the level of critical sensibility has sunk so low? The threshold for pain is so high, that people can sit through abysmal ''conventional'' reproductions of classical masterpieces in the theatre or in opera or in music. Rather than experience something quite new in a contemporary work or a dangerous or innovative re-staging of a classical work. I don't understand that. Do you understand it?

MARRANCA: Well, certainly part of it, but not all of it, is that the commentary is so bad in the papers of note—that's one major issue.

SAID: Well, there it becomes an important thing to talk about. This is where some of Gramsci's analysis of culture is very important, where you can look at the papers of note and the people who write commentary as sort of organic intellectuals for theatre interests. In other words, they are advance guard, in the military sense—advance guard organizers of opinion and manufacturers of consent for important interests in the theatre, whose role is to colonize and narcotize and lobotomize audiences into accepting certain kinds of conventions as the norm. I think that's an important part of one's work: to raise dissatisfaction at this time.

MARRANCA: You know, the other thing is that, unlike the art audience, for example, which always wants to see something new, the theatre audience and music audience basically want to see the greatest hits in familiar settings. And so the audiences are fundamentally different, even though they might be the same people.

ROBINSON: But sometimes that struggling with those greatest hits can be very fruitful, and writers are doing it all the time. Hofmannsthal will deal with the *Electra* story as handed down and absorb it into a creation of his own. Heiner Müller will write HAMLETMACHINE in order to kill *Hamlet*.

SAID: Or, in some cases, to keep adapting to the changing conditions of performance imposed by the patrons.

ROBINSON: It seems like there are two ways for contemporary artists to deal with the classic tradition, and the canon. One is just to keep pushing it aside and write or compose new work. And then the other one—Heiner Müller, Hofmannsthal—is to try to absorb it and then remake it somehow, to kind of neutralize it, recharge it in a subversive way.

SAID: I'm of the second opinion. In all of the discussions that have been going on in literary studies about the canon, and the whole question of the Western tradition, it seems to me that one of the great fallacies, in my view, has been the one that suggests that you, first of all, show how the canon is the result of a conspiracy—a sort of white male cabal—of people who, for example, turned Hawthorne into one of the great cult figures of American literature and prevented a whole host of, for example, more popular women writers of the time, or regional writers, and so on. . . . Therefore, what is enjoined upon holders of this view is you push aside Hawthorne and you start reading these other people. But that is to supplant one canon with another, which, it seems to me, really reinforces the whole idea of canon and, of course, all of the authority that goes with it. That's number one. Number two—half of this is my education and half of this is my age and predilection—I'm interested in the canon. I'm very conservative in the sense that I think that there is something to be said, at least on the level of preference and pleasure, for aspects of work that has persisted and endured and has acquired and accreted to it a huge mass of differing interpretations, ranging from hatred to reverence. It's something that I find enriching as a part of knowledge. So I'm not as willing as a lot of people to scuttle it. My view is to assimilate to canons these other contrapuntal lines.

You could take the extreme view of Benjamin: every document of civilization is also a document of barbarity. You can show—and I've tried to show it in this book that I've been writing on culture and imperialism for ten years—that the great monuments (well, I did it in the *Aida* case) the great monuments of culture are not any less monuments for their, in the extreme version, complicity with rather sordid aspects of the world. Or, in the less extreme case, for their participation, their engagement in social, historical processes. I find that interesting. I'm less willing to toss them overboard and say, ''Let's focus on the new.'' I mean, I find the idea of novelty in and of itself doesn't supply me with quite enough nourishment.

ROBINSON: The whole canon becomes an incredibly sharp weapon for a non-Western writer, too. Somebody like Soyinka can take *The Balcony*, or *The Bacchae*, or *Threepenny Opera* and rewrite them as parables of colonialism.

SAID: And not only that, but in the best instances—I think more interesting than Soyinka is the work of the Sudanese novelist Tayeb Salih. He's written several novels, but his masterpiece is a novel called *The Season of Migration to the North*—it came out in the late '60s—that is quite consciously a work that is reacting to, writing back to, Conrad's *Heart of Darkness*. This is a story, not of a white man who comes to Africa, but a black man who goes to Europe. And the result is, on one level, of course, a reaction to Conrad. In other words, this is a post-colonial fable of what happens when a black man goes to London and wreaks havoc upon a whole series of English women. There's a kind of sexual fable. But if you look at it more deeply, it not only contains within it the history of decolonization and reaction to

Western imperialism, but it also, in my opinion, deepens the tragedy by showing that this man's reactive revenge, which to many readers in the Third World, in the Arab and African world, is a just revenge. But Salih does it fresh because it's futile, pathetic and ultimately tragic. Because it reinforces the cycle of isolation as insufficiency of the politics of identity. It is not enough to just be a black wreaking havoc on a white, there's another world that you have to live in. And in that sense, it's a much richer and more interesting work than Conrad, because it dramatizes the limitations of Conrad. And I'm second to none in my admiration for Conrad, but this is a quite amazing type of thing which is in the novel, which is quite powerful in its own sense—it's in Arabic not in English—depends on the Conrad novel, but is independent of it at the same time. It's quite fascinating.

ROBINSON: And that may be a solution, as it were, to the whole problem of locality of a work of art. Because what you are describing can be both a very potent work in a local context, but it's also an intercultural work.

SAID: Absolutely. And that's where I finally disagree with Bonnie's idea. In the implied contrast between the local and the universal, I think the local is more interesting than the universal. It depends where you look at it from. If you look at it from the point of view of the colonized world, as Fanon says, the universal is always achieved at the expense of the native. I'll give you a perfect example—look at the case of Camus. Camus is the writer who, practically more than anyone in modern French culture, represents universality. A more careful reading of the work shows that in every instance of his major fiction, and even the collections of stories, most of them are set in Algeria. Yet, they are not *of* Algeria. They're always parables of the German occupation of France. You look even more carefully at that and you look for the point of view of Algerian independence, which was achieved after Camus's death in 1962—and of course, Genet answers to this, because Genet was involved in the same issue in *The Screens*. If you look at that and you see what Camus was doing throughout his work was using the cultural discourse of the French Lycée—which gives rise to universalism and the human condition and the resistance to Nazism and Fascism and all the rest of it—as a way of blocking the emergence of an independent Algeria. . . . It seems to me, *there* is the importance of local knowledge which you bring to bear upon this text. And put it back in its situation and locale. And there it doesn't become any less interesting, it becomes more interesting, precisely because of the discrepancy between its universal reach and scope on the one hand, and reputation; and on the other, its rather more complicit local circumstances. But maybe we're making too much of it . . .

MARRANCA: I think in some sense we're talking about different things. Because literature and the general secular intellectual life lead a more on-going life in terms of debate and internal politics than drama does. I simply wanted to point out, if drama was no longer going to add in some sense to an international repertoire, and we were only going to have a local drama, which I value also, then that means something entirely different. For example, in drama we don't really have secular theatre intellectuals in the sense that literature does. Almost all discourse and dialogue and debate on theatre issues is either in the reviewing mechanisms of the popular papers, which don't have any kind of interesting debate going on internally, or in marginalized journals like our own, or in the academic world. So that theatre issues are not brought to bear on general cultural-political issues in the same way that other subjects are treated now, in science or in literature. So I think that this kind of loss is more serious for theatre than it would be in the novel.

SAID: I think you're absolutely right, and I think—yes, I see your point. That's a much larger way of putting it.

CHAUDHURI: In the light of what you're saying about the burden on the public intellectual, and how you get caught up in this machine of duplications and spinning out of ideas, it may be a kind of blessing or gift for the theatre to be local or private in that sense. To have it occupy a space where it can do its intercultural practice and experimental thinking without too many public pressures.

III

CHAUDHURI: About the canon—this idea of not just throwing over one canon and putting another one in its place—it really seems that what's missing in that approach is that many people are not looking at how these things are taught and how they're presented. They're really only looking at what is taught.

SAID: Yes, exactly, although "what" is important, also. The exclusion of certain "whats" is very interesting.

CHAUDHURI: But it's almost as if one doesn't want to give up something deeper, which is certain models of evaluating texts . . .

SAID: I call them models of veneration, and that's what they are.

CHAUDHURI: That veneration is transferred to something else, and it leaves you in the same abject position *vis-à-vis* the text or the art work or whatever.

SAID: Well, it is one of the constitutive problems of academic debate in general, but it's basically unanchored in real engagement with the real world. It's largely theoretical. So the ''what,'' on the one level, is equally important. It's a claim to certain kinds of authority and turf and so on. But the ''how,'' you know, the ''how'' becomes relatively weightless, in a certain sense; it becomes one method among others. I'll give you an example of what I'm trying to say. Look at the result of all the massive infusion that American literary, and I suppose, cultural studies in general, have received through ''theory'' in the last thirty years: structuralism, poststructuralism, deconstruction, semiotics, Marxism, feminism, all of it. Effectively they're all weightless, I mean they all represent academic choices and a lot of them are not related to the circumstances that originally gave rise to them. For example, Third World studies in the university are a very different thing from Soyinka or Salih in their own immediately post-colonial situation trying to write a narrative of the experience. You know how sometimes a critic like Ngugi talking about decolonizing the mind is one thing for somebody who's been in prisons, lived through the whole problems of neo-imperialism, the problems of the native language vs. English, etc. They're very different things than somebody deciding, well, I'm going to specialize in decolonization or the discourse of colonialism. So that's a very great problem.

CHAUDHURI: The academy is actively rendering them weightless . . .

SAID: In a certain sense you can't completely do away with that, because the university is a kind of utopian place. To a certain extent, these things should happen. Perhaps the disparity between the really powerful and urgent originary circumstances of a cultural method, and its later transmutation as a theoretical choice in the university, is too great.

CHAUDHURI: Do you think it should remain utopian? Maybe that's part of the problem, that this is a model that has outgrown its usefulness.

SAID: I think that's where we are right now. We're watching a very interesting transformation. Most students, I think, the good students here, my students—and I know this from direct contact with them—are really no longer interested in theory. They're really interested in these historical, cultural contests that have characterized the history of the late twentieth century. Between racism and imperialism, colonialism, various forms of authority, various types of liberation and independence as they are reflected in culture, in aesthetic forms, in discourses and so on. So that's where I go. The problem is how you relate that to social change; at a time when it seems

56

everything is now moving away from the contests that determined the history of the twentieth century hitherto—the contests between socialism and capitalism, and so on. So it's a very troubling moment. I think the important thing is to be exploratory.

MARRANCA: You know, in fact, in the little piece in *The Guardian* that you wrote, you mention that you felt somehow the history of philosophy and politics, and general drift of intellectual life, was really almost inadequate to deal with the new situations.

SAID: I think it is. I think it certainly is.

MARRANCA: What directions might this view of the arts and sciences coming together somehow in some new understanding take? Where would you like to take it in your work?

SAID: Without getting too specific and detailed, I think that if you take a general thing that you've been interested in, interculturalism, I think that's obviously where it's going. That is to say, various types of integration between formerly disparate or different realms, like politics, history and aesthetics. But rather than just leaving it at that, it seems to me that new kinds of formations seem to be particularly interesting and important. One would be relationships of interdependence and overlapping. We've had a tendency, you see, to think of experiences in national terms. We say there's the Polish experience, there's the French experience, there's the Haitian experience, there's the Brazilian experience. It seems to me that that's pretty much over, where one could give a certain amount of fidelity and attention to basic national identities. What's interesting is the way the national identities have historically, in fact—and the present moment facilitates that—interacted and depended upon each other. I mean the relationship between Brazil and North America is very, very dramatic now in the situation of the rain forests. The relationship between North Africa and the European metropolis, is very dramatic now, because of the presence of a large number of Muslim immigrants in France.

What you begin to realize is the universality, therefore, not of stabilities, which have been the prevailing norm in cultural studies, but of migrations: these massive transversals of one realm into another. That seems to me an entirely new subject matter. Refugee studies versus the studies of stable cultural institutions which have characterized the paradigms of the social sciences and the humanities of the past. That would be one major thing. Another would be the study of what I call integrations and interdependence versus the studies dominated by nationalities and national traditions. The conflict between emergent transnational forces like Islam which is a subcontinental presence, it's an Arab presence, it's now a European presence. There's a total reconfiguration of the cultural scene, it seems to me, that can only be understood, in my opinion, historically. You could see elements of it already in the conflict between Europe and the Orient, for example, which I talked about twelve or thirteen years ago.

MARRANCA: Do you have any thoughts on interculturalism as it relates to performance or any of the other kinds of things you might want to take to your work, besides the *Aida* model of doing theatre history?

SAID: Not at this stage, no, because I'm so mired in *contested* regions between cultures. I'm very much, I'm afraid, marked by that. In other words, I'm really a creature whose current interest is very much controlled by the conflict between the culture in which I was born and the culture in which I live at present. Which is really quite a strange phenomenon. It's not just that they're different, you know, but there's a war going on and I'm involved on both sides of that. So it's very difficult for me to talk about interculturalism, which would suggest a kind of sanity and calm reflectiveness.

MARRANCA: Do you think of interculturalism as a kind of Orientalism?

SAID: Well, it can be. Yes, absolutely. Because I think there's a whole range of what is acceptable and what is not acceptable. We haven't gotten to that stage yet, I don't think, of being able to talk about it in an uninflected way, in a way that doesn't bear the scars of contests between the North and the South, or the East and the West. I mean, the geographical configuration of the world is still very strongly inscribed, at least in my vision of things.

ROBINSON: Drawing out of what's just been said, it seems that there's good interculturalism and bad interculturalism. But after I read *Orientalism*, a great paralysis set in.

SAID: Sorry about that.

ROBINSON: Every time I consider or reflect on another culture, I feel my "power" position coming into relief. But is the alternative to that power just a greater distance or isolationism? I don't want that.

SAID: No, no, no. I don't think it's possible. You know, I think one of the great flaws of *Orientalism* is the sense that it may have communicated that there is no alternative to that, which is a sort of hands-off sort of thing. That's not what I would imply. And I think, at the very end I say something like that. That there is a kind of "already given," you know, a sort of messiness and involvement of everyone of everyone else. It's just that I would like to think that the inequalities, as between, say, a native informant and a white ethnographic eye, wasn't so great. I don't know how to talk about this without seeming to congratulate myself, but it was interesting, to me at any rate, that *Orientalism*—partly because I think that it was already in the air—seemed to have released a lot of quite interesting work that went way beyond it. It instigated a certain kind of self-consciousness about cultural artifacts that had been considered to be impervious to this kind of analysis. And the irony is it didn't make them less interesting, it made them more interesting. So I think the history of Orientalism—I don't mean the book, I mean the problem—is really the history of human—how shall I put it?—human meddling, without which we can't live.

Look, any time you globalize, let's say East vs. West, you can come up with convincing formulas that always suggest the triumph of the West. That's why Naipaul is successful. I mean, that's the basis for the Naipaul appeal. He says the world is made up of people who invent telephones and those who use them. Where are the people who use telephones? We don't know that. See, you can always fall into that trap; the trap that C. L. James never fell into, because he said if you're a white man you can say you have Beethoven, and the black man's not supposed to listen to Beethoven, he's supposed to listen to Calypso. That's a trap you can't fall into. You've got to be able to make the distinctions and use what you want and think of it as part of the possession of all mankind or humankind. I don't know how to get to that point without waging the struggle on some very local and clearly circumscribed level.

So on one level it seems to me that there's a need for historical understanding of various contests. That's why I don't believe in "literary studies." I don't believe in the study of English literature by itself. It should be looked at with West Indian literature, with American literature, with French literature, with African literature, with Indian—you understand what I'm saying? The deep historicization of the circumstances of production of culture and along with that, an acute understanding of the extent to which every cultural document contains within it a history of a contest of rulers and ruled, of leader and led. And third, that what we require is a deep understanding of where we would like to go.

Transculturating Transculturation

Diana Taylor

I

A GIVEN: THEORIES TRAVEL. The question Edward Said poses in the "Traveling Theory" chapter of *The World, the Text, and the Critic* is "whether by virtue of having moved from one place and time to another an idea or theory gains or loses in strength, and whether a theory in one historical period and national culture becomes altogether different for another period or situation." In a move that echoes the crossing and blurring of national boundaries, the social sciences and the humanities are crossing disciplinary boundaries to ascertain how cultural material passes from one society to another. Terms like "transculturation," "acculturation," "neoculturation" have been used by anthropologists and literary theorists alike to describe the impact of one culture on another. My intention is to examine the changing usage of the term transculturation in relation to theatrical activity to illustrate not only how theories travel and how they change their meaning and function in different contexts, but also how the socio-economic and political power of one culture also impacts on, without altogether determining, another. However, it is essential to emphasize from the outset that transculturation is not a theatrical phenomenon but a social

60

one. The existence of theatrical hybrids (such as Peter Brook's *Mahabharata*) does not necessarily represent the deeper and more global shifts of transculturation in a society. Transculturation affects the entire culture; it involves the shifting of socio-political, not just aesthetic, borders; it modifies collective and individual identity; it changes discourse, both verbal and symbolic. Therefore, before discussing transculturation, it is necessary to clarify what we mean by "culture."

Culture, for my purposes here, involves two facets. The "first face of culture," as David Laitin calls it in *Hegemony and Culture*, is the one studied by social system theorists like Max Weber and Clifford Geertz, who hold that culture is tenacious and that cultural identities are "given" and self-reinforcing. For Geertz (in *Local Knowledge*), culture is "an historically transmitted pattern of meanings embodied in symbols, a system of inherited conceptions expressed in symbolic forms by means of which [people] communicate, perpetuate and develop their knowledge about and attitudes towards life." These theories emphasize the difficulty of ascertaining "meaning" across cultural borders. The "second face of culture" is comprised of the conscious politicization of culture, the strategic use of cultural symbols, and the recognition that "cultural identity becomes a political resource" in group action. The theory of transculturation involves both faces of culture. On one hand, it delineates the process by which symbols, discourse, and ideology are transformed as one culture changes through the imposition or adoption of another, and examines the historic and socio-political forces that produce local meanings. On the other, the theory of transculturation is a political one in that it suggests the consciousness of a society's own, historically specific, cultural manifestations—in contact with but differentiated from other societies. The various uses of the theory of transculturation examined here exemplifies the political positioning and repositioning of collectivities in their pursuit of empowerment. The issue in transculturation, then, is not only one of meaning (what do symbols mean in different contexts). It is also one of political positioning and selection: which forms, symbols or aspects of cultural identity become highlighted or confrontational, when and why.

This said, it is possible to turn to the original Latin American theories of transculturation and chart how they undergo change as they are adopted by "First World" theatre theorists.[1] The term "transculturation" was coined in 1940 by the Cuban anthropologist Fernando Ortiz to denominate the transformative process undergone by a society in the acquisition of foreign cultural material—the loss or displacement of a society's culture due to the acquisition or imposition of foreign material, and the fusion of the indigenous and the foreign to create a new, original cultural product. Ortiz defined the concept in opposition to the term *acculturation* which had been coined by U.S. anthropologists in 1936. He writes that "the term transculturation better expresses the different phases in the transitive process from one culture to another, because this process does not only imply the acquistion of culture, as connoted by the Anglo-American term *acculturation*, but it also necessarily involves the loss or uprooting of one's preceding culture, what one could call a partial *disculturation*. Moreover, it signifies the subsequent creation of new cultural phenomena that one could call *neoculturation*." One of the interesting features of Ortiz's paradigm, as Bronislaw Malinowski noted in his preface to Ortiz's work, is that it is not merely an uneasy fusion of two belief systems held simultaneously, a "mosaic." Rather, it accounts for the historic specificity and artistic originality of the new cultural phenomena. Hence, it goes beyond the syncretic model, so prevalent in current anthropological discussion, that emphasizes the co-existence of two cultural systems. The transcultural model simultanously notes the *co-existence* of elements but, just as importantly, underlines the element of *loss* of the two systems in the creation of a third.

The notable Peruvian ethnographer and novelist, José María Arguedas, expanded on the theory of transculturation. He stressed the survival of an indigenous culture "differentiated from Western culture" not in that it was unadulterated or unaffected by its contact with the West, but rather in that it was precisely a product of that contact, the "result of the long process of evolution and change experienced by the ancient Peruvian culture since the moment it suffered the impact of the Spanish invasion." The Peruvian culture Arguedas studied, like most of the inhabitants of Peru themselves, was neither "pure" Indian nor "pure" Spanish, but a mixture of both and, hence, *differentiated* from both. Uni-cultural paradigms set up to analyze their *mestizo* culture either by Eurocentric standards or by ahistoric indigenous ones were bound to misunderstand the hybrid nature of the phenomenon.

Arguedas, and the important literary critic from Uruguay, Angel Rama, go beyond Ortiz to map out the progressive or expanding nature of transculturation over time and space; both consider transculturation a shifting process, not a static, deterministic state. The areas which most directly experienced the impact of foreign culture were the ports of entry and large cultural centers like Mexico City, Buenos Aires, and Lima. Geographical accessibility was an important factor, although certainly not the only one. Class, too, played a role: the upper classes, mostly based in the cities, were more closely allied with the foreign metropolis, historically and ideologically, than were the lower ones. Gradually, however, both the foreign and the partially assimilated versions of the foreign spread to rural areas, by which time they were partially diluted by their contact with native elements. The "transcultured" people of indigenous communities, the *mestizos*, for example, were often anxious to leave traditional indigenous societies of which they no longer felt a part. Beginning in the 1950s and 1960s and up to the present, they left rural areas to try their luck in the large cities. As these groups moved to the cities, sometimes in numbers exceeding thousands a day, the urban culture too underwent profound changes as it assimilated the rural subgroups. What we are looking at, then, are ever shifting patterns—historical, geographical, economic, and linguistic—of cultural transformations. Without at the moment developing the migration pattern delineated by Arguedas and applying it to other contexts, Arguedas's study already suggests a number of connections that could be made between transculturation and "minority," and other oppositional discourses.

Transculturation is not inherently or necessarily a minority or oppositional theory, as its different uses in First and Third World contexts will illustrate. The term applies not only to other colonized or dominated cultures, but, I will argue, to dominant ones as well. Yet, while commentators like Malinowski and Arguedas would agree that both the dominant and the dominated are modified through their contact with another culture, it is clear that the interaction is neither *equal* in power or degree nor, strictly speaking, *reciprocal*. We must not minimize very significant imbalances in the crossing of cultural borders: conquest, colonialism, imperialism, tourism, or scholarly interest all involve choice and require power, even if only buying power. When the dominated cross over into the "First World," however, it is more often as slaves, refugees, exiles, or illegal "aliens" than as tourists or scholarly researchers. There is no dialogue insofar as the word connotes equality and give-and-take, in intercultural perspectives or expressions. It is clear that for all the First World "interest" and research in the Third World, the Third World knows significantly more about First World culture than the other way around.

Nonetheless, the theory of transculturation is interesting, even beyond its specific formulation in Latin America, because it allows the "minor" culture (in the sense of the positionally marginalized) an impact on the dominant one, although the interactions are not strictly speaking "dialogic" or "dialectical." Transculturation suggests a shifting or circulating pattern of cultural transference. The measurable impact of the "minor" on the "major" can be a long time coming. First World commentators often refer to intercultural exchange as if it were a conscious project, a decision to rejuvenate one's exhausted culture by those who, like Brecht, exploit, adopt, or mine other cultures "like a quarry." The Latin Americans allude to no such choice; for them, the concepts of loss and displacement are fundamental (yet noticeably absent from most First World discussion). The Latin American theorists acutely reflect the sense of loss of their native cultures while they proudly re-affirm the vitality of their new ones. By stressing the cultural survival and creativity of transculturation, they offset the implication of passivity and reification implied in a term like "quarry."

In spite of Latin America's history of colonization, which included the imposition of Western forms of self-expression and identity—such as language, artistic models, and religion—the fact remains that the native peoples of Latin America do not by and large speak, worship, or create like their dominators. Their languages, their world-views, and their art are *mestizo* to varying degrees, just as they themselves are. From the perspective of Latin American thinkers, the urgency of focusing on transculturation had to do with socio-political, rather than aesthetic, issues. They had to examine their own paradoxical reality: while 90% of the indigenous population of the Americas was decimated in the century following the conquest, by the twentieth century the indigenous and *mestizo* groups were the great majority in Latin America.

Ideologically, then, this theory was counter-hegemonic. Arguedas stated that his ambition as a white ethnographer/writer raised by indigenous people was "to unload into the current of creole Peruvian wisdom and art, the artistic and epistemic wealth of a people that was considered degenerate, debilitated, 'strange' and 'inpenetrable,' but which, in fact, was nothing but a great people oppressed by social disdain, political domination and economic exploitation on the very ground where it had once achieved its greatness."

Rather than merely revalorize the undervalorized (the indigenous), Arguedas took the colonizers' discourse (again, verbal and symbolic) and used it against them. This amounted to appropriating the signs and symbols of the *other* to express the world-view of the now defining self. As we shall see, this move involved both faces of culture—altering the meanings embedded in dominant symbols, and manipulating those symbols to create new political alliances. After all, this strategy had proved effective in the marginalization of the indigenous populations in the first place.

One example must suffice: Shortly following the conquest, the missionaries learned the autochthonous languages in order to convert the conquered to Christianity. They initially allowed the various groups to maintain their languages, and encouraged theatrical productions with all the native adornments and trimmings. In 1541, the Catholic missionary, Motolinía, described how the "*auto*" of Adam and Eve was "represented by the indigenous population in their own language, so that many of them

64

cried and showed much feeling, especially when Adam was exiled and sent out into the world." The recognizable indigenous trimmings, however, only obscured the fact that the entire world-view expressed in these outwardly familiar languages and productions had radically changed. While Adam and Eve's loss of paradise superficially resembled the indigenous peoples' loss of their world, the similarities resulted in the mystification of the vital fact that Christianity, to a large degree, *justified*, rather than *reflected*, the indigenous loss and displacement. The supposedly recognizable performances were instrumental in the transformation of the social construct that excluded native Americans; they legitimated the Spaniards' appropriation of their land (it was now represented as God's will); they rendered the familiar into a foreign, and ultimately unrecognizable, world. The *making foreign* turned the indigenous onlookers into strangers in their own land; they became positionally "marginal"; it decentered them as the "new" cultural, economic, and political center (the Spanish metropolis) re-mapped the "New" world from afar; the numerical majority became the political minority. In other words, the Spaniards co-opted the indigenous discursive and symbolic apparatus (performative, linguistic, religious) and gutted it, thus carrying out the domination of the indigenous that had been inititated with the conquest. The appropriation of indigenous discourse through theatre accompanied the forceful appropriation of land to such a degree that Maria Sten asserts, in *Vida y muerte del teatro Náhuatl*, that "theatre was for the spiritual conquest of Mexico what horses and gunpowder were for the military conquest" (my translation). In short, the colonizers realized it was more effective to take native rituals and symbols and transform them than to attack them or forbid them.

Arguedas, in turn, appropriates and subverts the language and art forms of *his* ideological (if not biological) *others*, the dominant, Eurocentric classes. He wrote novels, a non-indigenous art form which, unlike oral performance arts like drama, poetry, or singing, were meant to be read and hence resistant to the indigenous orality. Arguedas wrote in Spanish, but he invented a Spanish that would capture the Quechua style and world-view. Arguedas makes Spanish strange; he writes Quechua in a language that is not Quechua but which nonetheless enables the indigenous voices to be heard outside their relatively small language group. His is a project of bilingualism; he yokes two symbolic systems together to emphasize the cultural and historical syncretism of both. And from these two, he creates a third, an original cultural product.

Arguedas's aim, by using Spanish, differs from other writers struggling against colonization in that he does not primarily address an indigenous audience. Nor is his position the common "salvage" ethnographical one critiqued by James Clifford in *Writing Culture*. By writing down an orality otherwise doomed to disappear without a trace Arguedas does not intend to save "the vanishing primitive." Nothing could be further from Arguedas's intention than to represent the indigenous as Clifford's lost other, "lost, in disintegrating space and time, but saved in the text." The indigenous/*mestizo* is not an endangered minority but a marginalized and exploited majority. So rather than "rescue" the dominated, Arguedas strives to decenter the dominant. Arguedas sabotages the hegemonic discourse by inserting the indigenous into the dominant culture.

II

Understanding the process of transculturation and its potentially counter-hegemonic function is essential when approaching Latin American theatre. I would argue that one of the greatest obstacles, perhaps even the single most important obstacle, to the reception of Latin American theatre outside the geographical or academic area of study, is not so much that this theatre seems different, but that it looks oddly the same, that is, recognizable. In emphasizing this particular obstacle I am not ignoring or underestimating other very practical impediments such as the scarcity of texts and translations. However, I am suggesting that we rethink the apparent cause-and-effect relationship for a moment to consider the problem in a new light: if there were a greater interest in this material, there would also be more material available. If Latin American theatre seemed "exotic" or "indigenous," more foreign commentators might take greater interest in it. Can this recognizable drama possibly be artistically "original," culturally "authentic," or politically "relevant," they ask themselves?

But commentators have seldom asked the following: With all indigenous forms either truncated or transformed, what traditions were modern dramatists to draw on? If First World commentators expected these forms to be non-Western, that is, non-recognizable from their own context, what does that leave the dramatists to work with, either in terms of language or dramatic traditions? And whose mythic fantasy is tied up in this indigenous past: First World commentators or Third World playwrights? Even if they could, would playwrights want to strip away five hundred years of history to go back to some supposedly unadulterated or "pure" pre-Columbian ritualist performance—even if there were such a thing? Would these writers be more authentic and relevant if they depicted their indigenous reality as something lying outside history, or in the nebulous *before* history implied by terms like *pre*-Hispanic and *pre*-Columbian? Would playwrights working in the 1960s, 1970s, and 1980s in such extremely volatile political situations such of those of Argentina, Brazil, Chile, Uruguay, Columbia, Peru,

Mexico, Cuba, Nicaragua, Guatemala, and El Salvador to name only a few, choose to give up their contemporaneousness by going back in time to rescue forms that are no longer their own? Is not indigenous culture, as Arguedas argues, something born of the confrontation between the multiple native peoples of what is now Latin America and their conquerors? The indigenous elements with which we deal today are not those that existed before the clash but those that came into being as a result of it. What we have, then, is a complex configuration of cultural elements that looks somewhat recognizable. Yet, in fact, this hybrid product is also foreign, culturally specific, and "original" in ways scholars following any literacy competence guide to "What Americans should know" (and, worse still, many of those who reject such guides altogether), were not taught to recognize or evaluate.

The deceptive *familiarity* of Latin American theatre, then, has led to errors in criticism. As no indigenous theatre survived intact after the century following the conquest, it goes without saying that all the dramatic forms currently used in Latin America are derived *in some degree* from Western drama. While certain dramatic forms were forcefully imposed during the colonial period, since then Latin American dramatists have tended to "borrow" models. (Commentators generally speak of *influence* on First World authors; Third World writers seem to borrow.) Nonetheless, they do not borrow indiscriminately. Given a choice, people tend to take what they need. From the broad gamut of possibilities open to them, modern Latin American theatre practitioners, for example, did not pick up the musical comedy. What they did adopt were forms that could help change their positions with regard to their socio-political exploitation and marginalization (the second face of culture). Instead of the theatre of the oppressors that had dominated Latin America since the conquest, the "serious" or committed playwrights wanted a theatre of the oppressed. Moreover, their particular use of Western theatrical forms became essentially different in their new context, for example, theatre of the absurd, Lee Strasberg's implementation of the Stanislavsky method acting, and Brechtian theatre, to name only the most obvious. As I discuss in detail elsewhere, these works function in radically diverse ways and "mean" something different in their new settings (the first face of culture). Here I will examine how the "second" discovery of Latin American theatre, occurring almost five hundred years after the conquest, replayed the damaging critical misunderstandings of the first.

The 1960s was a period of revolutionary zeal. The Latin American revolutionary movement was linked to a larger, polyphonic revolutionary discourse the world over. The Cuban revolution of 1959 directly contributed to other liberation movements, not only to the civil rights movement and the feminist movement in the U.S. but also to resistance in South Africa (black consciousness movement), Angola (MPLA) and Mozambique (Frelimo). Without reducing the Cuban revolution to a spectacle, it is important to notice that it had spectacular, epic proportions. The powerful images of anti-hegemonic struggle, perhaps best embodied by the compelling figure of Ché, captured attention the world over. The revolutionary movement promised to cast Latin America in a leading role on the world's political and cultural acceptance, not as inferior *other*, but as a revitalizing, revolutionary self, theatrically as well as politically. Yet, even a brief look at a few major theatre practitioners of the late 1960s illustrates the degree to which familiar features disabled foreign commentators from comprehending "meaning" and function in cross-cultural settings. (While the situation continues basically unchanged, an examination of Latin American theatre in the the last decade must be postponed for another study.)

The first example comes from revolutionary Cuba. What does a revolutionary play look like? Whatever commentators might have envisioned, it was certainly nothing like José Triana's so-called "existentialist" or "absurdist" play of 1965, *Night of the Assassins* (published as *The Criminals*). Staged in Cuba's new revolutionary society, *Assassins* looked something like Sartre's *No Exit* or Genet's *The Maids*. Trapped in a filthy cluttered room, three adult children rehearse, or represent, or exorcise themselves of the murder of their parents, whose corpses, they claim, lie just beyond the door. Is this a game? A rehearsal? A cathartic liberation of murderous rage? Are the parents dead or alive? As we, the audience, can never see beyond the door, we have no way of knowing, no way of interpreting the meaning of the incessant abreactions onstage. From the perspective of foreign commentators, the play looked "universal," an example of Artaudian theatre of cruelty, a new "absurdist" piece, a Genetian ritual, or a "danse macabre." While some critics were enthused by this Cuban manifestation of the avant-garde, others were not impressed because the play looked too familiar to be a relevant commentary of its revolutionary context.

In Cuba, on the other hand, the play's avant-garde or "universal" trappings were considered meaningless, irrelevant to its underlying function, which according to various commentators was an anti-revolutionary denunciation of the revolution as futile and of the revolutionaries as assassins. Although Triana won Cuba's prestigious Casa de las Americas prize (the judges come from Latin America and Spain), over the next two or three years, he was completely marginalized from all intellectual activity in Cuba and eventually he went into exile. Does the play have nothing to do with the revolution, as the foreign commentators believed? Did it have everything to do with the revolution, as Cubans believed? The play exemplifies the conscious strategy to say the unsayable under the guise of acceptable (avant-garde in the 1960s) theatrical experimentation—to express the shortcomings of the revolution due to its gradual compliance with Soviet communism. *Assassins* might have looked like Sartre's *No Exit*, but nothing was more alien to Triana's thinking than a universalized, atemporal depiction of hell and suffering. And although ambiguity created by the restrictive set was considered ahistorical, and therefore anti-revolutionary by his colleagues who maintained "the problems of our times are not abstract; they have names and are concretely localizable," Triana's point, to my mind, was that the restrictive revolution was creating the ambiguity it tried so hard to erase. If the parameters of discourse were as tightly defined as Castro maintained—"Inside the Revolution, everything. Outside the Revolution, nothing"—then self-referentiality was unavoidable. As a meditation on the political exigencies of naming and locating, *Assassins* calls attention to the contradiction of the undertaking. On one hand, the ambiguity within the frame cannot be clarified unless we see beyond the frame, for we cannot judge what goes on inside the room until we see what lies outside it. Yet, the revolutionary discourse demands unequivocal definition and localization: is one in the revolution or outside it? For the revolution or against it? Triana's play, then, did reflect on the revolution but not in a way that made sense either to commentators outside or inside Cuba. Yet it was not "absurdist," unless by that we mean that it was dialectically opposed to the "reasonable" path of those in command.

Griselda Gambaro's "theatre of the absurd," on the other hand, is an invention of the critics. From 1963 onwards, she in fact was warning her audience about the escalating nature of politcal violence in Argentina by depicting the abductions (*The Walls*, 1963) and death camps (*The Camp*, 1967) that actually did come into being a decade later, as a result of Argentina's increasingly fascist politics. Moreover, from her first play on, it was evident that Gambaro's universe had nothing to do with Ionesco's ideas of art as "an autonomous creation, an independent universe with its own life and its own laws." As early as her first play it is clear she sees art as inexorably linked to the criminalized society she lived in. In *The Walls*, her first play, she depicts a young man who had been abducted and is being held hostage because his "host" thinks he is Ruperto de Hentzau or Hantcau from *The Prisoner of Zenda*. The young man clings to the illusion that life is separate from fiction (art is an autonomous universe), and reassures himself that he is not in fact a villain in a novel. He waits patiently for his release in his room (in fact a cell), decorated with costly furnishings and heavy curtains. Gambaro situates him in front of a painting of a young man sitting in front of an open window which hangs in a heavy ornate frame in his room. We see two images juxtaposed, two static, rather two-dimensional, young men looking out at false freedom. From the point of view of the protagonist, there is a radical difference between himself and the painting; he is alive, the painting is art, framed, autonomous, separate. From the point of view of the audience, both young men belong to the realm of art; both are framed representations, autonomous, separated from us by the proscenium. However, in the course of the play, the painting "disappears," so does the young man, and so over the next two decades, did 15,000 Argentines. Framing does not protect the victims from harm; it does not keep violence out. Rather than suggest false separations, Gambaro urges us to look beyond the artificial confines of the frame, to recognize not only what frames keep in, but also what they keep out. Her plays of the 1970s and 1980s—*Information for Foreigners*, *Saying Yes*, *Strip*—all emphasize the reality of abduction, torture, political violence; in short, everything we know to exist but cannot see.

Lastly, Augusto Boal's "Theatre of the Oppressed" borrows from J. L. Moreno's 1920s experiments in sociodramas and psychodramas. This in no way suggests, however, that Boal's theatre is anything like Moreno's. Moreno, a psychoanalyst working in Vienna in the 1920s, began his dramatic exercises with warm-ups and group discussion, and then proceeded to spontaneous representations in which the participants of the group acted out scenes from their everyday life, aided by others in the group. Afterwards, the entire group discussed the scenario, raised questions, proposed changes or alternative behaviors that might lead to better solutions and so forth. For Moreno, the exercises were designed to bring cathartic relief and behavioral modification to psychiatric patients so that they might adapt to society more successfully. While the psychodramatic techniques superficially resemble Boal's, nothing could be further from Boal's project. Boal works to turn disempowered, oppressed peoples into active protagonists in their socio-political and historical dramas. He wants to channel energy for revolutionary action rather than diffuse it cathartically. "Perhaps the theatre is not revolutionary in itself," he admits in his *Theatre of the Oppressed*, "but it is surely a rehearsal for the revolution." While his followers are politically marginal, their intention is to alter the social system, as opposed to Moreno's patients who strive to adapt to it.

These, then, are only a few examples of the selectivity and creativity, often denied to Third World artists, that go into adapting foreign cultural material and making it work in a profoundly different context. The motivations behind the borrowings or appropriations, in this and many other cases, are fundamentally socio-political rather than aesthetic. The playwrights need forms that will allow them to communicate with their specific audiences. In the tradition of Ortiz and Arguedas, the goal expressed by Latin American playwrights is that their audiences learn to change their role in an oppressive society. In spite of the many very important differences between them, they all believe that theatre can help bring about that change. That anti-hegemonic stance entails taking up the instruments traditionally associated with domination and using them to bring about liberation. Selectivity, as Rama stresses, applies not only to the Latin Americans' use of the foreign but, more importantly, to the "rediscovery" of their own "buried traditions." It entails, he continues, "searching for resistant values, capable of withstanding the erosion of transculturation," a task which Rama considered to be also an inventive one (Ortiz's *neoculturation*). The search for resistant values, however, does not imply a nostalgic return to the past. The cultivation of "indigenism" or the "exotic" that one finds in folkloric dances for tourists and touring national companies is not at all what these thinkers mean by "buried traditions." If Third World culture could be reduced to the exotic, to feathers, wide hats, and mariachi bands, there would be no current intellectual debates about protecting the Western canon and dictating what "every American should know."

III

The importance of stressing the liberating potential of the theory of transculturation is that it is one of the few theories that allows an opening to the impasse usually set up in relation to minority theories. Transculturation is a theory that explains how theories travel even as it travels and undergoes change. It does not lock cultures into binaries; it eschews simple oppositions that characterize much of the discourse on hegemony and counter-hegemony, such as Deleuze and Guattari's major/minor, and Arif Dirlik's ironic "the West" and "the Rest." The problem with "oppositional" or "resistance" theories, as the feminist theorist Toril Moi notes in relation to feminism, is that they "abolish [themselves] along with its opponent. In a non-sexist, non-patriarchal society, feminism will no longer exist." This applies to all emancipatory theory. However, the same does not apply to transculturation because it is not essentially or inherently a resistance theory. It describes a process; it is only partially defined by the *other*. Rather than being oppositional or strictly dialectical, it *circulates*. It is applicable to other dominated cultures and, unlike dominant theories, it highlights their vitality rather than their indebtedness to First World culture. Potentially, the hope might be that by engaging the many, previously marginalized *others*, these cultures may be able to decenter (not replace) the hegemonic. Currently, dominant cultural centers function like the hub of the wheel—the only contact between marginal cultures is mediated through the central hub. We need theories linking the peripheries without reinforcing the center. And by adding discourses, and emphasizing process and cultural specificity rather than "universality" and reified "tradition," the interaction might become too complicated to reduce to simple binaries. The dislocation of a centered hegemony might lead to the progressive borderization of culture, to a sharing, rather than crossing, of borders.

We can now develop Arguedas's and Rama's migration pattern further to understand how transculturation affects First World culture (the U.S. specifically, in this example) in ways it fails to credit. Both Arguedas and Rama noted that young *mestizos* tended to leave their quasi-traditional societies to move to the cities. We can continue to map the process of transculturation with a reference to the performance artist, Guillermo Gómez-Peña, who describes himself as a Mexican-Chicano-Latin American-*chilango*-Hispanic-Latino-*pocho-norteño* in his recent article, "Documented/Undocumented" in *Multi-Cultural Literacy*: "My generation, the *chilangos* [slang for Mexico City native], who came to 'el norte' (the U.S.) fleeing the imminent ecological and social catastrophe of Mexico City, gradually integrated itself into otherness . . . became Chicano-ized." Insofar as Gomez-Peña dismantles one social identity (*chilango*) in order to recode it, it seems appropriate that his description of de-territorialization should ring of deconstructionist punning: "We de-Mexicanized ourselves to Mexi-understand ourselves, some without wanting to, others on purpose."

It also illustrates the dynamic nature of social identity. In dismantling an identity, the second face of culture, one finds another—the Chicano is positionally related to the *mejicano* (or MexChicano, from which the term Chicano is said to derive) although physical distance is as fundamental to the relationship as is proximity. The process described by Gómez-Peña involves the de-territorialization of the displaced, loss, and a partial re-territorialization. He writes: "Our deepest generational emotion is that of loss . . . Our loss is total and occurs at multiple levels" and he proceeds to name country, culture, class, language, literary culture, and "ideological meta-horizons." The hope for him, however, lies in "a vision of a more experimental culture . . . a multi-focal and tolerant one." The move toward national-cultural-linguistic-ideological borders, suggesting both de-territorialization and re-territorialization, results in what Gómez-Peña calls the "borderization of the world."

"American" culture (if by that we refer to the mainstream, dominant culture, the ones American "should know") though itself in a process of transculturation, is changing in a way that most commentators either do not realize or are not willing to accept. The degree to which Mexican-American culture (to name just one) has affected, and will continue to affect, "American" culture and cultural institutions has not begun to be recognized. The effect of black culture, to name another obvious example, has only barely been acknowledged. While most people may like jazz or so-called Mexican food, political struggles indicate how hostile the dominant culture is to the presence of "minorities," especially when these seem to be competing for the same resources. The terms used to discuss the interaction between and among these cultures are not usually the celebratory ones used in hegemonic spheres to describe transculturation, that is, *their* acquisition, adoption, and embrace of the foreign. And while the insertion of black and Hispanic culture into the U.S. certainly qualifies as an act of transcultura-tion, the hegemonic resistance to accept the "minor" discourses, and the hostilities these intercultural relationships provoke, point to the important facet of transculturation that is completely missing from most analyses: the sense of loss. Those associated with the dominant groups resist losing what they see as their rightful place at the economic, historic, and cultural center of things.

As long as First World commentators speak of acquiring or otherwise assimilating the foreign features that they admire, all is well and good with interculturalism. Undesirable cultural manifestations associated with the disenfranchised groups can be dismissed as somehow "impure," as cultural concoctions unworthy of the term transculturation. The implication seems to be that the powerful who "acquire" and "exploit" foreign cultural quarries are involved in "pure" transculturation while the powerless simp-ly make the best of a bad job. When the possibility arises, as indeed it must, that foreign cultures could eventually displace or marginalize the previously dominant or central ones, then talk begins of preserving cultural purity and Western traditions. This variation on the strategy of "salvage" criticism suggests a new "endangered species."

The theory of transculturation points to long term reciprocities, to the degree that the dominant groups that define, acquire, and impose culture are themselves transculturated sooner or later, whether they want it or not.

NOTES

¹In referring to Latin America, I feel obliged to use terms like "Third World" and "non-Western," for lack of better ones, although I feel the terms are misleading and denigrating. "Third World" is a term coined in 1952 by a Frenchman, Alfred Sauvy. Like the term *L'Amérique Latine*, coined by the French in the nineteenth century, "Third World" im-poses a false unity on diverse countries. As Régis Debray (another Frenchman) recognized, the term functions as a "shapeless sack into which one could simply dump peoples, classes, races, civilizations and continents so that they might more simply disappear." Moreover, the term First World also gives a false sense of consensus and cohesion to the dominant societies, and glosses over important oppositional or outcast groups within them.

The term non-Western not only relegates Latin America to a non-space and non-identity, it is misleading insofar as it minimizes or erases the importance of Western influence on Latin America. Alain Rouquié claims ''that culturally [Latin America] belongs totally to the West. Conquest and colonization did not simply influence these societies; it created and molded them, imposing on them the language, religion, values, and attitudes of Europe. Thus, whatever the impact of the pre-Columbian past and its resurgence, Latin America is the part of the Third World that is Western.'' While Rouquié overstates the point, and overlooks the varying degrees of *non* or even *anti*-Westernization, from Argentina at one extreme to Peru and Bolivia at the other, there is substantial truth to what he says.

The Mahabharata
Peter Brook's Orientalism

Gautam Dasgupta

JULY 16, 1945, JORNADA DEL MUERTO, near Alamogordo, New Mexico. Indra was not yet fully awake from his night of lengthy repose under the eastern skies. Yet the horizons were ablaze, irradiated by the lethal rays of ''a thousand suns in the sky.'' With these words from the *Bhagavad-Gita*, J. Robert Oppenheimer, one of the architects of this conflagration, anointed the birth of the Kali-yuga, our nuclear age. How fitting, indeed, that when the sun rose from the east to gaze upon the charred and stillborn sandy plains of a New Mexico desert, it brought in its wake a wisdom from the ancient land of the Bharatas.

Now, forty-three years later, when the life-sustaining light of Indra is no match for the thousands of genocidal suns we possess, comes yet another warning from the land of Shiva and Kali. The howls of doom and terror cry out from within the cavernous walls of the BAM Majestic Theatre as the Pandavas and the Kurus line up under Peter Brook's direction on the battlefield of Kurukshetra. *The Mahabharata*, an Indian epic of immense prolixity, adapted for the stage by Jean-Claude Carrière, draws to a close after nine hours, its climactic image one of bloody carnage and tragic desolation.

The Mahabharata is a compilation, in over 90,000 stanzas, of vast Brahamanic lore. The dates of its composition cannot be fixed with certainty, but scholars generally agree to place it somewhere between 400 B.C. and 200 A.D. Although tradition has it that the creator of this vast poem was the sage Vyasa, it betrays the handiwork of a succession of priests who, during the course of their storytelling sessions, interpolated sections on morality, ethics, theology, and statecraft into what may have been, essentially and originally, a secular tale of war and strife. In any case, the epic in our time has come to symbolize, through its interconnected tales and legends and the morals attached to each, a virtual exegesis on the Hindu way of life. The *Mahabharata* I grew up with in India is a vital source of nourishment, a measure of one's thoughts and deeds. It is no mere epic constrained by literary and narrative strategies, but a revolutionary injunction, ethical and theological in purpose, that determines and defines the social and personal interactions of millions of Indians.

Given the scope of the epic, it goes without saying that any attempt to dramatize *The Mahabharata* is a task worthy of admiration. It is also a far more ambitious undertaking than Brook's earlier intercultural adaptations—*Orghast*, *Conference of the Birds*, *The Ik*, and *Ubu*. In all instances, he has drawn upon an international cast of actors, employed diverse acting styles and a variety of theatrical modes of representation. Underlying all this experimentation is, I suspect, a belief in a syncretic cultural universe, where the stage is all the world. A grand and perhaps even a noble vision, granted, but one that inevitably raises the problematic specter of what Edward Said has termed "Orientalism."

It is from this perspective that the Brook *Mahabharata* assumes an air of equivocation I find hard to dismiss. Obviously, all cross-cultural work would have to confront the idea of representing the Other. But as Said has argued in his book *Orientalism*, interest in the Orient and the field of study labeled "Orientalist" discourse was generated by Occidental scholars in the eighteenth and nineteenth centuries to accompany ongoing political incursions into the Orient. The Orient, according to Said's study, was not allowed to represent itself, but had to be represented by the Occident. In other words, it had to be re-presented in a manner so as to align itself with the prevailing heirarchy, with imperialist powers on top, the Orient on the bottom, of the political, social, and cultural scale. Although such political hegemonic divisions do not prevail in our time, the question to be posed is whether the thematics of "Orientalism" nonetheless still continue to haunt us.

On the political level, it cannot be denied that such thinking continues to play a role in international affairs. Even in terms of social intercourse, "Orientalist" prejudices have not ceased to exist. Generalities about

cultures abound, and this is of course by no means the sole prerogative of
the Occidental mind. But the question that concerns me is why so many artists in the West, particularly in the past few decades, have drawn upon
Oriental themes and myths to spur their own creativity? Is it because, in all
honesty, they do see the world as an organic whole, or is there implicit in
their cross-fertilizing instincts a recognition of their own paucity of ideas?
And, at worst, does the exoticism of the Orient, its different values and
norms, somehow permit them to evade criticisms of their cultures, supplan-
ting what ought to be a vital discourse on issues generated by their own
society by a surrogate other-world picture. These are by no means easy
questions to answer, and nor am I suggesting that we do away with all cross-
cultural artistic endeavors. What concerns me is that the representation of
another culture's artistic product address the lived, sensate fabric of that
borrowed cloth. And more, that such expressions of cultural give and take
not descend to banal generalities about the foreign culture, but seek to uncover its specificities, in actual, and not merely perceived, links with its own
society. What is it that makes *The Mahabhrata*, for instance, of such paramount significance, first for its own people, and then for the rest of the
world?

It should be clear that I am not remotely suggesting that representations
of the East be the sole prerogative of non-Western artists. Nor am I naive

enough to argue that any and all representations of this grand epic staged in India—the episodes of *The Mahabharata* are performed throughout India in theatrical forms that range from the classical Kathakali to the rural Jatra—lie any closer to the originary intent of the poem. But what is indisputably true is that such stagings do address, implicitly or explicitly, a deeply-ingrained structure of ritual beliefs and ethical codes of conduct intrinsic to its audience. *The Mahabharata* is nothing, an empty shell, if it is read merely as a compendium of martial legends, of revenge, valor and bravura.

And that, precisely, is the reading attributed to *The Mahabharata* by Carrière and Brook. How else can one explain the shockingly truncated *Bhagavad-Gita* sequence, the epicenter of the poem, the fulcrum on which rests the entire thrust of this monumental drama of humanity, here rendered into whispered words never revealed to the audience? It is as if one were to stage the Bible without the least mention of the Sermon on the Mount. I admit that there are ponderous speeches in the epic, and many cuts implemented by the creators of this *Mahabharata* are judicious, but the *Bhagavad-Gita* is, most assuredly, not one of them. Aside from its paramount thematic and contextual placement in the body of the work, it is also one of the supreme achievements of classical Sanskrit verse. Its eloquence and majesty of thought surely deserves a more prominent place than that given to it in this staging.

It could perhaps be argued, as Brook and Carrière have intimated in the published text of the play, that they chose to stage an earlier, and perhaps a vulgate, version of *The Mahabharata*. Although such a claim cannot be substantiated with any degree of accuracy—historical, philological, or theological—it does raise important and problematic questions about the "Orientalist" bias of their readings. Foremost among these is their impacting a Homeric idea of the epic onto the apocalyptic skein of an Indian legend. There are obvious parallels to be drawn between the warrior heroes of *The Mahabharata* and *The Iliad*: the rivalry between Karna and Arjuna is sure to evoke that other long-standing feud between Hector and Achilles, as will the saga of heroes born out of union between gods and mortals.

Where these paths diverge, however, is of the utmost significance. Karna and Arjuna, by virtue of their unique and personal relationships to deities of the Hindu pantheon who continue to be worshipped to this very day, are viewed in much the same way as the gods themselves. This is to a large extent true of all the characters in *The Mahabharata*, be they men, women, children, *rakshas* or *apsaras*. The hero of a Greek (or, for that matter, a Western) epic, on the other hand, remains a mortal who may on occasion, licensed by the gods, engage in superhuman feats. In India, the heroes of

78

this epic are perceived as some variant incarnation of a deity or as a member of a lower spiritual heirarchy. The feats performed by the characters in *The Mahabharata* are always, and invariably, seen within the context of a religious framework. There is no dramatic or epic kernel to *The Mahabharata* outside of its theological value system. When Carrière says in the introduction to his version that ''Any historical or theological truth, controversial by its very nature, is closed to us—our aim is a certain dramatic truth,'' he misses the point. The ''dramatic truth'' of this epic does not reside in the aesthetic or narrative pull of the story, but in a very human exchange of beliefs that grounds, for the average Indian, even the most elementary reading of the many tales woven throughout *The Mahabharata*.

The Homeric compaction is felt most poignantly in the characterization of Krishna, who comes across more as Ulysses than as a personification of the god Vishnu. Within the confines of *The Mahabharata*'s grandiose themes, the recklessness of Brook's Krishna is oddly out of place. That ungodlike aspect of Krishna remains reserved for the *Ras-Lila*, and I can find no justification for transferring the Krishna of that legend to *The Mahabharata*. True, the Krishna of the *Bhagavad-Gita* attains a more radiant visage, but at all instances of this colossal poem, he is beheld as nothing less than the Krishna of divine inspiration.

Martha Swope

Interestingly enough, one can also pose the question of whether Brook's adaptation is a prime example of an intertextual reading, or an illustration of the West misreading the literature of the East? That Brook and Carrière should bring their own subjectivity to the work is to be expected. It is perhaps no mere coincidence that many of the extrapolations that go to create the bulk of their adaptation resonate with Shakespearean themes. After all, it was with his justly praised Shakespeare productions that Brook attained worldwide prominence. And although I am in favor of intertextual readings on the stage, I also believe that such disjunctive devices only work when the primary text itself, on some level, has been apprehended by an audience. Contemporary stagings of episodes from *The Mahabharata* within India do take on intertextual guises. I recall once seeing a Marxist revisioning that brought to the fore and questioned the alarmingly revisionist high-priest and royal-caste ethics imbedded in the text. Its impact on the rural audience was considerable, and the reason for it obviously rested on their prior familiarity with the story.

The intertextual elements in Brook's production, most significantly the Shakespearean ones (Dhritarashtra comes across as King Lear; Krishna as Prospero; Kunti, Gandhari, and Draupadi as Lear's daughters), may have served as easy referents to his Western audience, but it fails to do justice to specific traits of these characters, traits that stem from a complex underpinning of Brahamanic and Vedic precepts. It is perhaps impossible to embrace the various threads of philosophical lore that this epic possesses in the course of a few hours; nonetheless, the responsibility to confront them is a grave one. One should not, under cover of universality of theme or character, undercut the intrinsic core of how *The Mahabharata*'s characters function within the world of which they are a part.

It is then understandable, perhaps, why Brook and Carrière chose to omit stories that, for the Indian viewer, belong to the heart of *The Mahabharata*. Why, for instance, were the legends of Rama and Sita, Savitri, Manu, Bhagiratha, Nala and Damayanti, Garuda, Soma, and others ignored? If time was a factor, surely some of the more drawn out sequences, particularly in the last third of the production—which resemble in scope the battle sequences of Shakespeare's history plays—could have been sacrificed for tales that would round out for a Western audience a fuller sense of the Hindu world-view.

It is, of course, entirely conceivable that such was not the intent of Brook and Carrière. Given the internationalist cast and the quixotic admixture of costumes and musical instruments, it seems obvious that coherence was not their primary concern. Unfortunately, however, despite the elegance of Brook's staging, the arresting theatrical effects, and, for the most part, the

seductive pacing of the production, the intentional hodgepodge of diverse accents and downright poor acting in a few crucial instances did little to alleviate the lack of theatrical coherence as well. It would indeed be sad if the restrictions imposed by the cast forced Carrière's hand in rendering the stately poetic lines of *The Mahabharata* in prose. The sixteen syllable line, the *Sloka* meter of the original Sanskrit, lends the epic a noble tread and adds to the grandeur of its theme. The prose adaptation achieves a poetic intensity in longer passages and in the narrative sections, but when it occurs at the level of everyday dialogue, it seems oddly commonplace and at variance with the characters who mouth them.

If, as I have suggested, Brook's *Mahabharata* falls short of the essential Indianness of the epic by staging predominantly its major incidents and failing to adequately emphasize its coterminous philosophical precepts, it does

81

however raise the specter, in no uncertain terms, of the fate that awaits us in the event of a nuclear holocaust. The play is completed on a note of cosmic desolation, with corpses littering the field of battle (an arena referred to in the original as the Field of Righteousness, or Law) and Yudisthira's descent into hell. (This penultimate sequence is billed as ''The Last Illusion,'' and the play ends with all the characters re-united, although this seems rather arbitrary and does not quite follow from all that has gone on previously.) It is also not the actual ending of the epic. In the *Aswa-Medha*, or the Sacrifice of the Horse, which is the proper ending, harmony once again is restored to the universe through a series of sacrificial rituals. The tragic *rasa* or mode, which the Brook production suggests, is inimical to Hindu norms of aesthetic decorum and religious beliefs. The tragic is irreversible, it is definite. It has no place in the endless cycle of birth and rebirth, the crux of Hindu thought.

Brook's tragic coda is appended to a body of prophetic writings that give daily sustenance to millions of Hindus the world over. Here again we might possibly glimpse another aspect of ''Orientalism.'' But now that even India possesses the bomb, *The Mahabharata*, yes, Peter Brook's and Jean-Claude Carrière's *Mahabharata*, apocalyptic ending in place, should be performed in the land from which it originated. The eternal cycle will be completed, for today both India and the West possess the ultimate weapon, the *pasupata* which Shiva bestows as a gift to Arjuna.

Interculturalism, Postmodernism, Pluralism

Daryl Chin

ALTHOUGH "INTERCULTURALISM" is a concept that is gaining a great deal of visibility as well as credibility, this situation is aligned to a number of issues, some of which are political and sociological, and others philosophical and aesthetic. Taking interculturalism as a specific philosophical and aesthetic issue, it continues the agenda set by postmodernism, pluralism, and marginalism. But what is postmodernism? What are pluralism and marginalism? "Postmodern" has become one of those terms, like "existential" for an earlier generation, which everyone tosses around like a beanbag, while aiming at different targets. For most of the commentators who insist on using the term, its meaning is not defined, but denoted by catalogues and lists.

I'll take the widest possible context for postmodernism on a philosophical level: as described by Jean-François Lyotard in *The Postmodern Condition: A Report on Knowledge*, it is a crisis in categorization, resulting in equivalence. The effect of this equivalence is the lack of hegemony in perspective. This break in unity has been the occasion for a crisis in cultural practice. Splintering in so many separate pieces, any aesthetic enterprise is fraught with suspicion, haunted by the possibility of misinterpretation. In order to grapple with even the most momentary meaning, art has now been occupied by the pastiche, the parody, the appropriation, on the assumption that nostalgic meaning is better than no meaning at all.

But the result of this nostalgia is the depletion of the centricity of artistic endeavor. Irony, reproduction, and simulation have become central to contemporary art, with all the distance that implies.

The attempt to define postmodernism is linked to a consideration of modernism, its limits and deficiencies. The problem of defining modernism is compounded by the multiplicity of ''modernisms,'' that is, modernism in literature, modernism in the visual arts, modernism in architecture, and so on. What is defined as the modernist epoch in each art form is not necessarily congruent with modernism in another art form. Thus, in architecture, the modernist movement was associated with the consideration of materiality, purity of line, and restrained monumentality, as exemplified in the work of Alvar Aalto, Mies van der Rohe, and Le Corbusier. Robert Venturi, one of the leading theorists of postmodernism in architecture, proclaimed: ''Architects can no longer afford to be intimidated by the puritanically moral language of orthodox Modern architecture. I like elements which are hybrid rather than 'pure,' compromising rather than 'clean,' distorted rather than 'straightforward,' ambiguous rather than 'articulated,' perverse as well as impersonal, boring as well as 'interesting,' conventional rather than designed, accommodating rather than excluding, redundant rather than simple, vestigial as well as innovating, inconsistent and equivocal rather than direct and clear.'' Venturi's theoretical proclamation of a postmodern ambition in architecture was defined through ''double-functioning,'' a recognition of pluralism in the living arrangements which must be acknowledged in architectural planning.

When pluralism is invoked, the assumption is that alternative perspectives are being permitted into the discourse, displacing the dominant hegemony. In the most basic sense, pluralism is an acknowledgement of alternatives so that additional perspectives have the possibility of being understood. Marginalism is an accreditation of these additional perspectives by defining a dominant, and ceding territory to the sidelines. During the last two decades, as an example, a feminist perspective has been established in the arts, with theoretical and artistic practices in theatre, in the visual arts, in film and video. The acknowledgement of that feminist perspective has occurred in ways which have preserved sharp demarcations, resulting in a continuance of marginalism for the feminist perspective.

The consideration of pluralism and marginalism is crucial to any attempt at comprehending contemporary aesthetics. More than twenty years ago, Susan Sontag attempted to define the new agenda in her essay ''One Culture and the New Sensibility.'' She proposed a relativism in aesthetic judgment, so that appreciation could embrace the beauty of a machine, the solution to a mathematical problem, a painting by Jasper Johns, a film by Jean-Luc Godard, and the music of the Beatles. During that period, critical debates in all arenas, from high art to popular culture, were engaged in the questions of modernism, pluralism, and postmodernism. Critical debate was joined to artistic praxis, as artists extended the boundaries of their work.

Annette Michelson had noted the ways in which artistic enterprise was aligned to philosophical and socio-political ideology in her essay ''Film and the Radical Aspiration.'' She had suggested ways in which formal radicalism could be seen as part of a general radical aspiration, and viewed as an answer to the social and economic hierarchies of late capitalism. As an instance of the pluralism of that period, Pop Art and Minimal Art were coexistent movements. Although stylistically opposed, both movements were identified by Michael Fried as antithetical to the modernist ethos, in that both were theatrically motivated because of an acceptance of audience perspective, as opposed to an Idealist pictorialism. Such attempts to define modernism without an account of pluralistic perspectives was one of the reasons for the collapse of critical authority. Criticism could not be prescriptive, but the alternative has been an abdication of critical autonomy.

Before attempting to address interculturalism, I would like to conclude with some remarks on postmodernism, pluralism, and marginalism. For most commentators on postmodernism, its unique contribution is the recognition of difference. However, this recognition of difference is then equated, as can be discerned in writers as varied as Jean Baudrillard, Peter Burger, and Andreas Huyssen, with complete indifference. To put this in the most extreme, stringent terms: the Eurocentric ego declares that, if recognition of the validity of ''otherness'' must be accorded, then there is total equivalence, an absolute breakdown of distinction. The Eurocentric ego is making a declaration, which is: if it can no longer claim dominance and superiority, if equity must be awarded, if the Eurocentric ego can no longer presume on self-importance, then nothing is important.

Hidden in the agenda of postmodernism is, I think, a rebuke, an insult, a devaluation. Instead of recognizing the status of ''the other'' as an equal, there is the undermining of ''the other'' by a declared indifference to distinction, while attempting to maintain the same balance of power. In fact, the very designation of ''the other'' is one such maneuver. This can be seen, for example, in Roland Barthes's *The Empire of Signs*, in which he discusses Japanese culture in terms of its sheer ''otherness,'' thereby rendering the working of a complex social structure as quaint, in the manner that Edward Said has described as ''Orientalism.'' At no point in Barthes's charming and elegant discussion is there any cognizance of the fact that, for a Japanese person living in Japan, the culture is not ''other.'' The culture is, in fact, the dominant culture, and the inscrutability, the impassivity, and the unfathomability of the culture are not constructs designed to tease the Western imagination. From a Japanese perspective, they are not inscrutable, impassive, or unfathomable at all.

* * *

When postmodernism, pluralism and marginalism, and interculturalism are proposed, there must be accountability for alternatives, that is, there must be a recognition of specificity, not just an accounting of equivalence. Extending the postmodern agenda, interculturalism has been a rubric to a cultural inclusiveness. An example of the way in which culture is perceived: although there has been a consensus that the power shift in world politics and economics is occurring, so that the Pacific Rim region has been gaining prominence, there has not been the same interest in the culture from that region. Although the technological advances in the Japanese culture have accelerated, there has been little interest in theoretical writing from Japan. The theoretical writing that is being considered still derives from European countries, in particular, France, West Germany, and Great Britain.

When Japanese culture has been considered, the emphasis is on issues of style, thus the prominence of fashion as the exemplar of Japanese culture. Rarely has the intellectual discourse in Japanese culture been given a hearing in international cultural circles. The fact that the most prominent theorists remain European, at a time when the sociological advances which they address have occurred in countries such as the United States and Japan, is indicative of a mind set so centered on European dominance that there is no way to redress the balance.

In any society, there are distinctions that are inherent in the social structure, distinctions between the sacred and the profane, between what is acknowledged and what is unacknowledged, between the good and the bad. The understanding of the symbol structure of that society, and aesthetics are, by definition, within the province of the symbol structure, crucial to an understanding of the products (artistic, industrial, craft) of that society. Is understanding of that symbol structure to be inductive or deductive? In Eric Wolf's terms, are the people of "underdevelopment" (an imperialist term) to write their own histories, or are their histories to be written by the culture of imperialism? And the objects of those cultures: are they to retain their meaning, or will their meaning be subsumed by imperialist domination?

The terms of relativism are supposed to be those on which anthropology lays claim to its inclusion as a science, but the questioning of that relativism has been non-negotiable. Trinh T. Minh-ha is a cultural figure at the very heart of the debate on postmodernism, pluralism and marginalism, and interculturalism. She is a Vietnamese filmmaker, writer, and composer who is

86

also an anthropologist living and working in the United States. Her two films, *Reassemblage* (1983) and *Naked Spaces: Living is Round* (1986), are ethnographic studies of African communities. But her films are not simply ethnographic films; rather, they question the very terms of ethnography and the filmmaking process, interrogating the presumption behind the anthropological world view of objectivity. The difficulties posed by her work, its self-reflexive questioning of perspective and point of view, are meant to be provocative and disconcerting, but so disconcerting has her work been, so threatening to the Eurocentric hierarchical views implicitly propounded by anthropology, that it has been consistently marginalized. The lack of certainty which her work engenders, the adherence to an ethic of continual vigilance, the sense of exploration which her aesthetic addresses: these have made her work problematic. Though the anthropological film community and the Asian-American film community claim they are dealing with an alternative to the dominant cinematic culture of the commercial industry, the (supposed) pluralism of their situation does not allow for the inclusion of a point of view which puts the pluralism into question.

The idea of interculturalism is one which is, in a sense, duplicitous. One question which must be addressed is the presence of a dominant power structure, and the presumptions of that power structure. In the context of the United States, the cultural power structure is one which is dominated by the ideology of a specifically white, Eurocentric, specifically capitalist establishment. In addition, all questions regarding interculturalism must be complicated by the pervasiveness of a commercialized popular culture. For those who have grown up with the artifacts of the American cultural establishment, the effects have become endemic, pervasive, and all-encompassing. Perhaps the first manifestation of this pervasive cultural infiltration could be seen in the movies of the French *Nouvelle Vague*; recent movies from cultures as disparate as Taiwan, West Germany, and Spain have shown the effects of American influence. In addition, the definitions of that cultural establishment have played a part in the valuation of those minorities within. The idea of interculturalism as simply a way of joining disparate cultural artifacts together has a hidden agenda of imperialism. When is interculturalism a valid expression of the postmodern crisis in information overload, and when is it merely a fashion statement of the ability to buy and sell anything from any culture?

One of the most egregious examples of the excesses of the intercultural approach, as it is connected to postmodernism, can be seen in Lee Breuer's *The Warrior Ant*. Although admirably ambitious in scope, the philosophical and aesthetic subtexts of the work consistently undermined any attempt at cohesion. In a sense, the formal disintegration of the piece could be seen as a statement about the disintegration of national boundaries implied by the collision of disparate elements from many different cultures. Thus, a Bunraku master, a Turkish belly dancer, and rap singers are all equated, rendered not so much equal as equally distracting. The distinctions between high art, folk art, and popular art which the different elements represented were blurred, without the implications being carefully considered. Instead of an attempt at synthesis, there was the formal placement of disjunction. This disjunction ultimately devalued all elements, as no element was allowed to exist within an appropriate context; appropriate, that is, in terms of the cultural context from which that element derived.

The collaborations between Robert Wilson and Heiner Müller represent another example of the collision of sensibility and, by extension, of ideology. In the case of Müller, his texts are highly reflective elucidations of a very specific political agenda. Like that of his precursor, Bertolt Brecht, Müller's political agenda provides the occasion for his most intensely lyrical speculations. However, Wilson's directorial work, founded on the visionary impulse of a post-hippie mysticism, is grounded in assumptions which could have arisen only in a late capitalist context, assumptions which are, at base, apolitical. Wilson's productions of HAMLETMACHINE and QUARTET have been marked by an inattention to the precision of language, so that the ideological and socio-political points in the dialogue are perceived in an incantatory fashion, and the specificity of the dialogue lost.

Peter Brook's recent productions, *The Mahabharata* and *The Cherry Orchard*, display the intercultural approach to nationalist texts in ways both overt and insidious. *The Mahabharata* has been the subject of much debate; suffice it to say that Brook's approach does not account for the distinctiveness of the text, its non-linearity, and its multiplicity of meanings. Rather, he extracts from the outline of *The Mahabharata* the rudiments of the narrative, to which he then imposes an ethnocentric meaning. In the case of *The Cherry Orchard*, Brook displaces the meaning of the work by denying its specificity. The equivalence of meaning, which finds formal correlatives in the international cast, the lack of dramatic emphases leveling the momentum of the play, and the bare staging, denies the structure of the play, stretching it out until the sense of dramatic impetus deteriorates. In this production, *The Cherry Orchard* is displaced, set in an empty space which does not reveal new meanings; rather, the production equivocates, rendering a sense of unvarying continuity all but destroying narrative logic.

The strategies of Breuer, Wilson, and Brook are not unique; to different degrees, they can be seen in the work of Peter Sellars, Des MacAnuff, Anne Bogart, Elizabeth LeCompte, John Jesurun, Robert Woodruff, and The Squat Theatre. For example, in Anne Bogart's production of *Danton's*

Death, the sense of the play was lost in a staging which was supposed to compensate through a sensual overflowing. There are many problems with this approach. For one, the attempt to update classical material often is an excuse to force disparate elements into conjunction without careful consideration, depleting the possible meanings. For another, the imprecision in the deployment of sensual means, such as the shouting, chanting, or recitation of dramatic dialogue, creates an effect of confusion. If a play has a specific text, with a rhythm structure and a dramatic development clearly defined, the disruptions of that structure and development must proceed to establish a viable alternative, rather than just a cacophonous negation.

To reconceive of an aesthetic in the most stringent terms of existent categorizations is one agenda much admired within postmodern circles. The total recreation of a thing so that the specificity of that thing is revealed has become an enterprise both critical and capitulatory. In the February 1989 issue of *Vanity Fair*, James Wolcott reviews the cable television station Nickelodeon in these terms: "By repackaging the sitcoms as camp artifacts, by recontextualizing them, if I may use a lit-crit mouthful, Nick at Nite has rinsed old pennies new. It's the approach of postmodernists from David Letterman to David Byrne, putting ironic quotation marks around stupid so that 'stupid' becomes smart. Kitsch is king—yesterday's dumb obvious is today's pop sublime."

This approach can be seen in everything from the comedy of Steve Martin and Robin Williams to the performance art of Eric Bogosian and Ann Magnuson to the appropriated advertising and commercial artifacts of Meyer Vaisman and Jeff Koons. When The Wooster Group positions an Amos 'n' Andy routine in blackface, are they displaying an underlying racism, problematizing that racism, or are they making an ironic comment on it, putting racism in quotes? Notice, though, that the context is carefully controlled: The Wooster Group is granted visibility and critical debate.

Two examples of performance artists who embody sensibilities and attitudes so totally that they become both these sensibilities and attitudes, and a comment on them, are Winston Tong and John Kelly. In both cases, their embodiment of marginalization is so extreme that their performances bring up disturbing questions. In the case of Kelly: he represents a certain tradition of dandyism within the gay sensibility. His intense self-dramatization, the melodramatic extremes of his recapitulation of "the diva," his operatic self-indulgence reflect an unnerving autonomy which places the audience at a remove, forced into reflexivity. This is also the case with Winston Tong, but Tong joins this to another aspect of marginalization: he turns himself into an "exotic," an object of delectation in the most extreme formulation of "Orientalism." During the period of his most disciplined work, Tong

WINSTON TONG

EACH TIME I SEE YOU, I FEEL IT COULD BE THE LAST TIME
AN INSTALLATION BY AL WONG

became the most intense personification of the "exotic" (in *Bound Feet, A Rimbaud, Nijinsky*), exemplified in "other" cultures (Chinese, French, Russian). By emphasizing their "otherness," Kelly and Tong have played into the stereotypes set forth by the dominant ideology in a way which explodes those clichés. Their extravagant self-definition becomes a way of defusing the definitions of the cultural around them.

The impulse to marginalize alternative perspectives is another problem that has surfaced in contemporary culture. The hidden agenda of condescension is always a possibility. During a gallery talk in November 1988, at the Whitney Museum, Al Wong was asked about the Asian influences on his installation piece, *Each Time I See You, I Feel It Could Be The Last Time* (1988). His reply was that he felt he was an American artist, and the influences were mostly Western. In formal terms, the piece was involved in the discourse about space and imagery which characterizes the most interesting installation work being done at this time. In short, Wong's aims are congruent with the aims of other media artists doing installation work, such as Dara Birnbaum, Dan Graham, Paul Sharits, Barry Gerson, and Judith Barry. Though the subject matter of the various sections involved Asian and Asian-American material, since that material was autobiographical, the piece itself, formally and structurally, was "American." Wong's assertion of his artistic enterprise within the American context was absolutely correct. Although there were critical questions implicit in the installation, questions concerning antinomies of "form" and "content" which could be considered in terms of, say, "East" and "West," the desire to exoticize the installation was one which should be resisted.

There has been a similar response to the performance work of Ping Chong. Although his work does deal with text and narrative, its aesthetic background relates to the type of imagistic movement work which is now being termed "dance theatre." Chong's work, with its multi-media components and its movement-oriented imagery, shares a common aesthetic with the work of Joan Jonas, Kenneth King, and, of course, Meredith Monk (with whom Chong has collaborated on several works). Though, in the most philosophical interpretations of his work, a case might be made wherein the thematic concerns of "foreignness" and "aliens" are tied to minority consciousness, the appellation of "Asian" is misguided. Whatever inflections Chong gives his work, its formal and stylistic vocabulary derives from a specific tradition in American dance.

The need to categorize and to compartmentalize is a way to marginalize and to ignore important cultural agendas. The whole issue of misinterpretation must be considered, specifically in intercultural terms. Nam June Paik once noted that La Monte Young and Terry Riley (and, later, Philip Glass

91

ANGELS OF SWEDENBORG BY PING CHONG/COMPANY

and Steve Reich) wanted to make music that would share the structure and form of Eastern music, but that they wound up making music that was more Western than ever. Similarly, Kazuo Ohno, noted as one of the founders of Butoh, the modern dance movement in Japan, began his career attempting to present what he believed was Western-style dance, but it wasn't modern dance as anyone had seen it in the United States or Europe. What he presented was more like the hierarchic poses of Kabuki as envisioned by the Norma Desmond character in *Sunset Boulevard*. So, when artists attempt to cross cultural boundaries, there are times when misinterpretation may prove to be stimulating, provocative, seminal.

The recent controversy surrounding *The Satanic Verses* by Salman Rushdie is indicative of cross-cultural misunderstanding. Rushdie's career as a writer was established within Great Britain, where comic irreverence is a tradition. Rushdie's use of Islamic tradition as a source of comedy is no more or less blasphemous than the Monty Python troupe's use of Christian tradition in *The Life of Brian*. Rushdie must have felt that, as an Indian-born author living in England, he could use his cultural and religious heritage as he saw fit, but the English traditions of satire did not coincide with the fundamentalist dogmas of the Islamic religion.

The Japanese performance group, Dumb Type, has been creating works which utilize the pop debris and mechanized environment of the contemporary urban center. The American-influenced iconography of commercial popular culture is everywhere in the landscapes which Dumb Type employs as the scenography of their work. The pleasure of Dumb Type's work comes from the precision and the fastidiousness with which the overdetermined electronic environment is depicted. At this point, the pop culture iconography, once derived from American mass media, has become universal: Tokyo is no more or less ridden with neon signs, billboards, and television than, say, Los Angeles, New York, Paris, London, or Rome. Dumb Type's acceptance of this environment is exploratory and open-minded, which removes a lot of the oppressiveness of the media overload which is presented.

The work of Hou Hsiao-Hsien reveals the pop corruption in Taiwan today. His most recent movie, *Daughter of the Nile* depicts working-class young people drifting in a displaced island landscape of Kentucky Fried Chicken franchises, rock and roll, walkmans, Japanese comic books, and the ever-present neon signs. *Village Voice* film critic J. Hoberman has described Hou Hsiao-Hsien's style, with its long-shot takes, as emblematic of loss, the abyss separating Taiwan from China, the distance of which is (culturally, politically, psychologically) unbridgeable. The ways in which foreign influences (China, Japan, the United States) have overtaken and become the culture of Taiwan are accepted as natural developments in the dissociated society. The determined contemplativeness of Hou Hsiao-Hsien's style is a way of neutralizing value judgments, moralizing, and imposed views, in

DAUGHTER OF THE NILE

order to examine the cultural confusions and the societal schisms without prejudice.

Pedro Almodovar crosses cultural boundaries as easily as he transgresses traditional morality. *Matador*, one of his most audacious works, takes the ritual of bull fighting as a metaphor for Spanish society, and extends that metaphor to the most extreme conclusion. The moral reversals in *Matador* are obviously akin to the moral reversals found in the writings of Jean Genet, but seen in terms of the *opera buffo* melodramatics of Hollywood movies (King Vidor's *Duel in the Sun* is the movie cited). Almodovar views contemporary Spanish culture as an amalgam of conflicting influences which melt together under the heat of the Spanish terrain. But Almodovar does not moralize about this morass of culture, he merely uses it as the basis for entertainment. In his movies, *What Have I Done to Deserve This!*, *Law of Desire*, and *Women on the Verge of a Nervous Breakdown*, he includes a dizzying variety of disparate elements, from martial arts to Jean Cocteau's *La Voix Humaine* to answering machines to Nicholas Ray's *Johnny Guitar* to fashion photography, and music of all kinds (and from all over).

* * *

Interculturalism hinges on the questions of autonomy and empowerment. To deploy elements from the symbol system of another culture is a very delicate enterprise. In its crudest terms, the question is: when does that usage act as cultural imperialism? Forcing elements from disparate cultures together does not seem to be a solution that makes much sense, aesthetically, ethically, or philosophically. What does that prove: that the knowledge of other cultures exists? That information about other cultures now is readily available?

Taking from other cultures can also be a form of connoisseurship, a new form of worldiness. At this point in world history, the interconnections of the geopolitical structure are so intricate and so intertwined that there is no way out of the dilemma of dependence. And that dependence, economically, industrially, agriculturally, means that diplomacy must be vigilant.

The intercultural agenda must be one of the utmost diplomacy. The problems of dominant culture, of suppression and rejection, of "underdevelopment," remain. Interculturalism can so easily accommodate an agenda of cultural imperialism. This is what happens when Lee Breuer tosses disparate elements together pell-mell as an indicator of disintegration; this is what happens when Robert Wilson's staging overwhelms Heiner Müller's text; this is what happens when Peter Brook distorts the narrative structure of Indian mythology and of Chekhovian dramaturgy. The sense of imposition is omnipresent in these enterprises.

However, I do not want to impugn these attempts, which seem more the result of clumsiness, a certain thoughtlessness, and lack of careful consideration. That is why I mentioned diplomacy in intercultural affairs. Interculturalism has a purpose in allowing for an opening of resources in the arts. The problem arises when interculturalism is cited as an excuse for work which closes options, curtails perspectives, and cuts off exploration in favor of imposing meaning, rather than allowing meaning to arise from the material.

The idea of the exploratory aspects of art is important, because, in recent times, the content of art has been pushed to extremes. The avant-garde sensibility of risk has caused art to extend into areas of human endeavor which had previously been suppressed. Interculturalism is one of the ways of bringing previously suppressed material into the artistic arena, by admitting into a general discourse other cultures, cultures which had previously been ignored or suppressed or unknown. But the general discourse (which we must define in terms of the dominant culture) must not deform other cultures by making them speak in the language of the dominant culture.

African masks, for example, have a beauty that comes from the boldness of stylization, which, in turn, derives from the magical connotations of the masks' conception and execution. Cubism, of course, influenced by African art, has helped us to appreciate the specific beauty of African art, but if we only appreciate African art as an influence on Cubism, there's something wrong there. (I once heard an Italian art critic say that he loved Cubism but he detested the barbarism of African art. But he assumed that African art must be tolerated because of its influence on Cubism. I love European critics and theorists: scratch the surface and you get the most wonderful, imperialistic, racist arrogance. He acted as if his statement wasn't a sign of his barbarism.)

There is, obviously, much more which might be mentioned in relation to interculturalism: that Marxist categorizations of cultural enterprise which have dominated discourse over the past century have been usurped, without having been replaced; that information retention systems have made available more information than can be understood by any individual; that socio-economic dependencies are now inextricably bound while geo-political structures remain demarcated, maintaining a rigid definition of boundary and border. These and other ideas are what we talk about when we talk about art.

II TRAVELS IN CULTURE

Dramatic Ritual/Ritual Drama

Performative and Reflexive Anthropology

Victor Turner

I'VE LONG AGO THOUGHT that teaching and learning anthropology should be more fun than they often are. Perhaps we should not merely read and comment on ethnographies, but actually perform them. Alienated students spend many tedious hours in library carrels struggling with accounts of alien lives and even more alien anthropological theories about the ordering of those lives. Whereas anthropology should be about, in D. H. Lawrence's phrase, "man alive" and "woman alive," this living quality frequently fails to emerge from our pedagogics, perhaps, to cite Lawrence again, because our "analysis presupposes a corpse."

It is becoming increasingly recognized that the anthropological monograph is itself a rather rigid literary genre which grew out of the notion that in the human sciences reports must be modeled rather abjectly on those of the natural sciences. But such a genre has no privileged position, especially now that we realize that in social life cognitive, affective, and volitional elements are bound up with one another and are alike primary, seldom found in their pure form, often hybridized, and only comprehensible by the investigator as lived experience, *his/hers* as well as, and in relation to *theirs*.

Even the best of ethnographic films fail to communicate much of what it means to *be* a member of the society filmed. A selected, often slanted, series of visual images is directed at a passive audience. Discussion in the classroom then centers on the items picked out for attention by the filmmaker. Though a good teacher will plausibly relate the movie to ethnographic contexts drawn from the literature, much of the socio-cultural and psychological complexity of those contexts cannot be related to the film. Anthropological monographs and movies may describe or present the incentives to action characteristic of a given group, but only rarely will these genres catch up their readers or spectators fully into the culture's motivational web.

How, then, may this be done? One possibility may be to turn the more interesting portions of enthnographies into playscripts, then to act them out in class, and finally to turn back to ethnographies armed with the understanding that comes from ''getting inside the skin'' of members of other cultures, rather than merely ''taking the role of the other'' in one's own culture. A whole new set of problems is generated by this apparently simple process. For each of its three stages (ethnography into playscript, script into performance, performance into meta-ethnography) reveals many of the frailties of anthropology, that essentially Western traditional discipline. And the process forces us to look beyond purely anthropological accounts—to literature, history, biography, incidents of travel—for data that may contribute to convincing playscripts. Where social dramas do find their cultural ''doubles'' (to reverse Antonin Artaud) in aesthetic dramas and other genres of cultural performance, there may well develop, as Richard Schechner has argued, a convergence between them, so that the processual form of social dramas is implicit in aesthetic dramas (even if only by reversal or negation), while the *rhetoric* of social dramas—and hence the shape of argument—is drawn from cultural performances. There was a lot of Perry Mason in Watergate!

The ''playing'' of ethnography is a genuinely interdisciplinary enterprise, for if we are to satisfy ourselves of the reliabilty of our script and our performance of it, we will need advice from various non-anthropological sources. Professionals in the field of drama in our own culture—scriptwriters, directors, actors, even stagehands—draw on centuries of professional experience in performing plays. Ideally, we need to consult, better still, bring in as part of the cast, members of the culture being enacted. We may, sometimes, be lucky enough to enlist the aid of theatrical or folk professionals from the society we are studying. But, in any case, those who know the business from the inside can help enormously.

I was given an opportunity to test these speculations in practice when, with fellow social scientists Alexander Alland and Erving Goffman, I was invited by Richard Schechner to take part in what was called ''an intensive workshop'' to ''explore the interface between ritual and the theatre . . . between social and aesthetic drama,'' and other limina between the social sciences and performing arts. I had often thought about the relationship between processual forms of social conflict in many societies, described by an-

100

thropologists and genres of cultural performance. Several years earlier, mutual friends had made me aware of Schechner's interest in the same problem from the viewpoint of theatre. The collaboration of Colin Turnbull *(The Mountain People)* and Peter Brook which converted Turnbull's study of the Ik of Uganda into a series of dramatic episodes alerted me to the possibility of turning suitable ethnographic data into playscripts. That experiment persuaded me that cooperation between anthropological and theatrical people was not only possible but also could become a major teaching tool for both sets of partners in a world, many of whose components are beginning to want to know one another. If it is true that we learn something about ourselves from taking the roles of others, anthropologists, those culture brokers *par excellence*, might be challenged to make this an intercultural as well as intracultural enterprise.

Though many social scientists frown on the terms *performance* and *drama*, they seem to be central. *Performance*, as we have seen, is derived from the Middle English *parfournen*, later *parfourmen*, which is itself from the Old French *parfournir—par* ("thoroughly") plus *fournir* ("to furnish")—hence *performance* does not necessarily have the structuralist implication of manifesting *form*, but rather the processual sense of "bringing to completion" or "accomplishing." To *perform* is thus to complete a more or less involved process rather than to do a single deed or act. To *perform* ethnography, then, is to bring the data home to us in their fullness, in the plenitude of their action-meaning. Cognitive reductionism has always struck me as a kind of dehydration of social life. Sure, the patterns can be elicited, but the wishes and emotions, the personal and collective goals and strategies, even the situational vulnerabilities, weariness, and mistakes are lost in the attempt to objectify and produce an aseptic theory of human behavior, modeled essentially on eighteenth-century "scientific" axioms of belief about mechanical causality. Feelings and desires are not a pollution of cognitive pure essence, but close to what we humanly are; if anthropology is to become a true science of human action, it must take them just as seriously as the structures which sometimes perhaps represent the exhausted husks of action bled of its motivations.

The term *drama* has been criticized (by Max Gluckman and Raymond Firth, for example) as the imposition on observational data of a schema derived from *cultural* genres, hence "loaded" and not "neutral" enough for scientific use. I have to disagree, for my notebooks are filled with descriptions of day-to-day events which, added together, undeniably possess dramatic form, representing a course of action. Let me try to describe what I mean by *drama*, specifically *social drama*. (For a fuller account of my theory of the social drama see my *Schism and Continuity in an African Society*.)

101

I hold that the social drama form occurs on all levels of social organization from state to family. A social drama is initiated when the peaceful tenor of regular, norm-governed social life is interrupted by the *breach* of a rule controlling one of its salient relationships. This leads swiftly or slowly to a state of *crisis*, which, if not soon sealed off, may split the community into contending factions and coalitions. To prevent this, *redressive* means are taken by those who consider themselves or are considered the most legitimate or authoritative representatives of the relevent community. Redress usually involves ritualized action, whether legal (in formal or informal courts), religious (involving beliefs in the retributive action of powerful supernatural entities, and often involving an act of sacrifice), or military (for example, feuding, headhunting, or engaging in organized warfare). If the situation does not regress to *crisis* (which may remain endemic until some radical restructuring of social relationships, sometimes by revolutionary means, is undertaken), the next phase of social drama comes into play, which involves alternative solutions to the problem. The first is *reconciliation* of the conflicting parties following judicial, ritual, or military processes; the second, *consensual recognition of irremediable breach*, usually followed by the spatial separation of the parties. Since social dramas suspend normal everyday role playing, they interrupt the flow of social life and force a group to take cognizance of its own behavior in relation to its own values, even to question at times the value of those values. In other words, dramas induce and contain reflexive processes and generate cultural frames in which reflexivity can find a legitimate place.

With this processual form as a rough guide for our work at Schechner's summer institute, I tried to involve anthropology and drama students in the joint task of writing scripts for and performing ethnographies. It seemed best to choose parts of classical ethnographies that lent themselves to dramatic treatment, such as Malinowski's *Crime and Custom*, with its young man threatening suicide from a treetop when his father's matrilineal kin urged him to leave their village on his father's death. But time being short (we had only two weeks), I had to fall back upon my own ethnography both because I knew it best, and because I had already, to some extent, written a script for a substantial amount of field data in the form I have called *social drama*. My wife, Edie, and I tried to explain to a group of about a dozen students and teachers, almost equally divided between anthropology and drama, what cultural assumptions lay behind the first two social dramas that I described in my book *Schism and Continuity in an African Society*. It was not enough to give them a few cognitive models or structural principles. We had to try to create the illusion of what it is to live Ndembu village life. Could this possibly be done with a few bold strokes, with a gesture or two?

Of course not, but there may be ways of getting people bodily as well as mentally involved in another (not physically present) culture.

The setting for all this was an upper room in the Performing Garage, a theatre in Soho where Schechner's company, The Performance Group, has given some notable performances, including *Dionysus in 69, Makbeth, Mother Courage,* and, more recently, *The Tooth of Crime* and *Rumstick Road* (directed by Elizabeth LeCompte). I knew that Schechner set great store on what he calls the "rehearsal process," which essentially consists of establishing a dynamic relationship, over whatever time it takes, among playscript, actors, director, stage, and props, with no initial presumptions about the primacy of any of these. Sessions often have no time limit; in some, exercises of various kinds, including breathing exercises to loosen up actors, may go on for an hour or so; in others, players may cast themselves rather than be cast by the director. In this complex process, Schechner sees the actor, in taking the role of another—provided by a playscript—as moving, under the intuitive and experienced eye of the director/producer, from the "not-me" (the blueprinted role) to the "not-not-me" (the realized role), and he sees the movement itself as constituting a kind of liminal phase in which all kinds of experiential experiments are possible, indeed mandatory. This is a different style of acting from that which relies on superb professional technique to imitate almost any Western role with verisimilitude. Schechner aims at *poiesis*, rather than *mimesis*: making, not faking. The role grows along with the actor, it is truly "created" through the rehearsal process which may sometimes involve painful moments of self-revelation. Such a method is particularly appropriate for anthropological teaching because the "mimetic" method will work only on familiar material (Western models of behavior), whereas the "poietic," since it recreates behavior from within, can handle unfamiliar material.

In an experimental session convoked by Schechner to rehearse Ibsen's *Doll House,* for example, we came up with four Noras, one of whom actually made a choice contrary to Ibsen's script. It happened that in her personal life she herself was being confronted with a dilemma similar to Nora's: should she separate from her husband, leave her two children with him (he wanted this), and embark upon an independent career? In reliving her own problem through enacting Nora's, she began to wring her hands in a peculiarly poignant, slow, complex way. Eventually, instead of detonating the famous door slam that some critics say ushered in modern theatre, she rushed back to the group, signifying that she was not ready—at least not yet—to give up her children, thus throwing unexpected light on the ethical toughness of Ibsen's Nora. Schechner said that the hand-wringing was "the bit of reality" he would preserve from that particular rehearsal and embody in the Nora-role in subsequent rehearsals. As these succeeded one another, a bricolage of such gestures, incidents, renderings of not-self into not-not-self would be put together and molded artistically into a processual unity. Depth, reflexivity, a haunting ambiguity may thus be infused into a series of performances, each a unique event.

Particularly since I had no skill or experience in direction, the task of communicating to the actors the setting and atmosphere of daily life in a very different culture proved quite formidable. In one's own society an actor tries to realize the "individual character," but takes partly for granted the culturally defined roles supposedly played by that character: father, businessman, friend, lover, fiancé, trade union leader, farmer, poet, and so on. These roles are made up of collective representations shared by actors and audience, who are usually members of the same culture. By contrast, an actor who enacts ethnography has to learn the cultural rules behind the roles played by the character he is representing. How is this to be done? Not, I think, by reading monographs in abstraction from performance, *then* performing the part. There must be a dialectic between performing and learning. One learns through performing, then performs the understandings so gained.

I decided *faute de mieux* to give a reading performance myself of the first two social dramas, interpolating explanatory comments whenever it seemed necessary. The group had already read the relevant pages from *Schism and Continuity*. The dramas were broadly about Ndembu village politics, competition for headmanship, ambition, jealousy, sorcery, the recruiting of factions, and the stigmatizing of rivals, particularly as these operated within a local group of matrilineally related kin and some of their relations by marriage and neighbors. I had collected a number of accounts of these dramas from participants in them. My family and I had lived in the village that was their "stage" or "arena" for at least fifteen months and knew it well during the whole period of my field work—almost two-and-a-half years.

When I had finished reading the drama accounts, the actors in the workshop told me at once that they needed to be "put in the right mood"; to "sense the atmospherics" of Ndembu village life. One of them had brought some records of Yoruba music, and, though this is a different musical idiom from Central African music, I led them into a dancing circle, showing them to the best of my limited, arthritic ability, some of the moves of Ndembu dancing. This was fun, but off-center fun. It then occurred to us that we might recreate with the limited props available to us in the theatre the key redressive ritual which was performed in the second social drama, and whose form we knew very well from having taken part in it on several occasions. This ritual, "name inheritance" (*Kuswanika ijina*), was an emotional event, for it marked the temporary end of a power struggle between the stigmatized candidate for headmanship, Sandombu, and Mukanza, the successful candidate, and his immediate matrilineal kin. Sandombu had been driven by public pressure from the village for a year, for it was alleged that he had killed by sorcery Nyamuwaha, a cousin on his mother's side whom he called "mother," a much loved old lady, sister of Mukanza. Sandombu had shed tears on being accused (even his former foes admitted this), but he had been in exile for a year. As time went by, members of the village remembered how, as a foreman, he had helped them find paid labor in the public works department road gang, and how he had always been generous with food and beer to guests. The pretext to invite him back came when a minor epidemic of illness broke out in the village while at the same time many people dreamed frequently of Nyamuwaha. Divination found that her shade was disturbed by the troubles in the village. To appease her, a quickset sapling of the *muyombu* tree, a species for memorializing the lineage dead, was to be planted for her. Sandombu was invited to do the ritual planting. He also paid the village a goat in compensation for his angry behavior the previous year. The ritual marked his reincorporation into the village, even though formally it had to do with the inheritance of Nyamuwaha's name by her oldest daughter, Manyosa (who afterwards became my wife's best friend in the village.)

Stirred by the dancing and recorded drumming, I was moved to try to recreate the name-inheritance rite in Soho. For the *muyombu* tree, I found as substitute a brush handle. For ritual "white" beer as libation, a cup of water would have to do. There was no white clay to anoint people with, but I found some clear white salt, which I moistened. And to pare the top of the brush handle, as Ndembu shrine trees are pared to reveal the white wood under the bark (an operation symbolically related to the purification that is circumcision), I found a sharp kitchen knife. Afterwards, I was told by one of the group that she was terrified that I would do something "grisly" with it! But truly there is often some element of risk or danger in the atmosphere of living ritual. And something numinous.

To translate this very specific Ndembu rite into modern American terms, I took the role of the new village headman, and with my wife's help prepared the surrogate *muyombu* shrine-tree with knife and salt, and "planted" it in a crack in the floor. The next move was to persuade someone to play Manyosa's role in this situation. Someone whom we shall call Becky, a professional director of drama, volunteered.

I asked Becky to give me the name of a recently deceased close female relative of an older generation who had meant much in her life. Considerably moved, she mentioned her mother's sister Ruth. I then prayed in

Chilunda to "village ancestors." Becky sat beside me before the "shrine," her legs extended in front of her, her head bowed in the Ndembu position of ritual modesty. I then anointed the shrine-tree with the improvised *mpemba*, white clay, symbol of unity with the ancestors and the living community, and drew three lines with it on the ground, from the shrine to myself. I then anointed Becky by the orbits of her eyes, on the brow, and above the navel. I declared her to be "Nswana-Ruth," "successor of Ruth," in a way identified with Ruth, in another replacing her, though not totally, as a structural persona. I repeated the anointing process with other members of the group, not naming them after deceased kin but joining them into the symbolic unity of our recently formed community of teachers and students. Then, Edie and I tied strips of white cloth around everyone's brows, and I poured out another libation of the white beer at the base of the shrine-tree. There was clearly a double symbolism here, for I was using Western substances to represent Ndembu objects which themselves had symbolic value in ritual, making of them, as it were, situational indices of cultural symbols. Surely, at so many removes, must not the whole performance have seemed highly artificial, inauthentic? Oddly enough, according to the students, it did not.

The workshop group later reported that they had gone on discussing what had occurred for several hours. They agreed that the enactment of the Ndembu ritual was the turning point which brought them both the affectual structure of the social drama and the tension between factionalism and scapegoatism, on the one hand, and the deep sense of village "belonging together" on the other. It also showed them how an enhanced collective and individual understanding of the conflict situation could be achieved by participating in a ritual performance, with its kinesiological as well as cognitive codes.

In the following days, the group began work on the actual staging of the ritual dramas. One suggestion favored a dualistic approach: some events (for example, when Sandombu, the ambitious claimant, having killed an antelope, gave only a small portion of meat to his mother's brother, the headman) would be treated realistically, naturalistically; but the world of cultural beliefs, particularly those connected with sorcery and the ancestor cult, would be treated symbolically. For example, it was widely believed, not only by Sandombu's village opponents but also in Ndembu society at large, that Sandombu had killed the headman by paying a powerful sorcerer to summon up from a stream a familiar spirit in the shape of a human-faced serpent, owned by (and also owning) the headman, and by shooting it with his "night-gun," a musket carved from a human tibia and primed with graveyard earth. Such snake-familiars, or *malomba*, are thought to have the faces of their owners and to creep about the village at night invisibly, listening, in wiretap fashion, to derogatory remarks made about their owners by rivals. They grow by eating their shadows, or life-principles, of their owners' foes, who are usually their owners' kin. They function as a kind of Frazerian "external soul," but when they are destroyed by magical means, such as the night-gun, their owners are destroyed too. Chiefs and headmen have "strong *malomba*," and it takes strong medicine to kill them.

Our class suggested that Sandombu's *ilomba* familiar (that is, his quasi-paranoid underself) should be presented as a kind of chorus to the play. Being privy to the political plotting in the situation, the *ilomba* could tell the audience (in the manner of Shakespeare's Richard III) what was going on under the surface of kinship-norm-governed relationships in the village. One suggestion was that we make a film, to be shown in the background, of an *ilomba* cynically disclosing the "real" structure of political power relationships, as known to him, while the *dramatis personae* of the social drama, on stage and in the foreground, behaved with formal restraint towards one another, with an occassional outburst of authentic hostile feeling.

During the discussion, a graduate student in anthropology gave the drama students in the group some cogent instruction in the nature of matrilineal kinship systems and problems, and, later, in the Ndembu system which combined matrilineal descent with virilocal marriage (residence at the husband's village), and asserted the dominance of succession of brothers to office over the succession of the sister's son—one of the causes of dispute in Mukanza village where the dramas were set. This invocation of cognitive models proved helpful, but only because the non-anthropologists had been stimulated to *want* to know them by the enactment of some Ndembu ritual, and the witnessing of the dramatic narrative of political struggle in a matrilineal social context.

To give a more personal idea of the values associated by the Ndembu with matrilineal descent, my wife read to the women of the whole class a piece she had written about the girls' puberty ritual of the Ndembu. I had described this ritual somewhat dryly in the conventional anthropological mode in my book *The Drums of Affliction*. Her account, however, grew from participation in an intersubjective world of women involved in this complex ritual sequence, and communicated vividly the feelings and wishes of women in this *rite de passage* in a matrilineal society. Trying to capture the affective dimension the reading revealed, the women in the drama section of the workshop attempted a new technique of staging. They began a rehearsal with a ballet, in which women created a kind of frame with their bodies, positioning themselves to form a circle, in which the subsequent male political action could take place. Their idea was to show that action went on

107

within a matrilineal socio-cultural space.

Somehow this device didn't work—there was a covert contemporary political tinge in it which denatured the Ndembu socio-cultural process. This feminist mode of staging ethnography assumed and enacted modern ideological notions in a situation in which those ideas are simply irrelevant. The Ndembu struggles were dominated by individual clashes of will and personal and collective emotional responses concerned with assumed or alleged breaches of entitlement. What was dominant was not the general matrilineal stuctures of inheritance, succession, and social placement in lineages but rather will, ambition, and political goals. The matrilineal structures influenced the tactics used by contestants overmastered by their will to obtain temporal power, but politics was mainly in the hands of males. A script should thus focus on power-struggling rather than matrilineal assumptions if it is to stay true to the ethnography. But perhaps the ethnography itself should be put in question? This was one view some of our female class members raised. And, indeed, such a question is legitimate when one opens ethnographies out to the performative process. Does a male ethnographer, like myself, really understand or take into full analytical account the nature of matrilineal structure and its embodiment, not only in women but also in men, as a powerful factor in all their actions—political, legal, kinship, ritual, economic?

Nevertheless, the fact remained that political office, even in this matrilineal society, was largely a male affair, if not a male monopoly. Hence, the attempt to bring into the foreground the female framing of Ndembu society diverted attention from the fact that these particular dramas were essentially male political struggles—even though conducted in terms of matrilineal descent. The real tragedy of Sandombu was not that he was embedded in a matrilineal structure, but that he was embedded in a structure (whether matrilineal, patrilineal, or bilateral) which played down individual political gifts and played up advantages derived from positions assigned from birth. In capitalistic America, or socialistic Russia or China, a political animal like Sandombu might have thrived. In Ndembu village politics, however, a person with ambition, but procreatively sterile and without many matrilineal kin, was almost from the start a doomed man.

The trouble was that time ran out before the group had a chance to portray Sandombu's situation. But all of us, in anthropology and drama, now had a problem to think about. How could we turn ethnography into script, *then* enact that script, *then* think about it, *then* go back to fuller ethnography, *then* make a new script, *then* act it again? This interpretive circulation between data, praxis, theory, and more data—a kind of hermeneutical Catherine wheel, if you like—provides a merciless critique of ethnography.

There is nothing like acting the part of a member of another culture in a crisis situation characteristic of that culture to detect inauthenticity in the reporting usually made by Westerners, and to raise problems undiscussed or unresolved in the ethnographic narrative. However, this very deficiency may have pedagogical merit insofar as it motivates the student/actor to read more widely in the literature on the culture.

It is hard, furthermore, to separate aesthetic and performative problems from anthropological interpretations. The most incisively or plainly reported extended case histories contained in ethnographies still have to be further distilled and abbreviated for the purposes of performance. To do this tellingly and effectively, sound knowledge of the salient socio-cultural contexts must combine with presentational skills to produce an effective playscript, one which effectively portrays both individual psychology and social process articulated in terms of the models provided by a particular culture. One advantage of scripting ethnography in this way is that it draws attention to cultural subsystems, such as that constituted by witchcraft/divination/performance of redressive ritual, in a dramatic way. The workshop group's suggestion that a film or ballet should be performed in the background of the naturalistic drama portraying the *ilomba* and other creatures of witchcraft (masks and masquerading could be employed) might be an effective device for revealing the hidden, perhaps even unconscious levels of action. It would also act as a vivid set of footnotes on the cultural assumptions of the Ndembu *dramatis personae*.

Our experience of the theatre workshop suggested a number of guidelines for how collaboration between anthropologists and practitioners of drama and dance, at whatever stage of training, might be undertaken. First of all, anthropologists might present to their drama colleagues a series of ethnographic texts selected for their performative potential. The processed ethnotext would then be transformed into a workable preliminary playscript. Here the know-how of theatre people—their sense of dialogue; understanding of setting and props; ear for a telling, revelatory phrase—could combine with the anthropologist's understanding of cultural meanings, indigenous rhetoric, and material culture. The playscript, of course, would be subject to continuous modification during the rehearsal process, which would lead up to an actual performance. At this stage, we would need an experienced director, preferably one familiar with anthropology and with non-Western theatre (like Schechner or Peter Brook), and certainly familiar with the social structure and the rules and themes underlying the surface structures of the culture being enacted. There would be a constant back-and-forth movement from anthropological analysis of the ethnography, which provides the details for enactment, to the synthesizing and integrating activity of dramatic composition, which would include sequencing scenes, relating the words and actions of the characters to previous and future events, and rendering actions in appropriate stage settings. For in this kind of ethnographic drama, it is not only the individual characters who have dramatic importance but also the deep processes of social life. From the anthropological viewpoint, there is drama indeed in the working out and mutual confrontation of socio-cultural processes. Sometimes, even, the actors on the stage almost seem puppets on processual strings.

Students of anthropology could also help drama students during rehearsal itself, if not by direct participation, at least in the role of *Dramaturg*, a position founded by Lessing in eighteenth-century Germany and defined by Richard Hornby as ''simply a literary advisor to the [theatre] director.'' Hornby and Schechner envision the *Dramaturg* as a sort of structuralist literary critic who carries on his research through a production rather than merely in his study. But the anthropological *Dramaturg* or *Ethnodramaturg* is not so much concerned with the *structure* of the playscript (itself a definite move from ethnography to literature) as with the fidelity of that script to both the described facts and the anthropological analysis of the structures and processes of the group. Incidentally, I am not calling for a mandatory exclusion of anthropologists from the acting role! Indeed, I think that participation in this role would significantly enhance anthropologists' ''scientific'' understanding of the culture being studied in this dynamic fashion, for human science is concerned, as we have said, with ''man alive.'' But I am aware of the evasiveness and voyeurism of my kind —which we rationalize as ''objectivity.'' Perhaps we need a little more of the disciplined abandonment that theatre demands! However, at second best, we can settle for the role of *Ethnodramaturg*.

The movement from ethnography to performance is a process of pragmatic reflexivity. Not the reflexivity of a narcissistic isolate moving among his or her memories and dreams, but the attempt of representatives of one generic modality of human existence, the Western historical experience, to understand ''on the pulses,'' in a Keatsian metaphor, other modes hitherto locked away from it by cognitive chauvinism or cultural snobbery.

Historically, ethnodramatics is emerging just when knowledge is being increased about other cultures, other world views, other life styles; when Westerners, endeavoring to trap non-Western philosophies, dramatics, and poetics in the corrals of their own cognitive constructions, find that they have caught sublime monsters, Eastern dragons who are lords of fructile chaos, whose wisdom makes our cognitive knowledge look somehow shrunken, shabby, and inadequate to our new apprehension of the human condition.

Cartesian dualism has insisted on separating subject from object, us from them. It has, indeed, made voyeurs of Western man, exaggerating sight by macro- and micro-instrumentation, the better to learn the structures of the world with an "eye" to its exploitation. The deep bonds between body and mentality, unconscious and conscious thinking, species and self have been treated without respect, as though irrelevant for analytical purposes.

The reflexivity of performance dissolves these bonds and so creatively democratizes: as we become on earth a single noosphere, the Platonic cleavage between an aristocracy of the spirit and the "lower or foreign orders" can no longer be maintained. To be reflexive is to be at once one's own subject and direct object. The poet, whom Plato rejected from his *Republic*, subjectivizes the object, or, better, makes inter-subjectivity the characteristically postmodern human mode.

It is perhaps perfectly natural that an anthropology of performance should be moving to meet dramatic performers who are seeking some of their theoretical support from anthropology. With the renewed emphasis on society as a process punctuated by performances of various kinds, there has developed the view that such genres as ritual, ceremony, carnival, festival, game, spectacle, parade, and sports event may constitute, on various levels and in various verbal and non-verbal codes, a set of intersecting metalanguages. The group or community does not merely "flow" in unison at these performances, but, more actively, tries to understand itself in order to change itself. This dialectic between "flow" and reflexivity characterizes performative genres: a successful performance in any of the genres transcends the opposition between spontaneous and self-conscious patterns of action.

If anthropologists are ever to take ethnodramatics seriously, our discipline will have to become something more than a cognitive game played in our heads and inscribed in—let's face it—somewhat tedious journals. We will have to become performers ourselves, and bring to human, existential fulfillment what have hitherto been only mentalistic protocols. We must find ways of overcoming the boundaries of both political and cognitive structures by dramatistic empathy, sympathy, friendship, even love as we acquire ever deeper structural knowledge in reciprocity with the increasingly self-aware *ethnoi, barbaroi, goyim*, heathens, and marginals in pursuit of common tasks and rare imaginative transcedences of those tasks.

WORKS CITED

Firth, Raymond. "Society and its Symbols." *Times Literary Supplement* (September 13, 1974), 1-2.

Gluckman, Max. "On Drama, and Games and Athletic Contests." In *Secular Ritual*. Edited by S. Moore and B. Myerhoff. 227-243. Assen, Holland: Royal van Gorcum, 1977.

Hornby, Richard. *Script into Performance*. Austin and London: University of Texas Press, 1977.

Malinowski, Bronislaw. *Crime and Custom in Savage Society*. New York: Harcourt, Brace, and Company, 1926.

Turnbull, Colin. *The Mountain People*. New York: Simon and Schuster, 1972.

Turner, Victor. *The Drums of Affliction*. Oxford: Clarendon Press; London: The International African Institute, 1968.

———. *Schism and Continuity in an African Society*. Manchester: Manchester University Press, 1957.

Invisible Cities/Transcultural Images

Johannes Birringer

1. "ZOBEIDE"

WHEN I LEFT WEST GERMANY LAST summer to return to Texas, I had just completed the first part of a performance work-in-progress, *Invisible Cities*, which is based on my experience of having lived in cities whose urban topographies are largely unfamiliar to me. I had begun to ask myself how I perceived and imagined Dallas or Houston, how these urban formations project and reproduce ideologies, myths, cultural values, communal relations, and a social order. Furthermore, how the visible symbolic economy of the contemporary post-industrial city (dis)continues the nar-

113

rative of the modern city.

During my stay in Europe I had seen the concrete effects of discontinuity in the decaying and abandoned harbor in the old industrial section of Genoa, Italy, or in the crumbling and ghostlike ruins of the old monuments in Rome, as I had seen the camouflage of wartime destruction in the rapid reconstruction of West German cities in the 1950s and 1960s. My visual memory of the historical and cultural landscape in which I grew up did not quite prepare me, however, for the unforseen collapse of space which I encountered in Dallas and Houston where the dispersion and decomposition of the *urban body* (the physical and cultural representation of community) have reached a hallucinatory stage.

It is this representational crisis, a crisis of visual space produced by the frantic concealment of the deterioration of the socio-cultural fabric, which I became interested in when I started to work on the performance project. I had just reread *Invisible Cities*, Italo Calvino's parables of the interminable work of building and rebuilding the city, the construction site of culture and history. I remembered that one of Calvino's key metaphors of cultural process in the tale of the construction of the multinational, corporate city of "Zobeide," presents a reverse image of the urban narratives of capitalist and technological progress which are our modernist legacy. "Zobeide" is a failed dream that has become phantasmatic insofar as it restages precisely and unfailingly the loss and displacement of its imagined center, the memory on which it was built.

> Men of various nations had an identical dream. They saw a woman running at night through an unknown city; she was seen from behind, with long hair, and she was naked. They dreamed of pursuing her. As they twisted and turned, each of them lost her. After the dream they set out in search of that city; they never found it, but they found one another; they decided to build a city like the one in the dream . . .
>
> This was the city of Zobeide, where they settled waiting for that scene to be repeated one night. None of them . . . ever saw the woman again. The city's streets were streets where they went to work every day, with no link any more to the dreamed chase. Which, for that matter, had long been forgotten.
>
> New men arrived from other lands, having had a dream like theirs, and in the city of Zobeide, they recognized something of the streets of the dream, and they changed the positions of the arcades and stairways to resemble more closely the path of the pursued woman and so, at the spot where she had vanished, there would re-

main no avenue of escape.

Those who had arrived first could not understand what drew these people to Zobeide, this ugly city, this trap.

Italo Calvino, *Invisible Cities*

As a topography of unconscious desire and symbolic reproduction, the image of the city described here can still be read paradigmatically in terms of the modernist topos of the prison, or in terms of the structural and psychoanalytic metaphors that identify the "scene" of repetition and failure in this theatre. The metaphor of the absent center and of the failure of memory and containment, however, points towards the end of the city as an imaginative or emotional focus even of cultural alienation. In contemporary urban fiction, the city (and the narrative itself) has lost all structural coherence. The people who roam the hieroglyphic urban landscape of Pynchon's Los Angeles (*The Crying of Lot 49*) have "no common or geographical ground" anymore, because a ground or an underlying logic have become unrecognizable.

Reading "Zobeide" during my traveling across the distance between Genoa and Houston, I realized that the speed of travel and the collapsing of geographical boundaries, which we are learning to regard as symptoms of a postmodern global culture that exchanges people, information, objects, and images across all and any territories, create conditions that make it rather more difficult to locate the place (the center) and the confines of cultural productions and of the objectifications of "identity" and "otherness." If my notions of "home" and "belonging" had become theoretical abstractions within the vast, sprawling, and depthless space of Houston, so did my performance work seem suspended, from the beginning, in-between itineraries, schedules, and different production environments. The initial workshop was held in Genoa at a cultural performance center which is part of a psychiatric hospital (it has been closed down in the meantime). The first fragment of *Invisible Cities* was created with a German cast and staged in a reconstructed medieval castle near Frankfurt; and the second part will be created with a Latin American cast in a warehouse in downtown Houston.

Does this mean that the work belongs nowhere in particular? Or that it is mostly a resource for building metaphors of its own contradictions and disconnectedness? In taking these questions seriously, I want to reflect on cities and culture, interconnected through performance. And what I have to say about theatre, its ground, cultural identity, and place as they were defined throughout different stages in history, will always be connected to my speculations on the disappearance of identifiable cities. This disappearance, which has produced a crisis of terminology for urban scholars,

115

demographers, and planners, is rarely discussed by students of theatre, however. I suspect that the current interest in intercultural performance has displaced the crisis of theatre in a terrain already occupied and traversed by the global media industry and the ideology of *"posthistoire."* I shall approach this terrain because it threatens to become our common ground.

What I am alluding to may be a common enough experience for many of us who follow the shifting points and winding roads of international exchange and collaboration in theatre, dance, music, and the visual media. One almost takes it for granted that, regardless of any language barriers, one would be able to see that Théâtre du Soleil's ''Asiatic'' Shakespeare Cycle (*Les Shakespeare*) side by side with Tadashi Suzuki's Japanese production of Euripides' *The Trojan Women* in a remodeled Hollywood film studio in Los Angeles. Or that one would see Peter Brook's ''Indian'' epic, *The Mahabharata*, travel from Avignon to Paris, Rome, Zurich, Frankfurt, and New York (and perhaps to India?); or segments of Robert Wilson's multinational opera, *the CIVIL warS*, reassembled in other parts of the world (the Minneapolis ''Knee Plays'' in Frankfurt and Paris; the ''Cologne'' Section in Boston; the ''Rome'' section in Brooklyn). While we have grown accustomed to such ''intercultural'' exchange at the institutional or organizational level (international festivals, touring exhibitions, collaborative productions), there have been surprisingly few critical responses at the level of the content of these works or the production aesthetics involved in the new(?) forms of syncretism or ''interculturalism'' which borrow and combine elements from diverse cultural materials, traditions, and techniques.

Unacknowledged as a continuation of hegemonic practices of appropriation and translation, the production of interculturalism in the West was never challenged or defined with regard to the ideological consequences of Western representations of other cultural materials. Likewise, it went unexamined with regard to the assumptions that underlie the engagement or design of the ''absent'' in our constructions of shared languages and commonalities (in the expansive spirit of the Western liberal, humanist tradition, of course). The promotion of cross-cultural research in performance is a recent phenomenon, however, and we might have to examine very carefully how the comparative study of performative phenomena has evolved over the past decades. Specifically, how Jerzy Grotowski's paratheatrical work or his Theatre of Sources, for example, influenced Eugenio Barba's Theatre Anthropology (ISTA) project and relates to current practices—in academic disciplines as various as ethnology, literary studies, film, photography, sociology, comparative religion—which seek to cover previously absent cultural spaces and performances.

What puzzles me most is the sudden vehemence with which Peter

Brook's *Mahabharata* has been elevated to its controversial status. How does his assimilation of alien ethnic styles or his "Orientalist" projection of images more accessible to Western audiences onto a sacred Indian epic differ from other commercial theatre, dance, or opera productions that have done the same? Or how does it differ from the more subtle (and more insidious) formalist aestheticism with which Robert Wilson constructs, expands, and repeats the dream images of his complete alienation from the subjects of his work? Why are these projections of images, and the screen effects (projecting our needs onto an "other" and eliding the conflicted source of the need) discussed at this particular moment? What absence is inscribed here?

The purpose of this essay is not to join these discussions but to return to my work and to the context of the alienation and dislocation I described in my response to the post-industrial city. I want to understand and perhaps thematize my own marginality, and to develop a point of view on the significance of the *place* and the position of my work/the work of others in relation to the theories and the visible culture which produce and determine our situations of viewing (absences, specular images, or the intercultural).

2. THE PLACE OF THEATRE

There is a remarkable statement by Stephen Balint, director of the exiled Hungarian Squat Theatre, with which I want to introduce a brief reflection on the cultural status (as both product and producer) and the physical and symbolic location of theatre at two exemplary moments of its history in the West:

> Theatre is not about something. It is from something, from a given place, from the social and personal forms of life.

My first example is the theatre of the *polis* in fifth-century Athens. Fully incorporated into the civic and religious life of the city, the annual dramatic festival (the spring festival of Dionysus) was sponsored by the city as a central cultural event which represented the city-state's consciousness of its values, laws, and beliefs to itself. The central place of the drama's cultural significance was accentuated by the topographical location of the open amphitheatre. With the altar of Dionysus in the center between chorus and actors, the audience enfolded the drama and was, in turn, enfolded and boundaried by the city which was visible throughout the daylight performances.

This architectonic, with its spatial organization and containment of the *agon*, can be seen as a map of Athenian culture and social structure. Richard Schechner has called the circular scenography of this theatre "sociometric": the performance incarnates in its space and design what

117

cannot take place anywhere else. Elsewhere in his *Essays on Performance Theory*, he writes that the surrounding city, the *polis*, "is not metaphorical: there were definite geographical, ideological, and social limits to Athens; and each person knew what it was to be a citizen. The shape of the theatre is a version of the social system which alternated agon and solidarity: which was open about debate and interrogation, but closed about who was or was not a member, a citizen."

In his comparative study of such *cultural performances*, which is primarily concerned, not with distinct and context-specific "interrogations" and agons, but with universal dramatic paradigms whose subject, structure, and action embody social process, Schechner claims the universality of ceremonial patterns (gathering, performing, dispersing) which center the performance event and transform spaces into "cultural places." He can therefore argue that the modification of space for a ceremony or theatre event, for example in ritual or processional performance in pre-industrial societies, but also in modern guerilla, environmental, or avant-garde theatre, is analogous to the construction of buildings for the occurrence of theatre in modern industrial societies. Here the proscenium theatre with its separation of stage and audience, of production and consumption, is a cultural version of capitalism in its classic phase.

If one follows this analogy in terms of urban location, one notices that modern theatre buildings, in contrast to the classical amphitheatre, are no longer a central structure at the heart of a clearly boundaried *polis*. Rather, they exist in urban areas that have themselves undergone reconstruction or modification, as in the case of many ill-defined downtown areas in American cities which seem evacuated at night except for the "entertainment" and "arts districts." In the current phase of late capitalism, we go to a barely existing and surviving non-profit theatre in the neighborhood or, more likely, we travel to one of the multi-purpose building agglomerations paradoxically named "cultural centers," where we watch a show that has been brought in from out of town. The ideological position of such "centers" in the decentered contemporary metropolis is purely nostalgic and anachronistic because it no longer defines or represents a culture of production and solidarity. As a decorative element within a landscape of real estate and commercial business schemes, the "centers" merely reflect a share in the space of commodified experience: the show takes place next to the bank, the restaurant, the fashion boutique, and the video store.

The dislocation of theatre culture had a very different meaning, as an eccentric phenomenon in a particular social and ideological setting, during the Elizabethan period of sixteenth-century London, which is my second example. Although we generally consider popular Renaissance theatre (with

Shakespeare at the center of our "world literature" canons) to have been a dominant cultural institution, we need to remember that Burbage's Globe Theatre, among the rest of the popular stages, was able to produce a new and complex form of cultural performance only because it was located on the margins (the South Bankside) of the city's limits. That situation granted it an ambivalent and powerful position in-between the topologies of power, law, custom, and cultural convention governed by what crown, church, and city demarcated as their jurisdictional boundaries.

The geographical location of the Globe Theatre, itself neither an open nor a fully closed building, was in the so-called "Liberties": a heterogenous area that was neither a part nor fully apart from the ritually and ceremonially constituted social order through which the city identified itself and its cultural and political authority.

> The Liberties served as a kind of riddle inscribed in the cultural landscape. The riddle was one of community, its limits and its threshold, and up until the second half of the sixteenth century it was the citizens of London who could correctly parse its message, and so reconstitute and define themselves as a community, through a ritual process of interpretation.
>
> Steven Mullaney, *The Place of the Stage*

If we reviewed the intense negotiations and multi-faceted adaptations of native and alien, residual and emerging, cultural traditions that became the subject—across ill-defined and easily transgressable genre-boundaries—of Elizabethan drama, we would more fully grasp the significance of a historical and cultural process which yielded a literally and ideologically removed position to theatrical representations. These representations, staged in an area that already modified the hegemonic conception of the hierarchical, ceremonial culture, contested the monarchical display of power because they were able to reinscribe and theatricalize the critical in terms of the rhetorical and contradictory margins of a cultural or communal territory (the city wall and its "other," the Liberties).

Elizabethan theatre, *from* its given and appropriated place, could embody an ironic and critical distance to the official Tudor ideology and its rehearsals of political, cultural, and religious legitimation. It could embody an image of absolute danger, "like the plague," as Artaud suggested, yet it survived, until the closing of the theatres in 1642, only by virtue of the irresolvable paradox—the cultural and ideological instability of the political system of absolutism which produced its own radical dissolution—that was built into the liberties of the margin. These liberties are another version, a specular image, of the historical contradictions of a dominant culture that cannot repress or recover the multiple and often conflicting identities it produces. These multiple identities, whether inside or outside of the center, inside or outside of "Athens" or "London," are produced in what I have earlier called construction sites of history and culture.

A poetics of interculturalism which would abstract them from their distinctly different social formations and urban topographies can only submit to a globalized historical consciousness that betrays its own alienation. This alienation is produced by the distance of, say, our post-structuralist theory or cultural anthropology not only from the past or from non-Western societies, but also from the present of our societies. Current culturalist or interculturalist assumptions, in other words, need to be continually examined in terms of their reliance on the role of the *center* with which they construct the "other" (the past, other societies) without recognizing that their universalizing abstractions participate in maintaining the hegemonic role culture now plays in relationships between and within societies.

I don't know how to resolve this problem, and I obviously claim no universal status for my metaphors of the city. They can function, however, as tropes of history because my mixed experience of a disordered reality—like metaphor itself—is defined by contradiction.

3. AUDIO-VISUAL SPACE/TRANSCULTURE

I return to Houston. The movement I shall describe is one from theatre (history) to theory, but there is no continuum between the different conceptions of city and culture addressed here. Or, rather, the model for performance no longer derives from a place and a cultural community, but from the spectacle that fills their absence. My critique of this spectacle in its transcultural dimension necessarily implies a critique of the current convergence of postmodernism and the new media technologies that absorb or transform the historically-determined identity theatre once had. If my return to Houston seems to reflect my own dislocation from the theatre, it also, on the other hand, provokes speculation on the visual metaphors and technologies which shape our perceptions of the transcultural. With the choice of the term "transcultural" I want to capture both the temporal movement, the space of time, which is at stake here, and the movement beyond cultural narratives of identity, difference, and opposition.

Moving from my previous historical example of the "ceremonial city" to the post-industrial, "overexposed city," there are no more riddles, if we were to trust contemporary theories of simulation and implosion, only transparent surfaces and equal visibilities of "everything that shares the same shallow space," as Jean Baudrillard writes in *The Ecstasy of Communication*. In Paul Virilio's conception of the "overexposed city," which is less cynical and ecstatic than Baudrillard's, the dissolution of constructed urban and cultural space is irreversible. The localization of "centers" and "margins," or the distinctions between public and private, reality and image, and among social classes and political positions, is subsumed into the single temporality of an instantaneous diffusion: the interfaces within a new technological/electronic topology.

The "overexposed city" has no "outside" or "elsewhere," which may or may not be a common experience for those who get lost in Houston or Dallas without recourse to the theory that the unavoidable fusion and confusion of geographical realities, or the interchangeability of all places, or the disappearance of visible (static) points of reference into a constant commutation of surface images, is the result of "the crisis of the whole" and the "crisis of a substantial, homogenous space."

What is more disconcerting, to someone who gets lost or confused, is the apparent interface between this post-historical theory ("technological time replaces historical time") and all concurrent postmodern theories of contemporary culture which screen out any meaningful opposition or aversion to the mass-media environment and its closed-circuit reproduction of aesthetic surfaces. Interestingly, the theories of Virilio and Baudrillard initially traveled in the same direction, from Europe to the United States, but they have now been elevated, like Brook's *Mahabharata*, to a powerful vision of "global culture," even though the vision mostly circulates in the metropoles of the West and merely belongs to the spectacle called postmodernism.

But since we must in fact confront the overexposure of mass culture and the effects of postmodernism on our relationship to the imposition of such a paralyzing theoretical hegemonism, I will try to decenter the crisis.

1. The postmodern vision of cultural hegemony, I believe, wants to eliminate all absences, including its own catastrophic lack of an oppositional or hermeneutic praxis. *It stimulates its own invisibility* since as a theory it collapses into the self-referential postmodern diffusion of forms and surfaces which it describes, and it imitates (cynically, no doubt) the all-consuming mass-cultural production of a perpetual present (cf. the fashion industry's erasure of history through an unbroken chain of stylistic recomposition).

2. It manages to explain its self-absorption by claiming the overdetermination of "the postmodern" within the logic of advanced capitalism which reproduces its hegemony through a transterritorial, international flow of images, information, and communications. This colonizing flow incorporates

all art or cultural forms as long as they can be made to reinforce the consumption of the "audio-visual space," as the French call the new technoscape and its interdependent media.

What is not explained is the possibility that the flow breaks down or gets interpreted according to very different understandings or alternative needs.

> The spectacle is the existing order's uninterrupted discourse about itself . . . [It] speaks for all the others.

> Guy Debord, *Society of the Spectacle*

What the French situationist Debord, in the 1960s, criticized as the totalizing power of promotional culture in advanced technological capitalism, we find affirmed, without interruption, in today's postmodernist theories of *implosion*. The abandonment of the situationist intervention, however, means that these theories focus on the promotional medium, its technological form and visual surface as such. (This, incidentally, happened to the reception of Wilson's *the CIVIL warS*, which promoted the non-interpretive consumption of the "look" of the synthetic images.)

Images are not treated as metaphors which translate material contradictions, but essentialized into interchangeable aesthetic screens that have absorbed any concrete social reality or specific "native"/"foreign" referent behind the image. As a consequence, the topography of boundaries between native and foreign, dominant and marginal, is made to disappear into the audio-visual space of a "global culture" modeled on a closed-circuit theory:

> . . . there is no longer . . . any judgment to separate the true from the false, the Real from Artificial resurrection, since everything is already dead and risen in advance.

> Jean Baudrillard, *Simulations*

Despite its self-mockery, this is a dead theory fully incorporated into the "hyperreal" and ahistorical "self-movement" (Debord) of the spectacle.

> Abstraction today is no longer that of the map, the double, the mirror, or the concept. Simulation is no longer that of a territory, a referential being or sub-stance. It is the generation by models of a real without origin or reality; hyperreality.

> *Simulations*

The abstracting and totalizing force of the spectacle could only produce a homogenous form of global postmodern capitalism if it were indeed capable of removing all borders (extensively and intensively, globally and locally) and masking all real conflicts and distinctions between local meanings with its images of a *transcultural culture.*

I should think, however, that such a vision only makes sense in the First World where the cultural homogenization among the advanced capitalist countries is based on a constant circuit of exchange which may have already supplanted or transformed the narratives of separate cultural identity or memory. As a way of thinking "global culture," the postmodern vision is only remotely suited to offering political understanding of the circuits of unequal exchange between the Western metropoles and the heterogenous cultural formations within the so-called Second and Third Worlds. Thinking "global culture," in Western theory, is a hegemonic modification of space, a performance which gathers and disperses, and which "re-centers" the already displaced realities of Second and Third World communities within the audio-visual terrain of international image markets that are exterior to the social processes of these communities.

3. The United States and Central America do not share the "same shallow space." If the history of colonialism and imperialism has produced different meanings of "global culture" for countries in Latin America, Asia, Africa, and Australia, it has also, however, returned the burden of internal colonization to us, to our own urban territories and war zones which are riddled with violence, racial division, confusion, paranoia, poverty, sterility, and waste—the concrete scenography of alienation and ghettoization. It is a scenography that also speaks of the failed replacement of History: the audio-visual space of the mass media, however dominant, cannot quite sublimate the exclusionary boundaries of class and race, and the abandonment of the various urban-others who are trapped in the ghettos of disease, addiction, poverty, or homelessness.

With its confusing cultural and ethnic amorphousness which defies urban categories, Houston could be read as an allegory (as a cultural ruin, in a Benjaminian sense) of the failed dream of an American cultural identity. Since the crash of the Texas oil industry in the 1970s, the city has lived the ghostly afterlife of its manifest destiny. Its riddle is one of community: fragmented and exploded in all directions. Freeway zones and tropical vegetation cover the spaces in between devalued property and bi-lingual billboards over empty parking lots. With its promise of unpredictability, visually portrayed by the sudden collapse of the steep corporate glass towers into the flat, deserted warehouse district next to "Chinatown," the city impersonates a speculative disorder, a kind of positive unspecificity on the verge of a paradoxical hyperbole (global power/local chaos).

Houston exceeds collective representations of its history. None of its immigrant residents remembers a particular reason for its construction or its existence. Houston thus exceeds any definition of culture and social organization represented by our topological models of theatre, and it comes as no surprise that there is no place for theatre in it. What creates a need for the projection of the ''transcultural,'' I suggest, is the desire to compensate for the lack of a culture that would be a meaningful and integrating force, both the ground and the destination, of representation for this invisible city. The dominant visual media in the city (television, movies, advertising) collaborate, not on the cultural recreation and integration of the urban topography of social relations (economic, ethnic, gender, and generational), but on a constant mutual conversion of the local and the global, in the images of historyless, weightless places, bodies and fashion-objects which float the seemingly universal regime of consumption.

But this regime, the *virtual space* of globalizing mass culture, cannot possibly project a *common* desire or fantasy, since the history of consumption itself, like the city, is built upon the social experience of division, dislocation, and disintegration. The theatre, in this respect, is more revealing in its limitation since it does not operate in a virtual space. It has always been closely connected to historical space, and the idea of inventing a transcultural space to supplant or transcend an older, failed one precisely hinges upon the question of history and memory. If we say that history has disappeared or can no longer be experienced through a collective conscience, then what exactly is it that we want to share across cultures and performances?

In my current work on *Invisible Cities*, the rehearsals in Houston are carried out with film and video cameras. We collect visual images of the disordered reality around us, and we examine how the technologies of the visual media can stage or construct what otherwise cannot be seen. It is an editing process of contemporary space; we are not interested in the imageability of the city, but in the process through which historical and cultural imaginations can rediscover what the city was and what it might become. In this regard, the work deals with history as an on-going process which influences the way we see. That movement is neither a closed circuit nor a mythic landscape as suggested by the screened images in Laurie Anderson's *United States* and Robert Wilson's *the CIVIL warS*, two recent performance/film/theatre works which obliterate history or render it invisible behind playful and inconsequential quotations.

Following the direction of my discussion of the place theatre has taken in relationship to contemporary visual media (film, video), I will conclude this essay with some reflections on their particular and contradictory potential for re-placing history and transforming our memory of culture.

THE ANGEL DAMIEL IN *WINGS OF DESIRE*

4. THE FALLEN ANGEL

A very different kind of transformation lies at the center of Wim Wenders' new film, *Wings of Desire*, a narrative movement across space which reverses the direction in which the protagonist of *Paris, Texas* had traveled towards final alienation and separation. Wenders' alienation from America has produced an astonishingly complex effort to recapture a sense of place and origin, to interrogate the *agon* of alienation and rediscover a meaning for existence within a (no longer) familiar historical space.

Ironically, Wenders returns to a historically and politically divided city, walled-in and contained, vibrant and bustling with energy but also bleak and depressed, shadowed by a past that has left its traces all over, not only in the bombed-out and fenced-in buildings. These buildings are the visible gaps and interruptions in a relentless and glossy reconstruction. Berlin's face is still disfigured and concretely marked by a German history which will not go away, burdening its dreams of a future *and* of a present. In a recent interview, Wenders commented on his return to Germany:

I realized finally that if I was going to stay anywhere in Europe, I was going to stay in Berlin. It is only in Berlin that I could recognize what it means to be German . . . for history here is both physically and emotionally present. My movie speaks of Berlin, not because it takes place there, but because it could take place nowhere else.

Even though the film starts out as a fable (''When the child was a child, he didn't know he was a child'') and eventually produces, in the nomadic trapeze artist Marion, the destination and embodiment of male desire, the questions of the fable (''Why am I here and not there? When did time begin? Where does space end?'') move towards her in a highly elliptical construction which replaces plot/story with stunning visual sequences. Dislocated and fragmentary as they seem, they gradually compose a kind of *cultural archaeology*, and the most striking aspect of this composition is the ostensibly incommensurable relationship between the observing eye (camera) and the city.

The observing protagonist, Damiel, is an angel whose point of view—and the spectator's point of identification with the camera—is *transcultural* to the extent that although his virtual presence in the film is central, he is invisible. He observes without being seen (except by children); his body is not subject to space and time; he floats in an ahistorical and undifferentiated dimension. I would not call it a transcendental dimension because Damiel, whose perspective on the world is shot in a stern black and white format, ceaselessly and carefully gathers information and collects events that can be transformed into cultural meanings once they are preserved in the memory.

In an important sequence which echoes the aerial longshots in the beginning, we see him in the municipal library where he overhears the writer Homer, a fragile old man, despairing of finding an epic voice for the present time, a voice that could give testimony to the collective experience of the culture. In another sequence he observes the American actor Peter Falk arrive ''on location,'' an abandoned, bombed-out building, to star in an American-produced film about Nazi Germany and the Holocaust.

The interchange between aerial longshots and increasingly intense closeups (on street level and indoors) points to Damiel's unfolding reconstruction work: his superior vantage point over human history and his unchangeable state above and beyond gradually come into conflict with his empathetic method. He no longer sees Berlin as part of a homogenous, eternal time, but begins to recognize, like Benjamin's dialectical angel of history, moments of danger that affect the experience of the viewer and must be seized ''as an image which flashes up at the instant when it can be recognized and is never seen again. For every image of the past that is not recognized by the present as one of its own concerns threatens to disappear irretrievably.'' Walter Benjamin outlines this perspective in his ''Theses on the Philosophy of History.''

Wenders' film pivots on the poignant and almost ritual process through which Damiel begins to see present reality (in color) and have physical, sensual experiences of the urbane culture. As the camera explores the specificity of mundane reality, and Damiel's desire to love and become human precipitates his fall, both he and the camera lose the ability to move effortlessly across boundaries and walls. Damiel falls onto the West side of the Berlin Wall. The irony of Damiel's fall into the narrative space of capitalism notwithstanding, *Wings of Desire* dramatizes what I believe to be an absolutely vital process of cultural understanding and experience based on physical integration with the place on which one's memories and desires will be grounded. The film thus moves into the opposite direction of the current postmodern vision of transcultural homogenization, a vision based on the assumption that the ''self-movement'' of the spectacle/capitalism congeals and annihilates history and memory as images. Wenders' film, for all its reliance on visual images, insists that the force of interruption, as historical perception of a culture-in-crisis, shares the same space of representation.

I vividly remember such a break in the visual flow towards the end of the film when Damiel enters a nightclub to search for Marion. In a sequence of sudden reversals of camera angles and switches between color and black and white formats, narrative space and the coherence of identification and point of view are disturbed. Instead of the anticipated seduction sequence between Damiel and Marion, we glimpse a view of Berlin through the voice of the subculture, the strained voice of a punk rock band (''Crime and the City Solution'') which tells another story of the divided city.

5. TRANSCULTURAL SCENOGRAPHY

The cinema shows us what our consciousness is. Our consciousness is an effect of montage . . . This is the recognition of the fragmentation of historical reality.

Paul Virilio, *Pure War*

I conclude with a reference to Francesc Torres' very problematic proposition, articulated both in his writings and his video installations, that art is antithetical to, and must necessarily decenter, history and socio-cultural coordinates if it wants to subvert the homogenizing effects of ideology and create a counter-memory.

BELCHITE/SOUTH BRONX
A TRANS-CULTURAL AND TRANS-HISTORICAL LANDSCAPE

In "Belchite/SouthBronx: A Trans-Cultural and Trans-Historical Landscape," a video installation recently exhibited at the Queens Museum in New York, Torres constructed a metaphorical counter-memory based on autobiographical experience as well as on his critical interpretation of current theories of *posthistoire*. In his examination of what constitutes "civil war," and how economic and power relations are sustained by the fluid passage from peace to war and vice versa (in international relations as well as relations within a nation), Torres develops a paradigmatic view of the state of war as a "trans-political," permanent process not contained by a unique historical duration but expressive of all cultural development and change. The total mobilization of warfare developed in this century is then perceived in the context of the evolution of high technical velocities which transcend territorial concepts. Torres claims that war-time destruction and social disintegration, produced in different historico-cultural situations, can show effects that are indistinguishable.

In his video installation, Torres' materializes Virilio's "pure war" theory by exhibiting a ghetto-like sculptural environment of ruined buildings (fragments of a tenement house, a basketball court, a bombed-out church, a Spanish house, and a wrecked car) which literally open up a view of the remains of war and peacetime devastation, and onto the twelve color monitors displaying multi-layered video and sound tracks. The video materials were taped in two different geographical locations: (1) in the destroyed town of Belchite (located in the province of Zaragoza, the region of Torres' origin), left behind—after the bombing in 1937 by Republicans and Francoists alike—as a monument-in-ruins to the Spanish Civil War; (2) in the physically and morally devastated urban space of the South Bronx, a monument to the disastrous effects of urban planning, economic inequality, segregation, violence, drug traffic, lack of education and social cohesiveness.

What makes "Belchite/South Bronx" so provocative is the fact that Torres, although he is fully aware of the radically different historico-cultural and ideological processes that produced these two "monuments," creates a floating paradigm by integrating and synchronizing the visual and acoustic images of his six-channel video exhibition. He even goes so far as to imply that his composite images, (re)constructed as a synchronic, ahistorical, and transcultural urban landscape, can make the scenographic space of the installation resonate with the "plasma of Beirut and Dresden and the slums of Mexico City and Port-au-Prince," which he demonstrated in "Absolute Fire/El Fuego Absoluto."

I am not convinced that a viewer from Long Island, or from Beirut or Dresden, for that matter, would in fact make these associations in a museum, in front of a monitor stacked into the carcass of a burned-out car, surrounded by the stylized ruins and the ritualistic ambience evoked by sounds of sacred music and a large number of votive candles. At the same time, the visual unity of the disparate image sources creates a powerful sense of urban space as a sacrificial site: in one slow-motion image sequence, the Black and Hispanic basketball players from the South Bronx, playing their game ritual in the midst of the rubble, come to look like the young Spanish civil war soldiers who fought for their ideals. The idealism of the Republican battle against the Fascists resulted in the complete destruction of Belchite. The town's eroding ruins, standing there as in suspended time, slowly fade into the images of the abandoned shell of a South Bronx building, burnt by arson. The camera slowly pans along the damaged walls, columns, and the black holes of windows; I hear the sound of gun fire and bouncing basketballs, linking the arenas of violence, aggression, and of stoic survival in the face of defeat.

The synthesis of images from these distinct political and cultural scenarios, in an almost surreal sense, creates a fascinating mutual decontextualization. Obviously, the political constellation of the Republican war against Franco's fascist forces has nothing to do with the decay and social disintegration of the South Bronx, even though it becomes possible —through the contra-diction of the two differently violated and consumed locations—to place them critically against each other in a larger context of fascism and capitalism. Then, they can be read "against the grain," i.e., against other, more conventional representations of cultural histories in the museum, the academy, in art and in the mass media.

Torres' transcultural synthesizing of video images inside the broken circuit of his sculptural environment (inside the museum just on the other side of the East River) is ahistorical and mystifying. It disregards the topography of cultural memory lived and experienced by the people whose absence is staged and whose faces and voices are recomposed, wiped, processed, feedbacked, and otherwise electronically transformed by the digital video technology. Inside the static scenery of Torres' installation, the loop of the video images projects a *continuous present*, occluding the diachronic and heterogenous movement of historical realities, and thus defeating the purpose of a "counter-memory" to *identical history*.

On the other hand, if we take video technology as the exemplary postmodern or, if you want, post-historical medium, then the question arises whether Torres' composite images within the circuit of the twelve monitors (different loops evolve at the same time) fall squarely into the synchronic model of postmodern formal aesthetics (the self-referential structure of the medium as a visual form, analogous to the serial repetition of television) and collapse all spatial relationships into one surface. Or, whether their virtual movement "across" Belchite and the South Bronx does not so much erase the historical and cultural specificity of these different places but transform them through the repetition of content. One could argue that the high-technological artificiality of the reproduction of "Belchite/South Bronx" makes the real movement of the images transparently illusory—it distances us from the medium and suggests a new and different temporality.

The way I understand Torres' conception of the "post-historical," the new temporality of his scenography, which has no point of departure and no point of arrival, proposes a critical momentum in our reviewing of the past and of other cultures from the position of the present (*the post-*). It calls into question, for example, the security and authority of such structures as "history," "context," "period," "center," or "identity," and indeed it questions our well-intended cultural critique of an ahistorical postmodern interculturalism and syncretism. In doing so, the transcultural scenography of "Belchite/South Bronx" demands that we interrogate the very distinction between local culture and "transculture" from the various points of view of our fragmented consciousness, and of our alienation from the places of memory.

These places are images, projections, barely remembered through the medium of some other representation. Invisible cities that are indecipherable because they relate to different "velocities," as Virilio might argue. Torres' transcultural scenography links up and synthesizes fragments of different cultural velocities, and their paradoxical "identity" can provide access to an extremely problematized version of how we construct the ''other.'' I cannot tell whether ''Belchite/South Bronx'' will be seen and read dialectically, and whether its theatrical staging of a virtual movement across ''real'' spaces of historical oppression presents to other viewers a moment of danger that explodes Benjamin's ''continuum of history.''

I can say, however, that Torres' insertion of the video installation into the space of the museum offered me a perspective of a new place for ''post-historical'' theatre. That theatre, if it could be imagined, would intervene in the fictions of continuity and civilizational progress written in the museum, and it would search for its own cultural memories in the absences between the images.

> The city toward which my journey tends is discontinuous in space and time, now scattered, now more condensed. Perhaps while we speak, it is rising, scattered, within the confines of your empire.
>
> Italo Calvino, *Invisible Cities*

The Forest as Archive
Robert Wilson and Interculturalism

Bonnie Marranca

NATURAL SELECTION

"ONE DAY I DISCOVERED THE HABITS of a porcupine fish,"
Charles Darwin recorded in his journal while traveling about the world on
the Beagle. Gilgamesh's Mother relates his curious pleasures in a
monologue that precedes Jean-Henri Fabre's lesson on the need for air.
Darwin's theory of natural selection finds a playful theatrical allusion in this
gathering in *The Forest* of texts and images that have no reason to be
together, mating in the same production, wandering in and out of each
others' realms. (Theatrical production is always reproduction.) A ballerina
walks a lobster, the forest overwhelms a great hall. Even the moon comes
down to earth. Words drift through centuries. All life forms cohabit
effortlessly in the desert, the city, the forest, the mansion, under ancient or
industrial skies. Adaptation is the cornerstone of natural selection.

This theatre is one of fortunate hybrids. Here the origin of species is no
longer an issue, genre courts possibility not principle. Animal and human
metamorphose, and reptiles, birds, fish, people, and rocks settle into narrative. Words are a form of sedimentation. In this new theatrical enlightenment natural history shares the scene with human history, for an alternative
view of culture. Aesthetics is a branch of natural science.

The ecology of theatre: Wilson chooses texts and images from the collective ancestry to situate in multiple environments, then documents (stages) their adaptability. The seasons are sensational. His theatre has biological perspective. A production is an organism, its very joints called "knee plays." Structure is a body of thought, nature and art inseparable.

Lizard, warrior, sea creature, raven, a Renaissance man, a child called Berlin: the already there is imagined in extraordinary landscapes. Oh, wonderful kind of rapture. Not since surrealism has there been a new visual ethnography.

HISTORY/MEMORY

Wilson treats history not as a body of fact but a landscape of experiences. An anthology of images, of texts: knowledge as database. A menu. Food for thought. (There is always a dinner table in the work.)

His theatre does not make history, only its poetic other side, memory. He lingers in myth, the space between literature and history. Intuition is the way to his encyclopedia, and one must have the watchfulness of an angel in a library. In the great sweep of his search for images in the dreams of cultures, Wilson adds a new chronotope to theatre: the archival.

(The interplay of history and memory suggests a way to consider the mysterious collaboration of Robert Wilson and Heiner Müller, the mystic and the materialist. Müller wants to be a machine, Wilson is always inventing the wheel. Müller believes in the blood of time, Wilson in the color red. Wilson prefers the cave, Müller the bomb shelter. Wilson loves the moon, Müller the sun. Their work plays out the struggle of the text and the image, or figuration and abstraction, in the art of the twentieth century. In this post-Brechtian world, theatre after the final purges from paradise, the collective now only alludes to myth. Symbolism is just an earlier mode of *Gestus*: it depends on the sign of the times. Artaud waits in the shadows, with Janus/Chaos, two-faced mask of time. Who better tells the story of the human race?)

THE DRAMATURGY OF THE DISPERSED TEXT

The cultural displacement of contemporary life finds its double in the lives of texts. These are the dispersed, refugee texts from lost civilizations, those of unknown or forgotten authors, the texts of books languishing on library shelves, texts found in archives, texts exiled into oblivion. They find a home in today's world, preoccupied by restoration.

A Wilson production elaborates distinctions between the "Text" and the "Book." In *The Forest* credit for the text is given to Darryl Pinckney who wrote several sections, including the kneeplays, and Heiner Müller, a portion of whose play *Cement* is used. Pinckney and Müller also collected texts of other writers. The Book is the actual literary document in which texts are arranged and fitted, and on which the staging is made. There is also a visual book comprised of lights, costumes, and gestures, research for which is drawn from photography, film, and painting sources. The *Book* then is the basis of the production. Wilson is the only visual artist working in theatre in the twentieth century who has a fully developed style conceived over a period of time, and embracing every aspect of a work: performance, narrative, design. Once the proscenium arch was thought to reflect the shape of perspective, now in Wilson's theatre it is the book that shapes the arch.

Wilson's way of making theatre, as the act of living and creating in many cultures, finds a parallel in his own displacement, precisely in his artistic emigration from the U.S. to work in European theatres. He inhabits the cosmopolitan's kind of homelessness, the capacity to live anywhere and nowhere. The natural state of his work is translation. If the idea of the "dispersed" describes the lives of texts, Wilson's own manner of working only stylizes this general condition of literature.

In this collection of texts that comprise *The Forest* there is a significant factor at work: the recovery of the dispersed text is not only a way of constructing theatrical narrative, but an attitude toward the past as an archive (remembered cultural artifacts). A remarkable hidden order characterizes the organization of literary material, not mere randomness, as even a few facts drawn from the program and outside research reveal.

Gilgamesh, a Middle East epic dating back to about 2600 B.C.E., and rewritten by multiple authors over a period of two thousand years, was discovered buried in the ruins of Ashurbanipal's library in Mesopotamia in the middle of the nineteenth century, then deposited in the British Museum. The epic began to be written down only centuries after the invention of writing, on twelve clay tablets. Parts of the text, which has never been completely recovered, were found in other cities besides Nineveh—Ur, Sippar, Uruk, Megiddo, Sultantepe, Ashur—in the languages of Sumerian, Akkadian, Hittite. Though *The Forest* is modeled after themes of *Gilgamesh*, it doesn't use the work itself as text material.

Another old text collected for *The Forest* is the *Florentine Codex (General History of the Things of New Spain)*, the pre-Colombian work originally written in Aztec, with Spanish added later, completed by 1569 by the Spanish missionary Fray Bernardino de Sahagún. Its twelve books were scattered during the Inquisition, and later found in the 1880s in the Laurentian Library of Florence where they have remained since the 1790s. This major historical document, whose text is supplemented by visual illustration, may have served as model for the frescoed ceilings by Buti in the Armory of the Uffizi Gallery.

Two stories by Edgar Allan Poe provide the organizing frame of *The Forest*. "Silence—A Fable," an 1839 work that was originally called "Siope," opens the production. Its Orientalist, stylized setting evokes the ancient world of myth and startling nature, ruled by mysterious forces. In "Shadow—A Parable," from 1835, a fragment of which closes the work, seven men grieve at the ghostly deathbed of a friend during a time of pestilence: outside the planets cross in an unusual configuration. The actual background was linked to an American cholera epidemic at the time, and, coincidentally, the appearance of a comet which greatly troubled the populace. Poe's tales weave through and around *The Forest*.

(The literary and the visual compel the restless voices of allegory "in the well-remembered and familiar accents of many thousand departed friends," the ending of "Shadow" that concludes *The Forest*. Here one finds resonance in setting this text beside the story of Gilgamesh and Enkidu, perhaps the first story of a great love between two men, and then placing both texts in the context of AIDS. So, too, does one recall that Gilgamesh and Enkidu cut down the Cedars of Lebanon to build a city, and the forests are still being cut down to build cities, and the forests are dying . . .)

The only Müller text in the work is the section HERAKLES 2 OR THE HYDRA from his own play *Cement*, which is based on the celebrated Russian novel of 1928 by Gladkov. Herakles had twelve labors, the second in the forest. (By now it should be clear that ''12'' and ''7'' are recurring numbers in *The Forest*.)

The methodology for constructing the visual book follows the same fastidious technique of composition: research culled from books of Oriental art, images from the period of the industrial revolution, sources of architecture and painting. Caspar David Friedrich's work suggested backlighting in silhouette for one of the scenes.

Perhaps the most intriguing visual source is the use of the book *New and Curious School of Theatrical Dancing* by the Venetian ballet master Gregorio Lambranzi. This recovered text, a manual with fifty engraved plates of dancers, was first published in Nuremberg in 1716, and discovered in the British Museum in the first quarter of the twentieth century. The movement, which looks remarkably like postmodern dance, serves as inspiration for the knee plays between the seven acts.

In our world where time is now told by the rings of trees, the forest of symbols is an archive. Dispersed texts then create a mosaic pattern in which the refracted light of ancient suns turns old books into illuminated manuscripts.

HANDS OF TIME

Splayed fingers on a surface, ravenous fingers, a wrist slightly bent, the palm held sideways, a hand pointed downward, palms turned upside down, arms pointed in opposite directions, one arm at an angle to the body, elbow angled behind the back, an arm a triangle.

Hands are the points of energy in Wilson's work. This is the feeling of portraiture he has brought to the theatre (where hands fall down at the sides of the body like defeated lines of dialogue. Or hide under the dining room table, its cloth their shroud.) Everything in his theatre exists in space. How one looks is what one is. Reality is geometrically beautiful.

These are the most beautiful hands in theatre, this theatre is hand-made. First it is drawn, then it is staged. Fingers are destiny.

Linda Alaniz/Martha Swope Assoc.

ECONOMIES OF THEATRE

In the world of global trade America is becoming more and more a purchaser of things, less a manufacturer. On the artistic level this situation is reflected in the example of Wilson who now creates most of his work outside the U.S., in countries where the culture industry is heavily subsidized.

The Forest then was experienced in New York as an import, a design from Germany. Many scenes quoted the overall "look" of German theatrical vocabulary, namely expressionism—the familiar captains of industry, a grid, a cabaret, the Krupp residence, the mask-like actors' faces, their language. David Byrne's music alluded to German musical references. The Oriental epic *Gilgamesh* was taken as a starting point for a work that treated the theme of nineteenth-century industrial Germany, for a presentation during the year (1988) Berlin celebrated its 750th anniversary as a city.

Work is made on the body of a culture, as dance is made on the body of a dancer. Every culture has the self-satisfied feeling of understanding the world, and the world of emotion, through its own artists. Experiences may

138

be "Proustian" in France, "Kafkaesque" in Central Europe, and life itself in the West is described more and more as "Beckettian."

But Wilson's success in Europe is due to his Otherness. Aesthetically, he can work anywhere outside his own culture because he lives entirely in artistic process as a form of travel, discovery, sights. His way of working subverts the sense of making, and (for audiences) of viewing theatre from one's own cultural center. If earlier in this century the avant-garde expressed nationalist tendencies, while at the other end of the spectrum reflecting interculturalism as an avant-garde theme and technique, now at this century's close the intercultural model Wilson presents—work that is, literally, between cultures—outlines a changing political economy. The worldliness of Wilson points to new possibilities for allegory, in art that lives here and there.

THE FRACTAL TEXT

Wilson problematizes the issue of rupture, dislocation. His *Forest* is part fable, part fiction, now epic, now science. Genres are temperaments that shout across millennia in long forgotten grains of the voice. Side by side, underneath, through and on top of each other, words are folded into a promiscuous forest of sounds, echoing the plenitude of species.

This text is *fractal*, chaos theory's word an aesthetic principle. Fractal now a way to tell of, to think about the surface that is irregular, broken-up, non-linear.

The shape of Wilson's book of knowledge: not smooth, casually ornate, crackling with strange attractors. The fractal text is the one without clear definition (border), the text that falls out of a book, an exile from its source. Elastic, punctured, cross-hatched by its own inner rhythms of image and sound: pattern inside of pattern, self-similar. At once turbulent and coherent, a self-organizer, infatuated with scale. A theatre of process rather than state, of becoming more than being. Pocked with promises of a glance into the texture of infinity. Wilson takes a quantum leap of the theatrical imagination over mountains of well-made play.

He welcomes chaos theory to the theatre. A remarkable coincidence: the application of the principle of chaos to a system is *global*, not local. Which is to say that this new knowledge of the way events can be described is unobstructed by borders. Wilson works, theatrically, by the same guidelines: he takes as his laboratory the art and artifacts of the world, measuring them with new technologies of time. His vision is global. A theatre of memory, which is a kind of mathematics.

This theatrical model outlines a new (scientific) perspective from which to consider the theme of interculturalism: the intercultural text as fractal.

In the year 2000 B.C.E. an Egyptian scribe lamented:

> Would I had phrases that are not known, utterances that are strange, in new language that has not been used, free from repetition, not an utterance which has grown stale, which men of old have spoken.

Yaqui Easter
A Reflection on Cross-Cultural Experience

Frantisek Deak

FOR TWO DECADES I HAVE BEEN living between two cultures. It's an every day, almost casual occurrence—the possibility of two worlds I can inhabit at will or slide into without even realizing it. As many others who have left their native country I can have at least two identities, take part in or distance myself from two cultures, and cherish or dread the experience, depending on circumstances or mood—to live two lives side by side, if ever that were possible. However, I don't dwell on it or turn it into a drama of displacement, a focal point from and to which everything in my life flows. On the contrary, I like to wear this double identity lightly, at times nonchalantly, but mostly as a matter of fact.

Coming to the United States was no travel in time for me. The cultures of industrialized countries used to be distinct, but today the differences among them are less obvious and the similarities more pronounced. The voyage from Prague or Bratislava to Paris, New York, Los Angeles or San Diego is relatively easy: one can retain the same interests and attitudes, at least those that matter, and acquire new ones. The world of modern art, literature, theatre has been international for some time. And it is in fact this world, besides personal relationships, that made my entry into this culture a relatively easy one.

* * *

Another way that I think about interculturalism is in the context of the continuous internalization of the arts which is one of the important characteristics of modernism and, of course, postmodernism. This again is in part a personal preoccupation since my generation acquired its attitudes toward art in the climate of modernist opinion, for which an openness to other cultures was an important prerequisite. The variety of contemporary attitudes toward non-Western cultures, mainly the perception of cultures as offering distinct possibilities for art making, to be freely incorporated and cross-fertilized with our own art and culture, were already part of the early avant-garde and modernism. By adopting aspects of African masks and sculpture (African tribal art), Japanese prints (Hokusai), ritualistic or hieratic gestures of rituals for their own works, artists not only accepted some formal aspects of non-Western arts as is often assumed, but also raised a more substantial question about the idea of art and culture.

This fundamental reappraisal of the Western tradition, which is one of the important characteristics of the avant-garde, was happening in the context of a resurgence of interest in other cultures. It was not only the new sciences of cultural anthropology and ethnography that were responsible for disseminating the information about distant cultures but also contemporaneous commercial and colonial ventures. A series of World Expositions that were held during the second half of the nineteenth century, and well into the twentieth century, not only informed people of distant cultures but also created great intellectual and artistic excitement. The colonial exposition of 1900 presented Parisians with the entire exotic world from the Orient, Africa, South America, etc., with their recreation of wondrous environments, staged scenes from life, exhibits of artifacts and performances. The fact that these exhibitions were commercial and colonial in nature does not mean that they had no relationship to art or literature, including the avant-garde. We should remember that Artaud wrote his seminal essay "On the Balinese Theatre" after a visit to such a colonial exposition.

The artists' crossing over into other cultures did not take place only toward geographically distant cultures. Moreover, non-Western, popular, and folk arts offered not only new formal and thematic possibilities but implied a different idea of culture. From the turn of the century on, non-Western, popular,and folk arts constituted a powerful triumvarite of alternative possibilities that influenced and even formed much of the artistic experience in the twentieth century. We can see this not only in specific works, but also in theoretical thinking about art. Jiři Veltruský writing about "Structure in Folk Theatre" in a 1987 *Poetics Today* pointed out how important the study of the avant-garde theatre, classical Chinese theatre, and folk theatre and customs were for developing a structuralist

142

theory of theatre in the 1930s. This to some degree was also true of early formalist and structuralist literary theory as well.

As time went on there was not only an acceleration in integration of non-Western, popular, and folk arts into the general culture, but perhaps a qualitative change as well. The description of the arts that freely mix a variety of genres, fashion themselves on popular arts, other cultures, a variety of folk traditions or all of the above as a distinct sign of postmodernism, suggests that the original avant-garde project was not abandoned but transformed or transcended. Historically, it is evident that the liberation from constraints of tradition, nationality, class, and culture were in fact important aspects of the avant-garde which was, in part, intercultural and highly international.

One can actually entertain the opposite view: that the recent, if selective traditionalism, in summary the new anti-modernism, is one of the distinct aspects of contemporary life. I do not want to suggest that postmodernism relates to the recapturing of a traditional identity or regional perspective but rather that one aspect of the discourse of postmodernism can be situated in a field delineated by further internationalization of culture and its opposite, an affirmation of an identity which is national, ethnic, religious, and cultural.

* * *

However, I had none of these concerns in mind as I left San Diego early one morning in March 1982, for Tucson, Arizona to see a Yaqui Easter ceremony. I could not have guessed how in this out of the way place, so unlike the United States that I found more or less familiar, I would encounter, at times with almost uncanny immediacy, circumstances of my past. Nor could I have presumed how the events of the Yaqui Easter would lead to reflection on many of my purely secular interests.

Early in the seventeenth century, Jesuits who had practiced and used theatre for religious education and indoctrination since the last quarter of the sixteenth century, taught Yaqui Indians their dramas, among them the Passion and Resurrection of Christ, which the Yaquis integrated into their own pre-Christian ceremonies. I was not as prepared for the trip as I would have liked. I knew little more about the Jesuit theatre than I did about the Yaqui ceremonies. I remembered Valentina Litvinoff's article in *The Drama Review* (T59), ''Theatre in the Desert: The Yaqui Easter,'' which got me interested in the first place. But since I was going with Jerry and Diane Rothenberg (Jerry is a poet and translator of Indian poetry, Diane an anthropologist) and knew that Richard Schechner and some anthropologists from Los Angeles were coming as well, I felt confident that I was among

143

people who could enlighten me if necessary.

Interstate 8 running West to East along the U.S.-Mexican border took us most of the way until we ran into Interstate 10 coming down from Phoenix (they meet around Casa Grande), which then led us to Tucson. If you continue East on 10 you eventually get to Las Cruces in New Mexico, and to El Paso, Texas, or if you turn North and take I-25 to Albuquerque and Santa Fe, you pass the town of Truth or Consequences right on the Rio Grande. This is the American Southwest: an Indian, Spanish, and Catholic part of the United States.

The landscape we drive through is bare—treeless, stony hills, and sandy plains, covered with scrubby dense chaparral. What can I recognize in this desert other than the wildly gesticulating Joshua trees (we pass whole forests of them), the brush-like mesquite trees and a saguaro whose blossom is the state flower of Arizona? This arid landscape is difficult to take hold of. It shimmers in the heat and throws unfamiliar shadows in the cool of the night.

We are at the large, elongated, dusty plaza of New Pascua Pueblo outside of Tucson. The Yaqui Catholic Church is on one end and the communal kitchen and wooden stands, where later in the week food would be served (Indian fried bread, tortilla, tacos and lemon, with a dry salted prune), surround the plaza on both sides. The small church with bell towers is very low. It blends into the desert. Its doors are wide, effecting an effortless transition from church to plaza. On the opposite end of the plaza is the Ramada Fiesta where the Deer Dance takes place. It is not certain when the ceremony will begin and there is no official schedule of events. The Yaquis, who started the ceremony on Ash Wednesday, much earlier than the beginning of holy week when we arrived, certainly knew their schedule—how and when to proceed—but they did not print it. Time is dealt with differently here. There is a lot of waiting, with nothing to do: standing, shifting weight from one leg to another, walking around, looking at other visitors, perhaps going into church to sit down. Then it looks as if something is about to happen. Since I do not want to miss anything (this was before I had accepted the fact that I would miss a lot), I rush to see what is happening. Anselmo Valencia, the Pueblo leader, welcomes us. He tells us that this is not a tourist attraction, but a religious ceremony of a profoundly devout community, and he asks us to behave appropriately, not to use cameras or any recording devices.

The ceremony of the Way of the Cross is different though familiar from what I still remember from my own Catholic past. The Stations of the Cross are on the outer perimeter of the plaza, behind the church, kitchen, and ramada. I do recall some of the stations, but my memory is rather vague and the recognition of events proceeds, not in some logical reconstruction of the

144

Way of the Cross that as a child I myself took part in, but in a sudden understanding of scenes and situations. The stop and go rhythm, kneeling, getting up and going again; teasing among participants, etc., are familiar. But the players are very different. The procession includes the masked Chapeyekas who as the soldiers of the Fariseos represent evil forces. They are all masked; some of them very abstract white masks, others represent animals and a variety of more or less contemporary figures, perhaps a policeman, a cowboy, or an implausible figure of a Jew. I remember that Litvinoff described the masks of these villain/clowns as ''startlingly Dada'' which, when I read it, seemed a forced comparison yet now I see her point: it is not just the masks and their juxtaposition but the energetic and anarchistic clowning that fits the description.

This is a colorful and fascinating spectacle. One of the visitors is busily taking notes. He leans on cars, pushing himself forward in order to see better and from the right angle. Just as I'm admiring his industriousness he is asked by Valencia to stop taking notes so obviously. Just a touch of discord but the Yaquis do in fact make us feel welcome.

A Catholic priest, perhaps of Irish descent, conducts Mass. He is the visiting parish priest who performs the sacraments and delivers a patronizing sermon: why don't you wonderful, religious people come to church every Sunday? If you would show as much of your religious devotion throughout the year as now during Holy Week it would please God more. This complaint must be at least three hundred years old, perhaps part of another tradition dating back to De Ribas who was the first to preach to the Yaquis. I walk out onto the plaza to look for something else to observe.

After about two or three days the masks and some of the events lose their novelty. I get tired of watching other people participating in a ceremony which is obviously very important to them but only, in part, understandable or relevant to me. Boredom and physical fatigue set in. I wish that I had come later, perhaps just for Good Friday and Holy Saturday, the finale of this spectacle. I think of anthropologists who go on long field trips: how, if ever, they deal with boredom and loneliness. Some of us take a trip to Tucson which turns out to be a pleasant city, we have a party, indulge in our own rituals of drink and conversation. Refreshed, we drive back to New Pascua Pueblo.

In the night, there are wood fires around the plaza. With the moon and the stars hovering over the desert the whole place is conducive to spiritual meditation. Throughout the night, the Deer Dancer will dance in the ramada. A handsome young Yaqui with a noble bearing dances the gentle evocative dance of a deer. He wears a white handkerchief on top of his head and over it a small deer's head. His torso is bare and his hands hold rattles that highlight and separate his movements. There is one particularly beautiful moment when he turns his head and glances over his shoulder. In this instant the deer becomes alive as if in that single gaze the hunter and prey meet in a spiritual realm.

Weary, I sit outside the church, by now accustomed to the rhythms of events. Some of the Yaquis seem to be as much observers as the visitors, going in and out of the church and generally hanging around. Obviously there are different degrees of participation among the Yaquis. A Yaqui who sits next to me stikes up a conversation. He has been a casual observer for some time. We talk the small talk of people killing time: of the weather, and of course the desert, until we stumble into gardening, the first obvious interest we share. A surprise is to come later. He takes several of us to see his garden behind the community center. His chilies, nicely in rows, look fragile in the dry, moon-like craters dug into the reddish soil, devoid even of the semblance of weeds, unlike the abundant vegetation that takes over the lot, the garden, and even the house, to which I am accustomed.

After a while he asks me where I am from. I tell him with some skepticism: Czechoslovakia. Excitedly he says, ''Oh! Czechoslovakia, I've often thought about the people of Czechoslovakia.'' It turns out that while he was in the army he was sent to Colorado to learn how to ski, and then shipped to West Germany. He ended up right on the Czechoslovakian border in a ski patrol, peeping in with binoculars and wondering about the other army and the people. He still remembers the names of some of the towns that are close to the German border. I wonder whether he was drafted or enlisted, a soldier by profession; anyhow that's how armies work. They can turn a Yaqui Indian from the Arizona desert into an expert skier. He still skis once in a while in the mountains. ''Those were dangerous times,'' he says. I nod, since there has never been a time in my life that I considered safe, as far as my native country was concerned. ''When were you there?'' ''During the Cuban missile crisis.'' I look at him in surprise, since I was in the Czechoslovakian army at the same time, drafted like every able-bodied young man of my age. Our Tank Division stationed on the other side of the same German border was ready to go. We certainly were not eager, but they had us prepared and if a war had started, we would have followed orders the same way they would have. But we don't talk about that. Rather, we laugh at the coincidence.

The narrative of the Yaqui Easter moves in several directions that come together at the end of the ceremony. The crucifixion of Jesus, the Catholic liturgy, the Deer Dance, and the conquest of the church by the evil forces are central events/stories that are enacted at times separately, at other times simultaneously. On Holy Saturday the Easter Ceremony is concluded

146

by reconquering the church from the evil forces. While church bells ring, children dressed in white rush against the black-veiled Fariseos and Chapayekas, throwing flowers on them. The Pascollas, Matachines, and Deer Dancer all attack the Fariseos. On the third attempt they defeat them and the church is liberated. This is a very moving action—the innocence and beauty of the children, obviously physically inadequate to the task, conquering the evil forces with flowers, which for Yaquis represent the blood of Christ. There is a great release, as if a miracle has taken place. The Chapayekas and Fariseos take off their ceremonial attire and burn it on a pyre with the figure of Judas. Supposedly, they are now in a vulnerable state. Their double role of serving Judas for the glory of Christ has ended, and they are rushed into the Church to be re-dedicated to him and receive benediction.

I came to New Pascua Pueblo for many reasons, simple curiosity among them, but I had particular interests in mind as well. When I read about the Yaqui Easter drama I was reminded in a certain peculiar way of the folk theatre of my country in which one finds the same presence of Christian and pre-Christian customs, the bi-lingualism (Latin and Slovak and Czech), the use of masks, the representation of the devil, the caricature of a Jew, clowning, singing, dancing, representation of animals, etc. (Subsequently, I read in *With Good Heart* by Muriel Thayer Painter that one of the figures of the infant Jesus which plays a part in the Yaqui Easter ceremonies is the Miraculous Infant of Prague, first blessed in 1945, and since then regularly brought to ceremonies. How this statue, which most likely is a folk rendering of Jesus, found its way to a Yaqui village must be an interesting story.) I was also hoping to see some remains of the Jesuit drama that the Yaquis were taught sometime after 1637 and, through them, to glimpse the faraway past. The performing tradition, whether it concerns specific theatre or dances such as the Deer Dance, can suggest to us very different experiences. I was not necessarily convinced that they would reveal any hidden secret, yet there were distinct moments when I knew that I was witnessing something different, perhaps not of this time, alluring but also distant.

Many writers who have commented on Yaqui ceremonies suggest a relationship to the European form of music or performances. Litvinoff believed the dances of the Matachines dance society (devoted to the Blessed Virgin) derived from Spanish dance steps. Edward S. Spicer in *The Yaquis* makes an argument that there are certain similarities to the European religious ceremonies of the 1500s and 1600s, also to features of Hopi, Zuni, Tarahumara, Pima, and other Indians not influenced by Jesuit ceremonies. He writes about the Chapayekas:

147

Are we to regard them as a modification of something which Yaqui had before the Jesuits, of ceremonial figures related to the
Hopi or Zuni Kachina dancers who also wore helmet-masks, performed in groups, carried out joking and burlesque behavior, and
confined their activities to a winter-spring ceremonial season? Or
should we look farther and consider as a possible origin the troupes
of "mummers," so common in medieval France, who played important roles (so long as the church hierarchy allowed it) in
religious drama. Some mummers wore helmet-masks in animal
form like the Yaqui Chapayekas and like them also played the fool
in serious situations. It is possible to go on at length pointing out
parallels between elements of native American and European
religious drama. Such listings are full of curious interest, but they
have not yet led to untangling the historical strands of twentieth-
century Yaqui religion.

There are certainly parts of the ceremony such as the Deer Dance that
are pre-Christian, and others clearly derived from Catholic liturgy and from
the Passion play; still others that can be ascribed to both traditions. But
what is interesting about the Yaqui ceremony is the way it all holds together. The ceremony is tri-lingual: Latin, Yaqui, Spanish. But English is
also spoken. It has pre-Christian aspects, Catholic liturgy, passion play, as
well as moments relating to contemporary Yaqui life. That all of this can be
included in a ceremony is not surprising. The concept of unity through
which works of art or performances are viewed is derived from stylistic concerns or considerations of genre or structure. The Yaqui Easter ceremony,
however, does not derive from art, but from religious ceremonies which
allow a variety of what is perceived as distant performance traditions,
genres, structures, and rituals to co-exist.

The same principle of reconciliation which initially allowed the Jesuit
theatre to be incorporated into Yaqui ceremonies is still in evidence.
Perhaps the Yaquis were unusually receptive to the Passion of Jesus Christ,
since it is well known that the relationship among various religions ranges
from happy syncretism to holy wars. Or it is possible to speculate that the
forms of medieval theatre practiced by the Society of Jesus were much closer
in spirit to the Indian ceremonies than can be imagined today. The same
kind of ritualistic inversion of the world, its religious and social order, that
can be found in medieval theatre carnival exists in a variety of Indian
ceremonies. Similarities can also be found in the roles of clown/villains and
sacred clowns.

The Yaqui Easter ceremony is definitively instructive from the point of

148

view of theatre and performance, and I was very glad that I had the opportunity to witness it. Yet my initial interest in Yaqui Easter as a form of theatre gradually lessened as I was watching it. I was certainly not disinterested in what was happening, but the focus was changing. I began to see it as a religious event, which it is, and relate to it personally. I also began to question the significance, for thoroughly secular people, of watching a religious ceremony. Whatever way we describe it or write about it, its reason for being will elude us, because in principal the experience of religiosity and of the sacred cannot be apprehended by the profane, even if there is a great variety of ways and intensity by which people relate to the divine.

As a result of this fundamental incompatibility, when we write about religious ceremonies we often transform them (into theatre, dance, or ritual) to fit our own interests and our own world. I wonder whether the observance of other peoples' religious rituals is not in part a nostalgic act of remembrance of our lost or perhaps imagined religiosity, tradition, or sense of community. None of these, particularly not the experience of the sacred, can be called back at will. Modern culture has been secular now for at least a century and maybe more.

Antonin Artaud, who saw the rediscovery of the sacred and mystical for modern society as its most urgent task, looked toward other cultures for examples to learn from. He went to Mexico to take part in the Tarahumara Peyote ceremonies. He was not too far from the Yaqui villages in Mexico which are located around the Yaqui river in Sonora. He would have had to descend from Sierra Madre where the Tarahumara live down to the Golfo de California to visit the Yaquis, their neighbors. Artaud would have appreciated the Yaqui Easter: the evocation of the sacred, the magic of the Deer Dance, the manifestation of evil, the ritualistic spectacle, and especially the service and ordeal of the Chapayekas who were performing the arduous tasks for well over forty days, observing many kinds of rules and prohibitions. Their ritualistic devotional transformation implies the kind of direct personal and physical relationship to the sacred and to evil that he, himself, was interested in.

Artaud wrote in "What I Came to Mexico to Do" that he went to look for a new idea of man. "Every important cultural transformation begins with a renewed idea of man, it coincides with a new surge of humanism. People suddenly begin to cultivate man exactly as one would cultivate a fertile garden." The Yaqui ceremony shapes man in a way that most Western religion or theatre in the twentieth century no longer does. For Artaud, to change culture meant to recover the idea of the conscious creation of man. Since religion for Artaud was already dead, theatre became the privileged place where the central ritual of civilization—the creation of man—would take place.

In talking about postmodernism today (let us suspend for a moment judgment of the term) we can agree upon the fact that we are discussing an important cultural transformation. Yet it is also very clear that, unlike Artaud, we are not concerned with the idea of the renewal of the human. Contemporary discourse of modernism versus postmodernism is concerned mainly with formal differences, and with underlining structural differences in relation to economy or technology. The idea of man was not a significant part of the discourse of modernism either, at least not explicitly. The idea of creation or transformation of man as well as an emphasis on personality were, with some interesting exceptions, foreign to it. Yet there was and still is an implied idea of modernist man. Roland Barthes described one version of modernist man as *the structural man*. This man ''[is] defined not by his ideas or his languages, but by his imagination—in other words, by the way in which he mentally experiences structure.''

Structural man looks for functions without identifying himself with any of them, he distances himself from them in order to see their interaction and codification. An identity which is national, ethnic, religious, and cultural interferes with the structuralist activity which is characterized not only by its distance from native culture, but also by its claim to objectivity and neutrality *vis-à-vis* cultural values. It is possible to argue that structural man, since he is distanced from his own culture, is perfectly suited to interact with other cultures. Yet, it is also possible to present the opposite argument, that because structural man, whom Barthes also calls the ''new man of structural inquiry, *Homo significans*,'' is concerned exclusively with the way meaning is produced, his relationship to any culture is a distant one at best, or distorted through his fictional objectivity, which will almost inevitably under- or over-value his image of tradition.

In this sense not only those who practice structural inquiry, but also those who live between two cultures or who are for some reason culturally displaced, are related to the *Homo significans*, who represents a very different idea of man from the one that the Yaqui ceremony implies and that Artaud envisaged.

YAQUI 1982

a poem by Jerome Rothenberg

"the eye of performance is cruel"

—H. Blau

1

the jews of the ceremony
dance in the thin sand of
pascua pueblo   in their pinhole
eyes new fires start
watched by ourselves & others
the bright memory of days to come
tomorrow   but the face
back of the mask
is fathomless
the jews march through the night
clack-clack their sticks
speak for them
red & white
the tips like dagger points
& voiceless
they are the purveyors of the death of jesus
yaqui-style
they stomp & whip each other
thursdays   the master jew
baldheaded man with droopy eyes
& half-a-beard
fresh crown of thorns over his ears
squats by the cross
black-coated
in white jodhpurs
it is the man without the belt
(el viejito)
who seeks the heart of jesus
in a box
white-covered
with lines of green above
the flat red heart
& silver rays
he looks into & sees

a crucifix   a water bottle
flowers & candles
then bangs his sticks
together   in a trance
they lead him with a silky rope
pinned to his shoulders
jews & clowns
how beautifully they walk
the stations of the cross
in yaqui
the plaza stretches to infinity
where the smallest freak is jesus
& angels sing

                                        "you smile & the angels sing"
                                                    —traditional

2

judas coyote rages
at altar   cracks
twin sticks for language
when the bell rings—
the virgin dangling
overhead—her name
her residue of fat he wipes
mindless down his thigh
mad dog mad judas
the first to poke his snout
under the altar
to sniff the linens on
the dead man's crotch
behind him packs of jews erupt
stalking the dead man's tracks
like flies
mad pharisees & litvocks
goat-faced dada jews
banging a klezmer tomtom
fiddles & accordions
they strum & dance to
faggot jews who hump each other
military jews
& jewish sheriffs

a pulpy cherub jew who bellows
an apache jew a lizard a highstepping jew
a nigger jew who chews a stogie
an arab jew with hiccups
a jew who dies of constipation
a two-headed jew
a jew without a nose
a jew who rolls by in a perfect sphere
a troop of jews with bells on
brushing past us, touching
the coyote jew who walks beside
a second jew like jesus
like judas riding backwards
on a mule
feet dangling
forehead aglow & bald
the body of the martyr
red with ants
astride the universe
they face & shake their hips
the accountant & the dog of heaven
whom we watch here
in the full moon over tucson
a true vision of the cross
they give us
comic deaths felt down the ages
judas burning
maestro who keeps the catholic
maestro's dribble
from our ears

3

only the clown plays jesus
here   the other jesus
remaining in wood or plaster
he is laid out in purple gowns
his bier is like
a birthday cake from which
a doll emerges
the babe's head of the other poems
to grace our dreams   it is

the ordinary insanity of art
my dear anselmo
enchanted worlds
we have all touched
on the green side of your purple house
in tucson   a white leaf
is very real
it has grown by leaps over the winter
(someone writes)
& fills the deep well
next to the cloud pump
stalking so slowly the deer
danger advances
that the church bursts with
anticipation
(someone else writes)
''trust the world to little max''
& if I do
seamlessly across the canyon rides
the dada financier
his head a squash
his heart a breadbox
with a mechanic's gift for flowers
he will match you
world for world anselmo
wheels & axles
thrown into the air to make them
sing   a dentist's drill
a meat grinder
the mist on railroad tracks
will fly around him
headlights will be deformed
—zimbrabim—
will light up shoes
& nylon hair
we will prepare our voyage to the desert
the flower world
anselmo
where a crazed stewardess will bring us
both a tray
a dish shaped like a funnel

a delay in glass that holds
a single eyeball

Yaqui 1982 is reprinted by permission of Jerome Rothenberg.

Performance in the Fourth World

An Interview with Ulla Ryum

by
Per Brask

I am writing
in a foreign language
(. . .)
on the page my words
become increasingly
blurred
they are pulled down into
the words below
as if
consumed
from beneath

(from the poetry collection *Skrift* by the Samek writer Ailo Gaup.
Translated from the Norwegian by P.B.)

SINCE HER DEBUT AS A NOVELIST in 1962, the Danish playwright and director Ulla Ryum has published four novels, three collections of short stories, and two collections of essays. She has had eleven plays produced, several radio plays, ballet scenarios, operas, and TV dramas. Many of these she has directed herself for different regional theatres in Denmark and at the Royal Theatre in Copenhagen. Her work is fueled by intense ecological concerns and by a meticulous analysis of human relationships. She has been extremely active in writers' organizations and involved in several governmental committees.

Ryum has also written extensively on dramaturgical theory. Her own dramaturgical model illustrates a non-linear, non-Aristotelian approach towards the elucidation of a dramatic question. The process as Ryum outlines it allows for greater audience participation, in the sense that the audience is not being forced to accept the conditions upon which the story develops, characteristic of Aristotelian dramaturgy. The audience is encouraged to relate to possibilities, suggestions. A play then does not move toward resolution but aims at insight into the conditions activated by dramatic issues. It is from this sense of dramaturgical democracy that she conducts her intercultural work with the Samek and with Faeroe Islanders.

The Samek are an indigenous people living in the Polar region of Fennoscandia inhabiting the northern parts of Norway, Sweden, Finland, and the Kola Peninsula in the Soviet Union. They have lived in these areas for over four thousand years. Only a small portion of Samek herd reindeer; many are involved in fishing (including whaling), farming and hunting, and other industries, depending on where they live. They have been exposed to many kinds of oppression from the countries in which they live; from being forcibly converted to Christianity to having their lands and their language taken away—a story not unfamiliar to many peoples of the fourth world.

The term ''fourth world'' as it is used in this interview includes what anthropologists would call traditional societies. The number ''four'' arises out of the rather ethnocentric sequence which sees industrialized Europe as the (old) first world, industrialized America as the (new) second world, and developing countries as the third world. It is clear that this terminology is not without severely problematic connotations. It is presented here, however, because the term is sometimes used by the peoples of the fourth world themselves in order to underline their distinction from the desire for industrialization expressed by the other three worlds; that is, in order to bring attention to the fact that they wish to retain their aboriginal cultures whether they live in the first, second, or third world. Another expression of this kind of assertion is found in the term ''first nations'' which Canadian natives, for example, often use when fighting for land claims. This term, too, is problematic as the concept of nationhood is also imported from a foreign value system. Be that as it may, I hope it is clear that here the term is used sympathetically to denote aboriginal cultures, many of which are now fighting against their complete absorption into industrialized worlds.

(The following is taken from a conversation with Ulla Ryum at her home in Farum, Denmark in November 1988. It was translated from the Danish by the interviewer.)

* * *

When did your first meeting with the Samek culture take place?

As a part of my hotel training—my training involved tourist hotels, resort hotels as opposed to business hotels in the cities—I apprenticed, starting in 1956, with the Swedish Tourist Association which runs a number of hotels in Sweden. I was sent to a hotel in Ammarnäss which is located in a part of Lapland. It was the first time I was that far North. Ammarnäss proved to be one of the most lively and still functioning church localities where twice a year—early spring and early fall—Samek gathered for a weekend of church activities. At these times an old Samek settlement would come alive again. It was one of the places where they'd built kata [hut-like structures built with wooden poles and covered with earth, often in the same shape as Samek skin-covered tents] to which people normally on the move would return from time to time.

It was here that I first made contact with Samek culture. I grew to have many Samek friends, including a boyfriend whom I would visit at his family's summer camp site about thirty-five miles from Ammarnäss. The Samek often mistook me for one of their own, due to my small size, the fact that I tan easily in the summer, and that I could move rapidly through the mountains. At our first meeting, my boyfriend's mother asked me if I was a Norwegian Samek. When he informed her that I was from Denmark she assumed that was a town in the Scanian provinces [in southwestern Sweden] which was the southern-most point in her map of the world. Since then I have been in Samek territory every year.

Very roughly, what has happened to the Samek culture in the thirty-some years that you have had personal contact with it?

Well, the most significant development has been the increasing sense of self-worth among the Samek, along with a growing pride in their own culture and the recognition that they must fight for the survival of their culture. This has, for example, resulted in demanding that the school system teach their children the Samek language. The problem here is that the Samek language only recently (in the past hundred years) has become a written

158

language. Therefore, most of the cultural material hidden in the language remains untold, or known only to a few very old people.

Didn't the process of the destruction of the Samek culture start with the enforcement of Christianity approximately two hundred years ago?

I'm not in a position to evaluate that. I can only say that much of the Samek culture moved underground then and that it started to express itself in new ways, such as through myths. But horrendous things have been committed against the Samek culture. In Norway, for example, the Samek were forced to take Norwegian family names which destroyed their knowledge of kinship relations, to mention only one among many devious means which have been employed to undermine Samek culture. They have naturally also been subject to the same economic forces as the rest of us and there is today a much greater gap between rich and poor Samek than ever before. In fact, a regular proletariat has evolved among the coastal Samek [in northwestern Norway], while in Sweden one can find quite well-to-do reindeer ranchers. Chernobyl has of course been devastating to many of these people. But it has affected the Samek differently depending on which country they live in, as each country has its own regulations concerning acceptable levels of radiation. So, the Swedish Samek were probably hit the hardest in economic terms. But it is impossible at this point to begin to estimate the devastation caused by Chernobyl.

There are about 40-50,000 Samek in Norway, 15-20,000 in Sweden, 4-8,000 in Finland, and maybe 3000 in the Soviet Union.

Are they allowed to move freely across borders?

Not at all to the extent they would like. There are some agreements between Norway, Sweden, and Finland, and there exists a pan-Scandinavian Samek Council. But the Samek on the Kola Peninsula are isolated. I was once involved in a committee under the Nordic Council which dealt with ways in which the Samek might participate in theatre education in the Scandinavian countries. It was also at these meetings that the first formulations concerning Samek theatre education were initiated. The Kola Samek were invited to participate but we never heard from them.

Do you have any sense of whether the Kola Samek have developed differently than other Samek, in cultural terms?

Yes, they have. But the Scandinavian Samek have also developed differently from one another depending on which country they lived in, and in accordance with the material conditions in which they found themselves.

How do the Samek relate to the four nation states in which they live?

They feel exploited. Their hunting and herding territories have been taken away through farming, and large hydro projects have destroyed grazing lands, etc. In some areas hunting rights have been sold to private interests, in others the right to fish salmon has been sold to foreign companies who protect their property with armed guards. And in all these areas the reindeer are not allowed. However, the reindeer follow the wind which still blows north, south, east, and west regardless of property rights. So, things have become quite difficult and complex. But the very big plans to destroy three or four towns through flooding, in order to build a large hydro dam by the Alta river in northern Norway, really activated the Samek in a huge protest where they had to fight the police. The Samek received massive support from Amerindian and Inuit environmental activists during this protest.

Why do you think that these kinds of assertions of rights are being expressed by the peoples of the fourth world at this time?

It's happening now because they have observed quite clearly that the peoples of the so-called "first" world are in the process of poisoning themselves and the rest of the planet. The aboriginal peoples therefore feel culturally amd materially threatened and in order to defend themselves they begin to assert their uniqueness—the fact that they are not mixed, that they are original cultures. Not to mention the fact that there are very few of these cultures left on earth.

We need to question the notion of "aboriginality," though, don't we? These fourth world cultures have also undergone incredible changes both within their own cultural histories as well as in response to "outside" contact. And they have often integrated with vigorous pleasure elements from the industrialized world, such as the snowmobile, a vehicle which is ruining much of Northern ecology. In other words, I don't think that the background of an original culture carries with it some kind of moral purity or innocence.

I agree. The equation of moral innocence, and the desire for moral purity, with a national and economic striving for independence can lead to some terrible conclusions, as history has shown. So, it is important to keep those two issues separate from one another.

In recent years, many of these cultures have taken to the use of theatre, in the Western sense of the term, in order to express their self-worth to the rest of the world. They have begun to use a form of cultural expression not indigenous to their aboriginality. Could you talk about this as it relates to the Samek?

They have discovered that there exists a form of expression, of communication which others make use of in television, in touring theatre productions, video, etc. And they wish to make use of these tools in expressing their own culture and their political and social agendas. My own role in this has simply been to teach dramaturgy which would have an effect through, for example, Swedish television. My function has been to teach them a tool whereby they could tell their own version of their history in a manner which could be understood by others. That process has been very simple, and then it's up to them if they want to use it—some do and some don't. The movie *The Pathfinder* [*Veiviseren,* written and directed by Nils Gaup] is a result of some of these efforts, a movie which certainly makes the most blatant use of Anglo-Saxon storytelling techniques. It is written completely according to [Syd Field's] formula, and it works extremely well as such, while it also leaves room for some moments of Samek *raisonements* concerning their own situation and their sense of self-worth. What is left behind is nine-tenths of a storytelling tradition and a singing tradition which is almost totally lost but for a few old people who remember.

So, when I work with the Samek I see it as my function to stimulate the development of these memories, these traditions which can become the basis for many different kinds of theatrical expression. "You have so many different kinds of performance in your own culture. Develop those, and make as much use of the dramaturgy I'm telling you about as is useful to you. But let's make use of your own cultural tools. For example, let's take a look at how you move when you dance."

They move very differently from us. Their movements while dancing certainly don't inspire one to start working on a classical ballet. Their movements are naturally in tune with their environment and with their work habits. They are used to moving through the tundra with its small bushes and through deep snow. They do not move about stretching their necks in a swan-like fashion. That means that their traditions of movement are quite different from ours. It is then not my job at any time to outline what they should or should not do. My task is rather to assist them in an attempt to systematize the residual effects of their cultural expressions.

But their initial interest in making use of the theatre lies in its usefulness as a propaganda tool.

Absolutely. Both in relationship to the outside world as well as internally, i.e., both in order to communicate with the outside world and in order to preserve their culture.

You are, then, also assisting in a project of cultural archaeology.

I see it as a project of cultural archaeology. The part involving teaching

161

them about Western storytelling techniques is rather simple. I am the one who is learning enormous amounts about life-cycles and multiplicities and expressions of generous inclusion when I work with them.

How did this work get started?

The Nordic Theatre Committee was approached by the Samek who requested workshops in dramaturgy. There were at that time a few Samek professional actors who'd started theatre groups. There are quite a few now. These groups arose to promote the Samek language which in many areas is completely lost. Among others there was a small group from Hattfjelldal in Norway for whom I went to do a workshop. The average age in the group was seventy-three and there were only six of them who knew Southern Samek. So they were in a hurry to get started working. They came to this workshop in dramaturgy because they wanted to make children's theatre, which they knew of through touring companies.

Are there any Samek playwrights?

There are a few who are in the process of becoming playwrights.

I am asking in an attempt to compare the Samek situation to that of the Inuit in Greenland where a professional theatre has existed in Nuuk since 1984, the Silamiut theatre. They tend to develop their shows through improvisation rather than working with playwrights.

The same holds true for a Samek theatre group like Raugos which is also about four years old.

Do you think there is a connection between Greenland's relatively recent achievement of home rule and the equally recent assertions of difference by other colonized cultures in the Nordic countries, such as the Samek and the Faeroe Islanders?

I think it fuels a hope as they witness the success of the Inuit in acquiring cultural independence. But I don't think that the Samek are modeling themselves on Greenland, although there are connections. When the theatre work began among the Samek at least one of the professional actors was educated at the Tûkak Theatre. [The Tûkak Theatre is located on a farm in the village of Fjaltring in northwestern Denmark, by the North Sea. It was founded in 1975 by its Artistic Director, Reidar Nilsson, a Norwegian actor who'd just left the Odin Theatre, and a group of Greenlanders. Until the establishment of Silamuit in Greenland, the main focus of Tûkak was the Inuit culture. Since then the theatre has begun more actively to include all cultures in the fourth world.] The Samek, and others, certainly see Tûkak as the only real place of theatre education for peoples of the fourth world.

When did the first dramaturgical workshop you conducted take place?

That was in September 1985 in Kautokaino (Samek spelling: Guovdageaid-
nu) in Norway. That was the first workshop in playwriting to which Samek
writers were invited. This past Spring (May 1988) we did a second one and
we are planning a third one for the near future. In between I am in constant
correspondence with the Baivas Theatre in Kautokaino. Baivas is the resi-
dent theatre in the cultural center up there which also houses an institute
for Samek research, as well as the Samek Council. I've also worked with the
southern Samek in Hattfjelldal where there's a very active group working to
preserve the Samek language.

You've mentioned the issue of preserving the Samek language twice now.
What are the real implications of the possible disappearance of a language?

A language doesn't actually die. It survives much, much longer than we
now have any real sense of. It lives on in various forms. As an example I can
mention the work of a wonderful Samek writer and academic, Agot
Vinterbo-Hohr, who does not speak Samek but Norwegian, and in whose
poetry a Samek consciousness and imagery is clearly evident in almost every
single poem she writes. In other words, one could say that images operating
in the mind which are based in a different language are being translated into,
in this case, Norwegian.

Through what kind of process is this possible?

I don't think it is a question of how this is possible, but rather whether it is
possible not to do it? It is then not possible to say that a language has disappeared because it still operates in the way we grammatically process into our
new language images and relationships originating in the former language.

Are these resonances then part of a genetic inheritance?

Probably. You will see this evidenced among quite a number of Samek
writers who write in Norwegian but who use the language structurally quite
differently—Ailo Gaup is another example. But you can see the same process at work among French writers of Arabic extraction.

What does a regular workshop look like?

At the last workshop I conducted the writers were asked to bring material
which they considered dramatic. They brought poems and scenarios. But
no matter what it was we would discuss their intentions with the pieces.
Then we discussed the specifics of how to translate these particular pieces
into works for the stage. There was a natural disposition towards expressing

163

things in non-Aristotelian ways and in visual terms, rather than in verbal terms. And the verbal expressions were frequently highly charged, lyrically speaking, in an almost musical fashion. The important thing for me in this process is always to facilitate their work because I have no sense of one cultural expression and shaping being more valid than another. Multiplicity and change are key notions. One has to listen to the grass grow. But I also teach Aristotelian forms of story construction as a valuable tool.

How does one "hear the grass grow" in a workshop?

I listen for repetitions. I become sensitive to repetitions. There is an African proverb which states that when you start writing down your poems you've forgotten how to dance. I understand this statement deep in my soul. And when I am with the Samek, I listen and I watch—that is the beginning of the dramaturgical process. My questions to the writers often relate to other ways of expressing the same thing. "How would your grandparents express this?" Eventually a certain rhythm is uncovered, sometimes related to song, sometimes to dance. And when they begin to move they start to seek relationships on the stage from which the language then arises. And slowly we try to get back to the point just before they started to write. When the poet commits the poem to the page he/she has forgotten how to dance.

How do you produce the dance along with the poem?

Through the fundamental rhythm. It must be sought in a space. Brecht says somewhere that what he seeks is the *Gestus*, the gestural material in a situation. Listening for the grass growing in this manner among the Samek is unbelievably rewarding. They are a people of such tremendous variety, of acceptance, with a sense of multiplicity and the ability to absorb and encompass, as opposed to our stingy demarcations and need for control.

What's the next step in the workshop process?

I get them to move. Writers seem to have a peculiar relationship to their bodies. So, wherever in Scandinavia (or elsewhere) I conduct workshops for writers movement becomes a very important warm-up exercise. I also require that the writers function as actors in one another's work. At the last workshop I did, all the actors and technicians of the theatre participated, so we ended up with about thirty people. This was a true gift to the writers. So, I began mixing them in groups, theatre is after all a joint effort. We were suddenly in an ideal situation. People began without my urging to exchange experiences. And we began to work practically with the materials that came out of that. We had very few theoretical discussions, because it's true you really do forget how to dance when you write down your poem.

Instead, we experimented with things like the stage picture, the visual elements, and so on. Quickly, we were moving towards political imagery, because they had specific things that they wanted to address: such as how the snowmobile was ruining the land, an issue which can only be addressed in Samek by the Samek—not by Swedish or Norwegian environmental activists. An issue like that belongs with other issues of Samek cultural affirmation. The discussion became very sharp and very specific which was wonderful because I could then assume the attitude that "your struggle for liberation is completely irrelevant to me, whether you belong to the fourth, the seventeenth, or the twenty-first world is of no interest to me. These are the issues at hand and we have to relate to them here and now."

Do you see a relationship between cultural preservation and progressive social change?

Progressive social change is impossible without cultural preservation. But the important thing is to learn from the mistakes as well as the positive collective experiences of the past, not to build a museum for the preservation of culture.

So you see cultural archaeology as a radicalizing process?

Yes indeed. Because it initiates change and understanding, insight.

How do you avoid becoming a "controller" in this process?

I never assume that I know more than they do. I move towards "I know something different from them" and then towards "I know nothing." When I arrive at that point I'm able to teach, become a facilitator of knowledge. How they use this knowledge is their problem: in a certain sense I function amorally in the situation. Whether they want to produce propaganda or save their language, or whatever, remains completely their choice. In this way I can function within the love, inclusivity, and philosophical multiplicity which characterize the circumpolar peoples, opposed to operating as a controlling, authoritative and therefore dangerous force. Their sense of the universe is much more holistic than ours.

Is there a connection between the growing interest among Western intellectuals in such matters as the increasing self-affirmation of the peoples of the fourth world on one hand, and the scientific realization that our universe is ungoverned and characterized by chaos on the other?

Yes, I think recent scientific considerations have made us much more responsive to and accepting of difference and change. As the world seems to become smaller it is actually becoming a much larger place as we participate in it with greater variety and with expanded senses, so to speak.

How do we find the path(s) towards a situation which will allow us to preserve our different cultural "uniqueness" while at the same time develop (a) world culture(s) which is/are multiple, non-exclusive, and accepting?

Let me put it this way: As long as one needs a sense of power, of control, to suppress others and claim special status, needing to be seen as better than others via one's culture, then one simply isn't present in the world. One is then removed from one's own expression and from one's own culture. Power is then necessary to achieve self-affirmation. Whereas acceptance of multiplicity produces the opposite. I really believe that it comes down to not being afraid of the multiple, of simultaneity.

Where is the culture which doesn't assume that it's better than others? Isn't there an inherent conflict between the self-affirmed uniqueness of individual cultures and the notions of acceptance and multiplicity?

Yes, but let the individual cultures remain limited, we know that they are, we've seen through them, and we can begin to transcend those limitations. Affirmations of uniqueness can then move our thinking to a higher level.

What about the intracultural expressions of oppression? Don't the Samek, for example, within the culture they are in the process of regaining give expression to oppressive power relations?

Yes, but it is up to them to solve those issues. And they, like the rest of us, are under the influence of the greater insight which recent scientific thought makes possible.

My sense is that Samek culture is more cooperatively based than Western cultures are, generally speaking. How does this express itself in the way they produce theatre?

They began by producing theatre in the same authoritative, hierarchical manner we do. But it didn't work for them so they now work more collectively, though they have somebody named as heading the organization because the funding state ministries require that kind of administrative structure.

Why then educate specific playwrights for the Samek theatre? One thing is to develop a certain competence, another is to encourage a specific division of labor.

I don't believe that one should. The case in point is the workshop which I mentioned earlier in which the actors and technicians of the theatre participated and everything began to work much better. So, I think that they themselves are dissolving that kind of structure.

That way the Aristotelian dramaturgy, understood as the expression of a single individual's singular, linear story line (which is then directed and finally executed by some actors) becomes less prevalent.

Yes, they are widening the territory. I always teach that the Aristotelian is only one among many possible dramaturgies. I don't see any problem in that and I have no sense of aggression in connection with it. The drive for control is then replaced by insight and collective knowledge. I also believe that insight rather than control is fostered through intercultural work, through interculturalism.

Zambia's Kankanga Dances
The Changing Life of Ritual

Edith Turner

RITUAL AMONG THE NDEMBU of Zambia has changed drastically through time and shows no signs of stabilizing. In 1985, after an absence of thirty-one years, I returned to the tribe where Victor Turner and I had worked to make a restudy of girls' intiation rituals. I found they had been greatly reduced and altered. However, during the few months of my stay further changes took place before my eyes, including a rebound to an older form, first ludic in style, and later by chief's decree. I had not realized that the tradition had never in fact been stable and that it was able to alter according to circumstances.

GIRLS' INTIATION 1951-54

To enable the reader to grasp the fluidity of the ritual style I will give the performative processes as they existed in the fifties and will follow with the variations I noted in 1985. The prime dramatic focus in the earlier intiations was *Kankanga*, the initiate herself, not the women as the case is to-day; the occasion I will describe is for Mwenda, a sulky romantic girl who has been teased continually about marrying her cross-cousin, whom she is a little keen on anyway. She is an active young woman, used to digging and pounding; she battles at every turn with her mother about why she should do the water-carrying, and so on. But her day is coming, for the cousin has given her an imba shell, the token of marriage.

Now this is an absolute personal situation. She *is* going to get free of her mother, by means of initiation. This shows the contrast with theatre performance where no actual social relationships are changed by what is performed. It is true effective ritual. The desires of a real person are going to be satisfied—elaborated and enriched by the older women she admires—in fact she can't wait for the hot development of sex (a strong element in the initiation).

At last the longed-for time has come. Kankanga's body is melting into a richer stranger form, sprouting in front with big teats. It is time for her to go into seclusion. This is an example of how the desire for the performance of a great ritual arises in Africa. Here it culminates in a final display dance by the girl—and in every initiation there is success. Let us compare that with performance among the general American public. Here and there a gifted child finds a gifted teacher, and enthusiasm for the art fires. But in our system such a one quickly ruptures through the social fabric. She or he leaves her original society, the world of ordinary humanity, and becomes a member of a professional group. In this way common society is looted of its talent by the professional world, leaving the dull mob to carry on without it, to be content to just watch; and such a tendency is very hard to combat. Among the Ndembu in the fifties every girl was in this elite.

Mwenda is taken by her ''midwife,'' the older cousin chosen to ''cause her to menstruate,'' and laid down at the foot of a milk tree in the bush. She has become a baby, lying in the fetal position, entirely covered in a womb of a blanket, where around her dance the women from dawn until dusk. This existential experience, say those who have experienced it, hatches out strongly the desire to be considered a woman and join the others. Physical experience is the basic power source for ritual, which, when carried out genuinely, feeding this desire, will in fact work. It is therefore likely that the performance of physical acts in the theatre has similar effects of power, waiting, as it were, to be transmuted into ritual—even though the theatre defines such performance as make-believe.

Kankanga lies there and becomes a baby-sex-sapling herself, in an entranced sleep beside the Tree of the White Sap where her male cousin's arrow is planted upright among its leaves. And atop the arrow hang her ''spirit-children'' beads, white beads which pre-image her future children. The world outside triumphs at the achievement of this phase. They sing in the jazziest shout, ''She has grown up! Her breasts have grown!'' There is nothing restrained or decorous about this dance, it is fun and the women teach me how to dance it too.

Kankanga lies there in the midst, all day long. The contrast between this girl, so negative and alone, and the singing women, so aggressive and feminist, has power, working up a dynamic potential, something comparable to an electric differential or sling-shot effect that actually propels the girl into womanhood.

The quarrelsome in-laws arrive and build her a seclusion hut, swaggering and defying the midwife and the mother. They appear to botch up everything; they really quarrel. It is accepted that they do and the episode becomes a combination of actuality and play-acting. The way the system is set up, the sheer biology of parenthood, marriage, and the resultant in-law relationship with its inevitable structural frustrations, produces strong emotion—all grist to ritual's mill.

I would comment that this ritual does not correspond to much postmodern intellectual theatre. Rather there are elements that match the crying of the Western mother of the bride, the scrawling of rude things on the bridal car, even such popular ritual as the beauty queen parade. However, some new theatre groups are determined to re-nourish popular performative culture. The Bond Street Theatre group, in keeping with their loyalty to the people, ran a paper hat parade in a small town in upstate New York; and Eugenio Barba has bartered popular entertainment with ordinary people in various parts of the world. These and other colorful ideas are becoming the business of the avant-garde. I believe, with Bonnie Marranca, that democracy will yet make artists of all of its people.

Late in the afternoon we women feast, lit up by beer and the triumph of our own sex. Kankanga has no food but is still lying ''dead,'' as they put it. Evening falls in the forest. We women remember Kankanga and gather around the milk tree. We do not regard the sun, who is the high god Nzambi, nor the males of the community, as beings of awe but as interlopers. When the sun has truly gone the girl can be lifted, like a baby or a corpse; the midwife heaves her up on her back, keeping her covered. All of us women pluck milk leaves which we hold hidden in our fists as in the womb: they are Kankanga's future children. We press around the midwife: the womb contracts around the baby. She is ours, a collective birth is on the way. We march-dance into the village, singing; and pause, contracting around our baby. All the time I'm very excited and can't hold the camera still.

We march again, shouting the song at the men; we circle the men while the drums thunder; we pause, and then head for the seclusion hut. The midwife/mother turns around backward at its door, at the vulva. Pop, out-in goes the baby, into the hut backward. We shriek trills of joy—and suddenly

170

we all set off running, in a classic sequence of simultaneity. The milk leaves in our hands are for Kankanga's mother, so we deliver them instantly into the mother's thatch at the opposite side of the village. We are very out of breath.

This is a complicated passage, very physical, very precise. Primarily we are acting ''as if'' (in the subjunctive mood) we were doing what we actually do, give birth. And we are doing it in unison. In that bunch we are one body made up of many individuals, with the nubile girl at the core. I remember that bunch well, we were one body for a magic moment. Nowadays they call this frame slippage; what had we slipped into, beyond the world of symbols? We had slipped off our defenses against each other and joined in one triumph, feeling the pleasure of it like a common bloodstream. This ''as one'' theme also dominates in the girl's own history in time. She is at once a baby, a trainee in sex, and a mother with her children, the milk leaves; all the periods of her life are as one. The accumulating condensation and resulting transmutation of symbols into this battery of oneness is triggered by the picking of milk leaves; what it triggers is the performance of the birth process, just as it is triggered unpredictably in the ordinary pregnancy of a woman. Now the woman, representing their sex, representing nurture generally, act together vis-à-vis the men, around whom they circle in the same circling action that their bodies skillfully perform at intercourse. The women are in the act of changing the girl into a woman. Thus we can see how the prophetic power of imaging—the setting down of patterns and templates before the event—known now as an important factor in biological processes—is well understood by the Ndembu. In this way the complex act of giving birth to a ''baby'' adult woman is enacted effectively, working very close to real physiology, but in a reflexive and not yet manifest relation to it.

Kankanga spends three months away from her mother in seclusion, not having to cook, dig, nor light fires because she is like a ''spirit from ancient times,'' an *ikishi*. She may collect honey, termites, and fish, she is one with the archaic hunters. She may not name a thing directly—she is a prelapsarian being, as it were, before Adam as we might say, a holistic entity. In seclusion the women attend to her body, which flowers at this time; they decorate it, they wet a peeled sweet potato and give her vaginal pleasure; they teach her a highly accomplished belly dance, so precise that it outdoes that of the Arabs. In her hut she keeps a secret harp on which she plays messages to the village.

The women also teach her the coming-out dance. She learns willingly and well, without competition or dread of failure. The dance step is again complex, and every girl learns it perfectly, or did before the missions started to

171

Photo A
Preparing for today's
initiation: washing and
oiling.

control the Ndembu. Her breasts are just beginning to show, and the dance focuses right upon them, for it consists of an extremely rapid shaking up and down of the naked teats—supplying this erogenous zone with unbelievable stimulation.

At the coming-out stage of this rite of passage the whole neighborhood is there awaiting the spectacle. Early in the morning Kankanga is taken to a screened-off area, washed, coifed, rubbed with red clay all over, given leg rattles, adorned with spirit children beads, also crisscrossed with beads over her bare breasts; and she is ritually fed by hand. After this she is led away, in the opposite direction from the crowd. Why away from it? The rest of us approach the crowd and form a wide circle along with the drums, we are wondering where she is. A mat is seen approaching from far over the other side, held carefully upright. As it reaches the crowd it is withdrawn. Kankanga is exposed, crouching, shuffling across the expanse toward the big drum. When she reaches it she beats it once, then springs upright, a fully-breasted woman. She dances: her hand is gracefully fanning a black swirl of animal hair over her shoulder—the headman's fly switch. She is one

172

rapid vibration from heel to skirt to shoulders, so that her breasts flash up and down, while her head falls languorously from side to side. Even her back is jingling, for now she is wearing a black pad stitched all over with bells which resound every time she shakes her back. She is a percussion system in full swing, she and the drums along with the frenzied singing. All the while her face is serene, with just a touch of ecstasy. She mimes the hunter dance, the honey gatherer, the fisher, and gives cloth "babies" to all. It is hard to know whether she's male or female, she has the strength of both.

She is a spirit, painted in red. And she comes as a surprise, as a spirit does. The mat screen, which is the prototype of our theatre curtain, enhances surprise, corresponding with the now-you-see-it, now-you-don't theme that commonly expresses spirit manifestation. So there we have the coming of the spirit both enacted and real at the same time; such performances are perhaps the most dramatic ones we know.

But now it is finished and she is led away, rendered passive again, the creation of the women. The midwife takes her to the door of her husband's hut. When she enters he rises and stands erect. Everyone knows what this means. His arrow stands erect at the foot of the bed and she comes to him, wearing her spirit-children beads in the part of her hair. She has power over him now because it is he who has to prove sexual competence this night. And she wants him. She does her circulating belly dance, and he follows with the same circling, closer and closer, until they are lying side by side, not one on top of the other. The insertion, devious and circuitous, is more tempting, more inflaming. At orgasm she says, *"Nafwi,"* "I am dying."

And so I left Ndembu, for thirty-one years, while Ndembu changed, and eventually I went back to the self-same village to see what had happened.

CHRISTIANIZED INTIATION

I found that Christianity and nationalist modernization had been devouring the ancient culture like a plague—a plague full of the best intentions but in fact the agent of tragic destruction. My original story was no longer true. For ten years there had been no spirit dancer, no spirit-children beads; girls' initiation had been seriously reduced and had lost its major symbolism. Under attacks from the missions and the rationalist government school system the milk tree was rarely honored—in fact there was little forest left. Scant forethought was being given during girlhood to the approaching event of initiation; no small girls or older ones practiced the dance. The girl was simply carried by her midwife from her mother's house and dumped in the separate kitchen nearby which she used as a bedroom until such time as the family could afford beer for a coming-out party; and even that often con-

Photo B
The initiate is passive:
she has been fully dressed
and will be adorned with
beads.

sisted of just dressing the girl up smartly and seating her down in the village plaza to receive gifts. The change altered the emphasis of initiation from the girl to the women themselves. There was little attention to her changing status, nor portrayal of alternating passivity and aggressivity. Any focus on sex and nubile breasts was frowned upon by the missions, therefore breasts were withdrawn and hidden behind clothes. Instead, among the adult women a generalized carnival spirit grew up around initiation; and a defiance of the missions among traditionalists began to surface in an even greater scurrility and violence expressed in the song's words.

I went from ritual to ritual carrying under my arm Turner's *The Drums of Affliction*, which contained the full script for girls' initiation; I was even invited to become an instructress myself. The book and its pictures were central to many conversations that arose about the old and new initiations. One morning I was up early at yet another coming-out ritual with my movie camera and notebook, and found that despite many reductions there was more to this particular celebration than I anticipated. The midwife brought the girl out of the kitchen along with her small girl helper and led the two to

174

a screened-off area behind where the village women and children collected to watch. One woman was wearing an initiation fashion from another culture area in Zambia, the Tonga. This woman had draped some beads on each side of her head, making them hang down loosely—hinting of the theme of the spirit-children beads. Now the midwife brought water and washed the girls, then braided their hair (Photo A). Kankanga was rubbed with vaseline to give her body a shine; she was passive throughout these attentions in the traditional manner. The women then proceeded to dress her fully in beautiful Western clothes, after which they hunted and found some ordinary beads (Photo B). They crisscrossed them over her clothed breasts in the time-honored fashion, then after feeding the girl ritually by hand, they prepared to lead her out.

And here to enrich this phase of the initiation, the Ndembu invented—and partly borrowed from the neighboring Kaonde peoples—a dramatic yet acceptable sequence which substituted for the girls' breast dance. When the two girls were dressed and ready, standing amid a large crowd of women, the midwife untied the mat which was our screen. Then

Photo C
The girl is passively
displayed, while women
throw money.

175

two women proceeded to hold it upright, while both girls got under one large tent-like cloth and guided themselves one after the other into position behind the screen, on our own private side. Kankanga bent low, holding onto the young helper in front. Four legs could be seen under the cloth. The legs walked, and the ''animal'' advanced, the screen being advanced by the women as they moved forward, with the head of the young helper continually butting into the screen in front. A lusty song broke forth from us all causing disturbances beyond in the village plaza as the men rushed for the drums. Excitement and din were set loose, we advanced right to the center of the plaza where the mat was removed. With the cloth over her head and body, the initiate seated herself on the mat. All gathered around singing and started to throw money into a dish at her feet. Her grandfather approached; he now enacted another Kaonde rite, first placing a coin on her head and with the same gesture lifting off the cloth—a male act of unveiling but also a matrilineal signifier, for he was her mother's father, not from the male line. All trilled: her father stood above her and peeled off a large sum of money in bills, casting them dramatically into the dish. Her elder sister and other women in wide carnival skirts and spotted faces danced before her, performing a kind of praise dance borrowed from the Lozi peoples. The song's words were largely sexual or horrific in meaning, often taken from Kaonde, Luvale, and Luunda sources: Zinia, my jovial consultant, sang the wicked words right into my face—''I tell you, it was Sela who did it, she killed her husband dead.'' Zinia had braids like sprigs standing out all over her head and brilliant white polka dots on her face, plus a broad smile. I shouted the song back at her.

COMMENTARY ON THE CHANGES

First, there has been much borrowing of ritual elements from neighboring peoples; clearly the Ndembu have become more osmotic in the modern context of greater mobility.

The fact that the screen episode has become enlarged and embellished highlights the private/public dichotomy, the idea that there is a hidden place in which techniques for effecting transformation can be put into effect. A further consideration is the absence of milk symbolism in the new versions of the ritual, but instead there is that striking episode of performance with money (Photo C), conveying a dynamic message in these days of economic stress in Africa. The animal physical message is kept under wraps and now exists in the form of an animal hidden under a cloth, within the women's sphere; but there it is still strong. The mock-animal episode is a rite that did not exist thirty years ago; it betokens a new inventiveness within the domain hidden from mission eyes. The girl may no longer take pride in her

176

own nubility nor express it in a solo dance. Her physicality is not supposed to matter; her clothes do. Yet that hidden physicality remains, expressed in a combination of cloth and an animal appearance in a circus-like parade, something like a two-person hobbyhorse. Does it rate as a folklore custom, then? The style of the whole more resembles that of the carnivals of popular culture.

Zinia came to my hut later to talk. She remembered dancing the breast dance at her own initiation. "Show me how you did it," I said. Zinia took off her blouse and somehow, with the long breasts that had fed six babies, she managed to flip them up and down in the classic manner while producing the shimmer, sway, and heel stamp of the ancient step.

A LUDIC VERSION

It was not long afterwards when I was called to greet a party of young women, men, and children who brought objects that had been used in girls' initiation long ago. One young woman held out a couple of bows, strung with gut. The bows constituted the musical harp of the seclusion hut. I was delighted and we had a try at playing it. Looking up from the bows I said, "Anybody dance the breast dance? Don't forget, you have to wear spirit-children beads on top of your head." The fat one smiled and found some beads which she fastened onto her hair by means of a twig. The beads flopped down, but her dance was genuine, for she knew how to vibrate her shoulders, hips, and feet to produce the real breast dance. They knew that I knew that they knew the dance. A five-year-old girl took up a cloth and draped it over her head and body, groping about like a shrouded Kankanga. They were actually play-acting initiation. They also had with them a conus shell threaded on a string; it was the *imba*, the gift that the bridegroom formerly presented to the future bride for her to wear around her neck. This one was from the days before money, and a priceless object.

Richard Schechner has described the revival of the Agni ritual in Kerala, India, produced for the purpose of making a film. He believes that such occasions are also genuine material for the student of performance and anthropology. By this means the past, even the garbled past, can come alive again and deeply affect the direction of culture in the present. As I watched this small Ndembu performance I thought of what he had said and realized that this too was an attempt at a revival. I also began to see the triggering mechanism for such a reenactment. In the present case they were the objects they brought: the harp, the beads, the covering cloth, and the shell—for the relationship of objects to performance is a long-standing one. People are transformed by means of these objects, some of which may even be costumes or masks. Central objects in ritual and celebration have the

Photo D
Dance practice: the midwife directs the girl's body with her hands.

power to attract, boost, and throw forward in a sling-shot manner the efficacy of action to an extraordinary degree. English missionaries used to hate fetishes—the missionaries correctly estimated the competition they implied; art fanciers admired the outside but did not see the power and meaning inherent in them; anthropologists have analyzed them purely as symbols, but may have to adjust to the idea, strongly insisted upon by the ethnic peoples concerned, that they have actual power.

BEATRICE'S INITIATION

A little later I heard that a Kankanga named Beatrice was about to come out of seclusion and dance the breast dance. I hurried to the village in time to see her bent under her covering cloth, in the act of leaving for the fields with her midwife. I followed with the other women and girls; as soon as we were clear of the village Beatrice pushed back the cloth—she was wearing a waist-cloth and scarf tied around her breasts.

"How do you think you'll do?" I asked her.

"I don't know, I'm shy," she said.

The women broke in, "We weren't shy when we were your age."

Further on they stopped at a secluded plain and formed a wide circle around Beatrice. A drum was fetched. As the music started the midwife,

178

whose name was Seriya, went inside the circle and gave a demonstration breast dance, sparking off comments like "The old woman's breasts are too fat, she'll never make it," followed by loud laughter. Manuel, a worldly bearded fellow with a leer, came by and stood on the outside. Beatrice was put in the circle to dance (Photo D). I gradually realized that this was only a practice, not the real thing. As I watched, Beatrice tried a pass or two here and there, with her breasts shaking a little; she even bared her breasts briefly for the dance, at which Manuel turned away overcome with laughter, his hand over his mouth. The women ignored him. Fwesa, one of the women, complained about Kankanga's performance. "Look, she has no notion of breast shaking. What are we going to do? Even the midwives themselves have forgotten it."

They turned to me. "Have you heard? Our local Chief Mukangala has decreed that if any persons prevent initiation girls from dancing at their coming-out they will be punished. Hear that, Kankanga?" Beatrice looked nervous and bent harder to the task of learning. This draconic but supportive message was news to me: I had heard that the far-off senior chief had warned the people not to forget their traditional dances; and also that even Kenneth Kaunda, the president of Zambia, had recently declared the same (in fact four national postage stamps pictured ethnic dancing). Now here was the same directive, from much nearer home. Of course Edie Turner with *The Drums of Affliction* under her arm had also been telling them the same, unable to stay quiet and refrain from influencing her fieldwork. Now I wondered, "How will they really respond to this—particularly Beatrice?" Beatrice was not doing too well as I watched. I was bothered by the fact that several girls had recently claimed they were going to dance at their initiations but had chickened out.

Beatrice's coming-out was postponed and postponed. On one occasion we were up most of the night at a healing ritual, and had barely sat down to breakfast when a message came through from Beatrice's village that she was once again "going to come out and dance." Unenthusiastically I took my notebook, loaded my camera, and got on my bicycle. When I arrived Beatrice was settled down on the ground behind her mother's house, covered with a cloth as usual, with two stick-like legs protruding from beneath. Nothing happened. Back in the village plaza it seemed doubtful if there would be any dancing at all that day. Yet the drums were standing in place. I wandered back behind the house and found that the washing was beginning at last amid a crowd of women. Beside the basin of water stood a small bowl from which they were taking body paint, red body paint. I blinked. They were going to paint her red?! The rites proceeded in front of my eyes. I was not allowed to photograph them, not the beautiful long body of

179

Photo E
The feast: feeding Beatrice by hand, for she is a "baby."

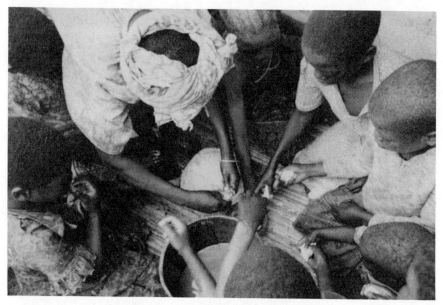

Photo F
The small girls feast after Kankanga.

the small helper, nor the bending poetry of Kankanga's body. Seriya the midwife, big and capable, was smearing red all over them, including their hair. Kankanga looked like an ocher statue with folding shy movements, maddening to an artist. The small helper's mouth hung open, ugly, but Kankanga's features were perfect and serene, though downcast. Now they put on her waistcloth, passing it through her legs as in the old days.

"Don't forget to tie the waist string." "The skirt's too long, make it shorter," the voices advised.

The midwife tied a silk square around Kankanga's breasts like a bikini. There was an immediate outcry from most of the women, "*Nkanga wanyi,* that's not initiation!" I joined the protest, "*Nkanga wanyi!*" But Seriya refused to take it off.

"Well, put on the crisscross beads," they urged, and Seriya put them around Beatrice's breasts, over the silk square. The feast was brought and Kankanga was fed by hand (Photos E and F). They brought in Kankanga's back pad and held it up proudly—it was decorated all over in patterns with hanging bottle tops that jangled together. Kankanga was now led off in the opposite direction from the gathering crowd. Everything seemed to fall into place once the red body painting started—waist cloth, pad, the strange direction.

Meanwhile the small helper met Kankanga who was approaching from way out in the bush. When Kankanga reached the plaza she crossed the small space in the middle of the crowd and touched the drum, a masculine act—then burst into a raging breast dance. The atmosphere was electric. Bill Blodgett, my co-researcher, and I were dizzy running around with cameras, holding our breath. This hadn't been seen for ten years. Kankanga's mother appeared in the ring, crying, her arms over her head, the sorrow of the traditional mother. Beatrice's face was serene with just a touch of ecstasy as she proceeded through the ancient dance (Photo G).

The chairman of the Branch Committee of the local black government came around the crowd to me and said, "I wouldn't have believed it." Nor would I. The clue was the red paint, the head of the comet that drew the tail of the other rites along with it to this final climax. That priming by a triggering object had reanimated an entire train of forgotten observances.

And I was part-instrumental in this development. We anthropologists are likely to become involved in the microhistory of some non-Western culture whether we intend to or not. The age of detachment, the age of modernism, is past.

Seriya, the fat midwife, and I shook hands. She had performed her role of dramaturg with consciousness, skill, and discretion; I left feeling somewhat awed. After a few days I tempted Beatrice with a present to come down to

181

Photo G
The breast dance.

my hut for a chat. Beatrice came, stunningly dressed in modern clothes. We sat down and I glanced at the familiar flat superb features—aiming, now that it was all over, to take a look at the underside of a teenager's life. So I started by describing how when I was a teenager I hated my mother. "I guess you were the same about yours."

"No," she said.

"Your work, that's a bore, isn't it, all that heavy hoeing?"

"I like it," she said, looking almost sad.

I was frustrated. Was there no conflict in her life? She must be kidding herself. I opened my mouth to say, "You think you're perfect, don't you?" Then suddenly I quieted down and asked instead, "Are you perfect?"

"Yes," she said. She had been a spirit.

In the course of these six versions, the original, the new perfunctory version, the mock-animal version, the ludic one, the practice, and the dance, the Ndembu have been playing with a basic theme which they can simplify or elaborate at will. They have successfully dodged the interdict of Christian missions and rationalist government, coming up from below with new elaborations to replace the old ones, developing a measure of defiance and cultural pride. In spite of restrictions the democratic, communal, and even spiritual character of the rite has been maintained; and largely because of the resourcefulness of the women it has neither succumbed nor become elitist.

Transiting from the "Wethno-centric"

An Interview with Peter Sellars

by

John J. Flynn

The Pacific Rim, and Japan specifically, has long been a source of fascination for Peter Sellars. Los Angeles is currently his staging ground, the place where, for three weeks in September 1990, the art and artists of the Americas and the Pacific Rim held forth. As director of the Los Angeles International Arts Festival, Sellars was as personal and as controversial as any of his theatre or opera pieces. He has also been directing and teaching at the University of California, Los Angeles, where, under the auspices of the Laboratory for Theatre Research and Performance at UCLA and the Museum of Contemporary Art, he produced his own radio version of Zeami's Kagekiyo, *entitled* Where Does the Exile Live? *This new* Kagekiyo, *and his radio production of Jack Kerouac's* Mexico City Blues, *were broadcast as part of "The Territory of Art" on National Public Radio. In 1990 Sellars also staged Mozart's* The Magic Flute *at Glyndebourne. Currently he is working on* The Death of Klinghoffer, *a piece about the hijacking of the Achille Lauro. This interview was taped in October, 1989.*

FLYNN: *I want to ask you about your initial contacts with Japan, your first experiences there. What interested you about Japan?*

SELLARS: It started, I guess, when I was young and apprenticing in a marionette theatre in Pittsburgh (The Lovelace Marionettes). The woman who ran the marionette company would go to a different place every summer—to Moscow or the Yucatan or somewhere to study and do puppet work and research. She went to Osaka and worked with Bunraku one year. She came back and for an important year, I was thirteen, the marionette theatre went very intensely Japanese. That was my first contact with Japanese culture and it left a very strong impression. We subsequently did, among other things, *Beauty and the Beast*, a marionette show based on a kind of Kabuki angle. Then when I went to boarding school one of my first projects was to make a Japanese Bunraku puppet for myself to figure out Bunraku construction, and I think I failed, but I worked very hard.

Have you given up on Bunraku? Do you still work with it?

No, no, I visit it. When I went to Japan, finally—well, two things happened. At Harvard I spent four years with Onoe Kuroemon II, a man who was one of the great *onnagata* of the '50s and '60s. His left side had been paralyzed by a stroke and he couldn't perform, and so he taught at Harvard for those years. I got to know him rather well, we became friends. My mother, it turned out, was living in Japan for four years, and that coincided with the year after I got out of college, and I went and stayed with her for four months or so. I keep visiting and revisiting Japan, but I spent a lot of time there with the Bunraku and with the Noh and investigating Matsuri (the local festivals). There's always been an ongoing contact.

When in your directing did you do anything with it?

From the beginning. Thinking in terms of those structures was completely logical, and I guess part of that is because I came from puppet theatre. The Oriental gift of separating sound from image, the sense that each of them have their own structure/systems which then intersect or don't intersect and create tensions or releases. And the idea that the image itself has power, which is something the traditional Western theatre almost ignored. John Gielgud does Hamlet and so on—the images themselves were very limited and didn't have that much power. English language theatre has primarily been verbally dominated, so theatre that stressed visual information at the same time was very appealing to me.

What particularly about Noh, and why Noh?

Noh to me is the one form with the most interest because it seems to be the

185

most profound theatre I know of. You can still see it, it's still being practiced, and its principles are many and still valid, and the idea that there is an existing corpus of rules, regulations, precepts, and a profound system of aesthetics—you can say that about very few other theatrical forms. The durability of Noh and its intractability in the face of the modern world is a source of instant fascination. The emphasis on place as opposed to space, the emphasis on really treating time as a specific element of the performance, and the kind of very gentle insistence that theatre is present as a transcendent possibility and for no other reason. It's not especially entertaining, it's not diverting. It's genuinely there to contemplate man's relation to nature.

When you put it into the media that you have—radio—you lose your images to a certain extent, but what do you gain?

Although the images come back much more intensely—that's the beauty of radio. In our society images are almost worthless, because they're eaten like potato chips off television, instantly disposable—every image has been so used and so over-used, squeezed dry. There are very few images that our society can conjure.

Do we have durable images in Noh? Is there a danger that if we consume Noh it will turn out to be potato chips?

No, I think . . . exactly because the form is so resistant. For one thing, the pace it moves at really discourages Sunday drivers. It's just plain boring. So right away that clears out half the people who weren't serious, and you genuinely have to decide that you're going to get into it if you're to get anything from it. It's not about a passive audience, it's really about an audience that is already bringing something to the work.

So, is bringing Japanese or Asian theatre generally into your work an attempt to make people pay a higher price?

Yes, it's a form that is insistent that values are not primarily related to success, and a Noh play is never successful, which is really wonderful. Theatre in the West is *so* absorbed with the notion of success. Success is such an evanescent and trivial concept up against the Noh tradition. The plays themselves are about that. And so it seems to me that the most interesting form of entertainment for a capitalist society in its last gasp of elaboration, as it chokes on its own prolixity, is to start with something that has this sort of concentration, where the point is you don't really know what's happening. I think that's one of the most important things about the Noh drama, it is truly about the unknown: what you don't know and what you can't know or are just beginning to guess.

186

What do you think about the way our culture is reflected in Japan?

I can't say, it's bad enough to make pronouncements about your own inheritance. Of course, I want very much to bring the Takarazuka dance company to Los Angeles—an all-girl performing troupe doing *West Side Story* in Japanese. I just saw Takarazuka do a musical comedy version of *War and Peace* as an all-girl revue for Japanese teenagers. You know, they stop halfway through the second act and start the Las Vegas revue. Andre returns to life and tap dances down the stairway from Paradise with chaser lights. And that's *War and Peace—Count* Leo Tolstoy to them. It's hard to say what the Japanese are making of *anything* right now, it's as diverse a situation as America. Just as you want to make one generalization, well there's the Wooster Group, and when you want to make another generalization there's the Metropolitan Opera, and when you want to make another generalization there's Mark Morris. There's so much going on right now, and it's going in so many directions. Some of the very important masters are attempting some experiments: Minotsuke, the youngest of the Bunraku masters, is only, at 55, about to come into his great years. He's extremely interested in different interactions that extend the Bunraku tradition. Obviously, the man who came from *The Warrior Ant* with Lee Breuer, Yoshida Tamamatsu, showed a genuine forsaking of everything he grew up with. . . .

I've heard stories from the program at the University of Hawaii about Kyogen and Noh performers who are, one might say, outcasts now because of things that they've done in the West.

Yes, and so certainly people are looking around. It's really too early to say, because what we're in the middle of now with all of this interculturalism business is what can be most charitably described as a transitional period. Let's face it—it's all over the map.

What are we transiting from, and toward what?

We're transiting from a ''Wethno-centric'' form of the celebration of the official culture that has brought us capitalism to a question of whether there are different cultures that are capable or would assist us in supporting other types of social relations. Obviously, capitalism has its strong points, but as we've come to some of the genuine dead-ends of capitalism as a society, as certain genuine crises in our society can no longer be papered over, making any kind of social progress calls for some different cultural models. I think one reason why American artists are so interested in looking elsewhere, to other traditions, and why it's so interesting that there are a number of American artists that come from other traditions now is that those traditions might help both the art world and the society out of the corner they've painted themselves into.

You seem to think that Los Angeles is the staging ground.

Only because, demographically speaking, you get the two important movements that are happening to America, the two things that America is confronting: Asia in the east and the other America to the south. The point where those two movements converge is southern California. This does turn out to be the staging ground simply from what the immigration figures are telling you, the geographical fact of it. This is where border issues are so absolutely hot, and it is the first region in the country that will have a white minority. Already, we know that there are certain built-in inevitabilities, the question is are we going to be ready for them? Are we going to prepare for them? Are we going to assist them? Or are we just going to keep driving around in circles? The basic idea of the L.A. festival is to try and share as much information with as many people, so that with a number of these cultures that have been marginalized and treated as something exotic or interesting we can make a statement that, "Excuse me, this is now central, not fringe."

You're talking about exoticizing cultures, but I wonder are there any rules of engagement for the Westerner? What are your rules of appropriation?

The usual rules that apply in art. What you do has to have its own kind of terrifying rigor within absolute freedom, and a kind of integrity—even if it's a violation it has to be a violation that has its own integrity. Sometimes people tend to confuse certain societal norms of polite behavior with questions of why would an artist make a certain gesture. Frankly, I think that we're at a time when a lot of these gestures are provocational and offensive.

Are you thinking of something in particular?

Well, I shouldn't name names, but there are certain things that I do that I know people find tremendously offensive, but I do the same with Mozart. I am mostly unqualified for most things I attempt. But then who is qualified anymore? And must the discussion be left as the exclusive property of the experts? Yes, in most departments of life it is advisable or even preferable to have some idea of what one is talking about, a considered historical perspective, and so on. But at what point do cultural phenomena become common property, points in a discussion rather than ends in themselves, and move beyond copyrights, priesthoods, and the narrowly-stated claims of the creators? To my mind this material exists so that we can enter it as fully as possible, and maybe it's not possible to enter it more fully than on a certain

188

level, and that other people will enter in a way that's more interesting than the way I enter it, I have no doubt. But it's a different rule of engagement for artists than it is for bureaucrats. People who are now writing the legislation for intercultural interactions, and who are deciding what is legal and what is not, what is permissible and what is not, what is officially offensive and what is not, have to realize that the artists have a different set of rules from the bureaucrats, the arts administrators, and the critics. We have to be able to cut loose.

The Wooster Group is now working on Kyogen in a way that I have no doubt will be completely offensive to most people in the same way that their work on black vaudeville routines offended everyone ten years ago. Their capacity for interculturalism is completely offensive, but it is that friction that produces genuine culture, as opposed to the sort of polite, respectful, "After you Alphonse," "No, no, Gaston," thing that actually keeps the barriers in place and has everybody walking on tiptoe. What becomes available and how it's purloined has to do with an artist's depth of feeling and range of response. It's something that happened. Speaking as a WAM—white American male—I have to just be honest about my reactions to things, and the degree of permissibility there has to do with the degree of my honesty and specificity about my own reactions. It's exactly the people who are having these artificial reactions about multiculturalism, where they want to like it or they want to have a certain point of view or they want to be politically correct—a great deal of wishful thinking replaces actual engagement. I find that kind of wishful thinking, that wish to be proper, frequently appropriate, but just as frequently condescending and counterproductive.

In the case of Where Does the Exile Live?, *how specifically did you plan to use Noh?*

Let's just get at a couple of issues of Noh drama that have been weighing on my mind for years and years: the issue of secrecy, and the issue of privacy. We live in a society that has no privacy, no value of privacy. There is no validation of a private life of the mind. Constantly, everyday, you are being told that if you're thinking independently or differently from the way everybody's supposed to be thinking something's wrong with you and, in fact, any life of the mind at all is highly suspect. There is a genuine assumption that you're kooky if you're thinking deeply about things. Part of what is valuable about Noh drama is the absolute sacrosanct quality of the private life of a spirit, and the fact that the only interaction permitted from the Waki (literally "side," or the person at the side who interacts with the *shite*—the primary character or "doer") is finally to watch—and I love that, and I find

189

that very beautiful. What was necessary was to create a secret world and an interior life. Most of our Western theatre tradition is geared towards a kind of extroversion, and not towards reaffirming an interior mode.

I think one of the most impressive things about Noh is that your mind wanders, and in fact you nod off, and so on. I wanted to work in a form that was not coercive, that would allow the mind to wander, and that would at the same time establish a completely interior life so that it was happening inside someone's head—without using the usual dream paraphernalia of Hollywood that has been borrowed by theatre. So radio was the ideal medium, because we internalize sound, and sound has a world of associations which are basically memory-oriented. When we hear a sound we link it to an image or a period of time, or something in our experience that we remember. Since the basic structure of Noh drama is a memory play, to deal entirely in a world of sound was appropriate. At the same time what I love about the world of sound in Noh drama is that it's frequently obscure. The *shite* wears a wooden mask without an aperture at the mouth, and therefore the chanting is muffled and you can't make out the words. That strikes me as interesting and useful.

On radio we could also deal with this notion of imperfect reception, of hearing something with clarity but also not being sure you heard something, also something missing or something muffled, or receiving signals that may be the wrong signals or may be accidental. That really calls for an extra level of concentration to make sure that you're listening, to make sure that you're hearing, that you're really hearing, and that you're hearing voices. Noh is about a priest, an itinerant scholar, sitting in an attitude of contemplation at a site of pilgrimage and, after a long period of quiet meditation, finally hearing a voice. And then after a while an image joins that voice.

I also wanted to deal with the structure of the chorus: what is the commentary that the chorus makes in a Noh drama? Of course, it represents again the interior thoughts of the *shite,* and the landscape. This idea of the landscape and the interior thoughts of the *shite* having a single manifestation is very beautiful, very profound. On radio, I could set that up so that landscape is created aurally and is utterly inseparable from the private thoughts of the protagonist.

What else are we getting from Noh for radio? Probably the sense of the mutability of time. In the theatre you are quite aware of the passage of time, and in a sound world you are just one step further removed, which is why I think records have timings on them, to reassure people that they're getting *this* much music. We know they're not sure. That panic to reduce our sound world to timings—that radio is formatted on these very specific

190

timings: this is a half-hour block, people tell time by their radios. The radio's on and you know that it's the hour because the news is on. That the chunk of time is delineated in that way is very interesting on radio.

Are you hoping people will get lost in this half-hour you've created?

Right. And then, by taking a form which is the most directional thing available to most of the American public—radio is so directed, so aggressive, so forward moving, every moment is packed with information but it is clearly going somewhere without going anywhere at all. To have a meander, where it's not clear which direction the information is going in at all, and to further have much too much information, an actual overload, and then to take that information, to process it, and chew on it for a while. . . .

Are you interested now in staging a Noh play?

About every three years I stage another Noh play. Before this, I did an evening of Beckett, a Noh play, and a Wallace Stevens play: *Ohio Impromptu, Tsunemasa,* and *Angels Surrounded by Paysans* with David Warrilow and Richard Thomas, and that was my farewell to the Kennedy Center. It was the last thing I directed there. Three years before that I did a night that was never shown publicly. I worked with three actresses in my loft for two months and we made *Ikuta, Hagoromo,* and *Sotoba Komachi.*

Last year you expressed a lot of interest in Hagoromo.

Well, for me that's a seminal play. It's about the gift of dance to human beings. It's about one's gifts and where one got them—under what circumstances they were presented. For every artist—which means for every human being—it's kind of required reading. It's the purest statement of the angel visitant and the dialogue that ensues is the dialogue that, of course, you *know.* Because, as you know, "One usually entertains angels unawares." Usually you're not precisely conscious of this process, and to see it dramatized so clearly, with the metaphor so simple and the speech so calm, is just shattering.

The Future of the Hyphen

Interculturalism, Textuality, and the Difference Within

Una Chaudhuri

THE QUESTION ONE NORMALLY ASKS about a new ''ism''—What is it?—is better transformed, in the case of interculturalism, from its general and definitional form into a temporally specific and normative one: What has interculturalism been, and what might it—should it—be, now and in the future? Since it appeared in cultural discourse little more than a decade ago, the subject of interculturalism has seemed murky and inchoate, its forms endlessly branching off like streaks of smoke from a sluggish fire. Now the question arises: what events, what changes in the world and in consciousness will provide the horizon against which the ''haze'' of interculturalism can finally take a distinct form?

In the area of performance, interculturalism has been several things, the least desirable but probably most powerful of which is an *effect* of global mass-communication. The wholesale export of films, videos, and television programming, not to mention also the worldwide dissemination of images of Western consumer culture through print advertising, has in effect ''interculturated'' the world to a degree and in a way that is obviously and profoundly disturbing, especially to artists. This deadly kind of interculturalism (so well captured in the title and so exhaustively documented in the text of

Pico Iyer's *Video Night in Kathmandu*) would be enough, by itself, to challenge artists to imagine another interculturalism, one which combats the flattening of cultural differences into a homogeneous mediocrity.

That other—conscious, even programmatic—interculturalism has developed as both a problematic practice and an ideological—and idealistic —project. In the former guise, it has sometimes seemed to collude in another version of cultural imperialism, in which the West helps itself to the forms and images of others without taking the full measure of the cultural fabric from which these are torn. This practice (of which the prime recent example, some have argued, was Peter Brook's *Mahabharata*) claims the interculturalist label for itself and often seeks to elaborate a moral-political model of theatre as a *vital* (in all senses) cultural *exchange*. Its critics, however, discern a less-than-equal dimension to its foundational trope: is the barter truly egalitarian, do both sides gain equally, or is there something of the ''glass-beads-for-land'' model of exchange at work here? Is this kind of interculturalism a sophisticated disguise for another installment of Orientalism, or worse, of cultural rape?

There is, obviously, no ready answer to this kind of worrying question; what it points up, however, is that the problematic of interculturalism frequently takes form on that slippery ground between intentions and effects which is also the traditional site of theatrical praxis. Like the theatre, which must always negotiate some kind of meeting between the heterogeneous orders of text and performance, of the written and the spoken, the intercultural project must reconcile the claims of disparate orders of being, various temporalities, historicities, ethnicities. This resemblance suggests that the view of theatre as a modeled *differentiality* could also be the site where the future of interculturalism might be imagined.

But before venturing into it I want to cast a brief look back to what interculturalism has been, or rather, to what it has been thought to be. For it may be that many of the problems of interculturalism in the theatre stem from the way it has been conceptualized. The fact that it has invariably been apprehended and theorized at the level of *performance* has, I believe, contributed to the instability of its status and the challenges to its legitimacy. Of course, the configuration of interculturalism as a practice confined to matters of display and presentation (rather than as of a property of certain *texts,* something inhabiting the deep structure of a work) is perfectly understandable in historical terms. It derives from one of the important origins of the practice in modern theatre: the experiments of artists like Grotowski, Brook, and Schechner in staging classical Western plays using non-Western performance conventions. That so much of the dynamism and interest of post-sixties theatre came from these experiments has given this notion of interculturalism a kind of authority, even a sense of inevitability, as if inter-culturalism could scarcely be anything other than this reverential appropria-tion of the performance techniques of other cultures.

More recent forms of interculturalism have extended this model con-siderably. In works like *The Mahabharata* or Lee Breuer's *The Warrior Ant*, the contents as well as the presentational techniques are borrowed from other cultures, and the intercultural label refers either to the mixing of various cultural materials in one work or simply to the displacement of the material of one culture into the Western performance context.

This development would seem to constitute a textualizing of inter-culturalism (and it does), but the form of textuality achieved is distinct from the textual mode most familiar in the theatre: the play-text. These perfor-mances generate texts that are lacking in the most crucial quality of dramatic scripts: repeatability, hence *performative reinterpretation*. The texts produced by such works are inextricably bound up with that *one* pro-duction (for example, it is quite inconceivable that another director and another group of actors will mount a new production of the text, published though it is, of Jean-Claude Carrière's *Mahabharata*). Thus, these examples do not really accomplish the crucial next step for interculturalist practice; they do not furnish the culture with lasting intercultural *artifacts* that can and must be re-interpreted, re-embodied, re-visioned. These interculturalist performances simply constitute a series of events that can be ordered historically but do not generate a history *of their own.*

I want to argue that interculturalism will come into focus when it is no longer a mere *effect* of heterogeneity but becomes a self-conscious *practice,* with a developing theory of its own, an awareness of the political meaning of various representational options presented by texts, and, most importantly, a recognition of its own cultural power. Such a development is not, I im-agine, a distant possibility; however, the ''future'' of my title acknowledges a degree of irreality to the model of interculturalism that follows.

* * *

My point of departure is, as I said before, a certain resemblance between interculturalism and theatrical praxis. Stretched as it is between varying and often conflicting subjectivities: playwright and director, director and actor, actor and spectator (the neat transitivity of the series is, of course, entirely illusory), theatrical meaning is by nature problematic and processive rather than ambiguous and fixed. The obligatory dispersal of dramatic sign-production between all those who collaborate in making a performance is a factor in all theatre, even the most traditional. That is to say, there is a flagrant heterogeneity (of signifying systems, of codes, of subjects) in all theatre, and every instance of theatre practice occupies a place somewhere on the continuum between the total denial and the total acceptance of this heterogeneity.

At one extreme of this continuum we find what I would call the Theatre of the Same, which gathers up the theatre's constitutive discontinuities and bundles them into effects of synthesis and harmony. This theatre's fundamental values are unity, hierarchy, order, Truth; its greatest theorist is, of course, Aristotle. At the other extreme is the Theatre of Difference, of which Brecht is only the most eloquent (and most systematic) exponent. It is this latter theatre that, in its many forms, has preoccupied this century, and it is this theatre which the terms of recent literary and cultural theory best describe. The deliberate multivocality of this theatre is especially consonant with accounts of meaning furnished by theories like semiotics and deconstruction; they could also, I believe, prove to be equally useful for understanding and theorizing interculturalism.

Both semiotics and deconstruction are theories of difference, which pay special attention to the heterological nature of discourse, the disjunctions, discontinuities and contradictions that are repressed and/or expressed in texts. Interculturalism (that is, interculturalism as self-conscious practice), which shares a historical moment with these theories of difference, may even conveniently be regarded as a political analogue of the formal multivocality which they valorize. As a discourse that is overtly and by definition heterological, interculturalism dramatizes and enacts—ambiguously but unmistakably—the world(s) of difference.

However, the identification of interculturalism as a discourse of difference does not get us very far. By itself, the only theoretical use it has is to resist the assimilation of interculturalism into a new version of the Theatre of the Same. This tendency is by no means remote. One theoretical representation of it is mythological feminism, yielding an interculturalism that seeks to erase culture itself by dedicating itself to the discovery of timeless truths. Its anti-historicism puts it squarely in the tradition of a universalist Western aesthetic, which frames all its encounters with difference, recoding otherness as sameness disguised, repressed, distorted.

Yet it would be misleading to construct the future of interculturalism in terms of a simple opposition to this latest version of the Theatre of the Same. The other option for interculturalism is not simple difference, that is, not merely a celebration (International Festival style) of cultural differences, but a plunge into difference itself, into (if I may be permitted so fanciful a formulation—an explanation follows) the differences *in* difference itself. Of the two kinds of difference which I see as forming the dialectic that will structure future interculturalism, the first kind, the difference *between,* that

195

is, the obvious and well-recognized differences between cultures, has already been fully engaged, especially under the new banner of postmodernism. The objection to this performance of difference is, often, that it trivializes the cultural materials it stages. Thus in *The Warrior Ant,* according to Daryl Chin, ''a Bunraku master, a Turkish belly dancer, and rap singers are all equated, rendered not so much equal as equally distracting.''

The alternative to an intercultural Theatre of the Same, it would appear, has been not a true Theatre of Difference but a Theatre of Non-consequence. And what this theatre risks is a simple reproduction of reified cultural categories, national and ethnic stereotypes. The sources of its problem lie in its acceptance of a definition of culture that is surely outdated and probably fundamentally erroneous. According to this definition, ''culture'' is a layered system of practices and convictions *rooted* in a certain geographical location and observed by a certain ethnic group. An inter-culturalism committed to this false idea of culture will be, as our inter-culturalism has been, an ''exotic'' interculturalism, bent on tracking down the remotest, ''purest,'' most ''ancient'' elements of other cultures and attempting, by imitation, to valorize tham. This is a kind of ''museum'' interculturalism, and it achieves all the pleasures as well as all the deadliness of museum display.

The crucial characteristic of this kind of interculturalism, it seems to me, is that it literalizes difference itself, reducing it to the grossest and most material of conceptions. Refusing any but a literal and geographical sense of otherness, it also refuses to displace the politically dangerous model of cultural difference as fixed, permanent, bound to race and place. Moreover, by identifying cultures as existing along and within the lines of demarcation settled upon by earlier periods, this kind of interculturalism risks reproducing the ideological structures which drafted those lines in the first place. Thus well-meaning intercultural projects can unwittingly perpetuate a neo-colonialism in which the cultural clichés which underwrote imperialism survive more or less intact.

A *practical* interculturalism would not simply reproduce already established (and hence already politically coded) images of cultural difference; instead it would *produce* the *experience* of difference. It would stage the detailed processes of differentiation which are the as-yet unrepresented realities of modern life. Instead of rehearsing and rehashing clichés about how this or that culture is different from ''the West,'' it would catch up with and show the levels and forms of actual cultural interpenetration in the world.

The drama of immigrants (in both senses of the preposition: by and about) furnishes more and more examples of what a truly differential interculturalism will look like. Its ultimate subject will be, I suspect, the distinction between two kinds of difference: one *between,* the other *within.* In the play between these two orders of heterogeneity, one "objective," already coded culturally, the other just taking shape, embryonic, pre-semiotic, lies the future of the hyphen.

Like all futures, this one has a past, indeed many pasts. One of the most fascinating of these is Barbara Johnson's brilliant essay, "Thresholds of Difference: Structures of Address in Zora Neale Hurston," in which she explores the ways in which Hurston's work "was constantly dramatizing and undercutting just such inside/outside oppositions, transforming the plane geometry of physical space into the complex transactions of discursive exchange." Johnson's discussion of what she calls "Hurston's joyful and lucrative gatepost stance between black and white cultures" adumbrates a transgressive representational strategy that I believe to be both the hallmark of a dynamic interculturalism as well as the site of its coupling with postmodernism.

In the following pages I will present three scenes, from three different works, which I consider to be loosely paradigmatic of a dynamic interculturalist practice. The works are, all three, British: two of them are written by writers who belong to immigrant groups, two of them (not the same two) are plays, one is a film. Two of them (again, not the same two) are fairly well known, one is not. In each case I will identify what seem to me to be the discursive or representational strategies that are characteristically intercultural. Chief among these strategies—and it is one that responds particularly well to semiotics analysis—is what I call trans-coding: the sudden movement of a perspective or a meaning from one familiar level or order of experience to another. Very often, the two codes between which a message is transferred are the political and the psychological, a procedure that has the effect of directing our attention to unexpected, even apparently idiosyncratic reactions to cultural displacement. Because it reveals effects not already associated with one or another culture, this practice—these moments—of transcoding function as reminders of the important fact that interculturalism is an incomplete, ongoing process, *constitutive* (and not merely demonstrative) of history.

The idea that interculturalism is something in-the-making animates the least well-known of my three works, with which I begin. This is *Migrations,* a play by Karim Alrawi, performed at the Theatre Royale, Stratford East, in 1982, which recounts the hopes and frustrations attendant upon building a playground in a poor neighborhood in contemporary England. The main characters are urban youth of differing ethnic backgrounds. Their situation on the margins of a modern metropolis designates them as key players in the

197

developing drama (the offstage kind) of displaced peoples. Indeed the link between interculturalism and the modern or postmodern city is the most conspicuous of representational strategies we will find in our brief survey. The many metaphors that have arisen to describe the inner nature and functioning of this link—the melting pot, the ''gorgeous mosaic''—are signs, primarily, of the pressure it puts on traditional ways of living. The city of immigrants—that is to say, the city in which newcomers are the majority and spread across many neighborhoods rather than confined to a few ghettoes—this new kind of city furnishes both the subject and the structure of much intercultural representation. Unlike the socio-political efforts to identify (and poetically name) the points of contact, cooperation or integration in such a community, interculturalist practice enacts and interrogates the *assumptions*—about community, about identity—that underwrite traditional ways of city-dwelling. For example, the poetically celebrated anonymity of city life, the romantic sense of ''public solitude,'' of being alone-in-a-crowd: all this is disturbed and reframed in the new context of radical displacement, which literalizes (and hence demystifies) the experience of ''apartness.''

These and other modes of interculturalist practice come together in the scene from *Migrations* which I wish to discuss, a brief but enormously affecting one. In it Selma, a teenager and daughter of first-generation Asian immigrants, confesses to her brother Zia that she is ashamed to eat the Indian food that her mother packs for her school lunch.

Alrawi's choice of food as a metaphorical site for an exploration of difference is precisely right for transcoding, and can also help us to distinguish this strategy from the more traditional literary technique of symbolism. Food is, in the first instance, a material element of cultural identity, and one, as Alrawi's young characters show, that is widely recognized as such, both from within and without an ethnic group. Yet the mechanism by which this materiality is connected to identity is notoriously, even mysteriously, subjective: namely, taste. Thus food, for all its cultural determinism, seems to be a prime instance also of the *transferability* of cultural meaning. This level of its meaning (prior to the symbolic level, where food = spiritual nourishment, emotional sustenance, and so on) is especially useful for intercultural writing, for it can be used to *distance* us from notions of fixed cultural identity in a way that the more intractable category of place cannot.

In *Migrations,* Alrawi transcodes food, moving from a socio-political perspective to one that is near-absurdist: rather than let her English schoolmates see her consume the foods of her shameful difference from them, Selma prefers to eat potato chips, or even to go hungry. Her brother wants to know what she does with the food her mother packs for her every morning. "Jocelyne and me, we feed it to the ducks in Victoria Park." "You feed chapattis and dal to the ducks?" asks Zia incredulously, and the girl, by way of reply, assures him: "They recognize us now."

The absurdity of the image is part of what makes it work; but more important than that is its *innocence*. The revelation that the awful gap of cultural difference suddenly yawns wide in the everyday experience of individuals with no power, no cultural investments, no strong identifications, swiftly removes interculturalist discourse from the grand accounts of difference *between* (how to "preserve" it, how to "respect" it), and situates it instead in the personalist terrain I call difference *within*.

The experience of Alrawi's teenagers inflects the political condition known as marginality by adding innocence. The result is an account of social experience that is quite different from the political discourses of power and victimage that are usually layered onto the subject of immigrants. To call these characters victims would not be adequate to the complexity of their case; they are more like accidental trespassers, not so much lost as "yet-to-be-found." Strangely "unmapped," they find themselves at a mysterious remove from the cultural "norm" and lack all resources for tackling the enigma of their difference. So they wander through the urban landscape, dealing with their predicament as best they can, noticing that they are now "recognized" somewhere, leaving us to negotiate the full meaning of this comic-pathetic *anagnorisis.*

* * *

The second of my examples, the film *Sammy and Rosie Get Laid*, written by Hanif Kureshi, works harder (from its title onwards, in fact) to deny the role of innocence, but succeeds in making that role even clearer. The innocence of Kureshi's characters—that is to say, their obvious *guiltlessness,* which is nevertheless quite irrelevant, apparently, to the harsh psychological realities of their lives—this innocence seems to exist in inverse proportion to the violent ruptures of the socio-political world they inhabit. Though so much more sophisticated than Alrawi's teenagers, indeed almost jaded by comparison to them, Kureshi's characters fully share both their marginalization and their innocence.

Kureshi's strategy for representing this experience makes explicit something already hinted at by Alrawi: that marginality is the paradigmatic contemporary urban condition. Kureshi, himself a second-generation immigrant with no home but England, restructures interculturalism away from the oppositional logic upon which past practices, including imperialism, were based. Unlike most explorations of the immigrant experience, the film dispenses with the often stereotypical representatives of the dominant culture. It gives no space whatsoever to figures of supposed traditional "power" and "authority." Instead it presents a world peopled entirely by those whose lives have suffered one or other kind of cultural rupture: immigrants, foreigners, homeless squatters.

Among these are Sammy and Rosie, a "mixed" couple whose marriage is strained to the breaking point by the barrage of discontinuities it must endure (adultery the least of these). Yet, as they pick their ways—now separately, now together—across the film's burning, riot-torn cityscape, a world of great desolation and brutality, Sammy and Rosie emerge as the unexpectedly proficient representatives of a possible new order, one that must be based precisely on the ubiquity of "differences within."

Their viability is figured less in terms of who they are as individuals than as a function of their history and their environment. Behind Sammy and Rosie (that is to say, both in their past and now obscured by them) stand two older figures, linked by an unlikely romantic association. One, the Englishwoman Alice, comes as close to representing the old, white, "civilized," Imperial Britain as any character in the film. The man she had loved and now meets again is the Asian Rafi who, long ago, traded in his immigrant status to return to his newly-independent country. Sammy, the son he left behind to contend unaided with English racism, has become a type of the gently cynical, alienated immigrant, listlessly promiscuous, deeply bewildered.

The film shows the return of the now rich and powerful Rafi, whose reputation for political corruption and brutality back home somewhat tarnishes such protestations as the following (about why he has returned): "And before I die I must know my beloved London again: for me it is the center of civilization . . ." The two people he had abandoned, his son and Alice, are willing to reconnect, but Rafi's "beloved London" gets in the way. The London of this film is an embodiment of the new multicultural city, a space/culture resolutely obstructing all attempts to retreat into any sentimental narratives of the past, especially the one that claimed it was *love* that conquered all.

The apocalyptic life of the city drives Rafi to despair and suicide, but not before his insistent nostalgia has forced others, his son especially, to experience and acknowledge the terms of a new sort of identity, based on a new sort of reality. This identity cannot yet be named, except perhaps circuitously and ironically, as when Sammy, refusing Rafi's invitation to return home to "your own country," tells his father: "We love our city and we belong to it. Neither of us are English, we're Londoners you see."

Being Londoners. Could this be a code term for a new, intercultural way of being, one which makes a creative use of urban multiculturalism to overcome the alienation and fragmentation of big cities? Sammy and Rosie (at least according to Sammy, who shares the film's irony towards himself) enjoy the urban-intellectual pleasures of London: "Then we go to the bookshop and buy novels written by women. . . . We go to an Alternative Cabaret in Earl's Court in the hope of seeing our government abused. Or if we're really desperate for entertainment, we go to a seminar on semiotics at the ICA which Rosie especially enjoys."

But the film defines being Londoners in another way as well, through the figure of Danny, the West-Indian philosopher-transient who befriends Rafi and then has an affair with Rosie. The historical and ideological displacements that so distress Rafi, Alice, Sammy, and Rosie are literalized in the existence forced on Danny and his companions: they live in tents and trailers which they gather into makeshift communities, occupying London's vacant lots, keeping just one step ahead of the developers' bulldozers.

This way of being Londoners, clandestinely yet ubiquitously, of establishing a community, paradoxically, on the basis of being denied traditional forms of belonging: this is the film's contribution to a new meaning for interculturalism. *Sammy and Rosie* speaks of a new form of self-definition, across boundaries of race and ethnicity and sexuality. The famous climactic scene of the film—involving a literal, sexual climax—fully expresses all the power and all the ambiguity of this new meaning. As the three misallied couples make ecstatic love in their separate spaces, the film's screen splits to accommodate the three transgressive images simultaneously. This "collage of . . . couples coupling" is further mixed with images of the film's several groups of vagrants and transients, "dancing in celebration of joyful love-making all over London."

The familiarity of the inane song on the sound-track ("My Girl"), together with the triplicated eroticism on screen, renders the characters as both less and more than real individuals. The split screen seems to comment ironically on their pretensions to difference, yet their "energetic, tender and ecstatic" love-making defeats any sociological reduction of their humanness. This balancing of passion and irony creates the precise tone, it seems to me, to speak of the new kind of interculturalism—ubiquitous, subtle, shifting, irreversible—that is being engendered here.

* * *

My final example, which comes closest to the mode of a textual (i.e., a repeatable) interculturalism in the theatre, prompts a prefatory word about the temporality of interculturalism. The future of the hyphen will, I believe, trace a path into the past as well. Just as every new literary or theoretical movement enables new readings of classical texts (did JoAnne Akalaitis not show us Shakespeare's postmodernism in her recent production of *Cymbeline?*) so also interculturalism will certainly reveal a rich hoard of dramas of difference from the past—making possible, perhaps, a whole hidden poetics of alterity. I am not thinking only of obvious examples, like *Othello* and *The Merchant of Venice,* but rather of a steady stream, subterranean but abiding, of "otherness" in drama, a presence neither superficial nor incidental but rather working at a deep structural level of the plays' meaning.

I would suggest that consciousness of otherness is tightly woven into the fabric of the dramatic medium, which—for all its vaunted commitment to liveness and presence—is always also projected into the future, into the other times and places of its potential reincarnation. This obligatory heterogeneity, this general accommodation of difference by the dramatic text is one of the subjects of the final work I wish to discuss, David Hare's *A Map of the World.*

The subject of the play is both a "real" event—an international conference on poverty being held at a luxury hotel in Bombay, India—and the future transformations of that event and its meanings into various media: a novel, a screenplay, and a film. Thus the play brings together the two kinds of difference that concern me here; cultural and temporal, and relates them to the frame of our discussion: representation.

In Hare's play, the future of the hyphen depends, quite simply, on goodwill. Every link in the representational chain between a real event and its meaning depends, it seems, on decency, respect, and—especially—goodwill. The play is not particularly sanguine about the availability of this elusive resource, but it does not quite despair of it either. After mapping out an expansive world of conflict: between First and Third Worlds, between conservatives and liberals, men and women, whites and non-whites, even between writers and directors—Hare leaves us with certain images of compromise, patience, and guarded trust in others. What status these images are to have in our response to his depiction of heterogeneity—and whether they can be usefully included in a model of a productive intercultural practice—will depend a great deal on how the conflicts themselves are staged.

While written strongly enough to be able to sustain several different interpretations in performance, Hare's text is marked in one way that no production can ignore: it is structured around a dramatic form with which we are very familiar—the intellectual *agon.* At the apparent center of the play is a debate between two men. There is the sophisticated, arch-conservative, hyper-anglicized, Indian-born but "Western-domiciled" writer Victor Mehta, who seems to have compensated for his over-hyphenated identity by identifying himself completely with the most conservative ideas and values of the West: "All old civilizations are superior to younger ones. That is why I have been happiest in Shropshire. They are less subject to crazes. In younger countries there is no culture. The civilization is shallow. Nothing takes root . . . a worthwhile civilization takes two thousand years to grow." The time span mentioned by Mehta is obviously coded to reverse the meaning of "old," to detach it from ancient civilizations like India and attach it to the Western, specifically Christian, world.

Mehta's antagonist is Stephen Andrews, a young left-wing British journalist whose idealism proves to be no match for Mehta's icy ironies. The stark ideological conflict quickly established between these two men promises a Shavian drama of ideas, with its attendant pleasures of systematic exposition, coherence, evidence, proof, refutation, and conclusion. When all this fails to materialize, we glimpse a significant fact about interculturalism in drama, namely, that it will be much more than a matter of content. It will revise the most stable forms, and reveal to us how much these forms were dependent on certain comfortable continuities.

One of these is the assumed link between one's ideas and one's sociological being that underlies so much Western drama (it was explicitly articulated among the neo-classical rules of decorum and has been especially forceful in realist drama, in which social status and ideology are depicted as mutually and deterministically constructive). In Hare's play, where an Englishman speaks for the Third World and an Indian defends "colonial" values, there is a flagrant lack of correspondence between the antagonists' ideological positions and their national identities. Thus the conflict that ensues is at odds with the extra-textual stereotypes of such conflicts. It is not, that is to say, a simple conflict between West and East, or imperialism and liberalism, because the spokesmen for the two positions have been "switched."

The non-congruence of ideology and national identity in the protagonists makes their views, at the very least, suspect. It introduces a note of subjectivity into ideas which would, if held by the "appropriate" people, seem "objective" or "natural." In the character code of realist drama, a character gains in authenticity exactly in the measure that his views and values coincide with those of his extra-textual, cultural "type." This code allows for several manipulations: a comic character is produced by exaggerating the stereotypical views and behavior of a cultural type, and when such exaggeration reveals political and ideological errors in the whole class or culture to which the type belongs, a semiological—or "epic"—drama results. Actually, this characterological rule was one of the few codes of realism that was *not* revised by Brecht's theory. Indeed, by distancing itself from the romantic individualism of the realist drama, epic theatre accentuates, even valorizes the social construction of character. This suggests that the theatrical mode that has been most thoroughly identified with political and social agendas in this century—the Brechtian mode—is nevertheless profoundly at odds with the project of a dynamic interculturalism. By maintaining the link between character and place Epic theatre perpetuates the model of identity based on difference-between and obscures the possibility of an identity derived with reference to difference-within. That possibility, then, depends for its realization on interculturalist dramaturgy. It is part of the future of the hyphen.

In Hare's play, only part of the realist code functions: places, events, and minor characters correspond to cultural types (the latter very pointedly so), protagonists do not. Or rather, they do so only partially: Mehta is the exact type of the conservative English intellectual, except that he is not English. This is interculturalism's characteristic *breaching*—not breaking—of social and ethnic stereotypes. In an effect that deconstructionists would call "putting under erasure," the stereotype is simultaneously evoked and undermined, recalled and revised. Perhaps the best term for this effect, so central to the interculturalist practice I have in mind, is suggested by Hare himself: let us call it "*unmapping.*"

One important effect that it has in this case is to inhibit easy spectatorial identification with either side of the debate. The spectator, that is to say, is dis*placed,* in an effect which is significantly different from the effects of alienation and disorientation which were achieved by various avant-gardes; here, it is specifically the nature of the spectator's relationship to those she has automatically considered as "different" or "foreign" that is in question, and not (as with the avant-garde) the spectator's general habits of seeing.

And this is only the first challenge that intercultural subject matter makes to the authority of the familiar dramatic structure—the intellectual *agon*—being used in Hare's play. A deeper kind of provocation is provided by a sexual *non sequitur* added to the debate. The political opposition between Mehta and Andrews is subordinated to a sexual rivalry which does not, as might be expected, simply "add another layer" to the conflict. Instead, this rivalry, the object of which is an American actress, Peggy Whitton—who has no direct association either to the conference or to the ideological issues at hand—cuts across and distorts the purely rational opposition represented by the two men.

Hare's way of "unmapping" one of the revered forms of Western drama, the drama of ideas—and its underlying value system, rationalism—differs from other iconoclastic practices like Brecht's and the absurdists' in that it shows reason unravelling under pressure of what I have called "the dif-

204

ference within'' (figured here as both cultural and gender difference). The play clearly shows that the great issue of our time is not inequality, not financial aid, not even poverty, but the *realization and representation of difference*. As one of the characters, the African delegate M'Bengue, puts it: ''We take aid from the West because we are poor, and in everything we are made to feel our inferiority. The price you ask us to pay is not money but misrepresentation.''

The play devotes its considerable structural complexity to the task of revealing and enacting the link between cultural difference and strategies of representation. The writer, in this case Victor Mehta, experiences this primarily as a problem of his control over the meaning of events he has witnessed and evaluated. But others in the play suggest a more general and more interculturalist dimension to the problem. For example, M'Bengue links the form of the *agon* to super-power politics: ''Pro-Moscow, pro-Washington, that is the only way you can see the world. All your terms are political, and your politics is the crude fight between your two great blocks.''

Countering this vulgar binary-oppositional formation, is the play's own design: a ''nested'' structure (a play about a film based on a novel about an actual event) in which the various frames or levels do not remain separate and distinct but break up, mix up, and match up in unexpected ways: the play dissolves into the film, the film contradicts the novel, the novel confirms the play, and so on. It is a structure that quite specifically uses the option of transcoding to develop an alternative to modernism's favored process of meaning-production, the dialectic. The orderly march of thesis, antithesis, and synthesis is disturbed here by the ubiquity of difference: the difference between forms, and the difference within selves. As the argument of the play traverses the gaps and disjunctions of cultures and of media, it eschews the comfort of a final resting place. The experience created is significantly different from that produced by rationalist dramaturgy, the experience of ascension to some intellectual high ground, some privileged perspective on the differences addressed in the work. Interculturalism replaces dialectics (and its power-reason nexus) with *transgression*: meaning shows itself as multivalent, subject to the shades and shadows of difference, a matter of circumstances, feelings, and perspectives—plural—not privilege.

A nice illustration of the link between multivalence and interculturalism occurs in the exchange between three characters, now in their role as ''actors,'' waiting for the shooting of a scene to begin. One of them, working on a crossword puzzle, asks: ''What on earth could be . . . seven letters, begins with Z, and the clue is 'It's the plague of the earth'?'' The black American actress guesses: ''Zionism,'' and the following awkward colloquy ensues: "What do you mean, Zionism?" "Well, it's seven letters, beginning with Z." "But are you . . ." "What?" ". . . just saying it because it's a word?" "It's a word." "I know it's a word. (*He pauses.*) I know it's a word . . . But are you also saying it's the plague of the earth?" "Well, obviously, if it's got seven letters and begins with Z, it scarcely matters what I think about it. What matters is what the compiler thinks, and obviously, I don't know, perhaps *The Times* has Arab crossword compilers these days. Perhaps they have some Libyan on the staff."

The discussion gets increasingly complicated and bitter, and goes on for some time, periodically interrupted by the "Peggy" actress, who is trying on different costumes and asking for another actor's opinion of them. Finally, the M'Bengue actor looks at the crossword, and remarks "It's not Z anyway." "What?" "Look, six down is 'evasion.' You don't spell that with a Z. You spell it with an S." Needless to say, this does nothing to soothe the enervated group; the quarreling continues down various other contentious tracks. When the long period of waiting is finally over, and the beleaguered director has assembled the cast and crew to begin the scene ("I beg you, let us act"), just then, at that penultimate moment before the play's version of "reality" gives itself up to its version of "representation," the M'Bengue actor solves the puzzle: "Slavery," he says. And to show us that even this moment of meaning is provisional and perspectival, the person who hears the word is the director, who knows nothing of what has gone before, and can only assume that he himself is the target of the cryptic remark.

Every detail of the scene, not least the fact that it appears to be mere "filler," just some idle chatter occurring in the wings or gaps of significant representation—every detail connects with the play's overall enactment of interculturalism's innovative aesthetic.

Finally, the relationship between the play's transgressive structure and its subject, cultural difference, is ostended in the explicit comparison a character draws between two kinds of meaning-production. Trying to reassure the writer that the film is not butchering his work, an actor says: "I can see from the outside it must be discomforting. Film is. It's so fractured, so broken up. To look at, at first, the first impression is chaos. As with India, I imagine, to the Western visitor. Nothing makes sense on the surface. Then, by a process, one absorbs. One is patient. The tendons of the place begin to show through." Here, it seems to me, are many of the key terms of the dynamic interculturalism that I find adumbrated in these works. Certainly, the word "process" is crucial to the conception, and also, obviously, "outside" and "fractured"; but perhaps most important are "absorb" and "patient."

* * *

The future of the hyphen has long been here; it is now a question of finding the right tone or vocabulary (or possibly even the right *grammar*) with which to express it. The rhetoric of contestation and contention that has dominated all the discourse on difference should now be seen to belong to the order of difference-between. The difference of interculturalism, the difference-within, must appropriate another semiotic and poetic register, one in which those long-time opposites, transgression and innocence, can somehow finally meet.

Behavior as Culture
An Interview with Lee Breuer

by
Gabrielle Cody

Lee Breuer has been an important figure in the American theatre as writer, director, teacher, and one of the founders of Mabou Mines. His recent works include The Warrior Ant, The Gospel at Colonus, Sister Suzie Cinema, *and* Hajj. *His early plays are published in* Animations: A Trilogy for Mabou Mines. *This interview was conducted in 1988.*

CODY: *Your theatre work has led you to deconstruct American culture in pieces like* Prelude to Death in Venice *and* The Shaggy Dog Animation, *then, it seems, to develop an intercultural aesthetic which culminated with* The Warrior Ant *and* Lear. *I wonder if, at this point, you have a position on interculturalism. How would you define it? What motivates you to blend cultural traditions? And what might be the political implications of such work?*

BREUER: I am desperately trying to develop an overview of what it means to be working interculturally in the theatre. There are a lot of underviews. They fall in the pattern of either I love the world and the world loves me, let's all get together and party interculturally, or, the notion of Western cultural imperialism—that we are ripping off every cultural icon we can get a hold of, and then selling it. These underviews of intercultural work are deeply enmeshed in the given politics of the moment. I'm trying to see the picture in a larger sense. But I realize that different positions are satisfactory and proper for different levels of points of view.

For instance, it is useful in contemporary politics to view intercultural events from the point of view of who owns what, which culture owns what bid, whose song belongs to who, what dance step came from where and who's ripping who off. It is equally useful, politically, to view intercultural activity as an attempt to get to know each other and appreciate each other's culture. But both of these approaches are morally informed, they stem from a moral point of view about what's right and what's wrong, and that morality is itself culturally determined.

I am more and more interested in the idea of behavior as culture, in cultural biology rather than cultural politics. If behavior is deterministic, part of the genetic picture, then it is a reasonable assumption that culture is part of the genetic picture as well. I think that what constitutes the basis of the form that we perceive as culture is really mass behavior, the collective behavior of various genetic groups, not single individuals. Cultures are, in a sense, the behavioral phenotype of a genetic grouping which manifests itself in certain imagery and form. What I have been trying to look at are the various cultural movements over the face of the earth through theatre. And in the same way that life is ultimately deterministic in that it replicates itself through genes, theatre is how culture duplicates itself. The idea of being theatrical—of theatre, in the abstract sense—is in itself the idea of adding energy to an image so that it will cross over and re-imbed itself in another individual.

Theatre is the business of constructing cultural icons, and icons are the semiotics of societies. Now the problem is that there has been a tremendous usurpation of these icons. For instance, in the Western hemisphere, there has been an intricate influx of what, in an interesting political coup, has been called "Hispanic imagery." But it's not Hispanic, it's Indian. There is nothing Hispanic about the entire Western territory from Guatemala on down. It's Indian. The Hispanic overlay is a European usurpation of pre-Colombian imagery and energy. Spain tried to usurp the Moorish culture too. But the idea of calling this Hispanic America is a double irony. Even in naming a Third World, we give it a European metaphor. The politics are fascinating.

There is no question that we are locked in a large-scale, profoundly Darwinian biological struggle for the advantage of certain cultures. I think each culture has to be perceived as a Darwinian competing agent, just like people competing for jobs or genes competing to be chosen. It's highly biological, particularly since European standards have so far determined world morality. But what's morally white is not morally black which isn't morally Asian. Our entire idea of what is right or wrong is culturally determined. There is no universal. What I am interested in doing is to put Europe in its place in American culture, because it is only about one third of the whole story. I am trying to work against measuring everything by European rules. But right now, in funding circles and throughout the critical establishment, all Third World aesthetics are still being viewed through European aesthetics. Third World art is defined as good, depending on how it approximates European standards. Minimalism is recognized, is considered good because Europe happens to understand minimalist art in this decade. The only way of moving toward a universal understanding is the complete interrelationship of cultures.

THE WARRIOR ANT

Yes, but I think there are some problems with that argument. You seem to be implying that culture is a strictly aesthetic notion. When a culture is introduced into another context, taken out of its own setting, isn't there a risk of de-politicizing it, of neutralizing it? What about the dangers of interculturalism?

210

Even though there is a thrust toward interrelationship of cultures, each culture is struggling at the same time, to keep its own sense while being usurped by larger and more powerful cultures. So what is absolutely imperative is to ask ourselves why this thrust toward the integration of cultures even exists? For whose benefit? To whose advantage? As a white man living in New York, is it to my advantage to suggest that we integrate Caucasian and African art? Would it be to the advantage of a Sengalese? Who is saying, ''Let's integrate?'' We've got to allow for some cynicism in looking at the ultimate purpose of interculturalism. But I also feel deeply involved with the side that says culture can be shared, without its power being taken away in the process of the exchange.

In fact, my interest is in seeing the resurgence of cultures that have been wiped out by the European imperative. Having just gotten back from the Yucatan, I have a strong sense of the Western world stretching across the bottom of Mexico including Guatemala and beyond. That culture is turning radically to the left, disengaging from capitalist economics, from white European thinking and theology which has attempted to quash the enormous force of pre-Colombian beliefs, and has been unsuccessful.

And do you think artists in the United States have to do the same thing?

Yes. When I got back to the United States in 1970, after five years in Europe, I found that my real interest was in trying to define an American classicism which didn't exist. I was angry and disturbed at the critical establishment's unquestioned purchasing of British culture as American culture. I constantly questioned whether Shakespeare should really be the key to American cultural classicism. Is Racine the culture of Haiti? Is language culture? No, language is not culture, it is just one element of it. American culture today is becoming triangular. The influx of African, Caribbean, and Asian cultural ideas, along with European ideas are creating a new culture—no longer a strictly European one. This is the ultimate melting pot. A country's classicism is its statement. Molière, Corneille, and Racine say it for France. Shakespeare says it for England, but nobody was saying it for America or they were saying it in such a minimal way, a neo-European way, that I didn't think it was really an American statement. Is O'Neill really an American statement? No, he is another Irish playwright writing another Irish play.

That's one reason you're doing a Southern Lear, *taking an English cultural statement and making it American?*

The idea and the fundamental question in *Lear* is whether power has its own behavior or whether it is tied to sex or race. My position is that power has

211

its own behavior. To me, it is interesting to see the violence associated with the manipulation of power in *Lear* as executed by women on stage. Their behavior becomes not only logical, but normal. They are shocking but not beyond the realm of imagination. We rarely see this on stage. I feel that since *Lear* is about power and the metaphor for power in bourgeois society is money, it becomes important to look at race and gender and what it can represent on stage.

Doesn't gender-blind and color-blind casting homogenize race and gender rather than recognize them?

I don't believe in color-blind and gender-blind casting. You can't say you don't see what you see. But I do believe in the idea of conceptualizing a particular production to allow for various races, actors, actresses to take part in this representation. Casting *Lear* in the contemporary South allows for roles to be taken by black actresses. Reverse gender casting is an attempt to perceive the behavior pattern of women in a way that represents the manipulation of power in the abstract. If dogs and cats had the same opportunities for territory and wealth as men and women do in terms of *Lear*, they would tear each other's eyes out. Anything alive will react the same way. It really is Darwinian. Of course it contradicts one opinion held, that the behavior of men and power are synonymous and that the behavior of women and power is not.

And you think it is?

It's a debatable point. It's a question, a discussion point. Since power is perceived in economic terms, it becomes logical that Gloucester might be Lear's servant and might have had an illegitimate child with a white man, and that therefore one of the two daughters passes for white. It is logical that Goneril would have a servant who is black. I feel that I am stretching things but always logically. When you cast Gloucester as a black rural woman and Lear as a white woman with the power, you see what the play is about.

You also deal with questions of power in The Warrior Ant. *There, you draw on the Japanese Warrior institution to comment on American culture.*

The *Ant* is a piece about machismo—about sexual politics, about contemporary political movements of feeling between men and women in the United States. It is a piece about the Women's movement but with a kind of different take on it than my earlier works. *The Shaggy Dog Animation* deals with many of the same elements but from a female point of view. *Ant* is a male look at these elements, but it is a mock point of view. Bushido—the Samurai tradition—is the epitome of macho, to the point of absurdity, which is an important aspect of this work. The Samurai warriors in Japan were barely five feet tall. It is a humorous look at the hero, at the maleness of heroism.

THE WARRIOR ANT

What is it about the Bunraku tradition that expresses you beyond your own writing?

Bunraku puppetry is perfect illusion. A head of wood and a bunch of cloth lying there . . . totally lifeless. It means nothing. It has no form. Then somebody puts his hand inside the puppet and suddenly it will drink, eat, make love, fight and die. When the hand comes out, it collapses again. This is how life is: a hand, or force of energy inside a piece of material. And this is the great lesson of Buddhist puppetry. Life is an imitation, a mechanism that can cease at any point in time. This kind of puppetry is really a prayer, a form of meditation. Plus there are other ramifications in that you see the black figures hovering around the Bunraku puppet. They are part of the mystery of where this energy comes from. You have the feeling that the puppet is both manipulating the puppeteers and they are manipulating the puppet.

Is one more present than the other? Who causes the other to exist?

It constantly fluctuates. That's the final dialectic. I feel that this experience is almost unspeakably exciting and astute because you are constantly aware—and this is what Beckett is all about—that every gesture is against nothing. In Beckett, every word is against the void, against death. There is no guarantee that the next word is going to happen. In this form of puppetry you have the sense that there is no guarantee the next gesture is going to happen. So the metaphysical experience of illusion and theatricality is for me readily represented in classic terms in this kind of puppetry.

Was the critical response to The Warrior Ant *part of the Darwinian battle you were discussing earlier?*

Yes, it was absolutely part of this battle. But the split operates on an economic level, too. There's a Marxist base to it as well. A culture is composed of any group of people that identifies itself as a group—whether economic, racial, aesthetic, or of métiers—artists versus non-artists—any group. My particular division is economic. I'm a borderline petit bourgeois or working class intellectual. The criticism from the upper-middle class is a criticism that is politically determined.

I think that a whole cultural grouping of people had problems with the *Ant* because they perceived it as politically committed even though it's not finished and a lot was unclear . . . the sense they got was that it was committed politically and that its political commitment is to the left. It's a political commitment that views Broadway and capitalist America as a lie. And since Frank Rich has already defined his favorite piece of theatre as being *Eastern Standard*, it's not surprising to me that *Ant* had nothing to say to him. I do not accept his criteria. I cannot credit him with an intellectual response to my work; it would be playing his game and the party line of the cultural elite's to pretend that there is anything motivating their criticism except self-interest. Anything that in anyway threatens their metaphysics, their politics, their sociology—their wing of culture—is threatening and must be eliminated.

I gave a showing of *Lear*, which is also a work in progress, at the Public Theatre. It was supposed to go to Spoleto. But it was refused. I was told it was too politically hot, too feminist, too black, too integrated and, basically, bad for funding. Money is doing the talking now. Deep right money. The only reason we got away with *Gospel* is because it fooled people. The music essentially is non-political even though the event was highly political, and

THE GOSPEL AT COLONUS

one of the things that actually made me uncomfortable is that I was getting support from people I didn't want support from. I don't need conservative support, I don't want it.

Politically, the country has moved too far to the right for me to have enough support for my kind of work. I've just had a long talk with Richard Foreman and he feels exactly the same way. He wants to go back to doing closet work in his loft. I'd just as soon write. But I don't want to do any more theatre. I'm tired of spending ninety percent of my time fund raising. I am retiring. *Lear* will be my last show.

Ta'ziyeh

Indigenous Avant-Garde Theatre of Iran

Peter J. Chelkowski

THIS TITLE IS DELIBERATELY controversial. But it is, perhaps, the most accurate description of the only indigenous drama engendered by the world of Islam. The Ta'ziyeh of Iran is ritual theatre and derives its form and content from deep-rooted religious traditions. But although it is Islamic in appearance, it is strongly Persian, drawing vital inspiration from its special political and cultural heritage. Its genius is that it combines immediacy and flexibility with universality. Uniting rural folk art with urban, royal entertainment, it admits no barriers between the archetype and the human, the wealthy and the poor, the sophisticated and the simple, the spectator and the actor. Each participates with and enriches the other.

The nucleus of the Ta'ziyeh is the heroic martyrdom of Hossein, the grandson of the prophet Mohammed. After the death of the Prophet (11 A.H., 632 A.D.) the still young Muslim community was faced with the problem of providing new leadership. Almost immediately the community found itself divided into two bitterly opposed factions, those who espoused the ancient Arabic tradition of succession by election and those who desired succession by inheritance, through blood-relationship to the Prophet. The former are known as Sunnites, the latter Shi'ites.

Three successive caliphs were elected; they had been companions to the Prophet. Then 'Ali, the cousin and son-in-law of Mohammed and the leader of the Shi'ite partisans, was recognized as the legitimate caliph. To Shi'ites, 'Ali, "the Hand of God," is so exalted that it is said: "Mohammed is a city of learning, 'Ali is its gate." But 'Ali was assassinated and later his elder son, Hasan, was poisoned and the Sunnite governor of Syria took over the caliphate and moved its capital to Damascus. 'Ali's younger son, Hossein,.however, persisted by championing the cause of the House of 'Ali and was asked by a Shi'ite group in Kufa, a city near today's Baghdad, to join them as their head.

Hossein accepted and set out for Mecca with his family and an entourage of about seventy followers. But on the plain of Kerbela they were caught in an ambush set by the Sunnite caliph, Yazid. Though defeat was certain, Hossein refused to pay homage to him. Surrounded by a great enemy force, Hossein and his company existed without water for ten days in the burning desert of Kerbela. Finally Hossein, the adult and some child males of the family and his companions, were cut to bits by the arrows and swords of Yazid's army; his women and remaining children were taken as captives to Yazid in Damascus. The renowned historian Abu Reyhan Biruni states: ". . . then fire was set to their camp and the bodies were trampled by the hoofs of the horses: nobody in the history of the human kind (sic) has seen such atrocities."

The siege began on the first day of the Muslim month of Muharram and came to its bloody end on the tenth day, called 'Ashura. It was in the 61st year of the Muslim calendar which corresponds to 680 A.D. Soon after, the battlefields and tombs at Kerbela became a place of sacred pilgrimage for Shi'ites throughout the Islamic Empire.

* * *

Ta'ziyeh literally means expressions of sympathy, mourning, and consolation. As a dramatic form it has its origins in the Muharram processions commemorating Hossein's martyrdom and throughout its evolution the representation of the siege and carnage at Kerbela has remained its centerpoint. Ta'ziyeh has never lost its religious implications. Because early Shi'ites viewed Hossein's death as a sacred redemptive act, the performance of the Muharram ceremonies were believed to be an aid to salvation; later they also believed that participation, both by the actors and spectators, in the Ta'ziyeh dramas would gain them Hossein's intercession on the day of the last judgment.

Perhaps, because of their tradition of hereditary kingship and strong nationalism, the people of the Iranian plateau were particularly hospitable to the Shi'ite form of Islam. According to Persian legend, the daughter of the last Persian king of the Sassanid dynasty was taken captive during the

217

Muslim invasion and married to Hossein. From the beginning, the annual Muharram mourning ceremonies were observed with great pageantry and emotion. Celebration of deceased heroes had long been an important part of Persian culture; the theme of redemption through sacrifice found parallels in such pre-Islamic legends as the death of Siavush and in the ancient Mesopotamian ritual of Adonis-Tamuz. By the tenth century impressive Muharram processions were well established. The reliable historian, Ibn al-Athir, tells of great numbers of participants, with black painted faces and disheveled hair, circling round and round the city of Baghdad, beating their chests and moaning the mourning songs at the festival of Muharram. It was at the time when the Persian Buid dynasty ruled from Baghdad.

In the first years of the sixteenth century, when under the Safavid dynasty Persia, which had always been a strong cultural power, again became a political power, Shi'ite Islam was established against the aggressive Ottomans and Uzbecks who were adherents of Sunnite Islam. The Muharram observances received royal encouragement; commemoration of Hossein's martyrdom became a patriotic as well as a religious act. Many accounts of the processions, written mostly by European envoys, missionaries, merchants, and travelers, tell of characters dressed in colorful costumes marching, or mounted on horses and camels, depicting the events leading up to the final tragedy at Kerbela. Living tableaux of butchered martyrs stained with blood, their bodies showing simulated amputations, were moved along on wheeled platforms. Mock battles were mimed by hundreds of uniformed mourners armed with bows, swords, and other weapons. The entire pageant was accompanied by funeral music and spectators, lined up along its path, beat their breasts and shouted, "Hossein, O Hossein, the King of the Martyrs" as it passed by.

Certain similarities between the Muharram processions and the European medieval theatre of the Stations are obvious. An important difference is, however, that during the Muharram ceremonies the spectators remained stationary while the tableaux moved and in the theatre of the Stations the tableaux were stationary while the viewer-penitents moved. The Muharram processions are, perhaps, more similar to the passion week celebrations which can still be seen in such Christian countries as Guatemala.

At the same time as the Muharram ceremonies were flourishing and developing under the Safavid rule, a second important and popular form of religious expression came into being. This was the dramatic narration of the life, deeds, suffering and death of Shi'ite martyrs. Virtually always connected, though sometimes only slightly, with the Kerbela ambush, these stories were taken from a book called *Rowzato'l Shohadah* or *The Garden of Martyrs,* written in Persian and widely circulated among Shi'ites from the early sixteenth century onwards. Unlike the Muharram processions, the Rowzeh-khani—garden recitations—were stationary, the narrator usually seated on a raised pulpit, his audience gathered in a semi-circle beneath his feet. Soon, readings from *The Garden of Martyrs* began to serve only as a framework and a springboard for the professional narrators who improvised creatively on the suffering and deeds of the many Shi'ite heroes. Through choice of episodes and modulation of his voice, the narrator was able to excite and manipulate the emotions of his audience, to produce in them a unity of feeling of great intensity.

For about 250 years the Muharram processions and the narrative recitations existed side by side, each becoming more complex and at the same time more refined and theatrical. Then in the middle of the eighteenth century they fused. A new dramatic form was born. Ta'ziyeh-Khani, or as it is more familiarly called, simply Ta'ziyeh. Interestingly, from the beginning, the antagonists recited their parts, while the protagonists sung theirs. The main theme was still the siege of Kerbela, but the focus was on individual heroes around whom separate plays were written. Martyrs who pre-dated and post-dated Kerbela were added to the repertoire.

Ta'ziyeh serves as an excellent illustration of the concept that the roots of drama are in funeral songs and commemoration of deceased heroes, and also that, in the development of the theatrical art, the text is one of the last elements to be added.

* * *

It is significant to remember that in the entire Muslim world Persia was the only country to nourish drama. This can perhaps be attributed to Persia's continuous attachment—in spite of religious prohibitions—to figural representation. Persia is justly famous for painting, sculpture and the other visual arts. Nevertheless it must be noted that, although the Persian literary heritage extends back over 2,500 years and is renowned for its carefully structured national and romantic epics, its only true drama is the Muslim inspired Ta'ziyeh, which took well over a millennium to develop. That this should be so, especially in view of Persia's close cultural and geographical ties with Greece and India, both of which had extraordinarily rich theatrical traditions, remains a puzzle. Indeed, no Greek amphitheatres have yet been discovered on the eastern bank of the Euphrates.

As a compromise between the moving procession and the stationary recitation, Ta'ziyeh was at first staged at street intersections and squares. Soon, however, it moved into the courtyards of caravanseries, bazaars, and private houses. By the nineteenth century, the nascent dramas were performed in arena theatres called *tekieh,* built, usually by the well-to-do and upper classes, as a religious and public service. Some tekieh could seat thousands of spectators, but most were for a few hundred people. Simpler ones were prevalent in the small towns and villages. Many tekieh were temporary structures erected especially for the Muharram observances. Even the British and Russian legations were drawn into the competition of arranging the most splendid tekieh for the annual Muharram celebrations in Tehran.

In the beginning, Ta'ziyeh consisted of a few loosely connected episodes with long elegiac monologues followed by some dialogue. Hardly any action was connected directly with these quite primitive recited and sung parts. In fact, the actors read their lines from scripts about 2'' wide and about 8'' long which they held in their palms. This tradition continued and is practiced even today. It is perhaps at least in part an expression of the Muslim proscription against representation of living things: the script serves as a barrier to any suggestion that the actor actually becomes the person he portrays. In this respect it bears some similarity to the use of masks in the Greek theatre. The spectacle of the pageant rather than the text was most important. Nevertheless, within a century, this art form produced a corpus of several hundred lengthy dramas.

The design of the tekieh preserved and enhanced the dramatic interplay between actors and spectators which was characteristic of the traditional Muharram rites. The main action took place on a stark, curtainless raised platform in the center of the building. Surrounding it was a narrow circular band of space used by the performers for sub-plots and to indicate journeys, passage of time, and change of scene. At the periphery of this space, extending into the audience-filled pit, small secondary stages were often erected. Scenes of special significance were acted upon them and sometimes players from these auxiliary stages would engage in dialogue or action with those on the central stage.

In addition, there were two or more corridors through the seating area, running from the central platform to the outer wall of the tekieh. These provided access for message bearers, armies, and processions including horses, camels and vehicles. Skirmishes and duels often took place behind the audience in unwalled tekiehs: sometimes actors in their fervor literally plunged through the audience to gain the central stage. The tekieh was indeed a model of the plain of Kerbela; it was a tradition that actors in plays about the Kerbela massacre never left the central playing area as a symbol of the martyrs encircled by the enemy. It would probably not be going too far to say that the tekieh was a kind of Shi'ite omphalos.

The following synopsis of the Ta'ziyeh play from the Northern provinces, called "The Marriage of Qasem," which was usually played between the fifth and the tenth day of Muharram as an introduction to the culminating martyrdom of Hossein, illustrates the dynamic interaction of audience and actor that took place in the Persian tekieh.

Qasem is a son of Hossein's elder brother, Hasan, who was poisoned shortly after his father, 'Ali, was assassinated. It was Hasan's will that Qasem be married to Fatemeh, the daughter of Hossein. Both Qasem and Fatemeh are among the besieged at Kerbela. They are still in their teens, but Hossein, realizing that their deaths are imminent, desires to fulfill his promise to his brother and orders their wedding.

While 'Ali Akbar, the elder son of Hossein, is singlehandedly fighting off the attackers' army (the fight is not staged, but is referred to), both actors and spectators make preparations for the wedding on the central stage and in the area surrounding it. Finally they bring in the colorfully beribboned nuptial tent and lead the bride and bridegroom through one of the pit corridors to it. Festive wedding music accompanies their march. Cookies are joyfully passed among the audience. Then suddenly, from behind the audience, the horse of 'Ali Akbar appears. It is riderless. At this sign of 'Ali Akbar's death, everyone in the tekieh freezes into position. Qasem leaves the main stage and rushes into the battlefield behind the audience. Almost immediately he returns, leading the procession that carries the body of 'Ali Akbar, raised high on shields, to the central stage. As it is the custom in Muslim countries for the entire community to participate in the last rites of the dead, the whole audience rises to its feet and weeps. Since it is also customary during the funeral processions that everyone should strive to help carry the coffin, those in the audience who cannot push close enough stretch their hands in symbolic gestures.

Finally, the body is laid on the main stage opposite the nuptial tent. On one side of the stage, funeral rites are performed with interludes of mournful music. The spectators dishevel their hair and beat their breasts. On the other side of the stage, the wedding ceremony continues accompanied by jubilant music. There is a cacaphony of sound, the audience turning from side to side alternating between tears and laughter.

When the marriage rites are concluded and Qasem is preparing to consummate the marriage, he is called to the battlefield. First he attacks the young sons of the besieging generals who, at the sight of the gallant son of Hasan, flee in a comical manner. Then at last he must fight the whole army and is slain.

The most famous and influential of the nineteenth-century Ta'ziyeh theatres was the Tekieh Dowlat, or Royal Arena Theatre in Tehran (construction started 1304 A.H.). Under the patronage of Naser-ed-Din Shah, who ruled Persia from 1848 to 1896, Ta'ziyeh reached the peak of its

221

development. According to many travelers, its dazzling splendor and its intensity of dramatic action overshadowed even the opera of the western capitals. The American envoy, Samuel Benjamin, who attended the Muharram celebrations, left this vivid description of the Tekieh Dowlat.

> I was invited to attend on the fifth day of the Ta'ziyeh. We arrived at the Tekieh toward noon. On alighting from the carriage I was surprised to see an immense circular building as large as the amphitheatrè of Verona, solidly constructed of brick. Ferashes, or liveried footmen, cleared the way before us. Thrashing their staves right and left, they opened a way through the crowd that packed the great portal; and entering a dark, vaulted vestibule I groped, or rather was impelled by the throng, towards a staircase crowded with servants whose masters had already arrived. Like all stairs in Persia, these were adapted to the stride of giants.
>
> A succession of springs upward finally landed me on the first gallery, which led around the building. A few steps in the twilight and then an embroidered curtain was raised and I entered the box of the Zahir-e-Dowleh (Shah's son). It was in two parts, the first higher than the other; stepping into the front and lower division, I was invited to recline at the left of my host upon a superbly embroidered cushion of velvet—the seat of honor is at the left hand in Persia. The walls of the loggia were of plain brick, but they were hung with cashmere shawls of price, and the choicest of rugs enriched the floor. A number of Persian gentlemen of lower rank occupied the back part of the apartment by invitation.
>
> On looking over the vast arena a sight met my gaze which was indeed extraordinary. The interior of the building is nearly two hundred feet in diameter and some eighty feet high. A domed frame of timbers, firmly spiced and braced with iron, springs from the walls, giving support to the awning that protects the interior from the sunlight and the rain. From the center of the dome a large chandelier was suspended, furnished with four electric burners—a recent innovation. A more oriental form of illuminating the building was seen in the prodigious number of lustres and candlesticks, all of glass and protected from the air by glass shades open on the top and variously colored; they were concentrated against the wall in immense glittering clusters. Estimating from those attached on one box, I judged that there were upwards of five thousand candles in these lustres . . .
>
> In the center of the arena was a circular stage of masonry, raised

three feet and approached by two stairways. On one side of the building a pulpit of white marble was attached to the wall. . . . But I soon discovered that all the architectural details of this remarkable building were secondary to the extraordinary spectacle offered by the assembled multitude. The entire arena with the exception of a narrow passage around the stage, was absolutely packed with women, thousands on thousands. At a rough estimate it seemed to me that quite four thousand women were seated there cross-legged on the earthen floor, which was made slightly sloping in order to enable those in the rear to see over the heads of those before them . . .

Refreshments were served in our box repeatedly, and cigars for myself. . . . But after the performance began, all smoking and refreshments were banned as indications of frivolity inconsistent with the tragical events of the dramas . . .

Ta'ziyeh, like other Muharram commemorations, was a communal event. Each individual contributed according to his means and ability. The men brought their most precious objects—crystal, lamps, mirrors, china, and tapestry—to decorate the walls of the tekieh. Even the most humble objects were accepted as they were given or lent with religious devotion. Athletes from the gymnasium eagerly donated their strength and agility to put up the tekieh. The women provided refreshments; the children of the aristocracy served water, a symbol of the Kerbela martyr's thirst, and sweetmeats to all spectators, rich and poor alike. Although the wealthy had their own gorgeously adorned loges, the poor could sit in them if there was space in accordance with the Muslim spirit of brotherhood. The purpose of Ta'ziyeh remained true to its essence; participation was an aid to salvation, for the suffering and death of the martyrs of Kerbela were instruments of redemption for all believers.

Good actors were paid very well by their patrons and also received favors and bonuses from the audience. Their costumes and props were rich. At Tekieh Dowlat many came from the royal treasuries. It is recorded that the Shah lent his own coach to carry Timur, and later a new royal automobile was used for King Solomon. Ta'ziyeh productions were lavish extravaganzas.

The texts of the Ta'ziyeh dramas were at first very simple, with concentration on universal truths rather than on the dramatic power, to be achieved through the skillful use of exposition, challenge, and complication. Gradually, however, during the course of the nineteenth century, they became more developed and refined as literature. They also became more secular in content as the "high" court tradition, resplendent in its external aspects, began to filter down to the rural areas, while the folk tradition, more organic and more natural, based on folk art, folk stories, popular religion and ingrained with social connotation, percolated up.

Digressions, or "Goriz" were introduced to extend the scope of the Ta'ziyeh and to add variety and secular detail. These were based on episodes from Biblical or Koranic stories, and from national legend and tradition. Spectators were led to identify their own sufferings with these lesser heroes. For women especially, they served as a wound-healing agent, for the point was always made that all suffering was slight when compared to that of the victims of Kerbela.

Despite criticism by the majority of the religious authorities who considered it sacrilegious for mortal men to portray any holy personage, Ta'ziyeh became more and more beloved by the people. Performances, no longer restricted to the first ten days of the month of Muharram, lasted until the end of the following month of Safar. Plays commemorating the birthday of a saint or a prophet provided an excuse to extend the dramas to other months. Eventually, popular demand induced troupes to perform Ta'ziyeh throughout the year as an act of thanksgiving, celebrating such occasions as the happy conclusion of a journey, the recovery of health after sickness, or the return from a pilgrimage.

At the end of the nineteenth century Ta'ziyeh was on the verge of giving birth to an Iranian secular theatre. But owing to fundamental social and political changes of the twentieth century it lost its patrons. Ta'ziyeh then became a commercial enterprise, centered not in the cities, which at that time were given to imitating Western art forms, but rather in the rural areas. Troupes fought for the most lucrative places to perform and were often forced to lease them from the provincial governors. Actors collected contributions from the audience, usually interrupting the play in the middle of the most crucial episode. Rivalry among Ta'ziyeh troupes led to theft of manuscripts and shifting of actors from one troupe to another. Dissident political groups began using theatrical gatherings to further their own goals, and subsequently the government imposed restrictions on the performances.

Although many critics have written that this retreat to the provinces had a swift and deleterious effect upon Ta'ziyeh as an art form, a strong case can be made to show that, to the contrary, it purified and preserved it. The Persian village tradition with its sources in popular religion is more simple, organic, and theatrical than the urban tradition. Its imagination is more closely attached to the essentials of life; it is less abstract and intellectual, less wedded to the spectacular effect. In the provincial setting there is far greater potential for coherence between actor and audience.

In fact, it may be said that the twentieth-century rural Ta'ziyeh is the unconscious avant-garde of the ''poor theatre.'' It totally engages the participation of the audience and it has extraordinary dynamic flexibility. There are no barriers of time and space. The text is not fixed; episodes from one play can be interpolated in another to suit the mood of the actors and the audience and the weather. The producer is omnipresent, regulating the movement of actors, musicians and audience. He remains constantly on stage, giving the actors their cues, helping children and inexperienced actors, and handling props.

Costumes are contemporary, as they always have been in Ta'ziyeh and other visual arts. In the past strict division into symbolic colors was observed, e.g., green and white for protagonists and red for antagonists. Today, if no appropriate costume is at hand, any that differs from the usual dress of the audience is acceptable. But, when possible, costumes conform to certain symbolic conventions. Warriors wear British officers' jackets instead of coats of mail. 'Abbas, the standard bearer of Hossein's troops, wears a long white Arabic shirt, embellished by a military jacket, Wellington boots, and a helmet. Bad characters often wear sunglasses, learned people wear reading glasses. The eminence of a character is signified by a walking stick. In the Western theatre, the use of everyday dress for historical characters has been practiced for some time as a shock device, but in Ta'ziyeh it has been traditional.

Props are casual, but often also have symbolic meaning. Gabriel may carry an umbrella to indicate he has descended from heaven. Automobile hubcaps have been used as shields. A bowl of water signifies the Euphrates river. Classical Persian musical modes form the basis of the interludes, but themes from currently popular songs and marches are often incorporated. The company makes use of whatever space happens to be available for its stage. None of these practices ever prove distracting to the absorbed audience and actors. On the contrary, they give each Ta'ziyeh performance special freshness and immediacy.

Since the decline of high court patronage there have been two strong Ta'ziyeh traditions. The first is in the hands of professional troupes; its practices form the basis of this discussion. It is active throughout the year both in towns and villages. The repertoire includes Shi'ite stories with the Kerbela tragedy at its core and the plays based on digressions. Usually the backbone of the troupe is a family for whom Ta'ziyeh has been a hereditary occupation. The actors are trained from childhood. The second is the non-professional Muharram village tradition. This Ta'ziyeh is usually organized on or around the day of 'Ashura by an ex-professional or semi-professional

225

Ta'ziyeh actor who brings together a group of villagers to perform, most commonly, the martyrdom of Hossein. This is an act of communal piety and has very little artistic value; its aim is to provide an archetypal framework into which the spectators can pour their own hopes and sufferings. It arouses their deepest emotions and permits them to express these physically and publicly. It is a primitive ceremony with frenzied shouting and chest beating. The performance is not only primitive, but awkward, and is generally responsible for the criticism Ta'ziyeh has received from the progressive elements of twentieth-century Persian society.

The advancement of film and television in the post-World War II period, together with the decline of religious ritual, has brought about a crisis in the theatre throughout the world. In order to preserve theatre, innovative producers and directors have been trying to break down the barriers which divide the audience from the actors, for film and TV cannot recreate the excitement generated by the close working together of living organisms. The touch, even the odor of the actor's sweat, the blink of his eye, the rhythm and warmth of his breathing create an intimacy between actor and spectator for which nothing can be substituted.

Grotowski, who exemplifies this effort as a director, has developed what he calls the "poor theatre." By "poor" he means stripping the theatre of extraneous outward appearances and achieving a purity of interaction between audience and actor that is based on their common humanity. This is only possible by reinvesting dramatic action with ritual and establishing a common denominator or archetype, such as the redemptive martyrdom of Hossein at Kerbela. Grotowski seems to be striving for what have always been the fundamental principles of Ta'ziyeh. The important difference is that Grotowski regards the theatre as his laboratory and controls intimacy by limitation of space, number and distribution of spectators; his is a chamber theatre. Ta'ziyeh, on the other hand, achieves the same goal in enormous spaces and with masses of spectators.

The actor-spectator confrontation in Ta'ziyeh and its archetypal themes induce self-analysis in all who participate, and create in them an inner harmony. Ta'ziyeh is such a personal and serious drama that it captures the very essence of thought and emotions embracing life, death, the Supreme Being, and fellow men. To students of the history of theatre and to those who are engaged in experimental theatre, Ta'ziyeh holds the promise of stimulating new theatrical ideas and experiences.

There are still living Ta'ziyeh producers who are a good source of information on this dramatic form. There are still Ta'ziyeh troupes who perform in this traditional manner. There are still thousands of Ta'ziyeh manuscripts fading in dowry boxes. We have much to learn from them.

The Condition of Ritual in Theatre

J. Ndukaku Amankulor

IN MANY SOCIETIES the cultural form known as theatre goes together with religious and cultural practices. Theatre, as performance intended for the education, enlightenment, and entertainment of the public, functions as an extension of the mythology and cultural conventions associated with a particular group or community as well as an artistic activity which other people outside the group derive pleasure from seeing. More often than not, the performance takes place within the context and environment of festivity, fixed at such periods in the year when the performers and spectators would have ample leisure time to prepare for and participate in the performance. Theatre cultures of this kind are still very much in vogue in Africa, Asia, the Americas, and Oceania.

In Africa, performances given by title or initiation associations and those used to mark the passage of the seasons or commemorate important historical events are invested with the best artistic traditions the group possesses and performed with a view, among other things, to advertising the people's performance traditions of excellence. The word ''play'' is frequently applied to such performances in ways that differ from other private sessions of the group's practices. Thus among the Igbo of Nigeria, for example, the *Okonko* or *Mmonwu* performances, given by initiation associations with those names, are freely described as *egwu* (play). The context of play here embodies both the serious and the pleasurable and not-so-serious. On the one hand, the public performances of a cultural group involve conventions such as masking which are protected by strict rules. Mask characters, for example, may not be unmasked in public nor are they supposed to fall while playing their roles. The spectators are therefore required to keep safe distances from them to avoid accidental collisions and irritations. On the other hand, the performances are presented to entertain and educate the spectators and to help them treasure memorable aspects of them afterwards.

If the integration of ritual and theatrical conventions is taken for granted in non-Western performance situations, it is highly questioned in contemporary Western theatre. The apparent divestment of theatre from the ritual origin in Western theatre practice is a foregone conclusion. It is taken for granted. Ritual, with its evocation of negative connotations of primitive, superstitious, and unscientific behavior associated with savage peoples, has no place in the industrialized high-technological Western world of today. In a popular sense, ritual has become what Orrin Klapp describes, in his *Ritual and Cult: A Sociological Interpretation*, as a "bugaboo word" for the modern man. It reminds him of other terms with negative associations such as voodoo, mumbo jumbo, cult, and superstition. Ritual has also come to be associated, like myth, with something false, and as Ronald L. Grimes observes in his *Beginnings in Ritual Studies*, it is also associated with boring, empty routine.

The negative associations of ritual, though not explicitly emphasized by anthropologists, are nonetheless implied in their writings which for the most part deal with traditional societies in Africa, Asia, and other places where religious ritual and theatre still co-exist. Unable to see the relationship between theatre performances in Europe and America and theatre performances in the largely non-literate cultures of the world, the anthropologists coined the phrase "ritual theatre" or "ritual drama" as a convenient label for distinguishing the "otherness" of non-Western performance traditions. This coinage changed the course of world performance studies as theatre scholars adopted the phrase, somewhat uncritically, specifically to describe or evaluate non-Western theatre and to isolate ritual in performance and theatre criticism. The term now has specific application to the performance culture zones of the world where they apply, but not in the West. This isolation has not only affected the healthy balance that should otherwise exist between ritual and theatre but it has also affected the course of intercultural performance, and obscured the creative interpretation and application of ritual in performance studies.

In his article, "Ritual in Contemporary Theatre and Criticism," published in the *Educational Theatre Journal* (now *Theatre Journal*), Anthony Graham-White warned theatre critics of the dangers in adopting the term "ritual" as a critical tool for analyzing contemporary American theatrical performances, the norms of which may by quite different from the ritual-based performances of other cultures. Graham-White felt uncomfortable with avant-garde and experimental theatre groups such as The Living Theatre, The Bread and Puppet Theatre, The Performance Group, and Polish Theatre Laboratory which may find the word ritual an attractive label with which to identify their performances. The literary or theatre critic cannot use the word indiscriminately, Graham-White warns, because it has specific cultural connotations. He explains that the difference between ritual and other forms of cultural expression is not the structure but "the attitude held towards it by participants and other members of the community, notably their belief in its efficacy."

Although Graham-White identifies "three different senses" of the use of ritual, namely as routine, as performance on behalf of a whole group or community expressing or touching upon its deepest values, and as ceremony, nonetheless, he emphasizes in his fullest sense of that term, the efficacious results attributable to ritual. By de-emphasizing the routine and ceremonious implications of ritual, Graham-White criticizes the avant-garde and experimental American theatre practitioners whom he accuses of seeking to project their performances in the fullest ritualistic and efficacious of contexts, in much the same manner as the ritual experiences in Africa and similar culture zones. The choice of cultures by Graham-White is instructive. The idea is to isolate those performance zones where theatre occurs as ritual as opposed to Western societies where it is practiced as art. In other words, though experimental and avant-garde theatre groups may pretend to practice theatre as ritual, critics must be reminded of the dangers of taking such pretensions seriously.

Hilary Ursula Cohen in her dissertation, "Ritual and Theatre: An Examination of Performance Forms in the Contemporary American Theatre," furthers Graham-White's argument. She studied selected American theatre groups "overtly seeking to create ritual in the theatre in its celebratory or ceremonial sense." Her major groups of study included The Iowa Theatre Lab, The Bread and Puppet Theatre, and El Teatro Campesino. The concern with the celebratory or ceremonial sense of ritual, without examining the other denotations of ritual such as habit or practice as they also apply to theatre practice, prompts Cohen to fall back to the narrow track which she believes constitutes the code which must strictly be adhered to by theatre practitioners as laid down for them by anthropology. "Anthropology," she writes, "has shown us that ritual, in the sense of ceremony of prescribed order, has a definite, identifiable form. By ignoring the form, scholars ignore the essence of what makes a performance ritual."

Like Graham-White, Cohen links ritual with the primitive state and therefore wonders how the actor could be "stripped of layers of civilization until his primitive core is discovered," as the work of groups such as The Polish Laboratory Theatre and The Living Theatre would suggest. At the back of Cohen's mind is the impossibility of reconciling the traditions of Western theatre bequeathed to contemporary society, as opposed to the attempts by avant-garde theatre groups to take this society back to the very primitive past with which it has severed all traditional relationships.

Ritual in theatre practice and criticism has either been so negatively conceived or narrowly applied that I believe a new interpretation is needed. Although Richard Schechner has convincingly drawn the attention of theatre scholars to the interdisciplinary advantages between theatre and anthropology, he does not suggest that one discipline interprets society for the other. The theatre scholar or practitioner cannot study the phenomenon of ritual in theatre without losing the creative spirit in theatre if he depends on any narrow framework dictated by anthropology. This creative spirit, used in the process of bringing theatre into being or evaluating its finished products, ranges freely but purposefully, in an effort to tap the denotative as well as connotative applications of ritual. Moreover, if anthropologists themselves have a wider application of ritual beyond the religious ceremonial or celebratory denotation as applied to non-literate societies, why must theatre critics cry louder than the relatives of the dead?, to use an African saying. Even the notion of celebration is so strongly shared by both theatre and religious ritual that what I have called the free spirit of theatre becomes somewhat ambivalent or non-specific. The play element, as Grimes observes in *Beginnings in Ritual Studies,* renders celebration at once the most relevant and most irrelevant to liturgical rites.

Victor Turner's "social dramas" do not refer to the art of drama but to a broader range of social relationships and group activities or behavior. In his *Schism and Continuity in an African Society*, Turner defines social drama as "a description of a series of unique events in which particular persons, impelled by all kinds of motives and private purposes, interact in many different ways." It is in the third phase of social drama, the "social dramatic," according to Turner in his study, *From Ritual to Theatre*, that theatre owes its origins. Turner's work portrays a conscious borrowing from theatrical language but he uses these to further his concepts in anthropology in much the same way as the political scientist, who borrows words such as stage, actors, and so on, uses them to enhance the political picture he is painting and not explicitly to create fun or entertainment as on stage. In the same manner, ritual in theatrical practice and criticism must reflect the variety of uses the word suggests and as they apply to the art of theatre, and not exclusively to anthropology.

Theatre's relevant and irrelevant relationship with religious ritual enables it to exhibit two different kinds of ritual, namely, sacred or rite-oriented and secular-oriented rituals. Rite-oriented ritual in theatre shows clearly in those performances linked with rites of passage and the festivals or ceremonies connected with them. Secular-oriented ritual defines performances the subject matter of which are social-oriented, including contemporary plays. There is no dichotomy implied in these ritual types as they are applied in theatre. On the contrary, there is an active integration of both types through the established practices of theatre as they operate in different cultures. The practice of theatre through the ages in cultures the world over has produced a variety of conventional practices or cultural rituals as the services of theatre are drawn into the religious domain or thrown out into the purely social circles of society.

Theatre and religious ritual have come to share common characteristics, including those identified by Oscar G. Brockett in his *History of Theatre* as knowledge, didacticism, influencing or control of events, glorification of the past, and entertainment or pleasure. These characteristics make it difficult to draw any clear line between sacred ritual and theatre in some cultures, such as Africa. Schechner emphasizes this phenomenon in his *Essays on Performance Theory* when he observes that theatre is "a mixture, a braid, of entertainment and ritual," no matter what culture is being considered or how far in the past one may search. "They are a twin-system, tumbling over each other and vitally interconnected," Schechner concludes. This suggests therefore that the contemporary theatre, even in its postmodern phase, comprises an active mixture of the conventional practices of an age-old past and the pleasure derivable from them, translated into contemporary needs and philosophy of life.

Taking the United States as the best example of a contemporary postmodern Western culture, I observe that the mainstream practice of theatre is much more of a social ritual than a religious one, but it continues to be meaningful or purposeful ritual to performers and spectators alike because of shared performance conventions properly observed. Observing the proper conventions in theatre practice creates an effect, an efficacy of a kind, which ensures that the bond between the actors and the audience of spectators is not broken. In fact, one reason why contemporary American experimental theatre groups are not always tolerated is that they are suspected of breaking down the traditional conventions of theatre practice which the actors and spectators have naturally come to take for granted. They play for smaller audiences with whom they try to develop the spirit of community or create a new social ritual. Their style creates new conventions and they hope that with time the new conventions will coalesce into a new mainstream tradition of theatre. Their emphasis on ritual should not be narrowly interpreted but properly regarded as an iconoclastic device which awaits future acceptance and mass application. This emphasis is a kind of weapon and a propaganda, as Eric Bentley comments in his book, *The Theatre of Commitment*. It will produce the effect of having to re-examine what Bentley aptly describes as ''something misleading about the history of drama from the primitive beginnings,'' a tradition which he observes has shown great sophistication and provided maximum satisfaction.

Theatre is a form of communication, like other arts, between the performers and the spectators. Communication is also an essential aspect of ritual because it is inherent in all its symbols which speak to those who know how to listen. ''Unfamiliar symbols,'' according to Klapp, ''may well be all that stand in the way of seeing how familiar a practice is to our own.'' Symbols here include not just the final product, the performance, but the process toward the production of it. This may explain why Graham-White would warn Western theatre critics and practitioners about the implications of ritual among avant-garde theatre practices which exploit symbols unfamiliar to Western audiences, and which are uncomfortable to them because they do not seem to strengthen their already strongly shared values or accommodate their world view. This view would create a permanent polarization in global theatre culture and prevent the much needed effort towards interculturalism in performance culture. Instead, the one thing that should be emphasized is that although there are many traditions of theatre in the world, what links them are similarities of their production processes. By emphasizing process rather than product, the interrelationships between ritual as religious rite and ritual as socio-cultural process would be better appreciated within the creative tradition of theatre and the wider interdisciplinary relationships. John J. MacAloon, in his introduction to *Rite, Drama, Festival, Spectacle: Rehearsals Toward a Theory of Cultural Performance*, which he edited following the 76th Burg Wartenstein Symposium, makes a very pertinent observation. He notes that Schechner's insistence on the importance of the rehearsal process caused the anthropologists at the meeting to rethink their discipline's traditional emphasis on the finished performance. This kind of healthy interdisciplinary influence should be the goal of theatre people who must first understand the basis and variety of their art before imposing external disciplinary theories on it.

The process of theatrical production obeys certain socio-aesthetic and artistic norms or conventions. Elizabeth Burns, in her book, *Theatricality: A Study of Convention in Theatre and Social Life*, defines convention as ''a mutual understanding about the meaning of action, which includes gestures and speech.'' These norms are so tacitly and mutually understood that there is no conscious realization that an agreement has been entered into. In contemporary theatrical production there is the rehearsal period during which the play is prepared for staging. What happens during the rehearsal process may be compared with Victor Turner's liminal period of the initiation process. Both involve the sequestration of the players or the neophytes from the wider community to a special place where they submit themselves to the authority of a leader or leaders who instruct them and prepare them for returning to that wider community as special persons and with something new. It is during the rehearsal period that the actors or initiands are taught the kind of relationship or interaction they must maintain with the spectators in their effort to create a fictitious world within defined bounds of place, time, situation, and character. Such a relationship Burns calls a rhetorical convention.

Authenticating conventions, on the other hand, help the actors to authenticate the world of the play. What happens in rehearsal is not for public consumption and as such only authorized persons are allowed to watch a rehearsal in progress whether of a play or initiation ceremony. A certain degree of social leveling characterizes the interaction of persons during the rehearsal process. Turner identifies this condition in the ritual process as *communitas*, ''a communion of equal individuals who must submit together to the general authority of the ritual elders.'' In theatre practice, this is especially true of the avant-garde theatre groups that see themselves not only as a cohesive community but also seek to bring the spectators into their fold during their performances, as would ritual elders. The traditional Western theatre observes this social leveling during rehearsals as actors seek the best creative vibrations from one another under the supervision of the director and his assistants. When the actors or initiands re-enter the society, they do so partly as a ceremony and partly as entertainment. The performance, as it were, justifies or accounts for their absence from the larger society. A place is chosen beforehand for the performance, the rules governing which are known to the participants. The breaking of these rules, whether in the theatre or ritual initiation ceremonies, attracts the wrath of other participants for whom it constitutes a break in the magic circle defined by the make-believe or ritual world. A code of conduct is conventionally observed in the way theatre patrons file into the foyer, acknowledging the courtesy of the house staff and settling into their seats. The dimming of the houselights, their eventual blackout, and the rise of the curtain, all prepare the spectators for the start of the performance. Conventions have a ritual aura, a momentary preparation and entry into another world, the theatre world. In traditional African and Asian societies some performances are heralded by the booming of guns, special music, singing and ululations which make spectators hasten to the place of performance or condition them for the entrance of the performers or special mask actors.

Beyond the immediacy of entertainment lies the subject of all theatre: man, in his society and its institutions. Man is the ultimate benefactor and object of the performance even where supernatural beings are characters in the drama. All major traditions of drama, whether in literate or non-literate societies, deal with man's social, environmental, and spiritual relationships. We cannot deal with the theatre in any historical period without a proper understanding of the socio-cultural and economic conditions under which they existed. The intensification or reduction in the ceremonial ritual content of theatre portrays the extent to which that society or group integrates religion and social ethos or the extent to which such integration is diminished. Thus Western theatre has moved from a time when sacred ritual was integrated with secular ritual, such as during the Greek and Medieval times to a time when its primary concern is secular entertainment, and as a business or industry. The indications are also showing through the new theatre groups that Western theatre is interested in reinventing that original communal base of the art. In the traditional societies of Africa, on the other hand, theatre remains a communal activity, not so much steeped in religious worship as practiced by groups such as title societies or associations whose performance conventions reflect their sacred religious origins.

In fact, the ritual to theatre origin does not suffice in the theory of theatre origins in some African societies. The theatre to ritual theory also indicates that in some performances, such as the Ekokon'ute of Ute near Benin City and the Iri Aha war theatre among the Ohafia-Igbo, may have sprung from purely creative inspirations, and later ritualized in the interest of their wider communities.

The spectators are perhaps the single most important aspect of a performance. Without them the performers cannot enjoy their roles. The action of the performance, which also includes symbolic action, is for the spectators to decode. Whether theatre is viewed from the background of secular or religious rite, the performance contains a multiplicity of symbols which must be decoded by the spectators if they are to arrive at any satisfactory level of cultural information, without which they could not have enjoyed the performance. The complex scenic backgrounds, costumes, and properties (or the lack of these) witnessed in the mainstream and avant-garde Western productions are symbols which help to explain human actions, be they natural, biological, technical, or expressive, to the spectators in much the same way that costumes, masks, music, and puppets help spectators to interpret such actions in the performances of non-Western cultures. In any culture the world over, the spectator must be educated in the processes of a performance before he or she can participate meaningfully and appreciate the action. An informed spectator does not just walk into a performance unprepared, but comes with some knowledge of the pre-performance or rehearsal processes and understands his relationship to the performers in the context of the performance space.

It is as serious for the spectator watching a traditional African performance of masked actors to unmask any of them in the performance arena as it is for a spectator watching Arthur Miller's *Death of a Salesman* to run up to the stage and challenge, for example, the authenticity of the actor playing the lead role or shout him down from his seat to stop kidding because he is not Willy Loman. The conventions governing a performance forbid such acts. A convention is shorthand for the expression of ritual in its sacred or secular forms. It is surrounded by taboos, which may not be wantonly broken without consequences be they sacred or secular or both.

In the foregoing pages, I have tried to identify the causes of the prejudices that the word ritual attracts, especially in Western society, and the narrow anthropological application of the term in theatre practice and criticism. I have indicated that the nature of theatre is such that both sacred and secular rituals apply to it and that a more inclusive adoption of the denotations of ritual should be adopted in theatre practice and criticism. The narrow adoption of the sacred ceremonial interpretation not only pushes certain types of theatre permanently into the religious domain and creates an unnecessary intercultural dichotomy, it also excludes the creative applications of the more inclusive denotations of ritual in theatre. The term ''ritual theatre'' is thus frequently applied to most indigenous non-Western forms of the art without much critical scrutiny.

Due to the efforts of the experimental theatre groups of the last twenty years, and to theatre practitioners such as Peter Brook, Jerzy Grotowski, and Richard Schechner, much light has been shed on various traditions of indigenous Asian theatre. Although Peter Brook has toured the North, East, and West regions of Africa to harness their indigenous performance culture, the performance landscape of the continent remains largely unknown internationally. The basis of the religious as well as social interaction found in the indigenous theatre of Africa would need to be studied in an effort to integrate our knowledge of world theatre as a viable phenomemon of intercultural performance studies.

* * *

Indigenous African theatre is communally produced by an entire village or the cultic associations contained in it. It is performed during cultural ceremonies of festivals, time periods which will afford enough leisure for the performers to prepare for the performance, and the spectators to come in large numbers to watch. Although the religious phase is distinct from the artistic, both are integrated within the environment of festivity and celebration during which the performance takes place. What happens is comparable to the Corpus Christi cycle plays of the medieval period which integrated the religious, economic, civic, and creative functions of the guilds as they prepared for the plays.

In the *Ekpo* performance of the Ibibio people of Nigeria, for example, the ancestral spirits return to their villages of origin to take a comprehensive social, moral, and spiritual stock of those they have left behind. The visitors are led by the founding mother of the village and mother of all the spirits. She is Eka Ekpo (Mother Ekpo) who must not be seen by any human. She plays her role in total darkness, lamenting the falling moral standards of her children and their greed for material wealth. The next day, however, the villagers gather at the ancestral or village square to be entertained by the rest of the spirits, the Ekpo masked actors. It would be naive to suggest that the spectators do not know or cannot guess the identity of the masked performers. They do know and do guess at who are behind the masks, but that knowledge is not openly discussed. It is a convention not to discuss the identity of masked performers openly or else some evil could befall the culprit. But the major reason is to protect the dignity of the performance and for the spectator to enjoy it in a proper manner.

A four-year-old boy once observed his father being masked during the outing ceremony of an initiation association in an Igbo village. During the performance the boy went to his mother who was with a group of women and said, "*Ubu Olokoro na-achu m oso. Obu Dede Dinne furu ubu.*" ("The Olokoro masquerade is pursuing me. It is Dede Dinne who is inside the mask.") Dede Dinne is what the boy called his father. The women laughed it off but they joked about it later, even within hearing distance of the men who merely pretended the secret of masking was always a secret. Isaac Delano in his 1937 book, *The Soul of Nigeria,* which studied his own Yoruba ethnic group to impress the British colonial administration of that time, wrote that it was an "open" secret that the *Egungun*, the Yoruba masked spirit, "is a full-grown man, covered in a big assortment of clothes, sewn on him in a way that leaves no part of his body uncovered." In indigenous artistic terms the truth of this statement would constitute a frivolity, an attempt to prevent the enjoyment of the imaginary speculative world of art. The truth of Delano's observation sours aesthetic appreciation.

The performances of the *Ekpo* are of secular rather than sacred import. A number of loose episodes on the moral failings in Ibibio society are artistically yoked together by musical interludes through which continuity is provided. In one episode a farmer catches his newly married young wife being seduced by an educated but lazy, amorous young man. With the help of his neighbors, the farmer beats up the young man while the neighbors boo the culprit out of the arena. Thereafter, the orchestra raises a song which condemns moral laxity and laziness among educated people who cannot do any hard manual work but find time to corrupt other people's wives and daughters. In another episode, a long-time rogue was caught stealing something as shameful as a woman's underpants. His public disgrace satisfies the spectators.

I am persuaded to think that the plays of the *Ekpo* cult portray a strong social drama with a strong moral message. If one thinks of efficacy in their plays, it is that which accompanies all dramatic art, namely, the aesthetic satisfaction of the spectators and the moral education it affords them. The incidents dramatized may have been taken from past events in the community, but the re-enactment of these incidents by masked actors removes the aura of individual condemnation by spreading the message to the wider population. The episodes are also not static but change from one performance occasion to another, depending on the latest moral infringements that occurred in the area, and are exploited by the *Ekpo* society for artistic and social reasons. Similar performances, such as the Odo among the Nsukka Igbo in Nigeria, which I studied for *The Drama Review* (TDR 26), and the *Egungun* of the Yoruba, can serve as additional examples. The *Ekpo* performance embodies many of the aesthetic and conventional characteristics in indigenous African theatre. It is a group activity which involves the whole community in an environment of festivity and celebration, during which the performance setting changes from one section of the community to the other as the visual and oral media of communication immerse the participants in what has come to be a known routine and entertainment activity for them. The spectators especially participate in the performance because they are entertained and educated in a routine renewal of their artistic and celebrative tradition.

* * *

The search for the ritual ideology among contemporary avant-garde theatre groups in the United States may not be found in the religious definition of ritual but in the creative process of theatrical production, which for these groups comprises research into new forms of theatre, especially those non-Western types identified by anthropologists as ritual theatre. These groups are known to be outside the mainstream American theatre tradition and as such their performances constitute a cultural revolt. Robert Brustein in a book of the same title calls the new theatre "the third theatre," being closely related to primitive religions and ideally taking the form of ritual ceremony and sacrificial rites. Theodore Shank describes the new theatre as "the alternative theatre" which forms the title of his study on these theatre groups. Every term used in describing this kind of theatre rightly portrays it as being on the periphery or fringes of culture because the models influencing their practices are also peripheral to contemporary Western culture. Whether or not they will be accepted as a mainstream tradition would depend on the commitment of the groups themselves and the performance community they are seeking to create.

The ritual some contemporary theatre explores is not the raw religious culture of non-Western cultures but the essence of theatre itself as an artistic process. Even if they tried, these groups could not hope to recreate the sacred rituals of foreign cultures exactly and with similar effects. Thus Peter Brook has been frequently criticized and accused of superficial understanding of the background of indigenous African or Indian religion and culture, in such productions of his as *The Ik* or *The Mahabharata.* The best way to appreciate the basis of the intercultural performance forays of the new theatre is through what Richard Schechner believes, that in seeking to relate to the practices among what he calls "whole seeking" primitive peoples, contemporary Western society would be "undergoing not a neo-primitive movement, but a post-industrial one." In other words, his belief that the rituals of pre-industrial cultures can be abstracted and performed in a postmodern culture indicates the technique of moving theatre back to a ritual. In this context, people do not come to performances and pay to enter because the show has been advertised but because the individual spectators can dissolve into the performance as participants. A performance that is significant enough must mean something to the spectators beyond being a mere social gathering for entertainment. It must strike the communal chord which evokes for the spectators their actual realities as well as fantasies: secular and sacred, temporal and spiritual.

The practice of theatre will always depend on individual cultural conventions invented, re-invented, or modified in the process of cultural and economic development. The postmodern ideology of ritual in theatre cannot be the same as in preliterate and traditional societies. Nonetheless, behind the postmodern concept is the enduring and communal idea of theatre from earliest times, an artistic form touched by the secular and sacred concerns of life and reflecting imaginative creative processes and the actualities of life, all of which go to enhance its aesthetic or pleasurable quality. To recognize this is to appreciate the continuity of the basic condition of ritual in theatre from primitive to postmodern times.

There can be no useful purpose served in theatre practice and criticism by creating an artificial concept barrier between the so-called primitive and contemporary postmodern ritual essence of theatre, using a narrow sacred concept intended merely to dichotomize the art into its primitive and modern forms. The danger here is that theatre scholars and practitioners may think they have clearly understood the concept of theatre in traditional non-Western societies, when they actually need to do more research in it in order to understand theatre better, and ultimately enrich its practice. Ritual in theatre as a narrow ceremonial sacred concept is a dead end for the criticism and practice of theatre. It is a rigid imposition which must be abandoned for the more creative concept that transcends this narrow path and incorporates the concepts of secular and sacred ritual which theatre as performance embodies. In the words of T. S. Eliot, in his *Four Quartets*:

> We shall not cease from exploration
> And the end of all our exploring
> Will be to arrive where we started
> And know the place for the first time.

Our exploration of the condition of ritual in theatre, even in this postmodern phase of the art, would necessarily take us back to the distant past when community and cosmos merged. Having arrived where the journey into the theatre began, we do not hope to recognize our starting point so easily because much of the artistic landscape would have changed over time. That we would ''know the place for the first time'' explains the phenomenon of the postmodern theatre practice and its efforts to re-establish the concept of ritual in theatre. Through its intercultural research on the earliest traditions of theatre, I believe that ritual in its sacred and secular emphasis or conventions is the major link in the understanding of the past and present traditions of theatre.

WORKS CITED

Amankulor, J.N. ''Odo: The Mass Return of the Masked Dead Among the Nsukka-Igbo.'' *The Drama Review* 26, 4 (1982): 46-58.

Bentley, Eric. *The Theatre of Commitment*. New York: Atheneum, 1967.

Brockett, Oscar G. *History of the Theatre*. Boston: Allyn and Bacon, Inc., 1974.

Brustein, Robert. *The Third Theatre*. New York: Simon and Schuster, 1969.

Burns, Elizabeth. *Theatricality*. New York: Harper and Row, 1973

Cohen, Hilary Ursula. *Ritual and Theatre: An Examination of Performance Forms in the Contemporary American Theatre*. The University of Michigan, Ph.D. Dissertation, 1980.

Delano, Isaac. *The Soul of Nigeria.* London: T. Werner Laurie Ltd., 1937.

Graham-White, Anthony. "Ritual in Contemporary Theatre and Criticism." *Educational Theatre Journal* 28 (1976): 318-324

Grimes, Ronald L. *Beginnings in Ritual Studies.* Washington, D.C.: University Press of America, 1982.

Klapp, Orrin E. *Ritual and Cult: A Sociological Interpretation.* Washington, D.C.: Public Affairs Press, 1956.

McAloon, John J., ed. *Rite, Drama, Festival, Spectacle.* Philadelphia: Institute for the Study of Human Issues, 1984.

Schechner, Richard. *Essays on Performance Theory 1970-1976.* New York: Drama Book Specialists (Publishers), 1977.

Shank, Theodore. *American Alternative Theatre.* New York: Grove Press, 1982.

Turner, Victor W. *From Ritual to Theatre: The Human Seriousness of Play.* New York: PAJ Publications, 1982.

_____. *Schism and Continuity in an African Society.* Manchester: Manchester University Press, 1957.

Culture is the Body

Tadashi Suzuki

THE MAIN PURPOSE OF MY METHOD is to uncover and bring to the surface the physically perceptive sensibility which actors had originally, before the theatre acquired its various codified performing styles, and to heighten their innate expressive abilities. I first began to think of the method when I was trying to search for ways to examine the differences in physical perception among different peoples, such as are found while the actors on stage just stand still, or have an impulse, take some action. I wished to integrate these differences into something we humans could share as a common property, beyond all differences in race and nationality.

First of all, I felt the necessity of inspecting our human orientation, in sensibility or feeling, toward the ground or floor—the attraction for the ground which the lower half of the body feels. I extracted some basic ways of using the body as perceiving various nuances of feeling, and then arranging them to formulate my method.

Technically speaking, my method consists of training to learn to speak powerfully and with clear articulation, and also to learn to make the whole body *speak*, even when one keeps silent. It is thus that actors can learn the best way to exist on the stage. By applying this method, I want to make it possible for actors to develop their ability of physical expression and also to nourish a tenacity of concentration.

In short, this training is, so to speak, a grammar necessary to materialize the theatre that is in my mind. However, it is desirable that this "grammar" should be assimilated into the body as a second instinct, just as you cannot enjoy a lively conversation as long as you are always conscious of grammar in speaking. These techniques should be mastered, studied, until they serve as an "operational hypothesis," so that the actors may truly feel themselves "fictional" on stage. For actors to realize the images they themselves pursue, they will have to develop at least this basic physical sensibility.

* * *

In my opinion, a "cultured" society is one where the perceptive and expressive abilities of the human body are used to the full; where they provide the basic means of communication. A civilized country is not always a "cultured" society.

It is true that civilization originated in connection with the functions of the human body; it may be interpreted as the expansion of basic functions of the human body or the extension of the physical faculties—of the eyes, ears, tongue, the hands and feet. For example, the invention of such devices as the telescope and microscope is a result of human aspiration and endeavor to *see more*, radicalizing the faculty of sight. The accumulated effect of such endeavors is civilization—the product of the expansion and extension of physical faculties.

What we have to consider, then, is the kind of energy required to materialize such aspirations. That leads us to think about modernization. A criterion some sociologists in the United States apply to distinguish between modernized and pre-modernized societies is the ratio of animal-energy to non-animal-energy. Animal energy here refers to the physical energy supplied by human beings, horses or cattle, etc.; while non-animal-energy refers to electric power, nuclear power and the like. One way of showing whether a country is modernized is to calculate how much non-animal-energy is used. Roughly speaking, in African and Near Eastern countries, for example, the ratio of animal-energy used is very high, compared with such countries as the United States or Japan, where energy derived from oil, electricity, nuclear power is used in all processes of production.

If we apply this thinking to the theatre, we notice that most contemporary theatre is "modernized"; non-animal-energy is fully utilized. Lighting is done through electricity. Elevators and revolving stages are operated by electrical energy. The building of the theatre itself is the end-

242

product of a variety of industrial activities from the concrete foundation to the props and scenery.

On the contrary, the Japanese Noh theatre is a surviving example of pre-modern theatre in which almost no non-animal-energy is used. Take music for example. In the modern theatre, it is recorded and reproduced through amplifiers and loud-speakers, whereas the voices of the dancer-actor and the chorus and the sound of the instruments played on stage in the Noh theatre are conveyed *directly* to the audience. Costumes and masks for Noh plays are made by hand, and the stage itself is built based on traditional principles of carpentry. Although electricity is used for lighting nowadays (which I still object to—in the old days it used to be done by candles and tapers), it is limited to the minimum, never like the elaborate and colorful lighting of the "modern" theatre. Noh theatre is pervaded by the spirit of creating something out of human skill and effort. So much so that the Noh can be said to be the epitome of pre-modern theatre! It is a creation of animal-energy.

As the theatre, either in Europe or in Japan, has kept up with the times and has come to use non-animal-energy in every facet of its activities, one of the resulting evils is that the faculties of the human body and physical sensibility have been overspecialized to the point of separation. Just as civilization has specialized the job of the eyes and created the microscope, modernization has "dismembered" our physical faculties from our essential selves.

What I am striving to do is to restore the wholeness of the human body in the theatrical context, not simply by going back to such traditional theatrical forms as Noh and Kabuki; but by employing their unique virtues, to create something transcending current practice in the modern theatre.

We need to bring together the physical functions once "dismembered"; to regain the perceptive and expressive abilities and powers of the human body. In doing so, we can maintain culture within civilization.

In my method of training actors, I place special emphasis on the feet, because I believe that consciousness of the body's communication with the ground leads to a great awareness of all the physical junctions of the body.

* * *

A basic part of my method of training involves actors stomping on the floor for a certain period of time to rhythmic music, or rather, walking around fiercely beating the floor with the feet in a semi-squatting posture. Then, the moment the music stops, the actors relax their bodies totally, falling on the floor. They lie completely still and quiet. After a while, music starts again, but this time it must be slow and smooth. In accordance with the change in the music, they slowly rise to their feet in any way they like, eventually standing upright, back in a natural posture. This training consists of a pair of contrasting movements, that is to say, the dynamic and static (motion and rest), in other words, emission and repression of physical power. The purpose of this training is to develop concentration on the body through controlling the breathing.

The essential point of the first half of this training is to keep stomping with a constant force, without swaying the upper half of the body. If the actor does not concentrate his consciousness on his feet, legs and hips which must be well-disciplined, it is impossible for him to continue to stomp consistently, however energetic he may be. Moreover, without the spiritual power and will to control his breathing, the upper half of his body gradually begins to sway and then the rhythm of the stomping becomes irregular. If you beat the floor with your feet, the force naturally influences the upper half of the body to make it sway. As I get actors to stomp as forcefully as possible, a reaction rises upwards so the more strongly they stomp the more the upper half of their body sways. If they try to minimize the sway, they have to repress the force with their hips. They have to stomp while always being aware of the relationship between upper and lower halves of the body which are pivoted together at the hips.

Of course, emphasizing the fact that the construction of the human body and the balance of the forces which support it are centered on the pelvic region is not thinking unique to my method; but almost all the performing arts invariably use such thinking. Only, I believe it is specific to my training that first of all the actors are made to feel conscious of this by stomping and beating the ground with their feet. This is derived from my belief that the basic physical sensibility of any stage actor depends on his feet. In our daily life, we tend to disregard the importance of the feet. It is necessary for us to be aware of the fact that the human body makes contact with the ground through the feet, that the ground and the human body are inseparable, as the latter is, in fact, part of the former, meaning that when we die we return to the earth—to make the body, which usually functions unconscious of its relationship, aware of this fact by creating a strong sense of impact through the beating of the ground with the feet.

This idea of mine has often been said to be quite Japanese, but it is not. Even in classical European ballet in which the dancers seem to aim at jumping from the ground to soar through the air, the basic physical sensibility consists of a feeling of affinity to the ground.

* * *

Again in traditional Japanese theatrical forms, such as Noh and Kabuki,

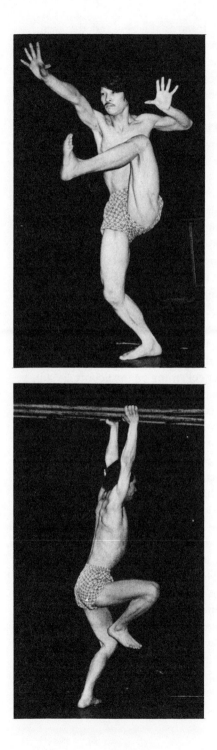
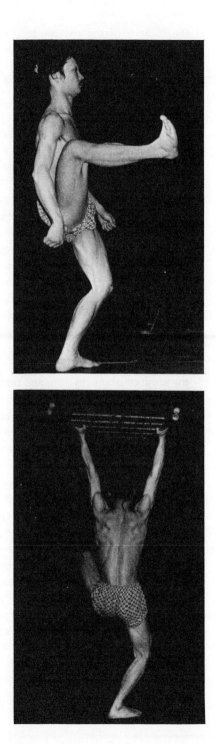

the balance of the two vectors leading towards the sky and the earth, towards the heights and the depths, has been very important in physical expression. Only, in the traditional Japanese theatrical forms, these two forces with vectors contrary to each other meet at the pelvic region, and the energy derived from this tends to radiate horizontally. Therefore, the higher the upper half of the body tries to go, the lower the lower half of the body tries to sink to balance this movement. The feeling that the feet are planted firmly on the ground is, thus, increased. This is symbolized in such movements as sliding steps (*Suri-ashi*) or stomping (*Ashi-byoshi*) which express the affinity with the earth.

The late Shinobu Origuchi, a prominent Japanese anthropologist and man of letters, said that when examining Japanese performing arts, he found that the performers invariably stomp at some part of the performance and that the appearing on the stage in itself signifies the treading down of evil spirits under the ground; the stomping is called *Hembai*. Seen from this point of view, the sliding steps (*Suri-ashi*) in Noh plays can be considered as preparatory movement to set off the stomping. According to Origuchi, the essence of traditional Japanese dancing is wandering around the stage, which originally signified sanctifying the place by treading down the evil spirits. The series of movements in my training consists of two parts—first, straining the whole body, concentrating the forces at the hips, stomping to the same constant rhythm; and then, after collapsing on the floor to lie still, getting up again to music like a marionette, by extending a calm strength throughout the body. All is achieved by completely changing the quality of what we might call the raw, unconcentrated body of everyday life. That is why many beginners feel that they are just forced to move mechanically and that the delicate nuances of their own bodies disappear. According to my own experience in giving this training, actors in the United States, who are close to realistic acting, tend to feel like that. Even though they begin stomping forcefully and seriously, they soon lose their concentration and their bodies "loosen." There are some people who watch this and consider my training particularly Japanese; who say that the training is unsuitable for American actors because their legs are long compared with those of the Japanese actors. However, it has nothing to do with the length of the legs or the stamina, but with the discovery of an inner physical sensibility or with the recognition of an inner and profound memory innate to the human body. In other words, it is to do with the ability to uncover this profound physical sensibility and to give it full play. Therefore, it is not necessarily only Japanese actors who are likely to assimilate the aim of my training into their body. Whether in Europe or in Japan, stomping or beating the ground with the feet is a universal physical movement necessary for us to become highly conscious of our own body or to create a "fictional" space, which might also be called a ritualistic space, where we can achieve a personal metamorphosis.

The stomping or beating the floor with the feet originates in ancient Japanese rituals.

In his "Six Lectures on the History of Traditional Japanese Performing Arts" Origuchi mentions the Opening Ritual of the Heavenly Stone Wall in the Japanese Creation Myth as the origin of the Sacred Dance (*Kagura*), and talks about the rhythmical dancing to calm down the spirits, which a goddess named Ameno-Uzumeno-Mikoto danced, turning over a wooden tub and stomping on it and striking it with the end of a stick. He says:

> Perhaps the tub symbolized the earth. The goddess stomped on it and struck it with a stick while making loud noises; actions supposed to wake up and bring out the soul or spirit that was believed to be under the tub, whether sleeping or hiding, in order to send it to the unseen sacred body of the god nearby.

What he means to say is that the purpose of the action of stomping and striking is not necessarily to tread down or suppress evil enemies but to arouse their energy in order to use it to activate human life. As a result, the same effect as of exorcism is brought about, for by acquiring the spirit of the evil it is possible to overcome it. The fact that Noh and Kabuki actors often stomp on the stage floor can be regarded as a practice related to this old tradition.

Thus the ancient Japanese stages were built on graves or mounds where the souls of the dead were considered to dwell. This has led to the custom that even now people hollow out the ground or bury a pot before building a Noh stage over it. That is not only for the sake of technical effectiveness—that the hollow ground makes the sound of stomping resound better—but it is a procedure to create an illusion that the actor can conjure up earth spirits or the spirits of ancestors who have returned to the earth, in order to acquire their energy. The resonance enforces the physical feeling of responding to the spirits. Even today such an illusion is necessary for actors on stage. For, the illusion that the energy of the spirits can be felt through the feet to activate our own bodies is a most natural and valuable illusion for human beings. Noh is well blessed because it has continued to cherish this idea right up to the present. Graves and mounds can be regarded as wombs from which we have been born. In that sense the earth is a "Mother" herself. Actors can undertake their roles on the premise that they are connected with all humanity integrating individuals.

Perhaps it is not the upper half but the lower half of our body through which the physical sensibility common to all races is most consciously expressed; to be more specific, the feet. The feet are the last remaining part of the human body which has kept, literally, in touch with the earth, the very supporting base of all human activities.

(Compiled and translated by Kazuko Matsuoka)

Cultural Nationalism

and the Cross-Cultural Product

Chidananda Dasgupta

INDIA'S KNEE-JERK REACTIONS to Peter Brook's *Mahabharata* film have been plentiful, many of them dismissive. Now that the film has done the rounds of the major cities, perhaps it is time to reflect a bit more on it. The first question that comes to mind in the context of the dismissive criticism is over the very idea of cross-cultural art; is it by nature contemptible or is there any valid possibility to it? Clearly, it is impossible for people of one culture to apprehend another totally in the terms of the first; perforce, an Indian audience will understand a Japanese film and an American audience a Kathakali performance in its own way. That understanding, misunderstanding, if you like, is bound to be absorbed and reflected within the culture of the receiver—even the most well informed. Even within India, one region has serious problems in the cultural product of others. Magnificent Naga dances often provoke laughter among audiences from the plains. Is that essentially wrong, corruptive of both? Should cultures, therefore, be hermetically sealed off except where the outsider can become an insider through a lifelong effort?

But it can equally well be argued that one lifetime is not enough to get to the heart of another culture; it takes generations to do so. What happens then to the creative energies generated by the inevitable contact between cultures in a shrinking world? The fact is that cross-cultural products are inevitable and cannot await anyone's pleasure, including that of the country from which borrowings are made. Hybridization has been, and remains, an essential part of the flow of cultures. We in India are constantly adapting Western films and plays into our languages, both in the elite and popular theatre and cinema. Indian culture today is the product of admixtures with Persians, Greeks, Shakas, Hunas, Mongols, Caucasians, with the Indus Valley people, the Aryans, and the tribals. What is hybrid in one century often represents the essence of purity in another.

What is more, the *Mahabharata* takes us back to a time when the nation-state of today was unknown. Borders shifted with the fortunes of frequent battle; borrowings and commonalities were plentiful. To attack another king's territory was a duty, a part of *Kshatradharma*. What we tend to see as a unique tradition today, such as the Hindu pantheon, was actually shared with the Greeks and large sections of West Asia. Shiva and Dionysius have uncanny similarities, and so have Krishna and Achilles; one of the names of the terrible Sumerian Goddess Innanna was Kali; the worship of Durga corresponds with harvest festivals across vast transnational territories and harks back to the days of matrilineal society dominated by the worship of the Great Goddess. The ancient Indian war chariot was the same as those used in Assyria, for instance. Indeed, the type shown in Brook's *Mahabharata* is very like the Hittite variety seen on Carchemish bas reliefs of the 12th-8th century B.C., very close to the period generally ascribed to the Kurukshetra war. Northwestern India of the first millennium B.C. was a polyglot mixture of races with varying physiognomies and many hues of complexion. It is in the nature of nation-state chauvinism today to ignore these past commonalities and see its own tradition as a uniquely national product uncontaminated by *mlechchas* and *Yavanas* and people across what was regarded as *Kalapani* until a few decades ago.

So the only valid way to judge a cross-cultural product like the Brook film is by its internal logic rather than the exactness of its correspondence, literal or otherwise, to our epic. As for its "essence," how many Indians understand it and how many understand it in even roughly the same way? The popular view of the *Mahabharata* reflected in B. R. Chopra's television series on Doordarshan is of a battle between good and evil. This is very far removed from the actual text which is laden with contradictions and ambiguities that in fact make it the great and universal work it is. All it needs to respond honestly to a foreigner's view of the epic is to see it with an open mind and to make allowance for differences of cultural perception.

This is easier said than done. Not so curiously, even the elite commentators seem to find it easier to accept Caucasians as opposed to Africans. Many find it impossible to see the remarkable individuality and character in Kunti, played with intensity and assurance by Miriam Goldschmidt— whose face is like a cubist painting—just because she is black. Similarly, the tall ascetic agelessness of Sotiqui Kouyate as Bhishma is unacceptable in its blackness. They do not object that Krishna and Arjuna, who are both described as black in the text, are played here by Caucasians.

There are many extremely unusual elements in Brook's film; the variety of races is only one of them. Take for instance the use of Rabindrasangeet. The opening scene has the song ''Antara mama bikasita karo, antaratara hay.'' It is the individual's prayer to the being within to open the mind, to make it pure and to illuminate it. In my childhood in Brahmo society, it was always sung on childrens' birthdays. It is the plain Jane among Tagore songs. To hear it at the opening of the *Mahabharata* is, to say the least, startling. But usually it is sung at a sprightly pace with a harmonium or cottage organ accompaniment by someone in the family with a very ordinary voice. Here it is almost unrecognizable, sung to an extremely slow tempo, making it almost into a chant. Sharmila Roy's limpid voice renders it with an exceptional purity and steadiness.

As the keynote to a story of massive destruction informed by a simultaneous quest for the truth of what is right or wrong, the song is deeply moving. I tried hard to forget the meaning of the words and to judge it as pure sound and it still seemed very profound in its impact as the camera panned across the future scene of disaster to be brought about by a throw of the dice. The song is later picked up on the *esraj* as the theme tune and is brought back in Roy's voice as the exile of the Pandavas is pronounced. It was impossible not to be struck by the sense of purification through suffering suggested by the words. The Rabindrasangeet in slow tempo had become a little like an Indian equivalent to the Gregorian chant. A similar effect is achieved at the end of the war when Roy sings the Upanishadic verse *Srinvantu Vishwe Amiritasya Putrat,* a lofty call to humanity by one who has seen the luminous being who lies beyond all darkness. Both the songs, at the beginning and at the end, underscore a spiritual quest in strange contrast to a war of total destruction around which the narrative is constructed. Toshi Tsuchitori's music does not try to enhance the effect of the visual or suggest the meaning of the particular event on screen, it is almost entirely introspective, meditative, and imbued with a sense of prayer for understanding—mostly through a gentle counterpoint.

Cinematically, the most successful aspects are the casting (if one concentrates on the sharp individuality of countenance and form), the battle scenes, and the images of Gandhari and Dhritarashtra sitting waiting for or listening to news of the war. Except in one or two cases (such as of Krishna helping the arrow into Bhishma's body—which is very Chopraesque), the battle scenes are impressive. There is both a sense of massive confrontation and of a misty past in which it is taking place. Considering that it is shot on the basis of a theatre performance, the sense of battle is remarkably well achieved.

However, the theatrical base of the film betrays itself in the grouping of characters in the other scenes. Characters are invariably huddled together, no cinematic sense of large spaces is created; dialogue never takes place between people far away from each other.

Camera angles are limited by the same factor. For instance, the scene of Yudhisthira's dialogue with Dharma at the pond after the death of his brothers cries out for a view from above, which could have been spectacular. In the epic, Nakula climbs a tall tree to spot water in the area; so a top shot is literally indicated. Similarly, a low angle shot from the point of view of Dharma who is in the water is also avoided. The eye-level shot predominates throughout the film.

One of the things that helps the film's sense of spiritual quest is the acting of Ryszard Cieslak in the role of Yudhisthira and particularly the use of his eyes, which have great depth. His quiet bearing contrasts vividly with Duryodhana's restlessness. Duryodhana is the body and Yudhisthira is the spirit, as it were. But Duryodhana is by no means all evil, just as no character in the *Mahabharata* is wholly good. He is wholly a prince, an embodiment of Kshatriya desire for wealth and power. He fights for them honorably, will not strike a fallen enemy without arms, always observes the rules of warfare. He has not time for the introspection that is Yudhisthira's life. Both actors convey the contrast to perfection.

Much has been made of the absence of Bidura whose moralizing commentary is an important part of the text. But this does not seem all that important in the style and content of Brook's presentation. The ambiguity of the epic is amply reflected without such commentary. Is Krishna God or man? Brook is as evasive on this as Ganesha who says in answer to young Janamejaya's question, "One can never be sure." The epic itself is not sure, no matter how much B. R. Chopra has tried to bend it. If Krishna is God, how is it that he can see some of the coming events but not others as the battle progresses? How can Gandhari curse him with the destruction of his own clan and an ignominious death? Why should his brother Balarama go against him and support the Kaurava claim to the throne? Most of all, why does he try to save the women of his clan by sending Arjuna to escort them from Dwarka? This episode is barely described by Krishna and not shown.

To my mind, it is the most serious omission, because in the epic itself it makes Krishna a protagonist in the drama and provides the biggest contradiction to his claim to divinity, which, as we know, is the creation of Brahamanical interpolators. The destruction of the Yadavas also gives a great sense of the end of an era and raises the question: what did Krishna gain by helping the Pandavas to regain their kingdom at the cost of *dharma* and of the annihilation of their world? In this unanswered question may lie the key to the historical meaning of the *Mahabharata*. Even if Brook has stuck mainly to the Kshatriya war story (as did the first 24,000 verse version of the epic, called *Jaya*), the end of the Yadavas should have been a part of his scheme. More than Yudhisthira's ridiculous climb (up a rope ladder) to heaven, it is the self-destruction of the Yadavas, Arjuna's loss of his heroic power, and the death of Krishna by an arrow struck in his heel (like Achilles) that spells the end of the *Mahabharata* war. Did Krishna, referred to as Devakiputra in the *Chhandogyopanished,* where his name is first mentioned in Indian tradition (he is never described as his father's son but as his mother's), actually lead the change from matrilineal, Goddess-worshipping, woman-dominated, polyandrous society to the establishment of patriarchy? He himself had 108 wives and 16,000 playgirls—the archetypal male, the exact opposite of the woman-dominated man in a polyandrous, Goddess-worshipping matrilineal society whose traces we see in Draupadi, in Kunti's premarital pregnancy, and in Gandhari's authoritative spirit, undaunted by Krishna's divinity. Obviously, this is too gray an area, fraught with modern interpretative controversy, for Brook and Carrière to enter. They are content to take the stunning story of the *Mahabharata* as it exists today, with all its interpolations and consequent contradictions, and to present it without over-emphasizing its miraculous or divine aspects, maintaining its link with earthly reality as also its spiritual quest. In that effort, they have succeeded eminently.

However, the *Mahabharata* is too great to be absorbed, not to speak of being exhausted by one film. It progresses in digressions and is a vast compendium of stories. In Indian performance tradition, it is treated episodically, in great detail. Perhaps there was need for a modern, linear narrative view as well (the *Mahabharata* is not lacking in one, as its original version *Jaya* clearly shows), compressed into one whole. One hopes that many films will follow, in India as elsewhere in the world, in a wealth of different interpretations, ending the monopoly of the traditional mythological genre's kitschy hold on it.

III KINDS OF HISTORY

The Universal Solvent

Meditations on the Marriage
of
World Cultures

Frederick Turner

AS A CONNECTED BUT TURBULENT series of meditations, this essay resembles the issue itself that it addresses: the issue of interculturalism, the mutual impact and result of the unparalleled mixing that has been going on in recent years among the world's cultures. This mixing process is a classically turbulent system—perhaps the most complex of all turbulent systems, its larger social movements echoed on a diminishing heirarchy of scales down to the cultural translation problems that beset an individual as he or she invents a viable self.

Interculturalism itself comes in a bewildering variety of genres, each with its own pressing and highly ambiguous set of moral and epistemological questions. Consider this brief and incomplete list of intercultural genres: tourism, international charity, evangelism, colonial administration, anthropology, true trade (as opposed to mercantile colonialism), political and military contacts, academic consultation and exchange, artistic collaboration, artistic influence, asylum, statelessness, refugeeism, education abroad, intermarriage, and emigration.

Anyone who walks the streets or campuses of the new tier of world-cities will be struck by the fantastic combinations of races in friendship, marriage, work, and study. My son, born in America, is half British and half Chinese; he plays baseball with a Slav from Poland and an Arab from Algeria; I eat at French/Lebanese, Thai, Salvadorean, and Israeli/Chinese restaurants, buy software from emigrant South Africans, celebrate the Zoroastrian New Year with Farsi friends from Iran, and collaborate on artistic and intellectual projects with a Macedonian Yugoslav, a Greek, a Hungarian Jew, a Japanese, a Latin American, and several Germans. Yet in a strange way the place I live in does not cease at all from being Texas to the core. Cultural information not only has the property of being transferable without loss, but also of being almost infinitely super-imposable. Many cultures can occupy the same place or brain without loss; there seems to be no cultural equivalent of the Pauli Exclusion Principle, which forbids two particles from existing in the same energy state and place at the same time.

Of course any celebration of a new era of tolerance and ethnic harmony would be premature. The collapse in our century of the great empires—the Austrian, the British, the Soviet, and soon the Chinese—has left large areas of the world in a state of Balkanized tribalism, and it well may appear that we are further away than ever from the interculturalism we anticipate. The Tutsi exterminate the Hutu, the Hausa and Yoruba the Ibo. Savage tribal pogroms and the intentional starvation of whole populations are the rule along the whole sub-Saharan rim. Serbian demagogues threaten their neighbors. The Bulgarians are oppressing their Turks, the Romanians their Hungarians, the Azerbaijanis their Armenians, the Chinese their Tibetans, and several countries their Kurds. Tribal/religious wars convulse Palestine and Lebanon. Tamils and Sinhalese murder each other's children without mercy. The ethnic Russians are now so hated and feared throughout Europe and Asia that when economics and demography have eroded their power they may be in danger of racial extermination. It may even seem a decadent luxury to trouble our conscience with the problems of cultural mixing when such a foul-tempered resurgence of racism and ethnocentrism is under way.

And yet it could be argued that these horrible events are belated but inevitable consequences of world forces that will eventually lead to a more comfortably intercultural world; that such places are undergoing processes analogous to the tribal wars of dark-ages Europe or to the religious wars of the Reformation, and that in each case a Charlemagne or Metternich will emerge, speaking for a new consensus superior to local loyalties. Perhaps the great empires had held those tensions in an artificial stasis, and now they are playing themselves naturally out. In this view the eventual result of the enormous mobility of persons and information will be something like the condition of the United States or the European Common Market; or like those countries which, having once possessed colonial empires, have now had their homelands peacefully invaded by their erstwhile subjects and find that together with the inevitable stress, there is also a surge of cultural revitalization that is not unwelcome.

But this cultural palimpsest is only possible in the presence of certain overriding conditions, which we need to explore.

It is, I believe, safe to assume that a particular constellation of political characteristics in a country will generally bring about greater contacts between its peoples and those of the outside world: political freedom, to minimize the restrictions on outside contacts usually maintained by tyrannical regimes in order to protect their flock from dangerous ideas; democracy, to ensure that freedom; capitalism, to provide both the wealth and the exchange system that makes such contacts possible; and a multi-racial and multi-ethnic home population. We may even rank human societies in terms of their openness, with communist and theocratic totalitarianisms at the bottom; precapitalist authoritarian or colonial regimes next; single-race and mono-ethnic democratic societies, like Japan, next; and multi-racial democracies, like the U.S.A., highest of all in this category.

Given this classification, we have seen in recent years a series of huge political changes whose net effect has been to open many parts of the world to the influence and conversation of the rest of the human race. Consider this list of countries which have undergone major political change in the last few decades: India, Egypt, Portugal, Spain, Greece, Argentina, Brazil, Singapore, Malaysia, the Philippines, the Soviet Union, Poland, Paraguay, Czechoslovakia, and Hungary; and consider too the temporarily aborted changes in Burma and China, and the hesitant dawning of democracy in Chile. In every case the move has been upward on the scale of openness. The major failures have been colonial countries, which have often exchanged one form of tyranny for another, and ended up as closed as before. But even here there are signs of progress. The countries that have become more closed, like Iran, are significant exceptions.

In 1786 a contemporary estimate placed the human population of the world at 775,300,000, of which 741,800,000 people lived under "arbitrary governments" and only 33,500,000, or one in twenty-three, were free. Today even the most pessimistic estimates would place the free population of the world at over 1/3 of the total; the list of countries cited by organizations such as PEN and Amnesty as egregious tramplers of freedom is shortening, and one might reasonably, though optimistically, hope for a strong free majority by the end of the century.

Perhaps the most remarkable fact of the modern world is that now for the first time all the member cultures of the human race now know of each other, and have, more or less, met. There really is no human Other now. Clearly the ethnocentrism of the old Right and of political conservatism in general cannot survive the enormous influx of information from the rest of the world. Nonetheless, the issue of Otherness has not gone away, but has been either artificially revived as an ideological weapon, or displaced to other species and even to some of our more human-like machines.

The formal complexity of interculturalism has not prevented some of our bolder, and paradoxically, more conventional, intellectuals from seeking to cut the gordian knot of the problem with a sword of neo-leftist analysis. A very crude reduction of their position might go like this: the rich are bad, the poor are good. The rich got rich by exploiting the poor, and then rigging the cultural value system to justify their privileges. The same goes for nations as for individuals. Nowadays the old form of international expropriation, colonialism, has been partly replaced by a new form, whereby the bad (rich, powerful, white, male, etc.) expropriate the cultural property of the good (poor, weak, etc.). The interest and sophistication of this argument lies in the fact that at least implicitly the Left now recognizes culture as having real economic value of its own, rather than simply being a smokescreen to conceal the true, economic, facts of coercion, power, and control; for otherwise the parallel between economic exploitation and cultural appropriation would have no meaning. If culture is a good that can be stolen by the powerful, then it is good.

Despite the remarkable enlightenment of this aspect of the new leftist argument, the rest of it is more problematic. A little thought will soon show how very flawed is the main body of the "cultural expropriation" theory of interculturalism.

This theory attacks anthropologists, collectors of tribal art, tourists, Western followers of Oriental religions, white jazz enthusiasts, performance artists who use foreign traditional artistic and ritual techniques, and even male collectors of quilts and women's arts, as expropriators of the cultural goods of others. Some kind of plausibility might be constructed for such attacks. But a few further examples serve to show how flimsy is the argument. Consider Japan's success in exporting its products, including much of its material and spiritual culture, to the United States. The expropriation model, to be consistent, would imply that the United States was expropriating the cultural property of Japan. More absurd still, the enormous penetration of American music, movies, TV, soft drinks, sports activities, and consumer goods into many of the poorer Asian, African, and Latin American countries would have to be interpreted as the expropriation on a huge scale of American cultural property by Third World cultural colonists.

Ah, but that's different, the determined neo-Leninist might say. But how is it different? Every answer leads to greater and greater betrayals of socialist articles of faith, some of them shared by all people of good will. Is it that the poor benighted natives (or poor benighted Americans) are in an unequal cultural contest and ought to be protected for their own good from our (Japan's) potent and corrupting forms of cultural firewater? Beside being rather condescending, this argument is virtually identical to that of the supporters of apartheid in South Africa. Or is it that the terms of the exchange are unfair?—that the Third World does not get a fair price for its cultural goods, while we gouge them for ours? This argument assumes either that there is some ultimate authority that decides which cultural goods are more valuable, ours or theirs, and does not trust either our valuation of relative values or theirs; or that there might be such a thing as *fair* trade (and thus the possibility of a free market, entrepreneurism, and the whole capitalist ensemble). And if we use the Japan-U.S. example, it is the cheapness, not the dearness, of Japanese goods that is the problem. When it comes down to it, the only difference between being culturally expropriated and conducting cultural imperialism is who we thought in the first place were the good guys and the bad guys.

The whole argument is based on a misleading analogy between cultural goods and industrial goods; which in turn is based on ignorance of the difference between information and matter. If matter is transferred to another location it ceases to exist at its first location. Moreover, it takes work to make the transfer, and if that work is paid for out of the matter that is being transferred, one ends up with less matter at the point of arrival than at the point of origin. A steamship gets to its destination lighter than when it left its home port. However, if information is transferred, it not only remains where it started, but it is not necessarily diminished by its travels. The sender of information by radio does not cease to know what she knew when she sent it off in the message; and the message can be made redundant enough to include an arbitrarily diminishing amount of error.

In the mysterious realm of physics which deals with the thermodynamics of information, the energy cost to a computational system—that is, a system which does work by creating and/or transferring information—is in theory incurred only when it comes time to destroy the excess information that has built up in the system. Thus one could in theory design a process for mass-producing pieces of information, whose only expense would be erasing the tape afterwards. If information is a kind of goods, then it is one which costs the maker nothing to make but which obliges its consumer to find an expensive waste-disposal system for the purchase once it is used. The logic and justice of such a transaction are almost unknown to contemporary economics, and the laws of intellectual property lag woefully behind the astonishing expansion of information-space that is now taking place in the world.

Yet do we not recognize, in these goods which it costs virtually nothing to buy but which clutter up the house and alarm environmentalists when we try to dispose of them, an increasing proportion of our own property? And if we are cultural workers, do we not recognize—though unwillingly, because it concedes how much fun our work is—those goods we create but cost us nothing to do so? And is not cultural property much more the kind that costs nothing to make or buy, that does not decay but is hard to get rid of, than the old kind, dear to Marxists and capitalists alike, that costs the groaning labor of workers to produce, which they lose by giving to us and must be compensated for, and which wears out only too swiftly as we consume it?

It is the ''expropriators'' of cultural goods, then, not their creators, that are the ones who are exploited. And thus the expropriation explanation collapses in absurdity.

But this meditation has already generated issues—or created information!—which it would be interesting to pursue. For instance, if it costs cultural creators nothing to produce their goods, why should they be paid? Yet if they were not paid, we would not have cultural producers, which would be a pity; even artists have to eat. Somehow there must be a medium and method of exchange between cultural goods and the material goods which, as we say, keep body and soul together.

Another problem: if it is the audience for cultural goods that is doing the work—erasing the tape—then shouldn't they, too, be paid? Do we not already pay them, in fact, by subsidizing out of the public purse the admission fees the public pays to go to the museum, the symphony, the university, the theatre? And if we pay both cultural producers and cultural consumers, who foots the bill? Can money itself, in such an economy, ''grow on trees'' the way information clearly can? But can we retain our traditional respect for artists and other cultural producers if we pay them *despite* the fact that, as artists (rather than draughtsmen, clerks, or athletes) they do no work; and that we pay audiences to go and see them, *and to selectively forget what they have seen and heard?* Can we replace the matter-based, or industrially-based, model of respect with another more suited to the age that is coming? Obviously artists do indeed do something like what we used to call work, but the many jokes and tragic stories about working parents who do not want their children to grow up to be layabout artists also have a grain of truth.

And again: are these economic paradoxes problems only for the cultural and information economies? Matter indeed cannot be transferred without cost; but to what extent are we actually buying matter when we buy as solid a thing as a car or a washing machine? In fact, increasingly, we're buying a very complicated and effective piece of information. The matter doesn't matter: some of the steel in my car was actually once a washing machine, and before that, another car. When my car no longer holds its information, I may pay someone to tow it away. What form—what information—the factory put into the matter is what counts. I wouldn't want or pay for a lump of steel; what I buy is the information the factory put into the steel; information increasingly transferred by robot machines without human labor. Steel itself is a kind of information imposed by atomic and crystalline structure upon neurons, protons, and electrons. Traditional economics still depends on the need for information to be embodied in, and thus tagged by, the matter of its incarnation; just as traditional copyright law still depends on the physical means of publication. The recent uproar over the importation from Japan of cheap high-quality digital tape recording machines shows that we have almost reached the limits of the old kind of economics, and the old kind of thinking, altogether.

By "old" I do not mean here ancient and pre-industrial, but rather pertaining to the conventional economic wisdom of modern societies. In fact we may have to resort to the thoughtways of traditional or folk societies, in combination with new imaginative constructs from the age of information, to be able to make sense of the new economics. Much of the riches of an ancient person was what she had in her head, as information; and as the new age develops, much of our riches will be in the form of totally intangible information contained in, but not confinable to, our cybernetic mental prostheses. As I write it, this essay becomes an immaterial process constituted by the interaction between my nervous system as I watch the screen of the word-processor, and a set of electromagnetic relations in its random access memory. But I still think of it as a text on paper, or at least as a picture of one. My son spurns the electric racing cars that I, as a boy, would have coveted, and prefers the meaningful pattern of electric charges embedded in the silicon of a computer video game. The computer game itself is not a picture of anything that ever was, in the modern sense of "thing." In a sense, my son is a more tribal person than I am, even though I have had access through traditional humane learning to the ancient tribal sources of non-materialist "oeconomics."

We may even, as we evolve toward an economics more like that of traditional societies than like that of our recent modern past, come to a wiser appreciation of their ethics—their amazing tolerance of the idea that persons can be a form of property, for instance, or their unquestioning acceptance of what we would regard as blatant inequality. If true riches are within; if nobody can copyright a great poem because everybody knows it by heart; if the chief value that society possesses is the information—the skills of beauty, weaving, prophecy, storytelling—embodied in the limbs and nervous systems of its Helens, its Cassandras, and its Penelopes; then economic injustice and human slavery largely disappear as ethical issues. Though we shall never bring back these abuses, for consciousness has a ratchet called memory, we are entering a time when the ethical economy itself is going to look very different and much of our moral outrage and enthusiasm rather quaint.

Already the West is getting tired of mere consumer goods, of commodities. On our urban beltways we can now find business establishments that rent storage space so that we can get rid of our possessions without ceasing to possess them. Possession is becoming very abstract. Our best possessions are empty space and time. We are becoming a "service economy" rather than a manufacturing economy. Strangely, it is the old critics of capitalist materialism that now chiefly complain about the change: but perhaps their complaints are inconsistent. Are we not becoming at last literally less materialistic? Should we not prefer service to things? The Japanese themselves, the heroes of manufacturing, are now rushing to export their manufacturing function to the little dragons of the Pacific rim; the socialist bloc has gone broke trying to hang on to a manufacturing economy. The paradoxes do not stop here: having persuaded the rest of the world to become harried producers and consumers of material goods, we may in a generation or two have so transformed ourselves by our information technology that we will have become the wise old sages, like Yoda in *Star Wars*, counseling brash young Asians on the mysterious ways of spiritual enlightenment and the traditional wisdom of the body electric.

We would seem to be approaching a time when cultural goods are going to be the only kind there are, and material, matter itself, will have dissolved into a brilliant and pliable haze of interpenetrating probability-domains. The requirements and luxuries of physical existence, according to this vision, will be supplied by self-reproducing, self-programming, and independently-foraging Von Neumann machines, nanotechnological miniature factories invisible to the naked eye—much like what ancient cultures and classical civilizations called spirits, genii loci, kamis, naiads, dryads, angels, nymphs, dakkinis, demons, gremlins. Nature is already full of such entities: the bacteria which ferment our cheeses, the DNA of plants and animals—but they are the results of evolution unassisted by conscious awareness. We ourselves, most potent of wood-demons, came about when our own consciousness, expressed and mediated by our kinship rules and mating rituals, took a hand in evolution. Now we have begun to extend that conscious hand to the evolution of the rest of nature.

Not that our productive processes and the goods that result from them will be utterly unconstrained by the limitations of physical existence. Our manufactures will not ever be of the pure stuff of intention. Nature has already invested an enormous stake in the existing structures of space-time, energy, matter, and life, and we can transform nothing but by calling upon nature's own processes of change. The "thinginess" of designed things will not disappear—their capacity to interact with each other in ways unexpected to their designers, the entailment of uninvited characteristics along with those demanded by their builders. There will still be in all objects of value a necessary inclusion of elements that are unknown and intended —the baser but more basic qualities—together with those higher but more abstract elements that are both intelligible and willed, and a tangled hierarchy of intermediate properties in between. Only thus will the world, after all, have any richness or interest, either in the economic or poetic senses of those words. A purely intended thing is as boring as the most pointless lump of matter. It is the tragi-comic realm in between that is interesting and valuable.

The difference will be that we will have overcome the recalcitrance of things left to themselves, and will now be confronted with a different sort of resistance: that offered by the feedback system composed of the matter itself *together with* our very attempts to mold it. Another way of putting this is to say, using the ancient Indo-European words for mother and father (matter and pattern) that the moment matter is totally reduced to pattern, we realize that pattern, when it includes knowledge of itself, has all the stubborn mystery and intractability of matter, and is what we really meant by "matter" all along. This further recalcitrance, the recalcitrance of the making process itself, will be insuperable, for it involves our own actions and decisions. It also ensures that the world will not cease to be surprising and difficult. However, in economic terms the shift from the one to the other will have large consequences. We may even perceive that shift as in part a shift *back*, to archaic kinds of valuation, and to human relationships based on them that resemble those of the distant past.

What kind of world economy will come out of the changes I am describing? Perhaps the closest analogy might be the Homeric economy, the world of gift-giving, hospitality, the ritualization of obligation, sacrifice, deed as performance, and bardic commemoration of deeds, that we find in the *Odyssey* and the *Iliad*. Such an economy is the only kind that makes sense when matter is no longer a reliable numerical index of value. That ancient world was one explicitly conceived as densely populated with intention, spirits, local dieties, and so on. The value of a sword or shield was the weight of story, of software, that it bore—the density of information, of spirit, embodied in Achilles' sevenfold shield is both what makes it a good shield and what identifies it as of divine make. Odysseus' story, the tale he brings back from the sack of Troy, is worth to the Phaeaceans a shipload of treasure; and those treasures themselves are worth only the stories stamped and embedded in them. Homer's own living is his tale.

But there is no copy-protection on this story-information. Thus no system of contracts, patent and copyright laws, bills of sale, and specie-backed currency, can ensure an orderly and just disposal of such goods if they are conceived of as material commodities. The only thing that cannot be copied in Homer's story is the power and immediacy of his own performance of it, his personal presence, that which cannot be measured as a commodity—his gift, as we say.

Homer's world is an economy of sacrifices, performance, and gifts; the greatest profit consists in the greatest sacrifice, the act or deed is not just the legal sign but the reality, the limits of this economy are not how *much* one is prepared to give in exchange for what one wants, but how *little*. It is the predatory givers of that world, the masters of the potlatch and the holocaust (in the old sense) that are the greatest dangers, not, as in the world of mercantile colonialism and early capitalism, the predatory takers. To take Troy, Agamemnon must first have given his own daughter Iphigenia. Beware of the Greeks when they come bearing gifts, especially Trojan Horses. According to an ancient etymology the gift (in English) may also be poison, "das Gift" (in German); the rhinegold is the kiss of death. Life is the performance, and thus the death, of the hero.

Already in our own time it is the entertainers—the pop singers, filmstars, sports heroes who create cultural information—that are the highest-status members of society, and often the richest. One year Paul McCartney was the richest person in England after the Queen. Ancient princes might well be described as the great public entertainers of their times, the sacrificial superstars whose exploits formed the basis of the stories that gave meaning to life. Agamemnon steps upon the magic carpet woven by Queen Clytemnestra, and his blood nourishes a cycle of stories—concentrated information—that define the wealth of the archaic Greek economy. John Lennon dies for our sins. We elect an actor for our king and watch while he is resurrected from the wound of the assassin's bullet; and so according to the logic of mythology, a dead king is reborn and the pollution of his death in Dallas is purified. What act or death will expiate the sacrifice of that other priest/victim, whose name was King?

But our theme was interculturalism; and though in our refutation of the expropriation theory of cross-cultural contact we discovered a way of making prophecies about the economy of the future, the task remains to apply that discovery to the original topic. How might the Homeric/cybernetic economy work *between* cultures, rather than within one? In Homer, if the hero comes across a tribe that is sufficiently barbarous as to be no part of the Greek world, the only possible relation he can have with it is as its food or indeed as its proto-colonialist expropriator: consider Odysseus' encounters with the Laistrygonians and the Cyclopes. For us, the whole world is as a Hellenized Mediterranean. What universal solvents will ensure the liquidity and translatability of cultural value? What new problems and dangers will be spawned by our very success? How do we preserve the cultural differences that we value?

The first of these questions, about universal solvents, requires some explanation. The human mind, and human culture in general, has admirable powers of compartmentalization. As any teacher knows who has experienced the coexistence in a student's mind of contradictory information (for instance, astronomical, biological, and geological book-learning together with a belief in the literal Biblical account of creation), "cut and dried" knowledge can leave the mind virtually unscathed. Contradictions do not even consciously arise; such knowledge has its own cocoon of insulation. To change the metaphor, the mixing of colors, or the metabolism of a ferment, or chemical reactions, or cookery, cannot take place without a liquid medium that presents the dissolved or suspended elements intimately and extensively against one another. Dry paints cannot mix.

The ready availability of multi-cultural information is not enough in itself to initiate the mysterious alchemy of interculturalism, whether that alchemy is the change in an individual's value system, or a transformation in the economic system and its underpinning of copyright law. All past bigotries and ethnocentrisms have coexisted with some, even much, information about other cultures. What is needed, and what our age has supplied, is a group of solvents that can serve as a common medium for all kinds of cultural information and insure that whatever processes of transformation they can engender in each other will actually happen. What are those solvents?

Most obvious, perhaps, is the instantaneous medium provided by worldwide telecommunications, especially television. There is a peculiar difference between radio and television in this respect, which has been ignored by the critics of television. Curiously enough, it is the age of radio which saw the last great spasmodic surge in nationalism, ethnocentrism, dictatorship, and mass ideology. It was radio that broadcast the mystagogic rant of Hitler, the brutal rhetoric of Stalin, the mouthings of Franco and Mussolini.

In a sense the Allied Powers in the Second World War were lucky in getting as leaders Roosevelt, Churchill, and de Gaulle, who had a patrician loyalty to democracy, because the power that radio and its associated technologies provided them might well have been a temptation to dictatorship; and they indeed did assume almost dictatorial powers at times.

Even though TV, like radio, is a broadcast medium, and thus would seem to favor the domination of a passive audience by a great authoritative voice, the nature of the visual medium subtly undermines the power and impressiveness of those who would use it. Somehow, if we can see the man live, see the play of expression on his face, his mortal human body taking up space in the world, turning its back, stumbling on the helicopter steps like Gerald Ford's, or dropping the banquet morsel from its chopsticks as Deng Xiaoping's did recently on TV, then we cannot take his speeches very seriously. Part of it is that we can see how old he is. If he is old, we can see the signs of decrepitude; if young, we feel superior to the fellow. I use the masculine pronoun here because, very significantly, female leaders do not seem to be afflicted by the TV feet of clay. The great warlords of the recent past have often been women: Golda Meir, Indira Gandhi, Chiang Ching, Margaret Thatcher. In the film medium, as Leni Riefenstahl knew, the visual awkwardness can be more or less edited out, but live TV is fatal to a demagogue. The only U.S. president to use TV well was, significantly, a film actor. Knowing the medium, he could use its deficiencies for his own purposes, and gain sympathy by playing subtly against his own mortal infirmities. His enemies did not realize this, and the more they attacked his apparent deafness, inattention, and wandering memory, the more affection he got. But it was affection, not obeisance.

TV is a humanizing medium, and a leveler. It also transcends, as radio does not, the barriers of language. That was why the students in Tiananmen Square put up their statue to Democracy: as a visual symbol that would speak across the variety of languages in the world at large and in China itself, where dozens of different languages are spoken. The man who stopped the tanks was making an utterance that is universally human. TV is thus a solvent for all cultural differences.

In the long run, other telecommunication media may be even more potent as solvents. Though the telephone is language-bound, it is not a broadcast medium, and thus, while enabling diverse populations within a language community to exchange ideas, cannot be used for domination of populations. Wiretapping is not a commensurate compensation for the authorities, as the Polish government tacitly admitted eight years ago when, after declaring Martial Law and outlawing Solidarity, it closed down the telephone exchanges, thus foregoing the potentially valuable intelligence it might have got by listening in. The fax machine, as the Chinese students found, is becoming another strong solvent, especially when there is a language problem. Here a picture is worth a million words. Computer logic and computer languages have begun to erode the acoustic language barrier, and perhaps eventually artificial intelligence may make possible the cybernetic translation of natural languages. In any case, the growth of telecommunications has tended to reinforce the development of the English language itself as a *lingua franca* and thus as a universal solvent. The expansion of English by the addition of hundreds of thousands of international scientific and technical words (themselves based on the old *lingua francas* of Latin and Greek) is part of this trend. I will deal later with the explosion of devices for recording and playing music, and the effect this has had on cultural liquidity.

Related to the cultural solvent of telecommunications, and technically based on it, has been the emergence of international financial markets, and the multinational corporations. Through new kinds of financial and investment instruments, ownership by union and pension funds of foreign securities, and the worldwide accessibility of government bonds issued by many nations, large numbers of ordinary people now own substantial property in other countries. In fact there already exists a loose and tacit world currency composed of a combination of old petrodollars, the U.S. budget deficit, and Third World debt. The world as a whole has discovered what Britain and America found in the late eighteenth century: the virtues of debt as a means of capital formation, its tendency to liquefy fixed assets and to put to work unused capital tied up in the real property of nations and, more intangibly, in the talents and education of their peoples and even in the probable political stability of their future.

Out of this world liquidity of value has come new institutions, especially multinational corporations. These entities constitute the first examples of the true world citizen. This is not to say that they are especially virtuous; but for them there is no escape, the world itself being their field of action. They cannot emigrate, and thus their loyalty must be to the world as a whole. The welfare of a citizen of a nation is partly bound up with the welfare of that nation, and thus that citizen's vote will be motivated partly toward the national benefit, a motivation that mitigates his or her special interests. When citizens of the world are numerous and powerful enough, there will emerge a political quality akin to patriotism, an identification of one's own interests with those of the whole globe.

Another universal solvent is the global ecological crisis and the increasing awareness that it cannot be resolved by purely national means. Such threats as Chernobyl, acid rain, the depletion of the ozone layer, species extinctions, and the greenhouse effect (with the accompaniment of global warming or a new ice age, depending on whose theories you accept) are world problems and require the liquefaction of different legal, industrial, and agricultural traditions in order to produce cooperative action. Related to this perceived crisis is the global danger of nuclear war and nuclear winter (or nuclear summer, according to some theorists). It is perhaps a blessing in disguise that the feedback mechanisms by which such changes might actually change the environment are as yet poorly understood. Even if alarm is misdirected, it is at least shared.

One of the most creative and positive solvents in world culture is the almost universal acceptance among the world's elites of the emerging scientific account of the universe. Here, though, there are dismaying counterforces: on both the right and the left there has been a backlash against the challenge and the cognitive expansion demanded by new developments in science. Evolution, for instance, is under attack by religious fundamentalists on one side, and by left-wing social determinists on the other, both anxious to avoid the responsibilities of creative and moral action demanded by the relationship between human nature and nature in general. The relaxation of social discipline brought about by cultural pluralism has itself been partly responsible for the new anti-science atmosphere. The hard disciplines of logic and mathematics, and the self-restraint and self-criticism required by scientific method, are now out of reach of many who, in a stricter academic climate, might have acquired the rudiments of them and so been liberated.

Nevertheless, I believe that science will win the race between enlightenment and reaction, because those societies and groups within society that have mastered science will generally be more effective, inventive, and moral than those that have not, and will thus have greater powers of cultural survival. "More moral," by the way, because more capable of self-examination.

The last, and in some ways the most intriguing, of the great solvents is the rhythm of contemporary popular music, specifically "rock music." Originating in a fertile combination of the sophisticated African musical tradition with European and Latin American elements, a new musical medium emerged in the '60s which is perhaps the most potent, because the most fundamental, of all forces for change. For many years jazz and blues coexisted with classical and folk music; but gradually a mutual translation took place. The names of Scott Joplin, the Gershwins, Leonard Bernstein, Dylan, the Beatles, and now David Byrne and Philip Glass chart the process of development. One recalls moments of musical insight in it: *West Side Story,* Procul Harum's "A Whiter Shade of Pale," which was simultaneously real Bach and the most psychedelic Pop, George Harrison's adaptations of Indian sitar music, Paul Simon's new work with South Africa's Ladysmith Black Mombaso, Glass's *Satyagraha* and *Koyannis-qaatsi.*

Essentially what happened was that a very simple, pan-human rhythmic beat was discovered, of no musical merit in itself, to which the music of all world cultures could be set and which served as a liquid medium that would enable musical syncretism to take place. What has followed has been a worldwide musical revolution, where a record made in London by a talented Indian singer using a reggae base and Brazilian arrangements will influence young Nigerian, Czech, and Japanese rock groups and perhaps form part of the raw material for a new classical opera. The extraordinary phenomena of *glasnost* and democracy in Eastern Europe and the Far East may have as much to do with the universality of rock and roll music as with anything else. This is not a praise of rock in itself, which is a rather insipid form of sound; but rock has been like alcohol, which can serve as the base for the most exquisite blends of perfume, the most delicate liquers.

The world of Homer and his Odysseus is one united by a liquid medium, literally that universal solvent that we call ocean, that Homer called *polyphloisboiou thalasses* , the multitudinously-flowing sea. The ambivalent and two-faced god of that medium, Poseidon, is the key problem of the *Odyssey*. The poem is about oars, about how to use the destructive element, as Stein calls it in *Lord Jim,* to do creative work and to get home with the story of Troy. The trouble with a universal solvent is what to use as a containment vessel. If the solvent is truly universal, it will melt down through any walls which hold it in. The solution to this riddle is the solution to the problems of our times. It is, essentially, the one barrier which stands in the way of those scientists attempting to achieve nuclear fusion, and thus a cheap, inexhaustible, and clean source of energy for all humankind. In physics, the universal solvent is plasma. What bottle can contain this genie? Uncontained, it is the principle of the greatest threat to humanity, the hydrogen bomb. Contained, it is the potential hearth of us all.

Interestingly enough, the best solutions suggested so far for the containment of this Thunderer, this Poseidonic universal solvent, is to use it as its own container; either by allowing it to power and to control an electromagnetic field that will constrain it, or by using it as an inertial jet-propulsion force to collapse it into a state of such density that it begins to produce more energy than it consumes. If we accept this answer to the riddle as having mythic force for the containment of the intercultural plasma, we must look for ways in which interculturalism will be self-controlling, or can be induced to enter turbulent but stable feedback states that maintain themselves. But first we must look more carefully at the dangers and diseases of the new informational economy that is emerging.

What are the main problems of interculturalism? One is immediately obvious: the issue of authenticity. It arises most clearly, perhaps, in the experience of tourism for both the tourist and the local population which serves and is photographed by the tourist. More subtly, but more disturbingly to the intellectual and artist, are such questions as: How authentic is my claim as an anthropologist to speak for the autochthones? Can I justify my ethnodramatic performance of their rituals? This haiku or Noh play I have written, or in which I am performing—is it genuine? Is my Buddhism authentic? Or again, how am I to feel about the modern factories on the outskirts of Athens, or the Kentucky Fried Chicken on Tiananmen Square? Or Japanese baseball and square dancing? Or Zimbabwean rock and roll? Or my Vietnamese student's appreciation of the novels of Jane Austen?

The problem is fundamentally connected to the characteristic reproducibility of the cultural (informational) goods: the fact that, unlike material objects, they are not destroyed at the point of origin when they are transferred to another place. When our fundamental model of the nature of cultural goods is pieces of matter, there can only be one original of anything. In other words, we can only worry about authenticity if we are materialists. A materialist knows that if there are two copies of something, at least one of them must be a fake. (Similarly, if two things apparently occupy the same place, at least one of them must be an illusion.)

The same suspicion can be found among materialist lovers of nature: for them a restored or artificial prairie can never be a real prairie. What they ignore is that all living things are by nature copies: reproduction is part of the definition of life. Nor does nature even bother to copy correctly: evolution can only take place because the copies are incorrect, and thus there is variation in a species, upon which natural selection can work. According to a materialist definition of nature, all life is inauthentic!

But suppose one understood culture to be, like nature, in its very essence a process of not-quite-correct copying, of transfer, of sexual and asexual recombination, of merging, mixing, miscegenation, and the mutual appropriation of information? Those who are nostalgic for the certainty of being they imagine among *les tristes tropiques* propose models of authenticity that are essentially closed semantic systems, hermeneutic circles impenetrable to any stranger. What they fail to take into account is that such systems must be as impenetrable and closed to their own younger generation as to any anthropological outsider. To put it another way, culture must always reproduce itself by indoctrinating its children, who start off as strangers; and irreversible slippage will happen in the process. The indoctrinators will be compelled to develop a subversive meta-consciousness of their own cultural material if only in deploying, enumerating, and organizing it so as to teach it and leave nothing out; the human child, as we know from rapid change in all living languages, delights in creative misreadings and playful inversions; and the human adolescent is hormonally programmed to question and subvert the wisdom of the elders.

In the strict, materialist definition of authenticity, then, there is no such thing as cultural authenticity; so we must, since authenticity is a valuable concept, look for other definitions than uniqueness, untransferability, cultural or natural indigenousness. Authenticity must be sought, where Jesus enjoined us to judge, by the fruits of something rather than its grounds. Authenticity is moral, artistic, and intellectual power; there is a lesser authenticity also in sheer economic effectiveness. Contain the plasma in the plasma; let the problem of authenticity become the authentic and central theme of the work.

How does this solution apply to the uncomfortable tourist? Here it is a matter of art. If the tourist is there for good, deep, complex reasons, and if the host country or city has a coherent aesthetic of what it means to entertain tourists, there need be no inauthenticity. The city of Stresa, on Lake Maggiore, has been entertaining tourists, mostly in summer from sweltering Rome, for the past two thousand years and has got very good at it. It would be inauthentic for the town to do anything else. And though the reasons its pilgrims might give for their visit have changed, Delphi is no more inauthentic now than it was when Oedipus consulted the oracle there three thousand years ago.

Related to the problem of authenticity is a peculiar perversion of the emergent system of value, that one might call moral consumerism. Homogenous cultures without much contact with the outside world tend to develop a consensus that delimits the area of ethical concern. Morality itself is a kind of informational goods; a relatively closed culture is able to restrict or "copyright" their extent or writ or relevance, rather as sumptuary laws restrict the use of consumer goods. This limitation can have horrible effects when a whole society excludes from its human sympathy some ethnic group over which it has power, as when for instance many Poles cheerfully permitted the Jews to be rounded up by the Germans and sent to their death in the camps. But there is an opposite problem, well exemplified by America in the sixties and seventies, where large masses of people learned to eat and use moral values from all sources, however mixed and exotic, without regard to their consistency, their cultural context, and their dependence upon modes of personal discipline.

This peculiar form of consumerism leads to disregard for the wholesome elements of one's own ethnic tradition, and a pervasive sense of guilt and moral inferiority to outsiders. Eventually there is a sort of breakdown in the moral immune system by which we distinguish what is a proper part of our own personal value system from something which, however valid in itself, is not in character. A kind of cultural AIDS sets in. Living by alien standards—adopting a principled communitarian gregariousness, for instance, when one's personal nature is private and introspective, or expecting the mystical insight and inner calm of the Oriental sage without the ascetic discipline and training that make it possible—can be so psychologically exhausting as to send one quickly back into the waiting arms of whatever narrow and bigoted system one originally escaped.

When contact with other cultures was rare, it had a certain scarcity value, like material goods which must be laboriously manufactured. A generation brought up in such an economy of cultural scarcity would indeed be inclined to gobble up alien ethical systems. However, newer generations are coming to realize instinctively that the expense involved in cultural information is not so much in acquiring it as in selectively discarding and editing it; that Nietzsche was right in prescribing a certain heroic forgetfulness for the sickness of cultural and historical surfeit. There is a renewed interest among the young in cultural limits and traditions, that is sometimes regarded with distaste by their more "emancipated" elders. The young may surprise us by recreating, though with much humbler and more prosaic ethical ambitions, a coherence and dignity that many of the sixties generation do not now find in their lives. But this turn toward more classical modes is, at best, not a return to old narrowness and bigotry. It is a conscious choice and discipline exercised after, not before, the exposure to and acceptance of cultural diversity.

Another great challenge to the twenty-first century is going to be a peculiar kind of insanity, wherein a person will not have enough of the traditional cultural tools to construct a stable and coherent self; and the consequent rise in addiction—to the drugs that imitate the neurochemical reward system of the brain, to starvation, to the feeling of will power, to religion, to moral absolutism, to ethnic identity, to superstition, even to sex. And our political problems will be to some extent the same things writ large. Some of these threats may cancel, others be mutually reinforcing. One will be an increasing division between the happy, creative and sane people who will be the competent knowers and makers of information, and those who, unable to meet the new integrative demands of selfhood, will be increasingly incapable of love and work. A second will be the implications of a geo-economic order underpinned by drug money. A third will be mass anomie and purposelessness, a sort of moral anorexia, with a decrease in participation in the political process. A fourth major political problem will be xenophobic and ideological backlash, as we have already seen in Iran and among fundamentalists of various religions. A fifth, related, problem, threatening to one of the very bases of the emergent world conversation, may be an erosion of the narrow majority of the population which generally accepts the methods and findings of science.

A sixth, which needs close discussion, will be the breakup of the institution of the family among some ethnic, ideological, and socio-economic groups: Europeans and Japanese, who are increasingly not having children at all; political liberals (in Israel, for instance, Labor party supporters have fewer children than those in Likud); the post-industrially affluent in general; feminists; hedonists; intellectuals; drug users; homosexuals. In combination with new diseases spread by more relaxed forms of social contact, this erosion of family ethics among certain groups will result in their demographic collapse after a few generations, so that their views and outlook will no longer be strongly represented in the general population. In America the population will be increasingly Hispanic and Asian, as these groups tend to have children and to look after and educate them when they have them. Even to refer to these facts is to tread on dangerous ground, and I shall draw no conclusions other than to say that these trends may be perceived as problems by those groups which will find themselves relatively underrepresented in the future. If these issues were not acutely uncomfortable to think about, they would not be problematic.

Given all these disquieting risks, one might be forgiven for wondering whether the hard intellectual and imaginative passage into the new informational economy of interculturalism is worth the trouble. We may console ourselves with the reflection that if this view of things is correct, the new problems will be side-effects of the gradual elimination of many old enemies of humankind: large-scale war, poverty, the idea of economic and social justice (as opposed to the old idea of justice), racism, the destruction of the environment, political and ideological oppression, and the cultural stagnation that attends materialist economies. Besides, there is not much, barring some equivalent to the Shiite/socialist revolution in Iran, that we can do to prevent the coming changes.

The intellectual and imaginative passage from cultural ethnocentrism is itself a good, and it might be worth summarizing some of the themes of this essay by means of a brief description of its main phases. The first step in the process usually involves institutions of which many now disapprove: empire, religious evangelism, and colonialism. Curiously enough, in order to break out of the bounds of their cultural limitiations most peoples have had to pass through one or two morally evil experiences: of being dominated by a foreign cultural hegemony, or of being a hegemonic dominator. India and

England are good examples. It is hard to say which experience is the more damaging in the long run; but the damage is necessary. It is the trauma suffered by any structure when it first encounters its corrosive, Poseidonic solvent. Very occasionally this first step can be accomplished when a group of refugees or emigrants which shares a common alienation from its parent cultures is able to band together to form a union, as did the American settlers; but even here a common hegemonic culture, embodied in the Enlightenment reasoning of the Constitution, was required. In effect, the hegemonic culture must *be* the solvent, and the experience of one's own world view as solvent is a profoundly unsettling one, manifested eventually in a kind of collective guilt, inertia, and anomie.

What follows the first stage, of hegemony, is what we might call naive relativism. Just like a child who discovers one exception to a rule, and who in a kind of cynical dudgeon dismisses the validity of all rules, so a culture at this stage, having found that its own rules are not universal, assumes a total cultural relativity of all rules. This phase actually comes from a generous impulse, itself the product of the colonial adminstrator's or anthropologist's need to develop an ethic of impartiality and self-criticism (or of an equally generous recognition by members of an oppressed colonial people that their oppressor's culture has its own sense and beauty). The effect is that the primary stance of the anthropologist, of respect for other cultures, becomes partly disseminated throughout the population. Sometimes this stance is adopted strategically, for the worst of reasons: as an excuse for hedonism and a relaxation of the demands and duties of adult human life. Margaret Mead's Samoa and the photographs of the naked tribespeople in *National Geographic* became in this way justifications for the ''playboy philosophy.'' The Huichol peyote cult served a similar function a few years later. Difference is interpreted as license, as permission; the very strict moral and ritual rules of traditional societies are ignored. Another use for cultural relativism is in its guise as cultural determinism. If a person's success in life is the result of overriding cultural forces, usually perceived as oppressive, then those who perceive themselves as unsuccessful have the advantage of being able to claim that it was not their own efforts that were at fault, but society; and that society owes them, regardless of their personal character or contribution, a handsome restitution.

Though superficially attractive, relativism is not a coherent intellectual position. Either it is uniquely, absolutely, and exclusively true, and thus the shattering exception to its own rule that all truth is relative; or it is no more true than any other intellectual position, in which case the absolutism of, say, Hitler's Germany or Khomeini's Iran is just as intellectually acceptable as relativism. Interestingly enough, it was on these grounds that Derrida was unable to condemn apartheid as roundly as his critics wished, and there were some intellectuals who found it difficult, for similar reasons, to condemn the Ayatollah's death sentence against Salman Rushdie.

Naive relativism is still a reigning ideology in the American academy, enshrined in what some have called ''oppression studies'' or ''victimology''; the general population, though, has to some extent moved on to a more mature perspective. One of the oddities of our time is how in many humanistic and social science fields the academy has ceased to lead the national consciousness, and has begun to drag behind it; rather as the Anglican clergy moved from being in the forefront of consciousness in the seventeenth and eighteenth centuries (witness Donne, Herbert, Herrick, and Swift) to being the butt of literary jokes in the nineteenth.

The more mature perspective—the third phase in the intellectual passage—is what we might call pluralism: the acceptance and recognition of cultural difference and a commitment to coexistence and to a world view that is not unified but diverse and disseminated. If it is objected that the general population is not as sophisticated as this, we may point to the values embodied in the most popular and even vulgar TV shows—*Donahue, All in the Family, Perfect Strangers, Night Court,* and so on—in which pluralism and tolerance have become not just one of a number of important ethical norms, but the supreme, even the exclusive one. The ideal of tolerance is indeed rather noble, and contrasts tellingly with the sometimes vicious exclusivism of minority and feminist academic societies, which one would suppose to be providing intellectual and moral leadership. The sheep, alas, are well in advance of the shepherds.

But pluralism itself has certain profound problems. One is that we are not neurally organized to perceive the world in a fundamentally pluralistic way. Even if, say, we were able to prove to our satisfaction that the vision of the compound insect eye gave a more accurate picture of things than the single eye of a human being, there is not much one could do about it. In actual fact, of course, a large part of an insect's brain is devoted to integrating all of its different views into a single program of action; and in another sense we humans do indeed have compound eyes, made of millions of retinal neurons, but again integrated into a single world view by the visual cortex. The universe itself has, by overwhelming selective pressure, evolved us as unifying and integrating animals. The strong inference is that a unifying perspective is, as much as anything can be said to be, more likely to be true than a pluralistic one: if it were not more accurate, we would not have survived.

Despite its claims, ''pluralism'' is itself, paradoxically, a unifying perspective, but a rather procrustean one: what it does is reduce all cultural

277

differences to a sort of grid of equal cultural black boxes laid out over an infinite plane, boxes whose external form is safely measurable but whose contents are incommensurable and thus unknowable, and which are, as it were, the fundamental monads and quanta of reality. Geometrically it resembles the characteristic grid-design of the American city, or the relationship between departments in an American multiversity. Though pluralism forbids any attempt to perceive one cultural box as containing another, and thus revealing a comparable and measurable internal structure, it is itself a sort of gigantic box containing all other boxes as its subordinate material. Thus, like relativism, it contains a subtle hegemonic ambition of its own.

One way of describing what is the problem with pluralism is to say that if the universe is curved, even a simple sphere, no grid of equal rectilinear blocks can cover (or "tile") it without overlap. Specialization, and the definition of smaller and smaller cultural units, might be seen as the desperate resource of an intellectual culture trying to resolve exactly this problem. If the squares are small enough, perhaps the distortions of the world's curvature will somehow go away. Pluralism is like a sort of oil, a liquid medium that merely holds its contents in suspension, and does not allow them to transform each other chemically.

Mere pluralism requires no change in one's own or one's neighbor's perspective; indeed, it is threatened by change, especially by any attempt to understand and imagine, and thus incorporate, the contents of another cultural box. It so fears hierarchy—one possible result of such an incorporation—that it would prefer ignorance. Its tolerance of other world views could well be described as neglect or even as a kind of intellectual cowardice. At its worst one could describe it as an abdication or shirking of the great human enterprise of mutual knowledge, communication (literally, "making one together"), and mutual transformation.

The final stage in the intellectual passage into a new world is beginning to emerge, prompted by an instinctive discontent with the limits of mere pluralism. We might give it various names: syncretism, evolutionary epistemology, natural classicism, dramatist ontology, the informational or Homeric/cybernetic economy. The nature of this stage of emergence has been hinted at in this essay, and I have dealt with it elsewhere; so a summary of its main features should suffice.

Beneath all cultural differences certain fundamental human powers and capacities are emerging, that require cultural triggers to express themselves. These powers and capacities include language, the fundamental genres of the arts (musical tonality, the dramatic/performative ability, poetic meter, visual representation, dance, and so on), fundamental moral instincts, a religious/mystical ability, and the scientific rationality by which we learn to speak the other languages of nature. These powers and capacities are genetic endowments, created by evolution and embedded in our neural structure. Thus true collaboration between cultures, and even a unifying syncretism of them, is possible on this shared biological basis. In this work ancient wisdom and traditional lore will join hands with the most sophisticated studies of genetics, paleoanthropology, cognitive science, cultural anthropology, ethology, sociobiology, the oral tradition, and performance theory. The word that describes our historical experience of the joining of old and new is Renaissance.

All cultures and all world views will be seen as competing or cooperating together in a single evolutionary drama, a dynamic ecology of thought that is the continuation by swifter means of the universal process of evolution. The relationship between cultural world views will not be that between black boxes, but between characters in an ongoing drama, who can change each other, marry, and beget mutual offspring. It is not simply that this drama establishes the truth of things; it is the truth of things.

In other words, we can have faith that once the bonds that hold human ideas and cultures locked into a solid configuration are loosed by the powerful solvents of our time, the elements of culture, being basically human, will have the hooks and valences to permit them to build up new, coherent systems not limited to one ethnic tradition. Moreover the new systems can be very flexible and need not purchase survival by a paranoid vigilance and rigidity. The conflict and miscegenation between and within such systems as they emerge is not a horrifying defilement or pollution, but the normal and healthy operation of an evolutionary ecology of ideas. Information will become the basis of a gift exchange economy, the inexhaustible currency of a new order of economics. The hard, the tragic, and the inflexible will not disappear, but will be valued aesthetically and treasured for its contribution to the richness of the world, rather than turned into a tyrannical fetish and a standard of conformity. As the human race recognizes itself more and more as a ''we,'' it will paradoxically be more and more surprised by the otherness of what was once considered familiar. How strange, how exotic, how attractive our own culture is! Is not this the strangest and most interesting of worlds?

Eventually, perhaps, that greatest of all Others, Nature itself, will be recognized also as part of the ''we.'' This is a mystical idea: it is prefigured in the lyre of Orpheus, that could make animals, trees, and rocks listen with delight; or the ring of Solomon, which gave him understanding of the languages of birds and beasts; the magic flute, the staff of Prospero, the double-helix caduceus or metatron of Hermes and Moses. We will, having learned to command Nature, find that it is sweeter to converse with it, and bury the staff certain fathoms in the earth; and that we are nature, and nature is ourselves. That time will mark the birth of Sophia, the divine wisdom, the long-promised accession of Athena to the presidency of the gods.

Interculturalism and Iconophilia
in the
New Theatre

Andrzej Wirth

IT SEEMS THAT FOR THE first time in human history we have the chance for global cultural understanding. Air travel and the media-created impression that we all are inhabitants of a global village enforce such a conviction. Is this conviction correct as far as theatre is concerned? Or, to speak in the terminology of Victor Turner, are we witnessing a "new transcultural communicative synthesis through performance?"

Contemporary presentational aesthetics are changing the proportions between theatre and performance. The development is moving in the direction of less theatre, more performance. This strengthening of the performative element occurs at the cost of diminishing mimetic, dramatic, and narrative elements. Literary theatre (generated from a verbal text) and live performance (on the "scripted" stage as dance, song, sculpture, etc.) do exist presently as a mixed form. To answer the general question about the role of transcultural communication in the new theatre it might be best to proceed analytically, limiting ourselves to a few pertinent paradigms. Those paradigms I have chosen are Robert Wilson, and as points of comparative reference Ariane Mnouchkine, Peter Brook, Eugenio Barba, and the Polish theatre group (now in exile), Teatr Osmego Dnia.

The interculturalism of Robert Wilson can be discussed on many levels, such as the aesthetics of production and re-production, performance aesthetics and theatre reception. This would apply not only to such obvious examples as the unique multi-national project of *CIVIL WarS* (from 1982 on), but applies equally on different levels to the majority of his works from the beginning. (Black performer Sheryl Sutton; Freud, Stalin as stage figures; Shiraz as location for the *KA Mountain and GUARDenia Terrace* project, etc.—the period of 1969-1972).

Wilson's interculturalism in terms of its production process has to be seen in the context of the geographical dissemination of his projects. An American, he works with the same ease in New York, Boston, Cambridge, Massachusetts, Minneapolis, Washington, Los Angeles, as in Amsterdam, Shiraz, Paris, Avignon, Lyon, Copenhagen, Rotterdam, Berlin, Cologne, Munich, Stuttgart, Hamburg, Frankfurt, Milan, Rome, Tokyo.

Since 1979 West Germany with its opulently subsidized state and city theatres has become an operating base for Wilson. He didn't become a German director, but he is surely one of the most outstanding directors working in German theatre in the last decade. Indeed, he has established a new intercultural model in theatre work. Unlike Peter Brook, an Englishman who works in Paris with an international cast of eclectic actors, Wilson works in Germany with German actors who are members of established repertory ensembles. The most universal German theatre, that is, theatre done in Germany with German actors for German audiences, is made presently by an American.

Intercultural praxis subverts the conventional view that theatre generated in a given country is an expression of its culture. Is this true in the case of Wilson's *Golden Windows* in Munich, or HAMLETMACHINE in New

Oda Sternberg

THE GOLDEN WINDOWS

York? In *Golden Windows*, the laughing aria of the great Munich actress Maria Nieklisch is composed of laugh quotations from her previous dramatic roles at the Kammerspiele. One could argue that this sequence of the play is made from indigenous material of the central European repertory theatre and therefore is an expression of local culture. This central European coding disappeared in the reconstruction of the work at the Brooklyn Academy because American actors don't have a comparable canonic reference system. HAMLETMACHINE with its many idiosyncratically European and particularly German textual references was staged in New York and "reconstructed" in Hamburg. A specifically American coding of some play sequences, e.g., the "Hamlet walk" of the original production, couldn't be preserved in the German reconstruction. These differences reflect some specific problems of interculturalism on the level of the aesthetics of theatrical production, which generates its kinetic matrix from the performative qualities of a "found" player.

This produces difficulties in finding adequate substitutes in "replicas" (cf. *Golden Windows* at BAM and *CIVIL WarS* in Cambridge). In the casting of "voices" in the performance, theatre problems are not different from those of the transcultural staging of conventional opera. In the reconstruction of the Roman part of *CIVIL WarS* in Rotterdam, Wilson's fans missed the Italianate charisma of Luigi Petroni's (Garibaldi) *bel canto*, in this case a price Wilson was ready to pay for the cultural transfer.

It is important to recall, however, that Wilson had initially a radically new and more radical concept of transcultural communication with chosen "target" cultures. His current theatre praxis of reconstructing single parts of *CIVIL WarS*: the Roman part in Rotterdam, the Cologne part in Cambridge, Mass., the Tokyo/Minneapolis part in Frankfurt, etc., is a compromise after the failure of a multi-national project for the Olympic Arts Festival in 1984, designed as a congregation of other cultures.

This project sought five or six production sites—Cologne, Rotterdam, Tokyo, Stuttgart or Marseille, Rome—and all realized parts received some mark of *couleur locale*: Orientalism of the *Knee Plays*; Frederick the Great of the Cologne part; Garibaldi of the Italian part; Dutch landscapes of the Rotterdam part, etc. Obviously, the original concept of Wilson's interculturalism didn't include a provision for "reproducing" Oriental, Teutonic, Italian, Dutch expressions, but *quoting* them from the source. The Dutch references of the Rotterdam part may appear as touristic stereotypes (Mata Hari, Queen Wilhelmina, William the Silent, cabbages and tulips), but the dominance of a language of the audience gives the piece a distinct *couleur locale*. In the Cologne part of *CIVIL WarS* the collaboration with Heiner Müller led to something more than a "tourist" view of

283

Germany.

Biographical references to Frederick the Great's youth, military career, and death, taken from Heiner Müller material, provided an illusion of a play-within-a-play and suggested a kind of central focus on a connotatively rich historical figure. Wilson assures us that he is interested primarily in the formal aspect of the ''picture book'' image: a parallel between the horse's neck line and the steep shoulder line of the rider. This is correct with respect to his formalist aesthetics. However, the stage figure of Frederick the Great can't be appreciated as an icon in Germany without diverse, heavily coded historical connotations. In a theatre which sees images as a vehicle for messages, such a gap between the aesthetics of production and reception could be considered a contradiction. But this is obviously not Wilson's concern.

Robert Wilson's intercultural praxis does not fit into an otherwise helpful dualistic model of *source* and *target* culture, proposed by Patrice Pavis (International Conference on Interculturalism in Theatre, Bad Hamburg, 1988). Pavis's model could be sufficient to describe the way Brecht used elements of Noh Theatre in his learning play *Ja-Sager—Nein-Sager*, but it would already be problematic if applied to his *Mahagonny* opera. The flow of exchanges and transformations in the realm of Euro-American cultures asks for another model in which the very notion of source and target is invalidated.

The Michelin-tire figurine with a ball-bearing ring in his hand in *DD&D (Part I)* is a grand example of Wilson's syncretic use of symbols from the reservoire of popular culture. Brothers Michelin were manufacturers of the first demountable pneumatic tires in France. Their company became a leading producer of tires in Europe at the end of the century and expanded to the U.S. before WWI. The Michelin firm became well-known to travelers in Europe because of its maps and guide books. Wilson transforms this trademark symbol, originated in Europe and popularized in America, through the addition of an icon from WWII Nazi propaganda (''*Alle Räder rollen für den Sieg,*'' ''All wheels roll for the victory'')—a ball-bearing ring—and lets the Michelin figurine recite an aria composed from numbers illustrating the production of ball-bearing rings in Hitler's Germany in the final stage of the war (this as quotation from the memoir of Hitler's war minister Albert Speer).

One directional source/target model of cultural transactions is superseded in Wilson's intercultural praxis through a model of *orbit*, with rotating motives which enrich themselves by passing through different cultural hemispheres. One could note many examples of Wilson's tendency to minimalize and familiarize any local ''foreign'' expressions. Wilson's intercultural glance: the perspective on the planet Earth from the U.S. space ship; Heracles as Tarzan; Hopi Indians dancing with Garibaldi's soldiers; Gilgamesh on the analyst's couch, etc.

To understand Wilson's stance on interculturalism, it is necessary to recognize that his is a *posthistoire* look, perhaps easier to achieve for an American than for a European (no irony!). This "look" can be accommodated in a theatre which sees itself as an exhibition, a public park, a landscape, a theatre that uses pictures not for their hermeneutic, but their contemplative, meditative value. Wilson's optics ignore the transparency of the signifier, and view it as opaque, denying its function of pointing towards the signified. Contemplation begins where representation ends. Such an approach admits the possibility of formal syncretism, which discovers a common denominator for the most diverse cultural manifestations. Asked about a possible link between Rudolf Hess and Franz Kafka as referential biographies for Parts 1 and 2 of *Death Destruction and Detroit,* Wilson answered that the analogy lies in the fact that Rudolf Hess (who was at that time still alive) does *not* want to die, and Franz Kafka *didn't want* to live. This is exactly a stance which stresses the *structural* analogy, and in a reversed symmetry sees a unifying syncretic moment.

My hypothesis: Paradoxically, interculturalism is for Wilson a vehicle *not* for cultural understanding, but for distancing, and luring the spectator into a meditative trance, as the only one comfortable position of appreciation in view of the displayed diversity. Statements to the contrary in the press releases for the *CIVIL WarS* should be considered as propaganda for an appeasement of conventionally-thinking sponsors. I am not suggesting duplicity here, but a strategical displacement. Wilson's interculturalism contributes to intercultural understanding on the level of collective, collaborative theatre team work.

It evokes a spirit of collaboration between artists (Lucinda Childs, Suzushi Hanayagi, Heiner Müller, etc.) of diverse cultures, and provokes a collaborative effort between theatrical styles which understand themselves as exclusive (Noh, Kabuki, Bunraku). The strategies which he invented and developed for intercultural collaboration in his global theatre project *CIVIL WarS* are unique in theatre history. Wilson's theatre allows one to appreciate aesthetically sounds, pictures, and movements as independent entities in a perceptually optimal display. The act of contemplation is a solitary one , and Wilson's artful displays "address" not an "audience" in general, but an *individual* spectator. The encouragement of intermissions at the spectator's own discretion in Wilson's *great operas* is not a theatrical provocation, but a provision to accommodate the solitary act according to its own pace and raptures.

Interculturally produced, Wilson's works are not intended to induce interacultural understanding, and as the experience with their "reconstruction" (replicas) shows, are relatively resistant to an intercultural transfer (remember *Golden Windows* at BAM).

Wilson's intercultural syncretism ignores distinctions between history and nature (Lincoln as tree, Frederick the Great as iceberg) and is designed not as a vehicle to promote understanding of cultural differences but an appreciation of their arbitrary aesthetic synthesis. Lincoln's *Übermarionette* appears in *CIVIL WarS* not as a symbolic figure of American democracy, but as a visual emblem de-anthropomorphized through scale, and an analogy with a tree stressed in the motto of the piece: "A tree is best measured when it is down." The Lincoln-tree is a stage object and its stage movement is suggestive of an abstract tension between *verticality* and *horizontality*. A Roman critic (a woman) wanted to see in it a representation of a penis, a guess as good as any in the discourse of Wilson's reception.

the CIVIL WarS: ACT V—THE ROME SECTION

The point I am trying to make is that Wilson's rich intercultural repertoire of images which includes Stalin, Freud, Einstein, Edison, Frederick the Great, Kafka, Hess, the Emperor of China, General Lee, Florence Nightingale, Madame Curie, Mata Hari, Hercules, Don Quixote, Captain

Nemo, Hopi Indians, and Gilgamesh serves a formal purpose which is to distance and to outfocus the conventional anthropocentric perception of theatre. His project in terms of postulated distance is much more radical than Brecht's (closer to Gertrude Stein's deconstructionist program: "the whole earth is covered with characters"). Brecht's *Galileo* play, compared with Wilson's *Einstein* opera, is an old-fashioned empathy piece. Wilson can play with any great figure in his theatre without inviting empathy. His "dignified aloofness," which Janny Donker describes in her book, *The President of Paradise: A Traveler's Account of Robert Wilson's* CIVIL WarS, requires a well-measured distance.

Wilson is a *Pythagorean*: he seems to believe in the transmigration of the soul, and sees numbers (proportions) as the ultimate elements of the universe. One of his favorite methods of distancing and *out*focusing the stage figure is its quantification and multiplication (*Einstein on the Beach, DD&D*). He denotes stage figures with numbers, uses counting as a measure of movement, indulges in classical compositional proportions (the golden mean, etc.).

Wilson's "trademark" players, whom he uses "interculturally" within different national ensembles—Sheryl Sutton, Christopher Knowles, Cindy Lubar, Jessye Norman, Lucinda Childs—are never cast as "characters," but as idiosyncratic performers because of their unique physical, kinetic, and vocal stage presence. They are displayed as opaque human emblems not to communicate anything *interculturally*, but as mere *presence* to be aesthetically contemplated.

Interestingly enough, if Wilson uses a famous "representational" actor, e.g., the actress Ingrid Andrée in *CIVIL WarS*, he transforms her into an historic, static, opaque emblem through mask, costume, and quoted gestures. The high points of the role are effects achieved through computerized, electronically-controlled light design.

A question arises concerning the function of a conventionally trained representational actor used as a mere physical carrier of theatre signs distributed by the *mise-en-scène*. In some instances the actor disappears totally under a de-anthropomorphizing disguise: a dinosaur in *DD&D* or a panther in *DD&D2*. On the other hand, such famous actors of German literary theatre as Peter Lühr and Maria Nicklisch of the Munich Kammerspiele are made productive for Wilson through an application of radical deconstructionist strategies: they are capable of using some of their idiosyncratic vocal and gesturing mannerisms in a kind of collage which derives its power from their conventional dramatic roles in the cultural canon of German literary theatre.

The culturally determined expressiveness of German actors is intentionally defused, outfocused, artfully blurred and universalized by Wilson as material for formal composition. Obviously, cross-cultural understanding is *not* a factor he considers. To the contrary, very diversified cultural material is saved from appearing eclectic through the synthesizing powers of Wilson's *iconophilia,* which is capable of transforming any material into an object for aesthetic contemplation.

THE MAHABHARATA

In contrast to Peter Brook, Wilson's position on interculturalism appears as a radically purist stance. He does not offer any rhetoric concerning trans-cultural understanding, as Peter Brook does in his *Mahabharata.* Under close examination, Brook's *Mahabharata* appears as a typical work of Orientalist aesthetics, and not as a representation of the unknown Orient, as Brook promises. This is to be seen in the imposition of a Shakespearean aura (*War of the Roses*) and of tragic perception of fate, principally foreign to the Indian original (cf. Gautam Dasgupta, *PAJ 30*). There is a greater honesty in the stance of Wilson who does not promise anything he can't deliver.

RICHARD II

Less maximalistic than Brook's, but more realistic as an assessment of interculturalism in theatre is the position of Ariane Mnouchkine in her Shakespeare cycle (*Richard II, Henry IV, Twelfth Night*—1981/1982). Mnouchkine retains the occidental cultural matrix of Shakespeare's chronicles, using stereotypes of *commedia dell'arte*, Noh, and Kabuki as a kind of overpainting, ornamentation, and stylization. No cultural transfer is promised, only a variation on a known melody in a new register. In this effort Mnouchkine succeeds, as she also does in *Mephisto*(1980). This is because the political opportunism of a prominent artist is an experience which the French share with Germans, and its exemplification is easier on "foreign" material.

I would put in the same category Eugenio Barba's *Brecht's Ashes* project, and the Mandelstam project of an exiled Polish alternative group Teatr Osmego Dnia, *Höhenflug* (1987). Barba, juxtaposing elements of Brecht's work and life, creates a new level of cross-cultural understanding of the German poet. The Polish group uses the biography of Soviet poet Osip Mandelstam to express the dilemma of contemporary political dissidents in Eastern Europe.

It is noteworthy that in all these instances the contribution to intercultural understanding does not exceed the realm of European experience. Wilson's sources and targets are pluralistic. He overcomes the danger of eclecticism through the fusion of iconophilia with iconoclasm. The iconoclastic moment is apparent in his unwillingness to draw a distinction between culture and nature, between man and animal, between ancient and modern, between holy and secular.

"A new transcultural communicative synthesis through performance," which Victor Turner hoped for, indeed took place in the new theatre, but, without a visible contribution to global cultural understanding. An edifice composed from the stones of an Egyptian pyramid, the wood from an Indian pagoda, and the bricks of an old Manchester factory does not provide any insights into the source cultures from which those elements derived. Nonetheless, we are capable of appreciating them in a new, arbitrary, totalizing context. In this respect, the aesthetics of the new theatre follows the way of postmodern architecture.

Interculturalism and American Music

Mead Hunter

AMERICAN MUSIC, IT COULD well be said, has been intercultural from its earliest days. Though the dominant (or at least more visible) heritage is European, the history of American music cannot be understood without charting the gradual, practically inadvertent infiltration of African forms.

Two more disparate bloodlines would be hard to imagine. Since the ancient Greeks, Western theorists have sought to ''rationalize'' music—define it, codify its functions. Pythagorean thought classified music with mathematics, a notion that mystified the nature of music by obfuscating its social basis. The medieval Church, by encouraging the development of notational devices, furthered music's reification from an auditory/sensory art into a quantifiable arrangement of readable (and thus predictable) tones. So it was not long before this process reached its immanent conclusion: the symphony orchestra, in which precision is everything, and individual expression occurs within narrow parameters, as overdetermined by the conductor. Such is the rational aspect of the European heritage.

By contrast, African music (West and North African, that is, these being the regions whose people would so powerfully influence American culture) was never set apart from other aspects of life and submitted to the rationalization process. Even in the one apparent virtuoso specialization of ritual drumming, percussionists played for what was essentially a collective experience.

According to critic Ortiz Walton, black music underwent a radical sublimation in the early American slave states, specifically because of edicts against drum playing:

Given the drum's retention, as was the case in all other 'New World' slave societies, it is likely that black music here would have sounded more like that of Trinidad, Haiti, or Jamaica, all these musics having retained more of an African percussive orientation. The enforcement of anti-drum laws in the United States made it necessary to transfer the function of the drum to the feet, hands, and body by way of the Spirituals during the slave era and by way of instrumental music after the Civil War in the new form of black music called Jazz.

Encoding lyrics with ambiguous language was another historically determined feature of black music during slave times—broadcasting geneology, whereabouts and news through apparently guileless ''field hollers''—and has remained so from then right up through rock. Blues, jazz, and rock have long been notorious for double-entendres and inside references; but it is rarely noted that this expressive aspect is also encoded into the music itself. The layering of major tonalities upon minor ones (made popular with the advent of Ragtime) is a musicological embodiment of psychological and physiological tensions that rock music would later exploit to the fullest (the Beatles being an excellent example).

Ragtime, as originated by Scott Joplin in the late nineteenth century, marked a milestone in American musical history by incorporating native African elements (notably syncopation and ''displaced'' accents) into melodic structures that were themselves descended from spirituals and other vocal forms. Also importantly, it supplied an overtly rhythmic base that in effect transmogrified and restored the long-disfavored African drums. And as it was the first African-derived musical style that could be converted into a widely popular synthesis, ragtime attracted a great deal of commercial attention.

The sad chronicle of its appropriation by white capital extended in even fuller force to ragtime's godchild, jazz. As an expression of alienation like all previous forms of American black music, blacks would see the music industry steal jazz from them, alter it, and sell it back. In his book, *Noise: The Political Economy of Music*, Jacques Attali records, ''the first market for jazz was composed of the workers of the ghettos of the Northern cities.'' Attali goes on to say:

> The economic appropriation of jazz by whites resulted in the imposition of a very Westernized kind of jazz, molded by white music critics and presented as music 'accessible to the Western musical ear'—in other words, cut off from black jazz, allowing it to reach the white youth market . . .

Of course white Americans had been evolving grassroots music of their own during the previous two hundred years. Irish and Scottish folk forms such as the jig and the ballad strongly influenced popular taste. In isolated ruralities (most notably the Appalachians), "hillbillies" synthesized ballad forms, black-inspired blues, and even church hymns to create a truly indigenous hybrid: the precursor of what is now known as "country-western." Rock history maintains that the coupling of European-derived country-western and African-inspired blues created rock and roll. Rock lineage from then on includes appropriations and reappropriations on both sides of the color line. To mention just a few of them, white rock versions have ranged from the simplicity of folk rock to the rococo excesses of psychedelia; Motown and the currently chic hip-hop are both black responses to white appropriation.

In American popular music, interculturalism is a new tag for an old phenomenon. Nevertheless, only recently has the process come full circle to affect the host countries whose music and people were formerly commodities for export. Popular music is now proliferating in consciouly worldwide terms; an increasingly conspicuous number of artists are producing work derived from music of other countries and blending it with their own, indigenous styles. Paul Simon's breakthrough album *Graceland* is still probably the most visible of American contributions; King Sunny Ade's Nigerian ju-ju music with its strong American followings, has been a high-profile import here for years. But week after week new bands are suddenly appearing, proving that this new interplay is global.

Zouk is emblematic of this—a music originating in the French Antilles, but basically a Paris-based studio phenomenon, sung in French and French Creole over Caribbean-based rhythms, known for using state-of-the-art recording techniques and high-style presentations in concert. Or you might look to Zaire, where musicians are taking call/response lyrics and setting them to electric piano. Or to Senegal, where several of its multi-national regions are recording a slick Afro-pop derived from traditional sources such as youth initiation rites and underscoring them with electric guitars and powerful percussion. Algerians, too, are adapting native songs; they set them to almost Disneyesque big-band arrangements, adding weightless, untethered vocals that sound nearly independent of their Western beats. Clearly, folk revival is not the point here; synthesis is.

"World beat," as these and other such hybridizations are often called, melds pop styles from around the globe. According to Don Snowden, music critic for the *Los Angeles Times*,

> Some world beat styles, like South African music, are pure, regional pop styles that evolved from local traditions. Others are

more in a classic melting-pot vein, with the musicians adding elements of Anglo-American pop (particularly black dance music) to local sounds. Or vice versa.

World beat is thus less a movement than an aesthetic—an approach to music, usually rhythm-oriented, that draws inspiration from ethnic musical traditions without being bound by them. Considered a highly social, "talking together" art form, it may borrow from African pop, from Caribbean forms such as reggae and soca, or any combination of regional styles from the Balkans to the Basque country, from Ireland to the Middle East.

Snowden observes that "soul is the unifying element" in these seemingly disparate strains—black soul, often in its fundamentally American strain, gleaned from sources such as Motown, gospel, blues, and folkier descendants such as zydeco. Black American music may not be the impetus for the intercultural explosion, but it is certainly providing a *lingua franca*.

For black Americans in particular, a major benefit of these interchanges is a psychic one; after long being considered *cultura non grata*, they may now contribute to, as well as borrow from, an ancestral heritage. However, it is not the Age of Aquarius yet; since world beat must employ the recording industry's technologies of production and modes of distribution to get itself heard, it is vital to ask who else this blending benefits. Specifically: what if this assimilative practice is not a true commingling at all, but rather a bankrupting, a surrender of cultural values that serve for export only? One assumption behind, say, yoking Berber riffs to dance-oriented rhythms is that the hybrid transcends native genres on either side (it's as bright as Western disco but as inscrutable as the Orient). Everyone can dance to it—together. Differences can be transcended and resolved into global village neutrality. But this is just the mirage of non-ideological utopianism with a popular gloss on it. If unscrutinized, intercult may offer only a prosthetic humanism in which the annunciation that we are all human gives way to the presumption that we are all alike.

Considering that the adoption of American dance beats—for they are now effectively American, however African their lineage—must to some degree insinuate an American sensibility, the end-product cannot be wholly value free. (The fact that the former president, Ronald Reagan, lauds the United States as a nation free of ideology should serve as an ironic caveat to intercult practitioners.) Regional cultures act not as barriers, but as permeable membranes; even with the best of intentions, their penetration can be a subtle strain of colonialism.

The problem is compounded by the fact that the marginality of the world beat leaves it with little ability to reach beyond itself. At the moment, most world beat acts more like a salve for alienation than a call to unity. The comments of Jacob Desvarieux, who plays guitar for and sings with Kassav', are illustrative:

> We know that life is hard and there are problems everywhere. How do you hold on? People answer, we have zouk. Zouk is the music that we play. They say that zouk is their medicine and when we listen to it for three or four minutes we forget our problems a bit and that helps us hold on. It gives us strength.

Not that anything is wrong with dissolving into transcultural euphoria for a few minutes. Or hours. But music must do more, much more, if it is to avoid becoming a statistical footnote to recording industry demographics. The recent ''Sahara Electric'' album is an excellent example of what music can do. This linchpin effort between West Berlin's Dissidenten and Lem Chabeb of North Africa is simultaneously a German affirmation of its inherited cultural diversity, and a North African movement away from tradition-bound themes and toward its transmarine neighbors. Lyrics on the album indict Parisian racism; but is there anything in the music to indicate this to an untrained ear? Of course not—not when they're sung in an Algerian regional dialect, over rhythms bound to sound upbeat and celebratory to all but the most well informed. The words are unavailable to most listeners; and yet it would be a loss if bands with agendas like Dissidenten's performed in French or English just to reach the broadest possible audience. How, then, to forestall the music industry's positioning of intercultural music as palatable but politically marginal?

Such music is political—inherently so, as Dissidenten and a few other bands have made explicit. But music alone, sometimes even music with words, can be as easily co-opted for one purpose as for its antithesis. (The extreme but apposite example is the facile translation of folk songs into nationalist anthems effected by the Hitler Youth.) It may be that world beat and allied efforts really do strengthen global village sympathies; it may also be that they elide differences that formerly were cultural strengths. If it is to be a positive force, intercult must be more than a way of consuming more and more images, of cannibalizing world culture. And so the question is: what is the responsible way of employing this dangerous but promising outgrowth of our postmodernity?

The solution is visual. Music integrated into a strong visual field is not easily disassociated from its original intentions; nor is it easily neutralized by those who would empty it of one meaning to replace it with an ahistorical one. In performance, music theatre can resist those who would suborn music's inherent polysignification.

* * *

Now interculturalism in music theatre is nothing new, even as a conscious project. In fact, Western theatre boasts an entire art form that has been aggressively intercultural from its inaugural work: opera. The Italian academics who composed Western opera's first few opuses believed (mistakenly) that they imitated the ancient Greek lyric-dramatists. And as if this set the agenda for the fledgling art form, it has even since either reverently enshrined cultural values or, in turn, irreverently plundered them. Often both.

As the example of opera makes clear, music theatre is only potentially an innoculation against political sabotage; it is no guarantee that the resultant activity will be revolutionary. On the contrary, opera is rightly viewed with suspicion because, among other good reasons, its proponents have often been less than respectful with their cultural scavengings. Edward Said has incisively demonstrated how *Aida* extends imperial France's sense of purpose in Egypt. For better or worse, though, the sheer level of integration required of these musico-visual gestalts makes even opera (the most pluralist of all art forms) an unwieldy agent for purposes *other* than those for which it was intended. It can be defamiliarized (Peter Sellars' *Don Giovanni*), or intensified (David Allen's *Wozzeck*), and, unfortunately, it can to some degree be defanged. But it cannot actually be pirated without rendering the work unrecognizable.

Opera is thus an outstanding (if suspect) model. But it is no longer the only one. Many of the best contemporary fusions of theatre and music are non-operatic *Gesamkunstwerk*s. Thanks in part to the intercultural impulse, we are now witnessing the interpenetration of theatre with popular music. Musicals, after long being considered suspect commercial products—ones whose success was directly and grossly proportional to public demand for kitsch—are again in vogue. Yet, for the most part, these new works are anything but throwbacks to *Brigadoon* and *Paint Your Wagon.* Excepting occasional bound-for-Broadway blockbusters like the palingenetic *Phantom of the Opera*, these new music pieces aim for a synthesis of musical styles, cultures, and perspectives. David Byrne scored Robert Wilson's abstract *The Knee Plays* for the Dirty Dozen Brass Band of New Orleans. Marc Ream interwove Arabian, African, and Asian motifs into the score for *RareArea*. Elliot Goldenthal combines multi-cultural musical elements with Julie Taymor's designs to create mythographic pieces such as their *Juan Darien.*

It is hardly surprising that music is fast becoming the solvent medium for intercultural experiments in the theatre. Ideally, by juxtaposing dissimilar perspectives, intercultural music becomes a direct conduit to the critical faculties, thereby availing itself of theatre's main advantage as an art form:

its ability to instruct.

Just as easily, though, music can be an emotional morass, swamping that same critical faculty. In the latter case the work is in danger of capitulating to social forces by the simple fact that it ignores them. In this case, the theatre piece succumbs to the same virus as much of world beat. Perhaps most damaging of all, since it passes itself off as authentic even as it reaffirms stereotypes, is music used simply for atmosphere, to evoke overfamiliar suppositions about unfamiliar cultures.

In a recent issue of *Theater*, Indian critic Rustom Bharucha objected to precisely this appropriation of Eastern musical exponents in Peter Brook's *Mahabharata*. According to Brook himself, Toshi Tsuchotori's score was deliberately "suggestive" as opposed to concrete; Brook feared that strongly Indian music would be a barrier to identification with epic narrative. But this half-measure itself proved to be a barrier—even more, a gross underestimation of the spectators' capacity for empathic identification. As with many other elements of the production, the synthetic Indian music read as generic, as redolent of Anglo-centric stereotyping, and not of culturally transcendent human experience. This variety of Orientalism has caused artists and spectators alike to question the validity of the interculturalist notion.

These are some hazards of the intercultural effort. They are not negligible. But to paraphrase opera critic Joseph Kerman, failures are no proof at all. I would therefore now like to consider the work of composers who are confronting these problems, and attempting to create global experiences by mediating drama through music. After all, the intercultural project at least begins with commendable intentions. Whether it takes the form of what theatre critic Glenn Loney describes as "dramatic communication between performers and spectators without the customary vehicle of a shared language," or whether it is an attempt to translate cultural myths into a universal archetype, the intention is certainly the transcendence of national boundaries. If we believe that the modernist moment of isolating art from its society was a boo-boo, the pluralism of intercult may well be one remedy. Let us examine what its possible uses are.

* * *

I. *Telson: The Acknowledgment of Culture*

Bob Telson is a composer who has not settled for half-measures in his work—which, it should be pointed out, is aggressively intercultural. Telson (a former member of the Philip Glass ensemble) has for years experimented with African-European and African-American fusions: R&B, salsa, reggae, rock and roll. He happens to be white, not black—a problem, for some, although interestingly enough these detractors are usually not black themselves. As a frequenter of Pentecostal churches who has performed and recorded with black gospel groups, Telson is hardly a cultural tourist; his explorations of black musical idioms are personal, not sociological. "For me," he says, "good pop music is the American haiku."

Telson's ethnicity became of public interest when he composed the music for Lee Breuer's performance piece *Sister Suzie Cinema* (1981). A "doo wop opera," to be sung by black men in the manner of The Persuasions—isn't it presumptuous of a white man to compose in such a style? As it turned out, however, no one contested the music itself; by the time it had been embellished by 14 Karat Soul, the New Jersey quintet that performed the piece, authenticity was not an issue. More problematic was Lee Breuer's text, which strained against the music's evident sincerity. Underneath the music, for example, one character intoned bits such as "Oh Veronica of the Lake / Oh Dolores of the Rios"—camp references that escaped some of the audience, and wrenched others out of the "doo wop" premise. Breuer, of course, can claim that this was precisely his intention, citing the postmod prerogative of fracturing art's frame to expose the scaffolding that supports it. But the dislocation leaves him open to the charge that faces many practitioners of intercult: condescension towards their subjects. The challenge for Telson, therefore, was to compose music that bridged this gap. In effect, he had to surmount a distancing that Breuer had deliberately imbedded in his lyrics; and at times the strain between music and text was obvious.

Fortunately for the next Breuer/Telson opus, *The Gospel at Colonus* (1984) evinced no such strain. This time the marriage of form to content was profound. Conceptually, the project sounded like the same uneasy amalgam of pop and pretension detectable in *Sister Suzie Cinema*: an all-black cast, singing the story of the erstwhile King of Thebes as though it were a parable for a Sunday revival meeting? Far from being pretentious, however, the play was an almost miraculous synthesis of disparate cultures.

Breuer's side of the collaboration achieved this by adapting Sophocles extensively but without transliterating him into Americanese. He did not remove Thebes to Georgia, say, or change the names to modern equivalents. While he did retain a few actors individualized to the point of having one continuous identity, he also followed classical practice by keeping a large, moving chorus, and using subsets from it to represent various characters (e.g., people at the gate of Thebes). Even the role of Oedipus was traded off between the chorus leader and other actors. Hence the narrative emerged from a reservoir of storytelling power: the undifferentiated but always emotionally resonant choral body. The actors seemed to be creating the show themselves; and hence no condescension existed, no pattern felt imposed by an unseen manipulator.

Much credit was due Telson for making this dramaturgical sleight-of-hand stand up in performance. By composing in the spacious gospel style, he could use the slow builds and room for improvisation of that genre to allow for apparently spontaneous choral interjections. In the Broadway production this contagion of feeling extended to the audience; at nearly every performance, there were spectators who danced in the aisles at his final apotheosis. Gospel proved to be so perfect a medium for the story of a man's redemption from exile that there was hardly a false note in the entire piece.

Breuer and Telson's most recent work returns their collaborations to the postmodern paradigm of pret-a-porter mixing and matching. Unabashedly intercultural with a vengeance, *The Warrior Ant* borrows from cultures worldwide. (Part Four, for example, "An Ant in Hell," had Dante's *Inferno* in mind as a metaphor for spiritual mid-life crisis.) In the course of the Ant's epic quest for self-discovery, Telson liberally employs Caribbean, Middle Eastern, African, and South American music. Breuer in turn pairs this with an almost bewildering smattering of theatrical styles. The Ant, for example, is represented by a Bunraku puppet; his speech sometimes lapses into movieland American slang.

A mess? Critics of *Warrior Ant*'s cultural acquisitiveness have said so. But more is going on here than just smelting down world iconography into personal slag. This is no deconstructive critique; Breuer is searching for a universal integument, not solvent. And therefore the stakes in *Warrior Ant* are very high. Just as with world beat, the play is not historical; it seeks not to discover links but to forge them. If "culture is the DNA of societies," as Breuer has written, then the task of the Telson/Breuer collaboration must be to go beyond synthesis to reformation.

Collage technique figures largely in *Warrior Ant*. Telson's work simultaneously localizes pieces with concrete musical modes, and then explodes them by juxtaposing these well-defined modes: Bunraku performance with Middle Eastern music with American street slang. Telson lets each reference remain fully itself, coexisting indissolubly alongside other references in dramatic enjambment. His ties to world beat come into full play here; he knows how to bind disparate motifs into a dissonant harmony. Yet Telson doesn't mix these motifs promiscuously. World beat in turn could learn from his tendency to compose by layering motifs rather than blending them.

At its worst, this approach can also look like the gratuitous exploitation of ethnicity for its own sake. Telson's music occasionally had difficulty compensating for the text's many troublesome ruptures of its own framework (as when the Ant's guide through the Underworld makes a point of declaring that his name is not Virgil but Maeterlinck). In time perhaps the Breuer-Telson tug-of-war (the former distancing the audience, the latter bridging the distance) will flower into dissonant harmony. But it is not there yet. Meanwhile, Telson is providing one of the most cohesive agendas for interculturalism to date.

* * *

II. *Glass: The Abstraction of Culture*

Although Philip Glass is well known for being a leading proponent of American minimalist theory, the ascription is, in his case, something of a misnomer. To prove this, it should be enough to intersect his career at the point at which he began composing opera—at that point where, one would suspect, ''pure'' music's irreferentiality would necessarily succumb to the pluralism of production, that is, the theatre. Yet initially, at least, Glass managed to have things both ways.

In 1976 the New York Met produced and presented Glass' first opera, *Einstein on the Beach*, much in the manner of a cultural festival, in the most generous sense of what Umberto Eco in his book *Travels in Hyper-reality* calls ''culture as show business.'' Director Robert Wilson created a hurly-burly of cultural images and references and set them onstage with little contextual framework in the ordinary sense.

A series of *mises-en-scène* looking like cultural debris (quasi-runic designs suggesting mathematical symbols, for instance) unfolded in a way that seemed to parallel Glass' music rather than correspond to it. No clear correlation was discernible in the collaboration between the director and composer. This was achieved through a kind of non-alignment pact (a characteristic *modus operandi* with Wilson): after initial meetings, both artists separated to work alone until the inception of rehearsals. Ultimately, then, their respective labors seemed unified only in that neither begged any operatic questions. Nor was there any parody of opera. *Einstein* disregarded formal issues altogether as something outside its existential scheme. The very nature of the presentation signaled an astonishingly casual approach to dramaturgy. (For example, a program note informed the audience it could come and go at will during the five-hour performance.) The play did not seem to need an audience at all.

In itself the lack of context was not so revolutionary. Earlier avant-garde operas—Stein and Thomson's *Four Saints in Three Acts*, for one—had banked on the mind's inevitable tendency to synthesize meaning where ostensibly none was prefabricated for it. But in *Einstein*, Glass and Wilson seemed out to short-circuit that very human faculty. What is intriguing about this in terms of the composer's incipient interculturalism is that here Wilson and he scavenged from the detritus of history and emptied their images of meaning. The opera's last spoken utterance, which is both a command and a question—"number the grains of sand on the seashore—impossible, you say?"—served to obscure the sense of a work in which images were liberated from context. They could mean anything—and didn't.

Yet Glass' next opera, *Satyagraha* (1980) eschewed *Einstein*'s radical solipsism by insinuating a cross-cultural agenda. *Satyagraha* was purposely intercultural: the opera had distant settings (it is a metaphorical portrait of Gandhi), and a libretto sung entirely in Sanskrit. For Glass, who had studied with Ravi Shankar and Allah Rakha, the piece might have provided the perfect venue for some fancy compositional tourism; but he avoided the trap of offering an exoticized "Indian" score. In fact, instead of ignoring the methods of mainstream Western opera, Glass used and transmuted them, bending the rules to accommodate his innovations. Most notably he used his technique of gradual harmonic progression to simulate the absorbing, meditative improvisations of Indian music. Emblematic of this was *Satyagraha*'s closing aria, which had exactly one line of text, repeated dozens of times, that metamorphosed almost imperceptibly with each reiteration. Now, of course, this is the very hallmark of Glass' music.

Akhnaten (1984) was at once both more immediate and more remote. This time Glass utilized a relatively conventional orchestra and traditionally operatic voices, yet his libretto, which was mostly in ancient Egyptian Akkadian, was even more distinctly exotic than ever. As with *Satyagraha*, there was little linear development; the work was closer to a series of tableaux, enacted to connote the freighted mystery of ritual. Scenography and context captured much of the cultural idiom; Glass did not use his music to supply "Egyptian" atmosphere, at least not in the way that *Turandot* denotes itself as "Chinese." While the score was replete with Eastern referents, Western notions of harmonic development played a larger part then ever in *Akhnaten*. In the opening procession, sharp chords puncture a polyrhythmic weave of percussion and structurally Western horns; a flatulent groan from an organ periodically sours the endlessly imbricated harmonics; and all this is underscored by a free-floating drone recalling an amorphous Orient to occidental ears. By beginning the opera with a metatheatrical scene of ceremony (it is a funeral), Glass establishes that Akhnaten will be a work of abstraction. Thus freed from historical reportage, he is then able to intimate the barbaric splendor of an ancient court without recourse to the pentatonic clichés used to signal foreignness. His Egypt was not anthropological, not European, but patently and peculiarly Glass.

However, if Glass' music was relatively free from Orientalism, the initial production at the Houston Grand Opera was not; critic Tim Page in *Opera News* described it as ''an ugly, pretentious production that resembled a *Saturday Night Live* sketch, 'The Coneheads Go to Egypt.' '' And this does matter—this gap between a composer's score and the director's realization. Glass is to blame if his work is so easily suborned.

Walter Benjamin quotes Hans Eisler as having once remarked that ''one must beware of overestimating orchestral music and considering it the only high art. Music without words gained its great importance and its full extent only under capitalism.'' Eisler's remark speaks directly to *Akhnaten*'s central problem. Though the work has a libretto, its arcane utterances are accessible to no one; the voices are only symphonic elements in an impressionistic mélange of sound and spectacle. As the Houston production demonstrated, a text-less *Gesamtkunstwerk* is as easily recuperable by the opera machinery as world beat is by the recording industry.

Glass' answer to this is instructive. In a different context he has said:

> Obviously modernism divorced opera from the public. There's a tradition of theatre composers who have always worked directly with the public. Benjamin Britten is such a composer. Virgil Thomson is such a composer. Menotti is another. I am also another one—a theatre composer writing for a general public. It's certainly true of Sondheim. It's true of Argento. These are people who are not writing theoretical music. We're writing theatre music. It's very different.

In other words, Philip Glass claims (ingenuously or not) to be creating populist art. ''It's not important to be prepared in advance for seeing my work. *Satyagraha* reveals itself. People don't need to buy the libretto and study it in advance.''

That he wants to be a ''popular'' composer cheapens Glass in the view of certain critics who routinely publish their umbrage at his ''tinkering'' with operatic idioms. But their objections sound small and shrill next to Glass' avowed objective: to shift opera from an elitist commodity to music theatre of universal accessibility. It is this desire that aligns him with the intercultural impulse—the urge toward popularization, for establishing a cultural *lingua franca* as an aesthetic tradition.

I do not believe, as Jurgen Habermas does, that intersemination of aesthetic disciplines (as in *Einstein*) or overlapping of cultural references (as in *Satyagraha*) necessarily results in the dissolution of the associated values. But there are attendant dangers; and, as Glass' detractors have been quick to observe, they may be slowly overtaking him. His most recent pieces have been in English, indicating a move away from his early hermeticism. But disappointingly, David Hwang's script for *1,000 Airplanes on the Roof* (1988) was a piece of stupefying banality; and Glass chose that moment to compose music that was merely illustrative, when an ironic score of resistance might have shored up the text's trivial throughline.

Always a composer of paradoxes, Glass' newest opera, *The Making of the Representative for Planet 8* (1988) sounds like the most overweening abstraction so far (it is set in a vague future on an even vaguer planet), yet it may well also be the most accessible. It is in English; and Glass' take on Doris Lessing's novel is that it's an allegory for a moribund society late in its cultural evolution. His observation that allegory allows music theatre to extend beyond itself, offering a dramatized anaglyph for societal concerns, hopefully points to a growing politicization for Glass. More than ever, he is placing the theatre public ahead of the opera lovers—and not apologizing for it, either. By using the well-heeled mechanisms of dissemination that the opera industry affords (translated libretti, supertitles, *et al.*), and at the same time regarding the idea that opera must be approached with erudition and respect, Glass creates art that travels well—inside the Unites States and out.

* * *

III. *Cage: The Transcendence of Culture*

> The past is not a fact. The past is simply a big field, that had a great deal of activity in it.
>
> —John Cage, 1973

Summer of 1988: the Pepsico Summerfare Festival is presenting the American premiere of John Cage's first operatic work, *Europeras 1 & 2*. The pre-opening publicity has done its job; the atmosphere is noisy, carnivalesque, pleasantly suspenseful; the audience is primed for a *Hellzapoppin'*-style review of Western opera. Already a film by Frank Scheffer, *Wagner's Ring*, is being projected onto the stage curtain; evidently it is snippets of the work we are about to see, played at fast speed on a continuous loop.

The film unceremoniously cuts itself short and *Europera 1* begins. With a bang. Singers traipse across the stage. Members of the ensemble play furiously, heedless of the onstage action. Lights go up and down where no singer performs. Voices of an enormous but unseen chorus go dopplering around the heads of the audience; somewhere in the wings a door slams.

Gradually the adjusted eye and ear can pick out recognizable snatches of melody or scenography: a flourish associated with *l'oiseau rebelle*, a bishop

303

trundling by in an open cart. A bewildering number of backdrops are wheeled on and off or lowered from a grid. The latter action doubles as an elaborate visual pun: many of the drops "flown" in are of birds.

Even when a particular opera is unidentifiable (which is most of the time), the operatic conventions are not. A pantalooned singer slowly grapevines across the stage, gesticulating grandly, accompanied by a backdrop emblazoned with busy arabesques. When she pauses in her circumnavigation, so does it; when she moves on, it moves with her, always backgrounding her. In this hurly-burly of an opera, she manages to take her own context wherever she goes.

It's enough to make the term "deconstruction" fresh again.

At first, John Cage would seem to represent the implosion of the intercultural mission. Until now, most works of his long career sought to refrain from acknowledgment of any musical tradition, Western or otherwise. However, this is not due to any spiritual valence with minimalist theory; Cage is utterly unconcerned with arpeggios, harmonics, and the rest of the West's musical architectonics. While his approach to music has always been a critical one, his investigations have been ontological rather than prescriptive. One of the most famous of these, *4'33''* (1952), was "a piece in three movements in which no sounds are intentionally produced"; the musician's function was to provide a context for listening by sitting at a piano and demarcating three consecutive stretches of time. Whatever happened to occur in that time was the concert. In this way Cage challenged the most basic notions of what constitutes music.

Though Cage's work was deeply influenced by Zen, and though he found models in Asian philosophy for the creation of his "indeterminate pieces," he never sought to transmit the "Easterness" *per se* of his sources. Rather his pieces have represented the degree-zero of composition, favoring humor and surprise over patently romantic devices such as atmosphere and referentiality. For as Daniel A. Herwitz has written in the same context,

> We pass beyond treating sounds as *themselves* both when we project formal or structural relationships onto them and when we hear them as expressive of human emotions. When we hear ninth chords as part of a tonal system resonating with the dying, unresolved weariness of the late Romantics (who were especially fond of them) or with the offbeat whimsy of Thelonius Monk (who is also fond of them), we are hearing more in them than is there and than we ought to.

Cage wants us to hear what is actually there instead of listening through the distorting filters of emotions and concepts. His *Europeras* behaves like a manifesto, insisting that the filtering tendency be obstructed.

Interculturalism for Cage is a strategy for doing just this—a way to attack the standard reception of music. And since he has a particular hegemony in mind, his subversive brand of intercult concentrates on collapsing the past's prize piece, opera. And a particular body of opera at that. As such, his purpose is far more insidious than mere pastiche. Opera is, after all, the West's most intercultural art form—a form capable of commissioning a French composer to write Italianate music for a "Spanish" setting and premiere it in Vienna.

Cage warmed up for his patchwork piece with *Truckera*, a collage of 101 fragments from seventy different operas mixed live during a broadcast on WKCR, New York, in 1987. Soon after he incorporated *Truckera* into the all-out pandemonium of *Europeras 1 & 2*. Moving from aural collage to operatic bricolage resulted in a surprising product: *Europeras 1 & 2* is not a blending of augmentative effects, as in *Truckera*, but a catalogue of surprisingly similar affects. Whereas worldwide interchange has usually meant an expansion of means, Cage's incestuous, hypo-European intercult serves to expose a conspiracy of sameness.

Needless to say, this is not an accident. Most of the operas quoted in the piece are culled from nineteenth-century works—not due to an aesthetic bias, so Cage says, but because it was legally imperative he use only works that had passed into public domain. Whether arbitrarily made or not, the choice is felicitous, since it means Cage has cut and pasted works launched from the lee side of European colonial imperialism—works often consciously created to represent jewels in the crowns of nations vying for continental prestige.

All of which works in favor of the project's alleged purpose: its much-ballyhooed destructiveness. Heinz-Klaus Metzger and Rainer Reihns, who commissioned the opera and served as dramaturgs while midwifing its world premiere at the Oper Frankfurt, boast that thanks to Cage's opera, no new operas are writable. Metzger says in his program notes that Cage is "abstractly negating opera." He calls "such a process irreversible," and hopes that contemporary opera composers "will immediately comprehend that their hour has come."

Actually, Metzger's apocalyptic press-hype notwithstanding, the pre-performance *Wagner's Ring* turns out to be the only truly anti-operatic event of the entire evening. In traditional museum-house opera, in which scenography is one of the principal compensations for attending overfamiliar works, this would be unthinkable: a production previewing its own surprises! The *effekt* of this *verfremdungs*, of course, is to inculcate the audience into complete familiarity with what is to come. The viewer's attention, then, will be on how the opera unfolds, not what it's "about."

And this is precisely what happens. What spectators behold in *Europeras 1 & 2* is an apparently random procession of stage elements ordered by a computer program (called "IC," because it simulates the I Ching's divinatory method). Actors, technicians, and musicians are "conducted" by this program, which cues people via video monitors set in front of the stage. Therefore the play is anything but chance-determined. The only true aleatory feature of the play is IC's kaleidoscopic imperative, which ensures the order of events will be different every evening. *Europeras'* program playfully points this up by providing twelve possible synopses for the opera.

This means that the human mind must make associations and cross-references that the play does not. And it does. Somehow it seems oddly apposite that a dirigible, for instance, floats into the auditorium just as a coffin is wheeled offstage. And so, as in the Wilson/Glass *Einstein on the Beach*, the joke would be on us, were it not that this process is such a rewarding one. Unlike *Einstein*, however, here Cage is not trying to frustrate that faculty, but to exploit it.

The problem is that Cage's distancing is soon easily ignored by the audience. In a play that is busier than a Bosch painting, it is hard work to keep the mind wide open for two hours while it watches the wreckage of Western civilization drift by. And so the opera turns into a cultural quiz for the audience, a high-brow game in which the winner identifies the most Great Works. Opera is not destroyed in this way; it is applauded and reaffirmed.

Probably Cage would not be bothered by *Europeras'* easy recuperability. He himself eschews Metzger and Reihn's pretensions to destruction; as Leah Durner reports in a recent *Ear* article, Cage set out to open territory, not close it. Whether or not *Europeras 1 & 2* does accidently celebrate operatic tradition, it is finally subversive in that it returns culture to people, as their property to splice up at will. Far from ending opera, Cage has given us a heightened awareness of its historicity.

* * *

A complaint currently in circulation about the art of the first half of the twentieth century is that in its search for purity, modernism broke with the past, rejecting history for spawning an uninhabitable present. In some disciplines (notably architecture and symphonic music), this break is demonstrable; but it is important to observe that this assessment is much less valid for the art of performance. Throughout this century, live performance has managed to retain a sense of responsibility to people, even when this responsiveness took homeopathic channels: provocation, for example (the Dadaists), or accusation (Brecht), or resignation (Beckett). No wonder then that theatre and the other performance-based manifestations of today are favored media for so many contemporary artists. One main plank of the postmodernist platform (in its developing sense of a conscious aesthetic), is that the historical context missing from much of art be reclaimed. Interculturalism, invoking as it does multiple frames of reference, is one way for art to reposit itself in history.

Each composer discussed above succeeds in fusing theatre and music for just this purpose. Cage's tactic is to transcend the cultural baggage of Western civilization. His clearing the table is an important gesture; but it is also one that must now transcend itself. Glass' best work comes closer to establishing a popular tradition, by utilizing the centripetal power of his abstract and yet strangely immediate compositional style. Bob Telson's cultural quotations are, potentially, the most ambitious and hazardous of all, for his work seeks a musical alchemy and a transmogrification of genres long considered too locally specific to speak to a global community.

In *About Looking* John Berger has referred to the potential of photography as "the prophecy of a human memory yet to be socially and politically achieved." The interculturalist project would do well to adopt the same working criterion. And since music alone, whatever its good intentions, can be appropriated for any ethos, its collaboration with theatre can make it indissoluble.

Adopting this vocation means rejecting the marginalization of art as a mere money-making item of consumption; and electing instead to establish a new, esemplastic mode of production. Music and music theatre have that choice today.

WORKS CITED

Attali, Jacques. *Noise: The Political Economy of Music.* Minneapolis: University of Minnesota Press, 1985.

Glass, Philip. *Artsreview* 5, no. 1 (Winter 1988).

Herwitz, Daniel A. "The Security of the Obvious: On John Cage's Musical Radicalism." *Critical Inquiry*, Summer 1988.

Metzger, Heinz-Klaus. *Europas Oper, Notizen zu John Cage's Europeras 1 & 2* (program notes, Oper Frankfurt Production.).

Said, Edward. "The Imperial Spectacle." *Grand Street*, Winter 1987.

Walton, Ortiz. *Music: Black, White and Blues.* New York: William Morrow and Company, Inc., 1972.

Intercultural Themes

Richard Schechner

1989

INTERCULTURAL THEMES ARE PRESENT in my directing, my writings, and my hopes for the future of the world. Like many other postmoderns, I've traveled a lot. Not because I've been a refugee, a starving person in search of food, a prisoner of this or that Gulag, or someone oppressed or victimized who must, as the police say, "Move on!" My journies as scholar, tourist, and artist have been privileged goings made by my own choice. In Asia, Micronesia, Australia, native America, Latin America, and Europe, I have exchanged information, ideas, techniques, feelings with people I've met. Some of these exchanges have been carried out in a more or less formal manner—lecturing, directing plays, participating in and leading workshops, talking to the press, arranging for the translation of my writings. Although I have not consciously on the individual level been a colonizer or exploiter, I have been enriched (yes, I know the metaphor) by my trips.

No culture is "pure"—that is, no culture is "itself." Overlays, borrowings, and mutual influencings have always made every culture a conglomerate, a hybrid, a palimpsest. So much so that we probably should not speak of "culture" but of "cultures." Racism is basically a myth of desired cultural purity played out against "others" who are perceived as being not only different but inferior.

The notion of "culture" though questionable is useful. Every apparently whole culture examined historically can be cut up into smaller and larger pieces, each with its own sustainable claims to ''integrity.'' Some ''stable'' cultures—for example, the British (or are they English? Scots? Welsh? Irish? Anglos? Saxons? Celts?)—are not homogenous, even today: for the influx of former ''colonials'' from India, Pakistan, the West Indies, southern Africa, and elsewhere is changing the cultures of the British islands as drastically as the invasion of the Normans did nearly 1000 years ago. Is this influx reducible to the collision of cultures, or does it mark the creation of new cultures: Anglo-Indian, Indo-Yoruban, and so on? Just how many hyphens does it take to specify what culture one is talking about? Can not the existence of distinct cultures be located down to the neighborhood, the family grouping, and possibly the individual?

But for all its problems, the notion of culture[1] is useful. The slipperiness of ''culture'' as a definite term is due to the extreme dynamism, lability, and volatility of any given culture. Every culture is always changing, even Japan during its period of so-called isolation that ended with the Meiji restoration of 1868. What is meant by ''culture'' is actually a snapshot, a stop-frame of an ongoing historical action. This ongoing action is a function of both endogenous and exogenous influences often so tightly intertwined as to make distinctions between en- and ex- impossible.

Attempting to fix cultures or stop them from changing is like trying to end or annihilate history.

Efficient communications and information networks, affecting not only the well-off but everyone, will make cultures increasingly less a matter of birth and more a matter of choice.

Performing arts—because they express behaviors and emotion through symbolic action, narrative of both the made-up and collective mythic kinds—are wide avenues of intercultural exchange.

Rituals and sports as well as arts, beliefs and agreed-upon modes of competition as well as styles, are being exchanged.

Not all of the exchanging is welcome. Certain cultures, under great pressure, are threatened with extinction. But cultures are not ''natural species,'' and care must be taken before applying ecological models to cultures using the same methods employed to save gorillas or rain forests. These attitudes barely conceal a kind of primitivism whereby threatened cultures (the Tagalogs of the Phillipines, for example) are perceived as ''living museums'' of the way humans ''used to be.'' Also, interventions based on ''saving'' or ''protecting'' cultures, although high-sounding, often are late twentieth-century versions of the racist patronization or imperialist ambitions that glossed, and glosses, the work of missionaries whose avowed purpose was, and is, to ''save'' and ''civilize'' people who were, and are, thought to be savages/heathens (ripe for exploitation). The alternative of allowing ''market forces'' or other kinds of social darwinism to prevail is equally unsatisfactory. Some kind of rule-governed exchange among cultures is the best course. These rules would guarantee to cultures autonomy parallel to the sovereignty guaranteed to nations, and prevent the more populous and geographically larger cultures from encroaching on and eliminating the smaller. It is easy enough to state this as an ideal, but as the experience of relations among nations has shown, there's lots of distance between cup and lip. Who is to set the rules of contact and exchange and, once set, enforce them? The best hope for such an arrangement is the growing awareness that cultural diversity is healthy for the human species.

The subjugation of one people, or peoples, by another does not necessarily lead to the extinction of their cultures. In the Americas, African cultures have flourished, deeply affecting the European cultures whose members are still dominant economically and politically. In Indonesia, the conversion of the population to Islam did not eliminate Hindu cultures anymore than hundreds of years of European colonization eliminated Islam. In India itself, Moghuls ruled for centuries, succeeded by the Christian English, but through all this, the Hindus of India effectively maintained their cultures. This is not to say that contact, and all the various forms of interaction which follow, do not change the cultures of both the conqueror and the conquered. My argument is, of course, that cultures are always changing—even if we do not (yet) know how to predict what changes will occur.

1974

Surely the tourist trade has influenced so-called ''genuine'' performances in Bali and elsewhere. I have no contempt for these changes. Changes in conventions, themes, methods, and styles occur because of opportunism, audience pressures, professionalism (itself often a new concept), and new technology. Tourism has been really important and worldwide only since the advent of cheap air-travel. Theatre historians will regard tourism as of as much importance to twentieth-century theatre as the exchange between England and the Continent was in the sixteenth and seventeenth centuries. Theatre people imitate popular imported modes, and the locals respond to the demands of rich visitors—or local audiences demand changes because they've absorbed the tastes of alien cultures. From one point of view these changes are corruptions—a clamor is raised to establish cultural zoos in which the original versions of age-old rituals can be preserved. But even traditional performances vary greatly from generation to generation—an oral tradition is flexible, able to absorb many personal variations within set parameters. And the cultural-zoo approach is itself the most pernicious aspect of tourism.

I hate the genocide that has eradicated [. . .] cultures. [. . .] But I see nothing wrong with what's happening in Bali and New Guinea, where two systems of theatre exist. The relationship between these is not a simple division betwen tourist and authentic. More studies are needed on the exchange between what's left of traditional performances and emerging tourist shows. And at what moment does a tourist show become itself an authentic theatrical art?

Tourism is a two-way street: traveler's bring back experiences, expectations, and—if the tourists are practitioners—techniques, scenes, and even entire forms. The birth ritual of *Dionysus in 69* was adapted from the Asmat of West Irian; several sequences in the Living Theatre's *Mysteries* and *Paradise Now* were taken from yoga and Indian theatre; Philip Glass' music draws on gamelan and Indian raga; Imamu Baraka's writing is deeply influenced by African modes of story-telling and drama. The list could be extended, and to all the arts. Many innovators since World War II (a great war for travel) have been decisively influenced by work from cultures other than their own; this means, for Western artists: Asia, Africa, and Oceania.

The impact of communal-collective forms on contemporary Western theatre is like that of classical forms on the Renaissance. The differences, however, are also important: in the Renaissance all that remained of classical culture were architectural ruins, old texts, and relics of the plastic arts. This material was frequently fragmented and corrupt. Also, Renaissance scholars looked with universal respect, even awe, at what they found of classical Greece and Rome. Today's cross-cultural feed is mainly in the area of performances; the shows have been seen intact, the originators of the performances are former colonial peoples, or peoples who were considered inferior by populations around the north Atlantic basin. In other words, it is logical that today's influences should be felt first in the avant-garde.

—"From Ritual to Theatre and Back"
Educational Theatre Journal 26, 4: 475-76

1979

[. . .] Cross-cultural feeding is very traditional. What is "traditional" is finally what's remembered and repeated over the years. There is no culture uninfluenced by foreigners—invaders, evangelists (Muslim, Christian, Buddhist), traders, colonizers. I enjoy the way a Madras musician handles a European violin as much as a thrill to Glass' Tibetan sounds. And what's more Italian than (Chinese) spaghetti?

—"Introduction: Towards a Field Theory
of Performance," *TDR* 23, 2:2

1981

Interculturalism is replacing—ever so tenderly, but not so slowly—internationalism. The nation is the force of modernism; and the cultures—I emphasize the plural—are the force (what word can replace force?) of postmodernism. As a world information order comes into being, human action can be mapped as a relationship among three levels:

PAN-HUMAN, EVEN SUPRA-HUMAN COMMUNICATIONS NETWORKS
information from/to anywhere, anyone

....

CULTURES, CULTURES OF CHOICE
ethnic, individualistic, local behaviors
people selecting cultures of choice
people performing various subjunctive actualities

....

PAN-HUMAN BODY BEHAVIORS/DREAM-ARCHETYPE NETWORKS
unconscious and ethological basis
of behaviors and cultures

This map may scare you as it sometimes does me. It can be of a totalitarian society, an Orwellian world. But it can also—depending on what people "predict" from it—liberate. It depicts three spheres, or levels, or actualities; but the dotted lines say that a lot of sponging up and down—transfers, transformations, links, leaks—joins these realms, making of them one very complicated system. Yes, that's what's most interesting to me: the whole thing is one system. I mean, without the overarching and the underpinning universals there is little chance for the middle—the multiplicity of cultures—ever achieving harmony, ever combining stability with continuously shifting relations among and in the midst of many different items.

Maybe the most exciting aspect of this map is the possibility for people to have "cultures of choice."

—"The Crash of Performative Circumstances,"
Triquarterly 52 (Fall): 100

1982

Peoples are going to have to learn to be intercultural if our species, and many of our sister species, are to survive. Clearly nationalism and its rivalries, armaments, boundaries—culminating in the nuclear catastrophe of mass extinction—is something we humans are going to have to learn to get rid of.

312

Learn to be intercultural? More like: unlearn what is blocking us from returning to the intercultural. For as far back as we can look in human history peoples have been deeply, continuously, unashamedly intercultural. Borrowing is natural to our species. The swift adoption of Western technology by non-Western peoples is only a recent example of very ancient patterns of acculturation. What is borrowed is swiftly transformed into native material—at the very same time as the borrowing re-makes native culture. So human cultures—the most traditional even—when viewed holistically, are something like the earth viewed from near space: a whirling mass of constantly changing patterns, incorporating what is introduced, sending out feelers into the surround: very active, yet very well organized. Syncretism and the making of new cultural stuff is the norm of human activity.

Only with the advent of a particularly virulent form of Western European-American exploitative nationalism, and its ideological outgrowths (including Soviet Marxism), was interculturalism foreclosed. We must work to make this foreclosure temporary. Thus, I am arguing both for an experiment and a return to traditional, even ancient values. This argument has been implicit in experimental art for a long time: it is the root of that art's "primitivism." Interculturalism is a predictable, even inevitable, outcome of the avant-garde, its natural heir. [. . .]

I'm not Pollyana about all this. Some very sinister forces are present in interculturalism. [. . .] First off, it is people from the economically advantaged places that are able to travel and import. Areas are culturally advantaged because of extensive and long-term exploitation of other areas. Many tourists, as well as some impresarios importing performances, are philistines, or worse. Also, multinational corporations who seem to be succeeding the nations as the Princes of the Earth are not any better equipped morally or ethically than their predecessors in government. I trust not Mobil. The multinational network has only one advantage: it is not in these conglomerates' self-interest to promote global war. It wasn't always that way. And "small wars," as well as the "arms industry," are still very good, and very evil, business. Good if you want to make a buck.

I am opposed to these trends toward one world under the aegis of state capitalism, corporatism, or international socialism. But I am opposed, too, to the national and ideological fervor that has brought us to the edge of nuclear annihilation—that has pushed us over the edge of squandering energy, wealth, and resources on the death industries.

So where does that leave me?

The more contact among peoples the better. The more we, and everyone else too, can perform our own and other people's cultures the better. To perform someone else's culture takes a knowledge, a "translation," that is different, more viscerally experiential, than translating a book. Intercultural exchange takes a teacher: someone who knows the body of performance of the culture being translated. The translator of culture is not a mere agent, as a translator of words might be, but an actual culture-bearer. This is why performing other cultures becomes so important. Not just reading them, not just visiting them, or importing them—but actually doing them. So that "them" and "us" is elided, or laid experientially side-by-side.

—"Intercultural Performance: An Introduction," *TDR* 26, 2:3

1983

Of course hundreds of non-Westerners have come to Europe and America to study theatre. At first these people mostly worked in the mainstream—brought back to their own countries versions of modern Western theatre. But more recently many non-Westerners, in America at least, have participated in experimental performance. This has led to the development of intercultural companies and a very complicated feeding back-and-forth of techniques and concepts that can no longer be easily located as belonging to one culture or another.

—"Points of Contact Between Anthropological and Theatrical Thought," *South Asian Anthropologist* 4, 1:24

1985

There will be more "in-between" performative genres. In-between is becoming the norm: between literature and recitation; between religion and entertainment; between ritual and theatre. Also, the in-between of cultures: events that can't easily be said to originate in, or belong to, this or that culture but that extend into several cultures. [. . .]

—"News, Sex, and Performance Theory" in *Between Theatre and Anthropology,* 322

1986

May I suggest to you that we are living in a convergence of epochs: one which we thought we had collectively escaped from—pre-industrial theocracies and city-states forever at war with each other, wholly caste-bound societies—and one coming at us from the nuclear and ecological tomorrow: a crowded, uncomfortable, dangerous world that can only be controlled by arousing and exploiting humanity's deepest fears.

—"Uprooting the Garden," *New Theatre Quarterly* 5 (February): 8

1988

The future I see is neither apocalyptic nor beatific. Approaching is a long period of human history where privileged individuals, sectors, regions, and continents protect their own interests while slowly adjusting their policies of greed to ones of conservation based fundamentally on not killing the goose that lays the golden eggs. The elites will do just enough to keep the world alive and their own privileges intact.

The underprivileged will boil with unrest and hatred but not have enough power to do more than annoy the powerful with terrorism, local wars, and other fitful expressions of desperation. Various media will ventilate all this as debate, rhetorical flourish, and entertainment.

A kind of postmodern medievalism, highly theatrical and stunningly elaborate, will emerge and prevail. Religious authority—both of the traditional kind and of new faiths—will be engines of inventing and vessels of transmitting ''comfort'' and beauty to masses unable to actually change in any substantial way the material circumstances of their existence.

What could change all this is contact with extraterrestrial intelligent beings or the ability to terraform and populate the moon or Mars.

Don't hold your breath.

Having said so much, what makes me feel optimistic? It is not irrationalism, religious faith, or confidence in the ET connection.

There is alive in the world an inquisitive, urgent, strong, and hopeful interculturalism. That is, the development of the world information order—with all its problems regarding hegemony, imperialism, exploitation, and so on—is not crushing local cultures but stimulating them. These local cultures once appeared to their own members as supreme and universal. When local people (French, Han, Yoruba, Javanese, Yaqui—you name them, there are many hundreds) came into contact with others, the illusion persisted that the others were inferior or superior, dominable or worthy of obedience. This illusion results in wars of conquest, conversion, exploitation, and extermination.

With the emergent world information order, a workable kind of relativism is beginning to glimmer and brighten. At some levels—the genetic, the informational, the shared responsibility for the decency of life on the planet (and beyond, if we ever get there)—all the individuals and all cultures are at least theoretically equal, even identical. At another level—that of individual, local, regional, and cultural expression, there is an abundance of diversity.

We have not yet learned how to balance these two levels of social existence.

But we are learning—as a world culture, as a world of many cultures—to respect these levels of existence. Even to the degree of recognizing the rights of other species and their cultures, of the planet as a unified ecosystem and its culture.

Perhaps in my lifetime, or in my children's, the rage of nationalism and appetite-driven ideologies will subside, giving way to celebrations of cultures within the framework of planetary systems. [. . .]

I have experienced an approximate model of this kind of living while reflecting on the terraced landscapes and systematic pageantry of Bali. Between the much worshiped high volcano Agung and the low fearful abode of the demons, the ocean—both largely out of human control and therefore still wild, from the Balinese viewpoint—exists a middle earth where the force of Agung and the sea meet and interact with human beings and the other animals and life forms of the island. All is not peace and plenty on Bali. The usual human forms of avarice, jealousy, rivalry, and the other belly-lusts are robustly exercised. But there is also—how shall I say it—a sense of manners, a certain courtesy owed to gods, nature, family, friends, strangers, even enemies. This decorum establishes limits, allows for tragedy and farce, framing life on the island. From time to time, one, some, or many Balinese run *amok*, unleashing violence, wholesale murder, and destruction on each other. So the Balinese system, too, has its bugs.

There is no perfection on this earth or any other (even of the imagination).

But the human species appears to be able to co-create the worlds it lives in. In other words, we will keep trying.

—"Letter Response," *ICIS Forum* 18, 3:3-5

1989: From Another

I was in Taipei, Taiwan, for five days last November. I had a hard time adjusting to being surrounded by people who looked more or less like me. There were other shocks as well—of a social kind. I find I no longer know how to behave appropriately in Chinese society, which is embarrassing for a person of my venerable age.

—From a letter written to me by a well-known Chinese-American scholar who for many years has lived and worked in the USA. This person wishes to remain anonymous.

NOTES

[1]Culture, these days, rarely means "excellence in the arts or scholarship" or "people with good manners and taste"—as in the cultivated rather than fallow or wild (field or forest), and

therefore the civilized (those who cultivate) as opposed to the savage (those who hunt or scrounge). These days culture signifies the determinable behavior, artifacts, architecture, customs, rituals, arts, and language that define a particular group of people. Formerly, there was a single standard of "culture" to which all people might aspire; today there are "cultures" not one of which is best. For what happened read Raymond Williams, *Key Words: A Vocabulary of Culture and Society* (New York: Oxford University Press, 1976): 76-82.

EPILOGUE

Interculturalism

A Lettrist Sampler

Gautam Dasgupta

[I]NTERCULTURALISM

I, the personal pronoun. Born in post-independence India to middle-class parents, schooled in the language of Shakespeare and Keats at a private boarding school, raised in two widely separated regions of the sub-continent whose languages and cultures are vastly different, and now having spent half my life in a country at the other end of the globe, I hope it is not too presumptuous of me to consider myself an exemplary interculturalist. To confer upon myself this privilege is, in all honesty, rather disingenuous, for who is not, and has never been, a product of multiple cultures. Perhaps more so than ever before in the history of the world, we are all intercultural selves, and if there is a difference, it is to be measured on a quantitative scale. It is on that scale that I hope to calibrate my own experiences with interculturalism and its increasingly agonizing discourse within the theatrical arts.

India. Born in the aftermath of bloody Hindu-Muslim riots in the state of Bengal, which itself was partitioned into West and East (the latter first East Pakistan, now Bangladesh), I grew up listening to family tales of ancestral homes left behind, of economic and geographic dispossession, anti-Gandhian rhetoric (Bengalis have never forgiven this universal cultural icon for his role, howsoever murky, in securing the division of their native lands), and an invincible pride in Bengali cultural supremacy that viewed the rest of India as a backward feudal entity. Born to an economically privileged class, there was little I had in common with the vast majority of Indians who were then living in sub-standard, if not primitive, conditions. Removed to an English-language boarding school high up in the Himalayan foothills—a Roman Catholic institution at that—I breathed in the cool, scented air of a climatic paradise while the rest of India sweated under a tropical sun way down in the plains. From Calcutta in the east to Mussoorie in the north, from a Bengali culture to a Hindustani one, from the folds of Indian family life to a life lived under the stern gaze of Irish Patrician Brothers, I had already traveled along the path of interculturalism without ever having left home.

Internationalism. It was a matter of no little pride to become familiar with the ways of the world. Born outside the yoke of imperialism, we were free to roam the political, social, economic, and cultural terrains of distant, alien lands. Invested with the formidable task of moving India forward on the road to progress, my generation was encouraged to cast our nets far and wide—inward and outward, eastward and westward—to glean the best that all cultures had to offer. So, in the fifties and early sixties, while still in school, I eagerly took to studying the great classics of Western civilization, for it was there, in ancient Greece, Europe, Great Britain, and increasingly America, that we located the font of advanced ideas in diverse fields of knowledge. This was what education was all about, an exercise in culture that would have made Matthew Arnold proud. No matter that Asian, Oriental, African, Arabic, Norse, or Oceanic classics and the stories of their cultures were left out. We first had to get the basics down, those fundamentals of culture without which one would be foolhardy to venture forth, let alone proceed with confident steps, into the modern age. Even Gandhi, the father of the nation, had known his Lincoln, his Tolstoy, and his Whitman. Nehru, our first head of state, was just as much a product of British jurisprudence as he was of Jeffersonian and Madisonian democratic ideals. Both had been educated in the West. The path of interculturalism was well-traveled.

I[N]TERCULTURALISM

Nationalism. In the desperate need to join the league of advanced nations, we had failed to acquaint ourselves with the cultural glories of our Indian past. Doubtless, we could boast of a grand and ancient tradition in philosophy, metaphysics, linguistics, mathematics, religion, dance, drama, music, and the epic. But somehow, to our cosmopolitan intellects, they were the riches of a distant and forgotten past, with little or no relevance to the urgent needs of contemporary society. Perhaps I could have learned to appreciate the trials and tribulations of life through readings of Kalidasa, of

322

Vyasa, of *The Ramayana* and *The Mahabharata*, the intricacies of linguistic and aesthetic thought through the formulations of Bhratrihari and *The Natyasastra*, rather than through Homer and Aristotle, Milton and Shakespeare. But how was I to escape the inflexible religious and spiritual rootedness of the Indian texts, their immutable character so impervious to interpretative change and elucidation? Although I had more than a passing acquaintance with those texts, in the intercultural mix of knowledge that was to prepare us for the social and technological advances of India's future, they seemed so monstrously inadequate to the demands of modernity. To walk that road was to betray the highest ideals of enlightenment thought and secularist beliefs. Neither I nor India in the final half of the twentieth century could afford to step back in time.

Nurture. It is indeed unfortunate that Indian culture continued to keep time in a vacuous eternity. Culture itself must be nurtured, fed with the cross-currents of a vitalist energy that derives from changing times and passions and needs. In its inability to recast itself in a new mold, the India of my youth seemed stuck in a rut of life-depleting spirituality, the exact opposite of what ought to be expected of contemplative and philosophical meditations on life. It was not the intercultural that was my enemy, it was Indian culture itself insinuating its poisons into the social arteries of the nation. It was not the intercultural that was an extension of colonial domination by other means, but Indian culture itself that was heavily politicized, using nefarious means to keep its people subject to the evils of poverty, both material and spiritual. The intercultural was to be our salvation.

Nature. The intercultural is widely seen, in India and elsewhere, to be a pollutant. Impossible to ward off, perhaps, but nonetheless a regrettable intrusion that undermines or denies our essential natures. Is there such a thing as being Indian? The question is not an easy one to answer. It is much easier to say that I was once a citizen of India, the way that I am now a citizen of America. Yet, it is a question that I have had to confront often, and that even while I was residing in India, though more so when I had moved to the United States. Curiously enough, in both instances, what was implied in being Indian was identical—to present to my interrogators the face and culture of an ancient civilization, with its outmoded belief systems intact. Refusing to offer up what was culturally acceptable and expected was to betray my Indianness and to despoil the culture of India. To be intercultural, on the other hand, was to be without a meaningful identity, an artificial social construct as a citizen of nowhere and everywhere, forever exiled, and forever constructing in whatever cultures one comes in contact with a renewed and shifting sense of self.

Theatre and culture. Extrapolating from the above, it could well be argued that there is an inner logic which links intercultural practice with theatre. In constituting myself as an intercultural being, I took on the protean role of a Pirandellian character in search of not one but many authors who would script the various dramas of my existence. And not unlike the evanescent quality of theatre itself, these dramas of cultures would float in a bed of quicksand, unstable and effortlessly moving from one cultural domain to the next. The process is best understood if an analogy can be drawn with Kurosawa's *Rashomon*, where the story is redrawn and reinterpreted from multiple perspectives. For me, living in intercultural space was to see myself as a player on a stage of infinite dimensions, re-inventing myself as a character (more precisely, characters) in the unending drama of life. By conscious choice and to assiduously fulfill my destiny in the world of the intercultural, there was no better medium to channel myself through than that of the theatre. Furthermore, it is no mere coincidence, I suspect, that the intercultural ethos has come to dominate our lives at the very same moment that everyday life itself has become overly theatricalized.

Theatre in India. As if deliberately to immerse myself in the flow of inter-cultural currents, I stayed away from the traditional theatre arts in India during the sixties. I do not confess to this with any degree of pride or cultural sophistication. At that juncture, having committed myself to inter-cultural practices, I felt a strong need to become engaged in forms of theatre that would enhance the dialogue between and within cultures, be they be-tween India and the rest of the world or between the various cultures of In-dia itself. To go back to tradition seemed mere academicism. I realize now how myopic my understanding of interculturalism was in those days, for tradition in and of itself is by no means detrimental to the movement of culture. It serves little purpose, however, if it holds fast to ossified forms, refusing to relinquish its old habits, structures, and subject matter that may well have spoken eloquently to earlier eras, but have little relevance, other than nostalgic or historical, for the current age. (I readily admit that "relevance" is a highly loaded and controversial term, much abused in contemporary theatre. The issue, for me, is not so much how to make works of the past relevant to our times, but how are we to be made relevant to those works. To do so, I submit, takes an intercultural frame of mind.) In any case, the theatrical temper to which I subscribed in India was mostly derivative of the West. The experimental theatre to which I was connected in Calcutta —Muktangan—put on plays by Ionesco, Sartre, Camus, Albee,

Chekhov, Brecht, and also plays by Indian playwrights whose works redefined the boundaries of symbolism, realism, naturalism, surrealism, absurdism, and musical and dance-drama genres. Translated into Bengali, most of the foreign plays were transplanted entirely into local landscapes, with native customs, dress, and behavioral patterns. Oddly enough, very little was lost in the cultural transposition, which may well suggest the universalizing, or better, intercultural, bias of these plays. If anything, a lot was gained in the effort, for to me and to most of the audience at Muktangan who were sympathetic to these experiments in the intercultural, it endowed us with a fuller and more complex sense of our own lives.

Theatre in America. On my move to America in 1970 as a graduate student in theatre, my knowledge of the Western dramatic heritage was viewed as a curiosity. It was virtually assumed that my research in the field of theatre could be none other than a study of Sanskrit drama or India's traditional art forms. Why would I, an Indian, be interested in the American theatre? Adamantly, I chose that very same path, this time with a certain degree of hubris. To my experience of the American theatre I could bring my knowledge of another culture, its aesthetic and philosophic determinants, if I so desired. If not, as was to prove the case, I would still carry within me the critical apparatus of interculturalism, employing it in my reading of other works of art. America, so like India in certain ways, with its commingling of diverse cultures, seemed a proper place to be interculturally and theatrically at home.

INT[E]RCULTURALISM

Emigration. Married Bonnie Marranca, an American of Italian ancestry and co-traveler on the freeway of interculturalism, and took American citizenship. What was (and is) intriguing about being here is that one can live comfortably within a neutral (or geographically and culturally diffused) space, for to this day I am unsure as to what it means to be an American. It is possible to be a cipher in America, just as it is to be interculturally complex. In both instances, however, the definition of an American is hard to come by. To be one is to be nothing and everything, and America today feels more and more like Alfred Jarry's description of Poland, which is to say nowhere. It is, to my mind, an attitude, a way of being in the world, an intercultural space with all the density and immateriality of a black hole. To adequately represent the emigrant in America today is to see him or her as a cubistically-reconfigured image, without clear definition but striated with the criss-crossing vectors of intercultural lines.

INTE[R]CULTURALISM

Representation. In a sense, my identity with each passing day in America was neither defined as Indian nor American, but was represented in the face, figure, and mind-set of an intercultural body. Curiously, though, whenever I would meet other Indians, I would introduce myself as an Indian. At other times, I was always an American. In the latter case, others would never question my Americanness, although they may well ask where I was originally from. It was a query not that unusual, for it is customary to ask the same of native-born Americans who are all children of immigrants. In the first instance, however, and this was revealed to me in no uncertain terms when I returned to India recently after 13 years, I have often met the response: "Yes, yes, you are from here, but you are not of here," the here meaning India. (The possibilities of exoticization—and representation—are numerous.) The "of" is the semantic semaphore of interculturalism.

INTER[C]ULTURALISM

Culture. I prefer to be of a cultured elite, not from a culture. Unless, of course, it is the culture of interculturalism.

Cultural. To embrace not only the theatre, but all cultural acts, in which I include artistic accomplishments, scientific developments, and intellectual activities of any and all persuasions. To live interculturally is to live in the domain of ideas, for ideas are the common property of humanity. Ideas enrich our lives, our biological selves, the way that micro-organisms or cells attain maturity through culturation in favorable environments.

Culturation. Here I must take pause, because the process of culturation has been the bane of the intercultural movement. Does the "favorable environment" of which I spoke above particularly favor the wealthier nations of the West, as some would have us believe, going so far as to suggest that the West has a monopoly on ideas as well? It is a fatuous argument, and doubly so in the theatre arts, where the circulation and exchange of ideas has been well-documented over the course of history. Yet, the notion of cultural hegemony persists, and it is crucial to ask why.

Colonialism. Yes, it is a fact of history that cannot be eradicated. And the West as much as the East, America as much as India, has been guilty of it. Its bitter lessons have been learned by all. But there are sweeter lessons that continue to be learned, lessons that are the product of interculturalism itself. They come in various shapes and sizes, from ethnic foods to household goods, from movies to international arts events, from travel in person to travel through that ubiquitous universal eye of the television set. Do the outrages of colonial pasts need to be avenged, particularly now when appeasement through intercultural means has, to a large degree, erased, if not obliterated, the scars of history? One needs only to look back upon Western Europe's emergence as a comity of nations to fully comprehend the feasibility of such a project.

INTERC[U]LTURALISM

Uses and misuses. Nonetheless, the battle rages on. And all of it stems from a misplaced anger that confuses the realms of art and its ideas, and politics. Not that art has nothing whatsoever to do with political, or with socio-economic, considerations. They may provide one of its many seedbeds, but the reverse must also be accepted as true. For was it not cultural *perestroika* in the Soviet Union that pre-dated and inadvertently prepared the political upheavals that were soon to follow? Art should not be seen as a powerless tool wielded by society. On the contrary, the power of its ideas, be they socially constructive or not, ethically useful or not, politically significant or not—so long as they are new, vital, and worthy of artistic inspiration and thought—is all that matters. The significance of art lies in the ensuing discourse that it engenders. To foreclose the argument by raising the banner of cultural hegemony or imperialism is to defeat the very purpose of intercultural practice. Could I myself have been guilty of the same? To a limited extent, yes, when I wrote of Peter Brook's *Mahabharata*. Had he used an Indian epic to further his own private explorations by imputing meta-Shakespearean and meta-Homeric literary and dramatic devices into it, in the process having misused (or even abused) the ethos and sensibility of the original? Yes and no. In a sense, how could he not have done otherwise. As an artist, one cannot deny Brook his subjective point of view. And in terms of the intertextuality that he brings into play, it is surely one of the more imaginative and trans-global readings of the epic I have ever encountered. But to be truly intercultural also requires an interpretative outlook that seeks to frame the other culture's philosophical viewpoint in a complex manner that goes beyond mere intertextual convergences, theatrical wizardry, and formalistic innovations. It demands a transposition in ideational terms, a reading (even a misreading) of the cultural map to which the original belongs. What Brook's version failed to do, I felt, was to sufficiently problematize the Indian epic within the sphere of intercultural practice, a provocation that might have enlarged our understanding (sympathetically or not is besides the point) of *The Mahabharata* from diverse perspectives.

INTERCU[L]TURALISM

Learning. Interculturalism entails learning that goes beyond knowing. It is an ongoing process of learning not only about diverse cultures, but also about learning how to know. One of the reasons for my refusing to study the traditional arts in India was because, in their codified forms, hermetically sealed, there was no opening by which to explore them. I could have mastered them perhaps, although that seemed insufficient a reason to quench my intercultural thirst. Furthermore, the intercultural needs to be activated by a hermeneutical motor, and that discipline was sorely lacking in Indian education. In a land of faith, where religion holds sway, the interrogative mode is widely seen as suspect, if not an outright Western imperial conspiracy. I write, of course, of the sixties; today India is vastly changed and seems committed to such change. In America, on the other hand, I found a climate receptive to intercultural learning, and that despite the fact that many of my friends would bemoan the mediocrity of cultural life here. Howsoever much that may be true, American cultural life was far from homogeneous. The rights of groups, communities, and other polities kept the American educational and cultural institutions forever on their toes. In servicing its democratic ideals, the country was awash in a torrent of questionings that left no cultural stone unturned. Democracy, it seems, will make interculturalists of us all.

INTERCUL[T]URALISM

Taste. The intercultural, like art, is a matter of taste. It is a process of refinement that comes with learning. It is not enough to know about other cultures, although that is a necessary first step. To appreciate interculturalism's gifts, one must work at it the way a master chef works at devising new and appetizing delicacies for the table. It is not just placing two or more dishes from different cuisines side by side; it is combining spices and sauces to create something new. To savor such a novelty, a product of plural discourses, enjoins diners (and audiences) to ask of the chef the secret ingredients of the recipe. Soon we begin to cook up that tantalizing dish at home, nurturing our bodies as we pamper our taste buds. So it is with interculturalism, if we have the taste for it.

INTERCULT[U]RALISM

United States of America. In this land of pluralism, where the freedom to pursue ideas is a constitutional right, I have felt more at home than in any other place. Or so it seemed, until quite recently, when the very strengths of its diversity, which would resolve themselves in healthy debate, civic tolerance, intellectual maturity, and personal growth, are losing ground to reckless political gerrymandering. The rights of individuals are being eroded by intransigent blocs of subcultures who subscribe to what is now referred to as "politically correct positions." Undoubtedly, political repositioning on the part of disenfranchised minorities is an integral part of how societies evolve, but when the political agenda, through its divisive tactics, intrudes upon and tramples underfoot the exercise of ideas and reasoned arguments in the name of ethnicity, race, sexuality, and other yet to be named categories (there is, alas, no end to such groupings which can, virus-like, multiply ceaselessly, effortlessly, and arbitrarily, if we so wish it), the essence of nourishment that accompanies interculturalism is all but lost.

INTERCULTU[R]ALISM

Representation revisited. Why is it that these very same issues that once helped to empower America's intercultural spirit now seem on the verge of fragmenting it? Part of the problem lies in the adequacy of social representation, which for many in these adversarial groupings appears to be woefully limited. Whether or not it is so remains a debatable proposition. But the greater problem, I suspect, has to do with the inability to properly comprehend the nature of interculturalism, which has little, if anything, to do with the tangible fact of representation, be it in carving out geographical or academic territories to be safely guarded, or in the imposition of quotas that compel an artificial pluralism on the body politic. For howsoever much these aspects of representation, now riddling the globe, are deemed necessary, contingent, or viewed as correctives to past injustices, they ghettoize and confine individual growth to a deeply polarized set of values which can only be nourished and given definition within a limited sphere. Interculturalism exists in the mind, in the sphere of ideas, in the imagination's ability to sort out differing modes of representation insofar as they have meaning to our individual lives. Each of us, I would argue, searches far and wide for those cultural representations that fulfill our innermost needs, and it is in the confrontation of the self with others that the intercultural comes into being and determines who and what we are. It is not something that can be forced upon us, for we are free to choose our own intercultural identities, and wear our disguises (our multiplex respresentations) with grace, civility, or abandon.

INTERCULTUR[A]LISM

Art. It is one of the privileges of art that it allows us to wear our disguises with impunity and without fear of reprisal. It is true both of the artist and of the audience. Art allows for representation that is conceived in the imagination free of any constraints (except those willfully employed by its creator), and can thus travel through the limitless expanse of intercultural space with an open-endedness that invites others to enter into its domain. It is often argued that no art is free of cultural and political biases. My answer to that, in the form of a question, is simple. So what? Works that proceed entirely from self-validating political premises are rightly considered propagandistic and undeserving of artistic merit. Kitsch belongs to the same world, a world that delimits the inter- (or intra-) cultural dimensions of art. Art that fails to engender further analytical or aesthetic exploration is, to put it bluntly, bad art. But art that moves us and speaks to us always carries within itself some degree of our personal representations, either of what we have been, or wish to be or not to be. And here, even mediocre, if not bad, art has its supporters. In all such instances, what cannot be denied is that art as a culture, and more so than other cultures, by being so integrally linked to ideas of representation, identity, and the socializing process, is the advance standard bearer of interculturalism.

INTERCULTURA[L]ISM

Latitude. Interculturality does not reside solely in the work of art; its burden must always be carried by the receptor. To exercise that option demands that the work of art have a broad enough scope to encourage further engagement with it. Such engagements take on various forms which in turn suggest the wide latitude of intercultural practice. The foremost amongst these is the interpretative faculty that ceaselessly re-frames and re-orients cultural artifacts, casting them anew for each successive generation. But there are other factors, such as political realignments, historical convergences, or economic contigencies, that play a significant role in how interculturalism enters the world's body. A case in point is the American television show "Dallas." Both admired and despised by differing factions of audience members at home, to some it validated the Reagan years of unbridled economic growth and boundless adventurism. To others, it was a vulgar display of near pornographic intent. High art it certainly was not. And yet if, as it is widely assumed, that "Dallas" in no small measure, and howsoever metaphorically, helped bring about the collapse of Eastern Europe's fealty to Soviet domination by displaying the wares of capitalist ingenuity, then who can deny the show's rightful place in the intercultural sun? I recall growing up in India with images of Hollywood westerns, seen not solely as a political exercise in justifying the eradication of American Indians, but also as a paean to American individualism and its frontier spirit. Cultures are to be used, ingested, and then stored away in the immense receptacle of interculturalism, only to be retrieved when they serve in-

330

dividual or group needs.

Levity. It is high time that we do not take culture, in the sense of meaning who and what we are, too seriously, for various crimes have been committed in its wake. Better to be intercultural, ungrounded or, more accurately, to be grounded in diasporic territoriality, for in and through its lightness of being, existing in today's world does become more bearable. Let us rejoice in the fact that all cultures are our own, and how we choose to make it so is up to each and every one of us. The intercultural is an attitude, it is not something out there. It belongs in our minds, an incorporeal presence that is the repository of all times and all places.

INTERCULTURAL[I]SM

Indo-U.S. In India, I have been accosted with queries about J. R. Ewing from people who live in shacks, with hardly a knowledge of what a leveraged buyout means. In America, when I first got here, a man at a bus terminal in Connecticut approached me and introduced himself as a Dravidian. He was an American black, and I soon realized he was putting me on. Sufficiently intrigued by this relatively obscure modality of representation, I entered into a dialogue with him, which soon turned into a monologue, for this man knew more about India's Dravidian south (where people are darker-skinned than those of northern India) than I had ever known. We learn what we can and what we wish to learn. In India, intellectuals talk of ''postmodernism'' and ''deconstruction'' with a familiarity that is ingrown and inbred, and so it should be. In America, scholars have written knowledgeably about Indian philosophy, religion, and arts with a sophistication that dispels any mistaken beliefs that culture is sedentary. In India, with its many languages and cultures, I go to the theatre with a synopsis in hand, for most of its languages are not known to me. I bring to those experiences the same outlook and criteria that I do when I see theatre from other non-English speaking countries. In America, I find artists who have grown to maturity and excellence through their exposure to Indian art forms. In India, even the traditional arts are being re-evaluated to create new and exciting hybrids. In America, I have heard Indian classical musicians and seen Kathakali dance-dramas and contemporary Indian plays at institutions and arts festivals the way I had first listened to live jazz sessions and seen modern American dance at cultural meets in India. The two geographies are now one as the world shrinks under the intense glare and solvent fury of interculturalism.

INTERCULTURALI[S]M

Syncretism. Cultural fusion today is taking place at an unprecedented pace, largely through the mechanism of information-processing systems. And like all such systems, the data enters the world's cultural bank without material loss. It belongs to the world's collective memory. To retrieve it, of course, is entirely our own responsibility. Those of us who choose to do so, the interculturalists amongst us, belong to a select group of citizens of a new world order, where the riches of the planet can be equally shared by all. That said, it only remains to be emphasized that equality does not necessarily mean complete and unequivocal parity. To think so is to fall into that dangerous trap of utopic thinking, which, if history is a guide, has led to dystopias of nightmarish proportions. It is just that cultures today are equally accessible to all. The rest is up to us. Synthesis, when it does take place, is first glimpsed as an idea in each individual's mind.

INTERCULTURALIS[M]

Me. The intercultural "I" reveals itself in the willed confrontation of the self with the other, reconstituting itself through various means. It is glimpsed in the cross-pollination of art and life, character and self, female and male that circumscribes Flaubert's response, "Madame Bovary, *c'est moi.*" From a spiritual perspective, it is inscribed in the language of the Indian Vedas: "I am the world." And finally, in recognition of the most pervasive intercultural medium of today, "We are the world."

Calcutta
Chaitra 1398

New York City
May 1991

Contributors

J. NDUKAKU AMANKULOR is Chair of Dramatic Arts at the University of Nigeria-Nsukka. He has published articles on African performance in *Performing Arts Journal* and *The Drama Review*.

JOHANNES BIRRINGER is a theatre and video artist whose works include *Invisible Cities* and *Border-Land*. He teaches at Northwestern University, and is the author of *Theatre, Theory, Postmodernism*.

PER BRASK, a director, fiction writer, and poet, teaches in the Department of Theatre and Drama at the University of Winnipeg in Manitoba. He edited PAJ's *DramaContemporary: Scandinavia*. PAJ will publish his forthcoming *Aboriginal Voices: Amerindian, Inuit, and Sami Theatre*.

LEE BREUER, a director and writer, is co-founder of Mabou Mines. He is the author of *Sister Suzie Cinema* and *Animations*, a PAJ title.

UNA CHAUDHURI is the author of *No Man's Stage: A Semiotic Study of Jean Genet's Major Plays*. She is an Associate Professor of English at New York University.

PETER J. CHELKOWSKI is Director of the Center for Middle Eastern Studies, and Professor of Persian and Iranian Studies at New York University. He is the author of *Ritual and Drama in Iran*.

DARYL CHIN is a Contributing Editor of *Performing Arts Journal*. He is a playwright, publisher, producer, and recent guest curator at the Whitney Museum.

GABRIELLE CODY is a doctoral student at the Yale School of Drama. She is a former Managing Editor of *Theater*.

CHIDANANDA DASGUPTA is one of India's most influential film critics. His recent book on Indian cinema is *The Painted Face*. He is arts editor of *The Telegraph* in Calcutta.

GAUTAM DASGUPTA is co-founder and publisher of *Performing Arts Journal*/PAJ Publications. He is a Professor of Theatre at Skidmore College.

FRANTISEK DEAK is a Professor of Theatre at the University of California, San Diego. He is the author of *Symbolist Theatre: The Formation of an Avant-Garde*, which PAJ will publish.

JOHN J. FLYNN is a doctoral student at the University of California, Los Angeles. His work has appeared in *Performing Arts Journal* and other publications.

MEAD HUNTER is a doctoral student at the University of California, Los Angeles. His work has appeared in *Performing Arts Journal* and *Theater*.

BONNIE MARRANCA is co-founder and publisher of *Performing Arts Journal*/PAJ Publications. Her books include *Theatrewritings*, *Hudson Valley Lives*, *American Garden Writing*, and *The Theatre of Images*.

MARC ROBINSON is a Contributing Editor of *Performing Arts Journal* and Associate Editor of *American Theatre*. He has also written for the *Village Voice*, *Theater*, and *Modern Drama*.

ULLA RYUM is a Danish playwright, director, novelist, and essayist. Her play *And the Birds Are Singing Again* appears in PAJ's *DramaContemporary: Scandinavia*.

EDWARD SAID is the author of *Orientalism*, *The World, the Text, and the Critic*, and *Musical Elaborations*. He is a Professor of English and Comparative Literature at Columbia University.

RICHARD SCHECHNER is the author of *Between Theatre and Anthropology*, *Performance Theory*, and *The End of Humanism*, a PAJ title. He is the editor of *The Drama Review* and Professor of Performance Studies at New York University.

PETER SELLARS is director of the Los Angeles International Arts Festival. He works in theatre, opera, and film. His Mozart opera productions were seen recently on public television.

TADASHI SUZUKI, one of Japan's most renowned theatre directors, is the founder of the Suzuki Company of Toga (SCOT). His writings on theatre are collected in *The Way of Acting*.

DIANA TAYLOR is the author of *Theatre of Crisis: Drama and Politics in Latin America*. She teaches in the Department of Spanish and Portuguese at Dartmouth College.

EDITH TURNER has done extensive fieldwork in Africa and, more recently, among the Inupiat Eskimos in Alaska. She teaches in the Department of Anthropology at the University of Virginia, and is the author of *The Spirit and the Drum*.

FREDERICK TURNER is the author of the recent *Rebirth of Value*. He is Founders Professor of Arts and Humanities at the University of Texas at Dallas.

VICTOR TURNER wrote many books, including *The Forest of Symbols*, *Dramas, Fields, and Metaphors*, and two PAJ titles, *From Ritual to Theatre: The Human Seriousness of Play* and *The Anthropology of Performance*. At the time of his death in 1983, he was the William R. Kenan, Jr. Professor of Anthropology at the University of Virginia.

CARL WEBER has translated and edited three volumes of Heiner Müller writings, *Hamletmachine*, *Explosion of a Memory*, and *The Battle*, published by PAJ. He heads the directing program at Stanford University.

ANDRZEJ WIRTH is the Director of the Theatre Institute at the University of Giessen in Germany. He had written widely for European publications, including *Theater Heute*.